Medication Errors
Lessons for education and healthcare

Robert Naylor

Professor of Pharmacology
School of Pharmacy
University of Bradford

RADCLIFFE MEDICAL PRESS

Radcliffe Medical Press Ltd
18 Marcham Road
Abingdon
Oxon OX14 1AA
United Kingdom

www.radcliffe-oxford.com
The Radcliffe Medical Press electronic catalogue and online ordering facility.
Direct sales to anywhere in the world.

British Library Cataloguing in Publication Data

A catalogue record for this book is available from the British Library.

ISBN 1 85775 956 7

Typeset by Joshua Associates Ltd, Oxford
Printed and bound by TJ International Ltd, Padstow, Cornwall

Contents

Preface

This project began three years ago as a review of medication errors, which was originally intended for publication in the pharmacological literature and as a teaching resource. Early advice from colleagues was that to target the manuscript to a pharmacological audience would probably miss the very groups who would benefit most from its message – healthcare professionals, healthcare managers and directors, the Government, academics who teach healthcare students and, by no means least, the students themselves and patients. A book was suggested as a more appropriate vehicle. I accepted and remain grateful for their guidance.

The book progressed in three phases. In the initial stages the understanding of medication errors in the UK proved to be a paradox. Although the existence of errors was expressed privately by many patients and healthcare professionals as a profound problem, it was quite clear that the expression of such concerns in the public arena was not the business of a polite society. Such reticence began to disappear in the second phase following the Department of Health's recognition of a very serious public health problem in a series of landmark publications, which included *Supporting Doctors, Protecting Patients*; *The NHS Plan: a plan for investment, a plan for reform*; *An Organisation With a Memory*; and *Building a Safer NHS for Patients*.

This marked the end of the age of innocence and denial of the problem of medical errors. Such was the rate of progress that the third phase evolved into the most difficult task of all – selecting a mere fraction of material from the daily deluge of relevant material. That remained the most frustrating aspect of writing the book. My sincere thanks to Jamie Etherington, Editorial Manager at Radcliffe Medical Press, for his continued understanding in allowing numerous amendments and inclusions.

My concern for the subject matter progressed from one of absorbing interest, yet frequent disbelief, into an indulgence or compulsion. The task of collecting and organising a substantial body of data from many sources outside my own area of expertise was particularly illuminating. If I have failed to interest, intrigue or enlighten then the enterprise has failed. Most importantly, whilst the book begins to provide answers to certain problems, it raises even more important questions, the solutions for which will require the united efforts of society acting together. All attempts have been made to verify the data and presentations, however, I remain entirely responsible for any inaccuracies and omissions. I would value comments if the reader discerns any faults.

This book could not have been written without an understanding of undergraduate teaching and the realities of student life. The students provide the teacher with an endless stream of abilities, interests and talents and make for instructive company. They quickly reveal any shortcomings within the system and their limited understanding of errors committed by healthcare staff was a major stimulus for the book. Such information was not readily available to them, or indeed, to their teachers.

Yet most importantly the book was written for anyone who has, is or will receive treatment at the hands of the healthcare system. Since this is almost everyone, the subject has wide appeal. I have focused on the crucial issues and tried to be comprehensible rather than comprehensive, and hope that the 'portions' of science, healthcare, education and law allow the reader a memorable meal. Bon appetit!

Professor Robert Naylor
r.j.naylor@bradford.ac.uk
April 2002

About the author

Robert Naylor is Professor of Pharmacology in the School of Pharmacy at the University of Bradford. A focus on neuropharmacological research relevant to psychiatric, neurological and gastrointestinal disorders, evolved into a 30-year period of drug discovery with Professor Brenda Costall (as a husband-and-wife team) and collaboration with many colleagues, students and friends in the neuropharmacological team at Bradford, and within the international pharmaceutical industry. It led to the identification of a number of drugs that were progressed as medicines to the clinic. For 30 years he has also taught pharmacology to students in many disciplines – pharmacy, nursing, medicine, psychology, biomedical sciences and others. He has also been chairman of a school of pharmacy. It was from his research, educational background and experience of pharmacy practice, the uncertain understanding of undergraduate and graduate students of the risks and benefits of medication and harm to patients, that the motivation for this book was born.

Acknowledgements

In writing this book I have corresponded with and undoubtedly interrupted, disturbed and intruded on a great number of people in many walks of life. Yet I have met with nothing but politeness and patience. My sincere thanks to all concerned. Particular thanks must be expressed to Dr Robert Dewdney, Dr John Blenkinsop, Dr Ian E Hughes, Professor Jeff Lucas, Dr Ian L Naylor and Dr David Wiseman for their valued comments on the text, and Andrew Murdoch for the use of unpublished data. Special thanks are due to Brenda Costall and Professor David J Johns for their detailed comments, and for their assistance in proof reading the final manuscript. I am also particularly indebted to Dr Kenneth Gulleforde, Barrister, for his comments on the content of Chapters 10 and 15, which address legal issues relevant to medical errors.

List of abbreviations

ABMS	American Board of Medical Specialists
ACGME	Accreditation Council for Graduate Medical Education
ADEs	Adverse drug events
ADRs	Adverse drug reactions
AHRQ	Agency for Healthcare Research and Quality
AMA	American Medical Association
APIL	Association of Personal Injury Lawyers
APSF	Australian Patient Safety Foundation
ASHP	American Society of Health-System Pharmacists
BMA	British Medical Association
BNF	British National Formulary
CI	Confidence Interval
CPR	Civil Procedure Rules
CPR	Cardiopulmonary resusitation
ECG	Electrocardiogram
EFAHP	European Foundation for the Advancement of Healthcare Practitioners
EU	European Union
FDA	Food and Drug Administration
FHSAs	Family Health Service Authorities
GMC	General Medical Council
GP	General Practitioner
HCFA	Healthcare Financing Administration
ICU	Intensive Care Unit
IHI	Institute for Healthcare Improvement
IOM	Institute of Medicine
ISMP	Institute for Safe Medication Practice
JCAHO	Joint Commission on the Accreditation of Healthcare Organisations
MDEL	Medical and Dental Levy
MPET	Multi-Professional Education and Training
NCAA	National Clinical Assessment Authority
NCEPOD	National Confidential Enquiry into Perioperative Deaths
NCPS	National Clinical Pharmacy Services
NHS	National Health Service (United Kingdom)
NICE	National Institute for Clinical Excellence
NIH	National Institutes of Health
NMET	Non-Medical Education and Training
NSAIDs	non-steroidal anti-inflammatory drugs

OHRP	Office for Human Research Protection
OSCE	Objective Structured Clinical Examination
PPA	Prescription Pricing Authority
QAA	The Quality Assurance Agency for Higher Education
QoL	Quality of Life
QuIC	Quality Interagency Coordination Task Force
RPSGB	Royal Pharmaceutical Society of Great Britain
SCOPME	Standing Committee on Postgraduate Medical and Dental Education
SERNIP	Safety and Efficacy Register, New Intervention Procedures
SHOs	Senior House Officers
SIFT	Service Increment for Teaching
TPN	total parenteral nutrition
UCAS	University Council Admission Service

Chapter 1

The two faces of medicines

Summary: Drugs used as therapeutic treatments: a two-edged sword

- Medicines are drugs which are chemicals. They are an essential daily aid to millions of patients in the relief of pain and suffering and the treatment of disease.
- This unquestioned and most valuable function, together with a sometimes casual indifference to their chemical nature, has hidden their serious potential for harm or 'adverse events' even when they are taken or administered with care.
- When compounded by the use of medicines in error by either the patient or the healthcare professional, the harm that can be caused to patients becomes an even greater problem.
- Yet there has been a genuine naivety or even unwillingness by healthcare professionals to begin the task of understanding the extent and nature of the problem.

The aims of this book are threefold.

1 to contribute to the global debate on the reduction of adverse events, particularly those induced by drugs and medication errors, in order to improve patient care
2 to provide students and colleagues in education and healthcare, those who resource and organise the healthcare system, patients, carers and society with a concise account of the nature of a serious public health problem
3 to identify possible solutions to the problem in order to begin to reduce adverse events and medication errors.

Introduction

On the available evidence, medical errors in the UK and the USA, including those caused by drugs and their medical misuse, are responsible for the death of some 4 and 8 patients and injury to at least 40 and 100 patients, respectively, every hour. The editor of a respected journal, *Quality in Health Care*, wrote a paper entitled 'Delivering safe health care' with the following introductory sentence: 'One fundamental guarantee that we cannot give our patients is that the faults and errors in the health care system won't harm them'.[1] Clearly, then, a serious issue is obvious to all. That issue is a major public health problem which probably exists in all developed countries. The extent and nature of the problem and the solutions that are needed to reduce faults and errors are the subject of this book.

Medicines are an integral part of life and their value is unquestioned. Examples of the many successes include insulin for the control of diabetes, antibiotics for the treatment of infection, beta-blockers and diuretics for the treatment of cardiovascular disease, chemotherapy for the control of cancer, anaesthetics and neuromuscular blocking drugs to allow complex surgery, analgesics to alleviate the distress of pain, anticonvulsants for the prevention of epilepsy, and the drug-dependent revolution in the treatment of psychiatric disorders.

The medical and pharmaceutical sciences can take great pride in these very real achievements, and indeed the great advances in therapeutics have encouraged a cultural belief by society and many in the healthcare professions that medicines are generally 'safe'. This view has been encouraged by commercial interests and those activities which have regrettably promoted the sale and use of medicines as a commodity. However, to consider drugs as 'safe' creates a dangerous illusion for society, patients and healthcare professionals which obscures the actual risks involved in medical treatments.

For example, aspirin and ibuprofen are perhaps the best known of a group of medicines described as the 'non-steroidal anti-inflammatory drugs' (NSAIDs). Such medicines, which have a common mechanism of action, are used extensively throughout the world as valuable drug treatments for the acute or short-term control of inflammatory or painful conditions such as rheumatoid arthritis, dysmenorrhoea and other disorders. It was reported in the USA that in one year 70 million prescriptions (representing 3.8% of all prescriptions) were written for NSAIDs at a cost of about $2 billion, with over-the-counter sales accounting for a further $1.8 billion.[2,3]

It is emphasised that, when used properly and under supervision as a short-term treatment, these drugs are invaluable and generally well tolerated. However, for over 40 years the NSAIDs have had known 'side-effects' ranging from mild to fatal. Probably at least 10–20% of patients have dyspepsia, and within a 6-month period about 5–15% of patients discontinue treatment for this reason.[4] The NSAIDs 'irritate' the gastrointestinal tract by removing a protective mechanism that normally prevents damage. This may cause a major problem with prolonged treatment with this group of drugs, because the doses of these drugs that cause damage are close to those which are required to relieve pain. A recent study has shown that for every 1200 people who take NSAIDs for at least 2 months, one will die from gastroduodenal complications.[5] This is the apparent risk of death from bleeding or perforated gastroduodenal ulcers with the chronic use of NSAIDs. It is equivalent to about 2000 deaths a year in the UK alone, and to about 16 500 deaths a year in the USA.[6]

Medication errors are the single commonest cause of medical errors, and in a Medical Defence Union study of adult deaths that were attributed to medication errors, over half were related to just three classes of drugs, namely the NSAIDs, anticoagulants (which may have been administered with the NSAIDs) and analgesics.[7] However, the risks are not evenly distributed within society. In an analysis of drug-related problems in elderly patients admitted to Tayside hospitals, no less than 5.3% of admissions were probably or definitely drug related. NSAIDs were the main group of drugs involved, being responsible for 28% of all such admissions.[8] In the USA, elderly patients show a 300–500% increase in the rate of hospitalisation and death from peptic ulcers,[9] and in this population around 30% of deaths are attributable to NSAIDs.[10] In the USA in 1983 it was estimated that $3.9 billion was spent on the management of the preventable adverse gastrointestinal effects of the NSAIDs alone.[11] This is a tragic indictment of patient injury and death due to a drug treatment.

Under proper medical or pharmaceutical supervision this risk may be greatly reduced or even removed by careful dosage adjustment and advice on the care required if the patient is taking other painkilling drugs (that may unknown to the patient also contain an NSAID drug) or other medicines that may exacerbate the gastrointestinal effects of NSAIDs. Furthermore, there are other medicines (e.g. misoprostol or the proton-pump inhibitors) which, when taken with the anti-inflammatory drugs, will protect against the gastrointestinal damage.[12,13] However, these interventions require expert knowledge, and in the UK the NSAIDs can be freely purchased even from supermarkets and petrol stations. The reader may seriously question whether this creates an appropriate culture for the safe use of medicines. Tramer has recently drawn attention to the problematic nature of this group of drugs in the title of his comment on a report on the NSAIDs: 'Aspirin, like all other drugs is a poison'.[14]

A recent and excellent article entitled 'Painkiller risks' published in *The Times* by Ingram[15] indicated for the lay reader the real risks associated with the NSAIDs, and referred the reader to patient information websites (pharmweb.net) and to the Oxford Pain Internet site, Over-Count (www.jr2.ox.ac.uk), which provide further guidance for individuals who believe that they may be misunderstanding or abusing over-the-counter analgesic drugs. However, such articles are rare.

Given the serious limitations to the use of existing NSAIDs, pharmaceutical and medical research has attempted to develop new and improved NSAIDs, called COX-2 inhibitors, which are designed not to adversely affect the gastrointestinal system. Celebrax and Vioxx are two such drugs, and are described as 'two of the fastest rising drugs in sales volume history, with $2 billion and $1.5 billion, respectively, in retail sales in the USA in 2000'.[16] Their potential is currently being evaluated.[16–19] Guidance on the use of the COX-2 inhibitors (celecoxib, etodolac, rofecoxib and meloxicam) in the UK has been issued by the National Institute for Clinical Excellence, which restricts their use to arthritis patients who are at high risk of developing serious gastrointestinal problems.[20,21]

Regarding and selling medicines as a commodity comes at a very real cost to patients' lives and professionals' reputations, and also at great expense to the healthcare system. The 'safety' of drugs can be a fatal illusion. Indeed, the number of deaths related to the NSAIDs alone is of the same order of magnitude as the number of deaths in road traffic accidents in the UK. Yet we try to reduce road traffic accidents by means of rigorously defined speed limits, active police intervention and widespread uses of camera and video surveillance of unsafe behaviour. However, no less than the Committee on Safety of Medicines in the UK, in agreeing that ibuprofen and other drugs are safe for general sale, has been criticised for being at odds with the Government's policy of promoting safe, effective and responsible self-care.[22]

The relative indifference to injury and death caused by the routine use of common drugs is curious, and appears to reflect a greater interest in developing and prioritising commercial activities. It may also reflect the lack of interest and attention directed to the problem by the media, as society cannot address a problem that is not known to exist. In addition, the mechanisms which exist for the reporting of adverse drug-induced events betray a voluntary and almost amateurish approach,[23,24] notwithstanding a structured system.[25] For example, it was as late as November 1999 that, *for the first time*, all community pharmacists in the UK were allowed to report adverse drug reactions via the 'yellow-card' scheme following a successful pilot trial.[26,27] They were asked to address in particular adverse drug responses associated with over-the-counter medicines and herbal products. In addition, the Consumers' Association has expressed concern about flaws in the black-triangle scheme which is used by the Medicines Control Agency to identify new medicines which are being closely monitored for adverse effects, based on an analysis of summaries of product characteristics given in the electronic medicines compendium (www.emc.vhn.net). In total, 54 out of 159 branded products in the black-triangle scheme were not listed in the electronic medicines compendium and 29 of those listed were not identified as black-triangle medicines.[28]

Yet this book reveals that injury and death caused by drugs and other medical interventions greatly exceed those caused by vehicular and many other accidents. Again, while the use of alcohol is a well-known risk factor in road traffic accidents, the possible association of road traffic accidents with the taking of prescribed medicines such as the benzodiazepines, antidepressants and other psychoactive drugs is much less well appreciated and researched.[29] Similarly, falls and hip fractures in the elderly are a major and well-known source of personal injury. What may be less well understood is that a recent investigation has revealed that during the initial 2-week period of medication, or after more than 1 month of continuous use of a prescribed benzodiazepine, the risk of hip fracture increases by 60% and 80%, respectively.[30]

Misunderstanding of the potentially unsafe nature of medication is not limited to lay people. Recently, during the design and teaching of new courses in pharmacology and therapeutics to undergraduate students in pharmacy and other healthcare disciplines, emphasis was given to the great care required in the safe use of medicines, and also to the problem of medical error. Even when used properly, it was clearly identified that drugs may cause injury and death and that their use in ignorance has been shown to be disastrous. Some students considered this to be an over-reaction, notwithstanding the (almost daily) deluge of media reports and even a television series in the UK devoted to serious medication and other medical errors. However, the students' confusion was understandable.

In one of the most widely used and respected textbooks, Goodman and Gilman's *The Pharmacological Basis of Therapeutics*,[31] the magnitude of the problem of serious adverse drug reactions is considered in a single page (out of 1900 pages!), and there is no mention of medication error. In Young and Koda-Kimble's definitive *Applied Therapeutics: the Clinical Use of Drugs*,[32] there is no mention of medication errors in the index.

It was only as recently as the year 2000 that the *British Medical Journal* (*BMJ*) courageously devoted almost an entire issue to medical errors.[33] It was reported that a previous attempt by the same journal 10 years ago to instigate a major study to investigate error had been roundly criticised by the President of a Royal Medical College for drawing the attention of the mass media to medical error. No detailed article on medication error has yet appeared in the *Pharmaceutical Journal*, although *Pharmacy Practice* is now publishing a series of articles.

The subject also appears to be an unwelcome guest at medical and other scientific meetings. For example, in the Millenium Festival of Medicine, entitled 'Celebrating the past and shaping the future', culminating in a Keynote Conference in November 2000, and at the British Pharmaceutical Society Conference entitled 'Medicines: the future horizon' in September 2000, and at the Pharmacy World Congress in Vienna entitled 'Pharmacy in the twenty-first century: the way forward' in August 2000, there were exciting programmes of medical and scientific events. However, no mention was made at any of these meetings of one of the most immediate and serious challenges facing every healthcare system in the developed world, namely medication and other errors.

A 'distasteful' subject: adverse drug reactions and medication errors

Against the undoubted potential benefit of drug therapy is the downside that, even when used properly, drugs can seriously harm, disable or cause death. These are variously known as adverse drug events, reactions, responses or effects, or drug toxicity. In Goodman and Gilman's textbook, the adverse reactions are considered to be 'a cost of medical therapy'. Although the mandate of the FDA is to ensure that drugs are safe and effective, both of these terms are relative.

Indeed, adverse reactions to drugs are cited as the commonest cause of iatrogenic disease (defined as an illness induced in a patient as a direct consequence of the physician's action) in humans.[34]

In summary, drugs may:

- cause serious injury, disability and death in their own right *even when used correctly* (i.e. these effects are not preventable)
- be safe in use *until used in error* (i.e. these effects are preventable).

An impression of 'safety' is even conveyed by the words 'medicine' or 'drug', which 'sanctify' their chemical nature – a simple but highly effective illusion. However, the terms 'adverse chemical events/reactions/responses/effects' or 'chemical toxicity' have a different connotation.

However, there is even distaste for the words 'disability' and 'death', which were considered 'hot and shrill' by McDonald and colleagues,[35] at least as used in the recent and highly influential Institute of Medicine report[36] on medical errors. Perhaps TS Eliot, the Anglo-American poet, was correct in saying that 'Human kind/Cannot bear very much reality' (*Four Quartets*, 'Burnt Norton', 1936). In the present account, injury, disability and death are expressed in these terms. This is precisely what the patient or family experience, and it also reflects the thoughts of the physician or healthcare staff member who has caused or is involved in these tragic events. Thus attempts have been made to avoid euphemisms, as the latter are not innocuous, and indeed are frequently calculated and designed to deceive. They create a protective patina of respectability which may afford a degree of comfort and distance a person from unpleasant facts. However, they inevitably distort the facts and finally start to conceal the truth and seriously interfere with a realistic understanding.

Yet errors remain a uniquely 'unpleasant' subject that many people, including some in the healthcare professions, would prefer not to consider or discuss at all. Indeed, a cultural hostility of fundamental proportions is revealed when the President of a Royal Medical College can criticise attempts even to establish the extent of the problem. However, since 1999 the extent of the problem of medical and medication errors has become only too clear to governments in terms of the human and financial costs to patients, their families and the healthcare systems. In addition, there can be devastating effects on reputations and serious damage to trust in the professions and in healthcare.

However, it is important to emphasise that the concerns must not be confused with 'accidents' and society's obsession with safety, the 'blame game' and turning bad luck into culpable negligence. For those wishing to climb Ben Nevis or Mount Kinabalu, the rewards can be tremendous. Yet the misfortune of injury and accidents is an essential part of the unwritten contract of such adventures, the excitement of risk and the human condition. To cleanse the word 'accident' from a medical journal,[37] in the belief that accidents are a failure to take precautions, while accepting that the word 'accident' is inappropriate when considering injuries,[38] may unintentionally contribute to a culture which believes that behind every injury can be found a neglect worthy of financial redress.[39] However, this may undermine a crucial sense of personal responsibility, and this is of paramount importance in acquiring an understanding of the risks involved in climbing mountains or taking medicines.

From a similar perspective, Furedi suggests that: ' "Safety at any price" is not a virtue of a rational society. It is a symptom of compulsive behaviour'.[40] The present account acknowledges that patients who accept medical treatments are inevitably exposed to degrees of risk. It is about minimising the risks cognisant of an acceptable and known standard of decent behaviour.

The aims of this book

These are threefold:

1   to contribute to the global debate on the reduction of adverse drug-induced events and medication errors, in order to improve patient care
2   to provide students and colleagues in education and healthcare, those who resource and organise the healthcare system, patients, carers and society with a concise account of the background and nature of a serious public health problem
3   to identify possible solutions to the problem in order to begin to reduce adverse events and medication errors.

The detailed objectives are as follows:

1   to identify more clearly the nature of the problem.
   • to attempt to establish the incidence and nature of non-preventable and preventable adverse drug events in patients in both primary and secondary healthcare
   • to analyse how and where drug-induced adverse events and errors occur in the medication process
   • to consider the risk factors which contribute to adverse events and errors
   • to assess the human and financial costs of adverse events and errors
2   to attempt to identify solutions to the problem:
   • to define human errors and the consequences of their recognition, acknowledgement, recording, reporting, analysis and response in healthcare
   • to address the issues of the major challenge of attempting to achieve a reduction in medical errors
   • to indicate the strategies that are available to reduce medication errors as the single commonest form of medical error
   • to consider the significance for both education and healthcare of a lack of knowledge by the clinical practitioner as the single most frequent cause of medication error

- to consider how the major changes in the civil and criminal law in the UK relating to complaints and medical litigation may influence standards of professional behaviour
- to consider the implications of error reporting for future professional aspirations and clinical competence, and the purported new roles for healthcare staff in the new National Health Service (NHS).

Given the intended broad nature of the readership of this book, the numerical and statistical findings are presented as briefly as possible. Frequently the data are displayed in a visual format in order to aid understanding and memory of the overall picture.

This book describes a journey of discovery which is frequently a cause of deep concern. However, it is also a journey in which there is real belief in an optimistic outcome. During the completion of the book, the report by the Department of Health entitled *An Organisation with a Memory*[41] was published, and *Building a Safer NHS for Patients*[42] was published after the manuscript had been completed. It became clear that the subject matter was being overtaken by events. Both of these very important reports attest to the intense interest and rapidly growing resolve of the NHS and other healthcare systems to address problems of patient safety. In addition, in the USA President Bush has increased the budget of the Agency for Healthcare Research and Quality by $100 million in order to promote research on the safety of patients,[43] and at the first Asia Pacific Forum on quality improvement in healthcare in Sydney in September 2001, it was reported that the meeting was over-subscribed.[44] This reflects current interest in Europe, where it is reported that over 1000 people from over 30 countries now attend the European forums.[44] For these reasons, different chapters were revisited and comments from the above reports and meetings have been included to indicate the global importance that is now attached to improving the quality of healthcare systems, and the challenging if not daunting task of reducing the level of harm to patients.

The incidence of adverse events, adverse drug reactions (ADRs) and medication errors in hospitals

Summary: The recognition of adverse events and their importance in hospitalised patients

- Studies of hospitalised patients in the developed world indicate that adverse events, defined as injury or mortality induced by medical management (operative, drug related, procedure related, diagnostic mishap or therapeutic mishap) are a leading cause of impairment, disability and death.
- This is equivalent to the death of at least 8 and 4 patients (and injury to over 100 and 45) every hour in the USA and UK, respectively.
- Drug-related adverse events (iatrogenic injury) are the single commonest adverse event, and around 50% of the adverse events are preventable.
- It is essential that educators, healthcare workers, patients, politicians and society grasp the scale of this major public health problem.

Introduction

Adverse events, reactions and effects are defined below. Their classification by Edwards and Aronson[1] can be found in Appendix 1.

Adverse events, adverse drug reactions (ADRs) and medication errors are to be found in healthcare systems throughout the world. However, the literature on adverse events, reactions and medication errors is a relatively recent phenomenon. In most countries it has not received priority status, and frequently it has received little attention.

However, in the USA in 1961, hospital pharmacists Barker and McConnell[2] conducted a study which showed that one out of every six doses of medication was given in error. As a result, many pharmacists began to focus attention on medication error (*see* review by Davis[3]). In retrospect, if pharmacists had published more widely in the medical literature, then the developing problems of medication error might have been addressed at an earlier stage. However, this was clearly an extremely sensitive issue, since publishing on the subject of colleagues' imperfections is still fraught with practical difficulties. Interest in ADRs was also stimulated by the thalidomide tragedy in the early 1960s, and in the USA the Senate passed a bill in 1964 requiring pharmaceutical companies to provide ADR data to consumers. In the same year, Schimmel[4] reported that 20% of patients who were admitted to a university hospital medical service were injured by medical treatment, and that 20% of the iatrogenic injuries were serious or fatal. In addition, prospective studies on hospital patients began to record all ADRs in defined populations.[5]

The definition of an adverse event/reaction/effect

An *adverse event* in a patient can be defined as 'an appreciably harmful or unpleasant event during the commission or omission of an intervention that may be related to a diagnostic test, surgical, medical or other healthcare procedure'. This would include the spectrum of minor to major adverse events or death, and does not necessarily imply error or negligence. These are assessed as a separate issue.

It is also important to note that not all 'events' are necessarily related to the primary challenge. For example, in clinical drug trials or surgery, an adverse event may be related to the pathology or other factors. It is not always possible to establish causality with the drug administration or surgical procedure.

With respect to an *adverse drug reaction*, the harm or unpleasant reaction actually results from the use of a *medicinal* product which is a complex preparation incorporating many different chemicals. It would be more accurate to use the term 'medicine' rather than drug. Frequently, however, there are many medical preparations containing the same drug. This book considers 'drugs' rather than 'medicines' as the cause of an event.

It is also important to note that an *adverse drug reaction* is seen from the *perspective of the patient*, who may also be taking other prescribed and over-the-counter medicines, alcohol, other recreational drugs, unusual foods or health products.

Drug reactions may be:

- *predictable*, based on the known preclinical and clinical pharmacology, or
- *unpredictable or 'idiosyncratic'*, occurring unexpectedly as an interaction between the individual patient's unique environmental or genetic factors. These reactions may be severe.

In contrast, an *adverse drug effect* is an outcome that can be attributed to the *drug itself*, whatever the mechanisms involved and the patient population.

Yet by the 1970s, the evaluation of ADRs in clinical practice remained somewhat arbitrary. The data on ADRs were described as:

> *incomplete, unrepresentative, uncontrolled, and lacking in operational criteria for identifying ADRs. No quantitative conclusions can be drawn from the reported data in regard to morbidity, mortality, or the underlying causes of ADRs, and attempts to extrapolate the available data to the general population would be invalid and perhaps misleading.*[6]

About 10 years later, the accumulation of quantitative information on the clinical use and adverse effects of drugs, particularly those drugs that had been marketed for many years, began to reveal an unwelcome perspective on the problem. On the basis of in-hospital studies,[7] some type of adverse reaction was reported to occur as follows:

- about once in every 20 drug treatments
- 10% of these reactions were regarded as life-threatening
- outpatient drug toxicity was the cause of about 3% of all hospital admissions.

These were astonishing claims of the serious hazards posed by the drugs themselves and/or by their medical or patient misuse.

However, it was the detailed and quantitative analyses which were reported in the 1990s that seriously challenged a reluctant understanding not only of the importance of ADRs, but also of the incidence of adverse events and medication errors *per se*. There was also a growing realisation that ignoring the problem was simply creating an ever increasing dilemma.

The following studies provide important examples of investigations which have made a major contribution to or challenged our understanding of the incidence and causes of drug-induced or medically-induced injury or death.

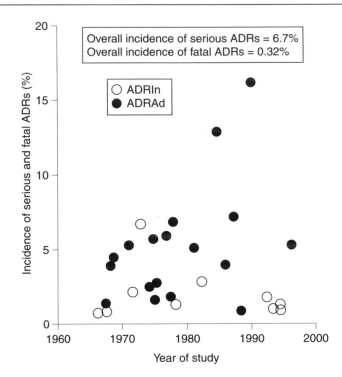

Figure 2.1: The inherently harmful nature of medication. The incidence of serious plus fatal adverse drug reactions (ADRs) in 39 studies of patients in the USA over a 32-year period incurred by drugs that were judged to have been properly prescribed and administered. All 39 points are not visible since several of them are superimposed. ADRs are shown for those patients who exhibited an ADR while in hospital (ADRIn) and for those admitted to hospital with an ADR (ADRAd). Prepared from the data of Lazarou *et al.*[8]

The inherently dangerous nature of drugs

A meta-analysis of studies in the USA

The objective of the study by Lazarou and colleagues[8] was to estimate the incidence of serious and fatal adverse drug reactions (ADRs) in hospital patients in the USA that were attributed to the drug itself.

It is important to note that possible ADRs caused by errors in drug administration, non-compliance, overdose, drug abuse or therapeutic failures were all carefully excluded. Briefly, the goal of the study was to estimate injuries incurred by drugs that were 'safely administered'.

Of 153 prospective studies reported in the literature between 1966 and 1996, 39 studies were selected. A serious ADR was defined as one which requires hospitalisation, prolongs hospitalisation, is permanently disabling or results in

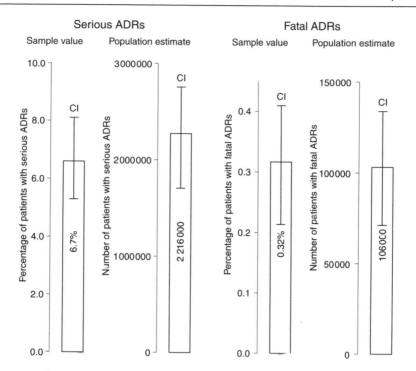

Figure 2.2: The inherently harmful nature of medication. The incidence of serious adverse drug reactions (ADRs) and fatal ADRs in hospitalised patients in the USA in 1994 incurred by drugs that were judged to have been properly prescribed and administered. Sample data and population estimates are shown. Prepared from the data of Lazarou *et al*.[9]

death. Serious ADRs therefore include fatal ADRs, which were also analysed separately.

The prospective studies were conducted on two separate populations of patients, namely those admitted to hospital because of an ADR (ADRAd) and those who experienced an ADR while in hospital (ADRIn).

Over a 32-year period, combining the ADRAd and ADRIn data, drugs induced in hospital patients in the USA:

- an overall incidence of serious ADRs of 6.7% (95% CI, 5.2–8.2%) of the patient population
- an overall incidence of fatal ADRs of 0.32% (95% CI, 0.32–0.41%) of the patient population.

The data indicate that the incidence of ADRs remained fairly constant over a 32-year period (*see* Figure 2.1).

The incidence of ADRIn was 2.1% (95% CI, 1.9–2.3%), compared with an incidence of ADRAd of 4.7% (95% CI, 3.1–6.2%) (the overall incidence of ADRIn and ADRAd of all severities was 15.1% (95% CI, 12.0–18.1%) of hospital

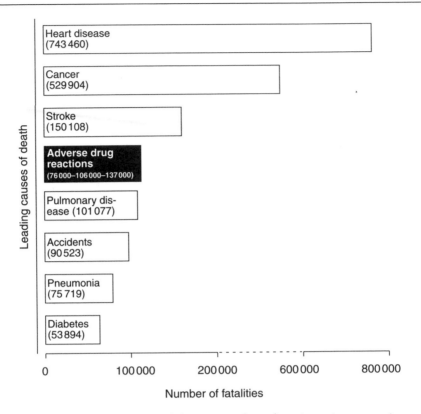

Figure 2.3: The inherently harmful nature of medication. A comparison of the leading causes of death in the USA in 1994 and the estimated deaths (and confidence intervals) caused by adverse drug reactions. The drugs were judged to have been properly prescribed and administered. Prepared from the data of Lazarou *et al.*[8]

patients). Estimates of the number of hospital patients in the USA who experienced a serious or fatal ADR in 1994 are shown in Figure 2.2.

The numbers appear to be large and difficult to comprehend. To illustrate their significance, Lazarou and colleagues compared the values with those for other major causes of death in the USA (*see* Figure 2.3). These comparisons were memorable, with conclusions indicating that fatal ADRs are between the fourth and the sixth commonest cause of death in the USA.

The authors concluded that ADRs represent an important clinical issue. Again, it is emphasised that *the figures relate to drugs that were judged to have been properly administered (i.e. the adversity was not preventable)*. Such information is important for improving our understanding of the inherently adverse consequences of medication and the drugs that cause these effects, and for contributing to the design of improved treatments.

Preventable and non-preventable adverse events

The Harvard Medical Practice Study

This major study was part of an interdisciplinary investigation of medical injury and malpractice litigation by Brennan and colleagues.[9] It was not designed primarily to study risk factors for injury, or indeed patient safety, for example, but to assess the extent of injury that could lead to malpractice litigation. Thus the authors excluded non-disabling injuries and focused on negligence. This inevitably led to an underestimate of the total number of adverse events.

In a retrospective medical record review study, data were obtained from 30 121 randomly selected patient record charts from 51 randomly selected acute state care, non-psychiatric hospitals in New York State in 1984. The process involved two stages. All records were initially screened by trained nurses or medical records administrators using 18 screening criteria. The detailed criteria used to detect adverse events can be found in Hiatt et al.[10] (see also Leape et al.[11]). Records that fulfilled any of the criteria were then reviewed independently by two physicians who identified adverse events and instances of negligence.

The adverse events included hospital-incurred trauma, adverse drug reactions in hospital, acute myocardial infarction, cardiovascular accident or pulmonary embolism during or following an invasive procedure, neurological deficit at discharge, death, cardiac/respiratory arrest, and transfer from general care to a special care unit.

The screening criteria were indicators or markers of an undesirable outcome that had already occurred, where the outcomes could have resulted from an adverse event. Patients had to fulfil only one of the screening criteria. Care was taken to exclude as far as possible patients who were severely ill or who had complicated conditions.

A limitation of the study was that it relied on implicit judgements made by physicians. Leape and colleagues[11] emphasised that:

> While extensive efforts were made to strengthen the accuracy and reproducibility of these judgements through training of physician reviewers, use of a highly structured data collection instrument, and duplicate review with rereview, and resolution of disagreements, errors undoubtedly occurred. It is possible that these errors 'cancelled out' (i.e. over-interpretation of medical error was balanced by under-interpretation), but that is unknown. A serious weakness of any retrospective review is hindsight bias, the tendency to impute causation to an action when the (bad) outcome is known. Hindsight bias would tend to overestimate the number of deaths due to adverse events.

In an uncompromising study the authors estimated the incidence of the following:

- adverse events caused by medical management (and not by the disease process)
- the subgroup of such events that resulted from negligent or substandard care.

Definition: the term medical management refers to physicians and any member of the healthcare team (e.g. nurses, pharmacists, physiotherapists and other supportive personnel) who may have contributed to patient injury following surgery, medication, diagnostic testing or any other aspect of healthcare.

The physicians identified a total of 1278 adverse events, which included 306 adverse events due to negligence. It was estimated that:

- the statewide incidence rate of adverse events occurred in 3.7% of the hospitalisations (95% CI, 3.2–4.2%)
- 27.6% of these adverse events were attributed to negligence (95% CI, 22.5–32.6%).

The investigators then developed population estimates of injuries and computed rates according to the age and sex of the patients as well as the specialities of the clinicians.

It was estimated that among the 2 671 863 patients who were discharged from New York State hospitals in 1984 there were 98 609 adverse events, and 27 179 adverse events involving negligence. Negligence was found more frequently in cases involving patients who had died (*see* Figure 2.4).

A number of specialities (neurosurgery, cardiac and thoracic surgery and vascular surgery) had higher rates of adverse events but not negligence. The data suggested that variation in rates of litigation between specialities does not reflect differing levels of competence, but rather differences in the types of patients and diseases for which the specialist cares.

(Leape and colleagues[12] further investigated the types of adverse events which were found, and included those related to operative procedures, such as wound infection, and also non-operative events, such as technical complications, diagnostic mishap, drug-related events and 11 other causes which are reported in detail on page 42).

It was concluded that there is a substantial amount of harm to patients resulting from medical management, and that many adverse events are the result of substandard care.

It should be noted that adverse events do not necessarily signal poor-quality care (the events may have been unpreventable), nor does their absence necessarily indicate good-quality care (the treatment, whilst not causing an adverse event, may have been ineffective).

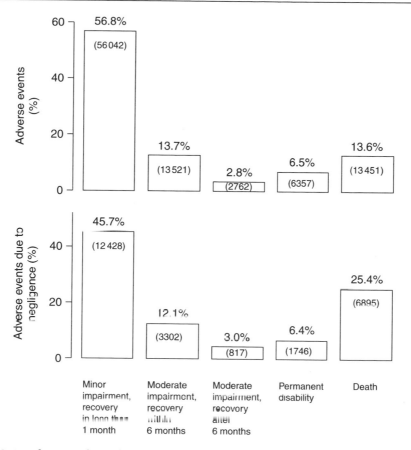

Figure 2.4: The number of adverse events caused by medical management that were judged to be the result of negligence. The estimated number of adverse events and negligent adverse events causing impairment, permanent disability and death recorded in the Harvard Medical Practice Study of 2 671 863 patients discharged from New York State hospitals in 1984. The population estimates of adverse events are expressed as the percentage and number (in parentheses) of patients in each category of injury. (Disability could not be reasonably judged in 6.6% of patients.) Prepared from the data of Brennan *et al.*[9]

In a further analysis of the data by Leape and colleagues[13] *to include injuries*, it was found that:

- adverse events *and injuries* caused by medical management occurred in 7% of admissions
- 69% of the injuries were the result of error.

In total, 37% of the errors in the use of a drug were judged to be negligent.

Again, it is likely that this underestimates the *error rate*, as the investigators defined adverse events stringently as 'disability and injury', and errors do not necessarily produce injury. For example, they may have been detected in good time, or the patient may have been resilient.

A study in Utah and Colorado

The conclusions of the Harvard Medical Practice Study were broadly corroborated by Thomas and colleagues[14] in a review of medical records of a random sample of 15 000 discharges from hospitals in Utah and Colorado in 1992.
   The study found that:

- adverse events occurred in 2.9% of hospitalisations
- 80% of these adverse events occurred in hospital, and the remainder occurred in the physician's office, the patient's home or some other non-hospital setting
- 53% of adverse events were preventable
- 29.2% of adverse events were due to negligence
- 6.6% of adverse events led to death (a lower value than that of 13.6% recorded in the Harvard study)
- the leading cause of non-operative adverse events was adverse drug events (19.3%); of these, 35.1% were due to negligence.

If one extrapolates the results of the above two studies to over 33.6 million admissions to hospitals in the USA in 1997, it would appear that at least 44 000 Americans die each year as a result of preventable medical errors.

Medication error deaths in the USA

The Harvard and Utah and Colorado studies, as well as the study by Lazarou and colleagues, were conducted on hospital-based material. Phillips and colleagues used a different approach which was designed to measure medication errors within the entire healthcare system and to compare inpatient and outpatient data.[15]
   They examined US death certificates for the period 1983–93, which indicate the cause of death (with International Classification of Disease codes), race, sex and patient status.
   'Medication error' was classified as accidental poisoning by drugs, medicinal substances and biological agents, which includes 'accidental overdose of drug, wrong drug given or taken in error, and drugs taken inadvertently', as well as 'accidents in the use of drugs and biologicals in medical and surgical procedures'. 'Medication error' deaths per year increased overall from 2876 to 7391 over the 10-year period, corresponding to a 257% increase (*see* Figure 2.5).
   A more detailed analysis of the data revealed marked differences between the increase in 'medication error' deaths of outpatients (848%) and inpatients (237%) (*see* Figure 2.5 inset). The increased number of deaths could not be

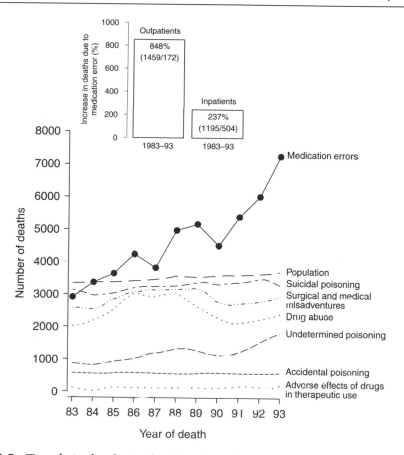

Figure 2.5: Trends in deaths in the USA based on the coding of death certificates according to the International Classification of Disease codes (ICD-9) from errors attributed to medication and from related causes during the period 1983–93. Inset shows a breakdown of the data into a comparison of the percentage increase (with numbers in parentheses) in deaths attributed to medication error in subjects who had received outpatient and inpatient treatment. Prepared from the data of Phillips *et al.*[15]

accounted for by the increased number of prescriptions (a 2.57-fold increase in medication deaths compared with a 1.39-fold increase in prescriptions). Furthermore, the increase in 'medication errors' contrasted with the lack of increase in deaths due to drug-induced adverse effects, and this is in agreement with the data reported by Lazarou and colleagues.

However, 'medication' deaths did vary according to race and sex. Black and white males showed 5.23- and 2.8-fold increases, respectively, and black and white females showed 2.27- and 1.53-fold increases, respectively. It was suggested that the high-risk groups might be those most likely to receive outpatient treatment, which fuelled a growing concern about the quality

Table 2.1: Medication error deaths for each of the nine pharmacological categories listed under medication errors (E850–E858) in 1983 and 1993 and the ratio increase or decrease during this period[15]

Pharmacological category	1983	1993	Ratio
Analgesics, antipyretics and antirheumatics	851	2098	2.47
Barbiturates	75	18	0.24
Other sedatives and hypnotics	43	17	0.40
Tranquillisers	95	65	0.68
Other psychotropics	156	315	2.02
Other central and ANS drugs	289	1184	4.10
Antibiotics	56	43	0.77
Anti-infectives	9	9	1.00
Other drugs	1302	3642	2.80

ANS, autonomic nervous system.

and continuity of the physician–patient relationship. The authors also analysed the nine pharmacological categories listed under 'medication errors', and for each category they determined the number of deaths (see Table 2.1). It was suggested that the identification of any particular group of 'problem drugs' might be helpful for the prevention of future medication errors.

The paper encouraged a spirited correspondence,[16–18] with concern that the category for accidental poisoning used by Phillips and colleagues[15] might have led to a mislabelling of data as medication error. Further analyses of death certificates by Phillips and colleagues[19] in order to test the hypothesis that alcohol might be a risk factor in medication error deaths revealed that a co-listing of medication errors and alcohol abuse had increased from 7 cases in 1983 to 315 cases in 1993, representing a 45-fold increase.

The Quality in Australian Health Care Study

In this major investigation of Australian healthcare, which was modelled on the Harvard study, the medical record charts of 14 179 admissions to 28 hospitals in New South Wales and South Australia in 1992 were reviewed by Wilson and colleagues.[20]

An adverse event occurred in 16.6% of admissions, in which:

- the disability had resolved within 12 months in 77.1% of cases
- the disability was permanent in 13.7% of cases
- death occurred in 4.9% of cases.

In total 51% of the adverse events were considered to have been preventable.

Disability and preventability varied between specialities, diagnostic categories and locations in which the adverse event occurred. The instruments used to measure causation and preventability are described in Appendix 2.

Population estimates were as follows:

- 18 000 deaths (95% CI, 12 000–23 000)
- 33 000 patients with permanent disability (95% CI, 27 000–37 000)
- 280 000 patients with temporary disability (95% CI, 260 000–310 000) per year.

The adverse event profile in Australian hospitals was even greater than that in the Harvard Medical Practice Study, indicating that one in every six patients who entered hospital experienced an adverse event. It was suggested that the differences may reflect the following factors.

- The Harvard Medical Practice Study was concerned with medical negligence and malpractice, whereas the Australian study focused on prevention, producing different incentives for reporting of adverse events.
- The quality of the medical records may have improved between 1984 (the time of the Harvard Medical Practice Study) and 1992 (the time of the Australian study).

A preliminary study in London

A recent study by Vincent and colleagues[21] provides the first epidemiological report of adverse events in the UK. A retrospective record review of 1014 medical and nursing records was undertaken in two acute hospitals in London during two 3-month periods in 1999 and 2000.

The study found that:

- 10.8% of patients experienced an adverse event
- 48% of the events could have been prevented with ordinary standards of care
- of the patients who suffered an event, 34% developed an injury or complication that resulted in moderate or permanent impairment or contributed to death
- patients who experienced an adverse event were older than those who did not experience such an event.

The authors estimated that around 5% of the 8.5 million patients admitted to hospitals in England and Wales each year experience preventable adverse events

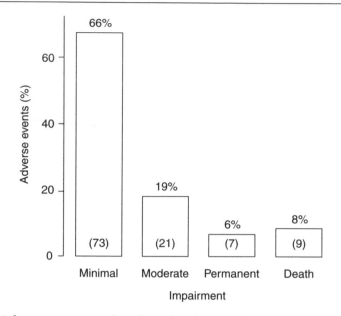

Figure 2.6: Adverse events related to the degree of impairment detected in a preliminary retrospective review of 1014 medical and nursing records in two UK hospitals in the Greater London area in 1999 and 2000. A total of 110 patients (10.8%) experienced an adverse event of the severity indicated; some patients experienced multiple events and the overall number of events was 119. The number of patients is shown in parentheses. Prepared from the data of Vincent et al.[21]

(see Figure 2.6). This is equivalent to injury of some 425 000 patients and death of 34 800 patients each year.

The incidence of drug-induced adverse events and medication errors in the UK

It is regrettable that, with the exception of the study by Vincent and colleagues,[21] very little has been published on adverse events and medication errors in the UK. Differences in culture and in the type of hospital in which the studies are conducted may affect the degree of adverse events and errors (see page 66). However, there is no reason not to believe that the general UK experience will broadly reflect the incidence measured by Vincent and colleagues and the values determined in other developed countries.

On the basis of government figures disclosed in the landmark report, *An Organisation With a Memory*,[22] Professor Liam Donaldson, the Chief Medical Officer, disclosed on 13 June 2000 that one in ten patients admitted to hospital (or at a rate in excess of 850 000 a year) become even more ill because of medical errors and negligent care, and that half of these mishaps could have been avoided.

For example:

- 400 patients a year die or are seriously injured in adverse events involving medical devices alone
- nearly 10 000 patients are reported to have experienced serious adverse reactions to drugs.

Gross under-reporting of ADRs

The incidence of ADRs reported by Lazarou and colleagues[8] is higher than is generally recognised, but this is not too difficult to understand. Most hospitals have relied on spontaneous reports of ADRs, which only identify about one in 20 events.[23] The reasons for this gross disparity seem obvious – reporting large numbers of adverse events attracts unwelcome attention and possible litigation. This may occur at all levels of clinical investigation, and appears to reflect a distinctive culture which has developed over many years.

For example, in 1994 the Food and Drug Administration (FDA) received 73 887 reports of adverse reactions, of which only 3863 (5.2%) came from clinicians.[24] A weakness of spontaneous anecdotal reporting is that 'it is difficult or impossible to estimate reliably how often adverse events might be occurring since, according to FDA estimates, only about 1% of adverse events are ever reported'.[25,26]

More recently, the death in 2000 of a research subject, Jesse Gelsinger, in a gene-therapy clinical trial using an adenoviral vector prompted an investigation by the National Institutes of Health (NIH) which involved all scientists conducting such studies. It was revealed that 652 of 691 serious adverse events were not immediately reported to the NIH, representing a non-compliance rate of 94%.[27] A spokeswoman for the NIH claimed that the NIH 'had served the public interest very well', but added that 'there is always room for improvement'.

The FDA has recently closed down a number of gene-therapy trials after investigating several violations of trial standards.[28,29] An editorial in *Nature*[30] indicated that:

> *Many gene-therapy researchers privately object to filing adverse events reports either to the FDA, where they remain confidential, or to the NIH, where they are made public. But, in retrospect, having more public records on adverse events associated with the vector used in Gelsinger's trial would have been useful.*

The reader may question whether the culture of either the researchers or the FDA may contribute to the decline of a duty of care to the patient or research subject.

The problems identified above caused the US government to establish the Office for Human Research Protection (OHRP) in 2000. It recently ordered the closing down of one of the nation's premier medical institutions at Johns Hopkins University. This followed the death of Ellen Roche, a previously healthy 24-year-old volunteer, in an asthma experiment.[31] The OHRP concluded that the Hopkins scientists had failed to obtain readily available information showing that the drug hexamethonium, when inhaled, has toxic potential, that the Hopkins review board never asked for data on the safety of inhaled hexamethonium, and that the consent form signed by Ms Roche failed to reveal that the drug was not for human use and had not been sanctioned by the FDA, notwithstanding the fact that it was described as a medication.[32] The Chief Executive Officer of Johns Hopkins Medicine commented that 'Hopkins has had over 100 years of doing clinical trials, and we have had one death in all those years. We would have done anything in the world to prevent that death, but (suspending the studies) seems out of proportion'. Hopkins has described the shutdown of its experiments as unwarranted, unnecessary, paralysing and precipitous.[32]

Accurate medication histories reveal previous ADRs, and their recording and analysis can prevent future problems. Frequently, however, ADRs are not recorded in patients' medical notes, and less than 20% of ADRs may be entered on drug charts.[33] A comparison of pharmacist drug histories with those of Senior House Officers found that the latter omitted 62% of medicines and identified fewer ADRs.[34] During a 12 month period at the Wirral Hospital NHS Trust in 1999, a change in practice to use anonymous reporting of errors rather than staff-identifiable instant reporting of errors, recorded no less than a five fold increase in the reporting of medication errors.[35]

A failure to record accurately deaths associated with care in the NHS is also apparent from the report entitled *An Organisation With a Memory*:[36]

> *(4.42) the experience of Confidential Enquiries in the NHS in general suggests that there are limits to the coverage which can be achieved by voluntary reporting systems. For example, the National Confidential Enquiry into Suicide and Homicide by People with Mental Illness achieved reporting rates of only around 15% for suicide until it was redesigned to draw on other sources of information – District Directors of Public Health and Office for National Statistics (ONS) data – for the initial identification of relevant incidents. Clinical information is now collected on 92% of relevant suicides and 93% of relevant homicides. The participation rate in the National Confidential Enquiry into Perioperative Deaths (hospital deaths within 30 days of surgery), the biggest Confidential Enquiry, varied between 71% and 86% (depending on specialty) in the most recent year of study.*

It is clear that, at all levels of medical practice, adverse events associated with medical treatment or investigation are being under-reported.

The incidence of adverse drug-induced events/ reactions and medication errors in primary care

Summary: The recognition of adverse events and their importance in primary care

- The incidence of adverse drug reactions (and errors) in primary care has yet to be established.
- Some recognition of the problem is revealed by studies showing that 2.4–3.6% of all hospital admissions in the USA were drug related, of which 32–64% were possibly or definitely preventable.
- The incidence of drug-related injury in the USA was shown to account for 11–13% of adult admissions to ICUs at several university hospitals.
- An analysis of general practitioners' prescribing patterns in the UK is indicative of possible adverse events and errors in an under-prescribing of drug therapies.
- The failure of patients to take their medicine as directed is a major and international cause of hospital admissions (0.2–21.7%) and the cause of relapse in 50% of some patient groups.

The international experience

Knowledge of the incidence of adverse drug-induced events in primary care is limited by the few studies which have investigated the problem. Similarly, the incidence of medical errors outside hospitals is a difficult subject to investigate and a cause for concern. There has been no immediately obvious way to measure errors in primary care reliably, and voluntary reporting would presumably be susceptible to the same under-reporting as in secondary care.

There is evidence that adverse drug events in ambulatory settings account for some admissions to hospital facilities, but the proportion of these events *that can be related to errors* is not known. Beard[1] found that between 3% and 11% of hospital admissions were attributed to adverse drug events in the elderly.

A review of Australian studies revealed that 2.4–3.6% of all hospital admissions were drug related and that, of these, 32–64% were definitely or possibly preventable.[2] Specific groups of drugs that caused problems included the cytotoxics, cardiovascular agents, anticoagulants and non-steroidal anti-inflammatory drugs. Schneitman-McIntire and colleagues[3] reported that in an analysis of 60 000 visits to an emergency department by patients enrolled in a health maintenance organisation, 1.7% of these visits were related to inappropriate prescribing or patient non-compliance. In an analysis of the 1987 National Medical Expenditure Survey data, physicians were found to have prescribed potentially inappropriate medications for *nearly a quarter* of all older people living in the community.[4]

Some measure of adverse events within the community can also be obtained from the study by Lazarou and colleagues,[5] in which the number of adverse drug reactions in patients who were admitted to hospital was found to be around twofold higher than that in inpatients. Furthermore, outpatient drug toxicity was recorded as the cause of about 3% of all hospital admissions in the USA.[6] In an evaluation of the complications associated with medications among patients at 11 primary care sites in Boston, 18% of 2258 patients who had had drugs prescribed reported having experienced drug-related complications.[7]

In other studies[8,9] iatrogenic injury accounted for:

- 11–13% of adult admissions to intensive-care units at several university hospitals
- 5–36% of admissions to medical services.[10]

Using anonymous incident reports collected from Australian general practitioners of 'an unintended event' that could have harmed or did in fact harm a patient,[11] of 805 incidents involving drug treatment, diagnosis and equipment:

- 27% were judged to have the potential to cause serious harm
- 76% were judged to have been preventable.

Prescribing patterns in primary care

An analysis of prescribing patterns of potential drug interactions offers a further measure of medication errors. In an analysis of all prescriptions ($n = 962\,013$) with potential drug interactions dispensed at all Swedish pharmacies ($n = 885$) in January 1999 involving two or more drugs dispensed to the Swedish population ($n = 7\,214\,509$) (age range 15–95 years), drug interactions were classified according to clinical relevance (types A, B, C and D) and documented evidence (types 1, 2, 3 and 4).[12] For example, D4 indicates an interaction which may have more serious clinical consequences and is based on more controlled studies than A1 (*see* Figure 3.1). In total, 13.6% (130 765) of the prescriptions dispensed included at least one potential drug interaction; 13 282 (1.4%) of the dispensed prescriptions were designated as those that might have serious clinical consequences (type D). For example, of the potential type D interactions, no less than 2358 were between potassium-sparing diuretics and potassium supplements, which may cause severe and even life-threatening hyperkalaemia. The combination of warfarin with an NSAID, which can increase the risk of gastrointestinal bleeding (*see* page 2), was found on 644 occasions. The adverse events associated with these interactions have been fully established for decades. The study provides an instructive example of the illusion created by an apparently 'low' incidence of 1.4% of potentially serious side-effects from the total of those recorded. It relates to no fewer than 13 282 ADRs in a 1-month period, or approximately 150 000 serious interactions per year possibly resulting in patient injury or death, complaints and litigation in a population of around 7 million people.

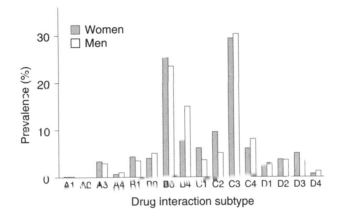

Figure 3.1: The prevalence of potential drug interactions on prescriptions ($n = 962\,013$) dispensed at all of the pharmacies in Sweden in January 1999 for a population of 7 214 509.[12] Of the total prescriptions dispensed, 130 765 (13.6%) included at least one drug interaction. The potential drug interactions were classified according to the following criteria.

1   *Clinical relevance*: A, probably no clinical relevance; B, clinical relevance not completely assessed; C, clinical relevance – interaction may modify the effect of the drug, but is susceptible to control by dose adjustment (this includes both beneficial and adverse drug interactions); D, clinically relevant – interaction may have serious clinical consequences, may suppress a drug effect, or the effect modification is difficult to control by dose adjustment. This type of drug interaction ought to be avoided.

2   *Documented evidence*: 1, incomplete case reports, *in-vitro* studies, or a drug interaction is assumed on the basis of evidence coming from similar drugs; 2, well-documented case reports; 3, based on studies in volunteers or on pilot studies in patients; 4, based on controlled studies in relevant patient groups.

The UK experience

The level of medication error within primary healthcare in the UK is not known, although it is established that there are significant differences in prescribing patterns and patient compliance. Moreover, it has been reported that *medication errors result in no less than 25% of all adverse incident claims* in general medical practice which result in litigation (*see* page 99). Wilson and colleagues suggest that patient care in the community is becoming more complex, with the use of more potent medicines, the pressure of short consultations and the increasingly fragmented nature of primary care.[13] Informal estimates of the number of medical practices that use 'significant event audit' in the UK is about 20%.[13]

Prescribing patterns in primary care

Even at an international level there are curious and distinctive features of prescribing which are sometimes difficult to explain. For example, the level of prescribing of tranquillisers and vasodilators is much higher in France than in Italy, whereas the Italians use more tonics and hepatic protectors (*see* review by Taylor[14]).

There is evidence that under-prescribing is a significant clinical problem. For example, in an evaluation of the prevalence of the use of lipid-lowering agents in a nationally representative sample of 13 586 adults, and despite the high prevalence of dyslipidaemia in English adults, the proportion of adults who were taking lipid-lowering drugs was found to be only 2.2%.[15]

There is also substantial variation between English regions and between medical practices within a region in terms of their prescribing practice. In 1995, the Department of Health published a report entitled *Variations in Health* in which it drew attention to variations in gender, ethnicity, socioeconomic status and geographical location.[16]

Patel and colleagues[17] published a preliminary report of a macro-analysis of prescribing patterns of lipid-lowering agents and the relationship with underlying factors of general practice, ethnicity and demography of 346 005 patients within 62 medical practices in a northern metropolitan health authority in the UK. Considering medical practices with a higher proportion of patients of South-Asian origin, regression analysis revealed a strong antithetic relationship between defined daily dosages of lipid-lowering agents and the percentage of South-Asian patients aged between 35 and 65 years within each practice. In view of the increased prevalence of both diabetes and coronary heart disease experienced by these patient groups, the direction of this relationship was wholly unexpected. Although the statistical analyses cannot address issues of causality, such findings provoke debate of the government document *Saving Lives: Our Healthier Nation*[18] which describes an action plan for tackling instances of poor health and its treatment. Micro-analyses are required to determine whether the low prescribing levels reflect a medication error or a failure to provide an appropriate standard of care.

It is important to note that differences in prescribing patterns do not necessarily relate to medication errors. Moreover, even within the same practice there can be variations in prescribing. Some of these may be explained by age and sex profile of the patient or the doctor, or by socioeconomic status or ethnic differences (*see* review by Taylor[14]). Systematic variation could occur as a result of clinical uncertainties, ignorance of relevant research or individual informed preference. A study of over 200 general practitioners showed that the size of their drug repertoire ranged from 50 to 220 different drugs[19] (*see* Figure 3.2). It is important that future research establishes the reasons for these significant disparities in prescribing practice.

However, it is still particularly disappointing that prescribing patterns in the UK have invariably been analysed from a cost perspective rather than from one of patient safety. The Audit Commission, in criticising the prescribing by general practitioners for being irrational and inconsistent, provides a typical example of this.[20]

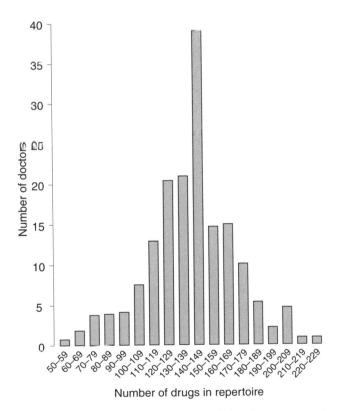

Figure 3.2: A frequency histogram of the size of the drug repertoire for over 200 general practitioners in the UK. Prepared from the data of Taylor and Bond[19] (*also see* Taylor[14]).

Within the UK there are additional concerns raised by medication practice in nursing homes. The use of neuroleptic medication is currently being investigated,[21] and a recent study showed that 71% of nursing homes which were surveyed sometimes resorted to concealing medicines in food or drink,[22] which gives rise to ethical and pharmacological problems of drug and food interactions. Such mishandling of medications inevitably predisposes to drug-induced adverse events (*see* page 228). Such concerns reflect those observed in the USA.[23]

Patient compliance

In the USA, a meta-analysis of seven studies estimated that 5.5% of hospital admissions (i.e. 1.94 million admissions) can be attributed to non-compliance with drug therapy.[24]

Using manual and computerised literature searches of data between 1989 and 1996, adverse drug reaction rates associated with patient non-compliance or unintentionally inappropriate drug use in 49 hospitals or groups of hospitals in international settings revealed that drug-induced hospitalisations accounted for approximately 5% (range 0.2–21.7%) of all admissions. Eleven of the reports indicated that non-compliance induced on average 22.7% of hospitalisations as a result of adverse drug reactions.[25]

In 1995, the Royal Pharmaceutical Society of Great Britain, in partnership with Merck Sharp and Dohme, conducted an investigation into the difficulties that patients experience in taking their medicines.[26] The problems that were revealed were astounding. In one study, as many as 25% of prescriptions were not even presented for dispensing. Rates of compliance with different long-term medication regimens for different illnesses in various settings tended to converge towards a value of approximately 50%. For example, in patients with schizophrenia the relapse rates while 'taking' medication were far higher than would be expected from the results of controlled clinical trials. One of the main reasons for the high relapse rates was that only 40–50% of schizophrenic patients comply with antipsychotic therapy prescribed to prevent relapse, and the non-compliance rate for first-episode patients can be as high as 75% (*see* review by Hummer and Fleischhacker[27]).

Even patients who may be assumed to be highly motivated to take their medicine (e.g. renal transplant patients) do not necessarily comply, and in one study 18% were not taking their medication as prescribed. Within this group, 91% of patients experienced organ rejection or death, compared with only 18% of patients who adhered to their treatment.[28] Patient compliance is discussed further on page 224.

Dispensing errors in pharmacy

Relatively little has been published on this subject.[29] In four pharmacies that were monitored in Glasgow, an internal error rate of 50 in 5004 prescriptions

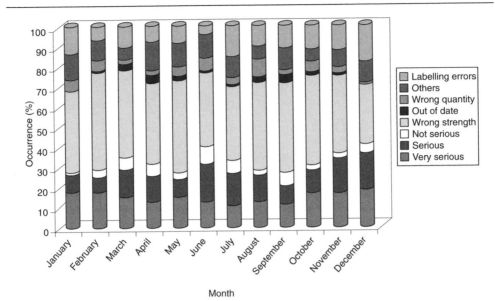

Figure 3.3: The occurrence by percentage of different types of monthly dispensing errors in a major community pharmacy group during 1999 (personal communication, Mr A Murdoch, Pharmacy Director, Lloyds Pharmacy[32]).

was identified. Nine of the errors (0.18%) were considered to be serious, but none of the potentially fatal errors left the pharmacy.[30] Dispensing errors should be viewed within the perspective that about 1.5 million prescriptions are written by general practitioners in England every day, and about 0.5 million in hospital daily.[31]

It should be noted that the major multiple community pharmacies have routinely measured errors for many years using mandatory systems. For example, monthly dispensing errors that are subdivided into labelling errors, wrong quantities, out of date, wrong strength and other categories allow the opportunity for recognition, recording and subsequent analysis to enable error reduction or maintenance of a minimum error rate (*see* Figure 3.3).[33] The opportunities for double checking within pharmacy also ensure that the majority of errors are recognised and do not leave the pharmacy.[34]

The stages at which adverse drug-induced events/ reactions and medication errors occur in hospitals

Summary: The stages at which medication errors arise

- Medication error is one of the most preventable causes of patient injury.
- Errors that result in preventable adverse drug-induced reactions may occur during prescribing, transcription, dispensing or administration of the drug, or as a result of patient non-compliance.
- Most errors occur during ordering/prescribing (56%) and drug administration (34%), with fewer errors occurring during transcription (6%) or dispensing (4%).
- The errors incurred by the patient in hospital are unknown, but are likely to be small.
- In primary care, the errors incurred by the patient as a result of non-compliance and taking other drugs, inappropriate medications and recreational drugs (e.g. alcohol, smoking) are a major source of potential error.

The limitations of chart review

It should be noted that both the Harvard Medical Practice Study and the Quality in Australian Health Care Study used patient chart review, which may under-report errors. Unrealistic under-reporting of drug-induced death or disability is damaging in that it leads to false perceptions both by society and by healthcare professionals that drugs are safer than is really the case. Also, and just as important, chart reviews generally provide few clues about the stage(s) at which events and errors occur.

Incidence and preventability of adverse drug events in hospitalised patients

In a preliminary study in the USA, Bates and colleagues[1] identified incidents and adverse drug events (ADEs) in an urban tertiary-care hospital using logs to record incidents, chart records and a twice daily solicitation of reports of incidents over a 37-day period (2967 patient days). They found that:

- 73 drug-related incidents occurred
- physicians were primarily responsible for 72% of the incidents, with the remainder being a consequence of errors made by nursing, pharmacy and clerical personnel (in similar proportions)
- 27 incidents were judged to be ADEs
- 56% of these incidents were judged to be preventable.

The authors concluded that ADEs were not infrequent, were often preventable and were usually caused by physicians' decisions.

Incidence of adverse drug events and potential adverse drug events: implications for prevention

Following the initial study described above, Bates and colleagues[2] conducted a pivotal investigation in which they employed a prospective cohort design using both a daily review of all charts by nurse investigators and stimulated self-reports by pharmacists and nurses to detect incidents. Over a 6-month period in two large tertiary-care hospitals in Boston, it was found that:

- 247 ADEs had occurred
- 194 potential ADEs had occurred.

The extrapolated event rates were 6.5 ADEs and 5.5 potential ADEs per 100 non-obstetric admissions.
   Of the total number of ADEs:

- 1% were fatal
- 12% were life-threatening
- 30% were serious
- 57% were significant.

Of the life-threatening and serious ADEs, 42% were preventable. The rate of serious medication errors (i.e. preventable adverse drug events plus potential adverse drug events) was 7.3%. This is an order of magnitude higher than the 0.7% rate of ADEs recorded in the Harvard study review. The data recorded in

Table 4.1: Frequency of adverse drug events (ADEs) and the percentage preventable by drug class[2]

Drug class	ADEs number (%) (n = 247)	Preventable ADEs number (%) (n = 70)
Analgesics	73 (30)	20 (29)
Antibiotics	59 (24)	6 (9)
Sedatives	20 (8)	7 (10)
Antineoplastic agents	18 (7)	3 (4)
Cardiovascular agents	9 (4)	3 (4)
Anticoagulants	8 (3)	3 (4)
Antipsychotics	6 (2)	5 (7)
Diabetes related	5 (2)	4 (6)
Electrolytes	3 (1)	3 (4)
Other	46 (19)	16 (23)

prospective rather than retrospective studies would be considered to be more reliable.

The 247 ADEs were associated with 101 different drugs. Combined analgesics, sedatives and antipsychotics accounted for 46% of preventable ADEs (see Table 4.1). Although analgesics, antibiotics, sedatives and antineoplastic agents were the main offenders, numerous other drugs were clearly contributing to ADEs. This supports the observations recorded by Phillips and colleagues.[3]

The importance of the investigation by Bates and colleagues[2] was that the stages at which errors occurred could be determined more reliably. There are six stages involved between the prescribing of a drug and the patient taking the medication (see Figure 4.1). In hospital the doctor prescribes or orders the drug, a nurse or pharmacist may transcribe the order, the pharmacist dispenses the prescription and the nurse generally administers the medication or ensures that it is taken by the patient. In most studies it has been assumed that the patient has taken the drug, has been co-operative and has not contributed to medication error. Although this may be a reasonable assumption for most hospital patients, it is a major variable for patients in primary care (see page 224). Within primary care it should additionally be noted that a carer may also play a crucial role in the patient's medication. However, it should be noted that the actual potential for the detection of errors within the six stages shown in Figure 4.1 is unequal. Thus the errors made by the prescriber may be detected by the pharmacist, nurse, carer or patient, the errors made by the pharmacist may be detected by the nurse, carer or patient, and the errors made by the nurse may be detected by the carer or patient.

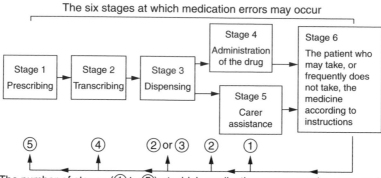

Figure 4.1: The different stages in the medication process at which errors may arise, from the prescribing of the drug by the doctor through to the patient taking the medication. Most errors at the prescribing stage are corrected by the pharmacist at the dispensing stage, or by the nurse at the stage of drug administration. In hospital, the drug may be administered by a nurse, or the patient may simply take the medication, as routinely occurs in primary care, with or without assistance from a carer. Most medicines that are administered to patients in hospital are given by a nurse or actually taken by the patient according to the instructions given. In primary care the dispensed medication is frequently not taken by the patient as directed, with potentially harmful consequences. To improve the reporting of errors, the government report entitled *Building a Safer NHS for Patients*, published in 2001,[4] identified a major future role for patients to report errors that occur to either themselves or to other patients.

Errors resulting in preventable ADEs ($n = 70$) most often occurred at the stages of ordering (prescribing) (56%) and administration of the drug to the patient (34%). Transcription (6%) and dispensing (4%) errors were much less frequent (*see* Figure 4.2). The errors caused by the patient as a result of non-compliance (if any) were not recorded.

It is particularly revealing that in none of the studies reported in this chapter is there any evidence that patients were requested to report perceived errors in their medication. Yet, where practicable, this would have provided important insights into errors that were undetected or under-reported by clinical staff.

The commonest errors were wrong dose of drug, wrong choice of drug, wrong frequency of drug, wrong administration of drug, wrong drug, adverse drug–drug interaction and known allergy to drug. These aspects are discussed in detail on pages 46–52.

The total number of adverse drug-induced events ($n = 264$) (as distinct from preventable adverse drug-induced events) is shown in the inset to Figure 4.2. Again the majority (75%) of the errors occurred at the prescribing and drug administration stages.

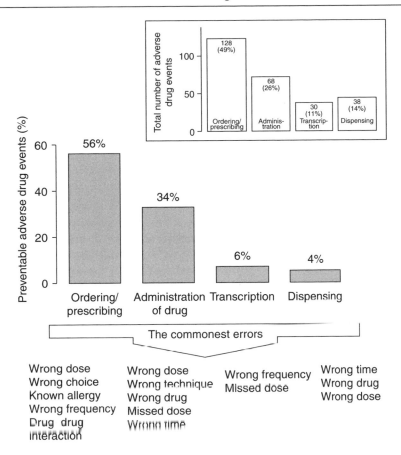

Figure 4.2: The different stages (i.e. prescribing/ordering, administration of the drug to the patient, transcription of the order or dispensing of the medicine) at which primary errors associated with preventable adverse drug events ($n = 70$) occured in two tertiary-care hospitals in Boston, USA. The percentage of errors at each stage is indicated, with the commonest types of error. The inset indicates the distribution of errors for the total number of adverse drug events (preventable, intercepted and non-intercepted potential ADEs) ($n = 264$). Prepared from the data of Bates *et al.*[2]

Medication prescribing errors in a teaching hospital

Lesar and colleagues[5] reported a landmark investigation of *prescriber-only* medication errors for the period 1 January 1987 to 31 December 1987 in a 640-bed tertiary-care teaching hospital in north-eastern New York. The medical staff consisted of a house staff and fellows (a total of 378 individuals who rotated between this and two other institutions), and attending physicians from an associated medical school and private attending physicians with privileges to admit patients from the surrounding community (a total of 840 individuals). Confirmed medication errors prescribed by a physician and detected by staff pharmacists were subject to evaluation for clinical severity according to the classification shown in Appendix 3 (all errors were detected and averted prior to implementation of the orders, and therefore the level of clinical significance could not be detected). Examples of significant prescribing errors are also shown in Appendix 3.

The total number of medication orders prescribed during the study period was obtained from the computer database (the pharmacy computer system had automated dose checking, duplicate therapy checking, allergy checking, drug-interaction checking and other facilities). In total, 905 prescribing errors were detected, of which 57.7% were rated as having potential for adverse consequences. The overall detected error rate was 3.13 errors per 1000 orders. Antimicrobial drugs accounted for a particularly high proportion of drugs that caused prescriber-related medication errors. However, the proportion of antibiotic drugs compared with the total number of dispensed drugs was not reported, and in any event over 70% of the errors were attributed to drugs from 18 other therapeutic drug classes.

Medication errors in paediatric practice in the UK

Wilson and colleagues[6] conducted a 2-year prospective cohort study, and standardised incident report forms were filled out by doctors, nurses and pharmacists. The simple Medication Error Report Form and the classification and grading of errors according to Hartwig and colleagues[7] are shown in Appendix 4 (it is interesting that no attempt was made to record the cause of error). The medication error reporting scheme was established in order to:

- determine the incidence and consequences of medication error
- institute changes in policy and practice in order to prevent recurrent medication errors and improve patient safety.

A total of 441 medical errors were reported in 682 children admitted for 5315 inpatient days to the Congenital Heart Disease Centre at the University Hospital of Wales, consisting of a paediatric cardiac ward and a paediatric intensive-care unit. It was noted that:

- errors were seven times more likely to occur in the intensive-care setting
- prescription errors accounted for 68% of all reported errors
- doctors contributed to 72% of the errors, nurses to 22%, pharmacy staff to 5% and doctor/nurse combinations to 1%.

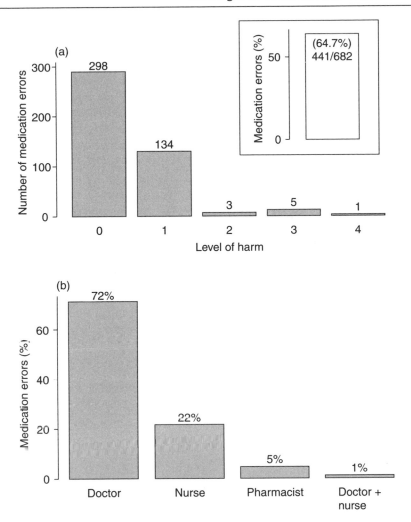

Figure 4.3: (a) The number of paediatric medication errors in a UK teaching hospital (441 reported errors in 682 patients; 64.7%) and the level of harm as defined in Appendix 4 (from 0 = error prevented by staff surveillance to 4 = error occurred that required extra treatment or increased length of stay in hospital). (b) The percentage distribution of medication errors among different members of the medical team. Prepared from the data of Wilson et al.[6]

The number of errors and their level of harm are shown in Figure 4.3. If level 0 (i.e. prevented) errors are excluded, there were 117 actual medication errors, corresponding to one actual error for every 5.8 admissions, or one error for every 45 inpatient days. The prescription error rate doubled when a new junior doctor joined the team.

The authors concluded that:

- medication errors are common
- the paediatric population is at greater risk than adult patients due to altered metabolism and excretion of drugs, as well as the need to tailor drug doses to specific body weights
- although the potential for harming paediatric patients was great, over two-thirds of the reported errors were prevented by the vigilance of nurses and pharmacists. Only four errors were associated with any overt clinical change.

The more you look for errors, the more you find

In the above studies the number of medication errors appears to be high, but even higher rates of error and injury have been recorded using observational studies.

For example, the study by Andrews and colleagues[8] used peer observers in a Chicago teaching hospital who recorded 'all situations in which an inappropriate decision was made when, at the time, an appropriate alternative could have been chosen'. They observed that:

- 45.8% of patients experienced an adverse event
- 18% of these patients experienced a serious adverse event (i.e. at least temporary disability).

The reader may wish to reflect carefully on these figures, as observational studies by expert peer review provide one of the most accurate methods for assessing adverse events and errors.

In a similar study in the medical–surgical intensive-care unit of a university hospital in Israel,[9] it was shown that clinicians made 1.7 errors per patient per day. An earlier study[10] had also reported a serious error rate of 58% in the treatment of patients with severe trauma in the emergency room, where the treating physician's lack of experience was the main cause of such errors.

Chapter 5

Types and causes of adverse events and medication errors in hospitals

Summary: The proximal causes of medication errors

- Within the combined processes of the physician ordering, through transcription, dispensing and drug administration to the patient, lack of knowledge of the drug (22%) was the single most important cause of medication error, together with lack of information about the patient (14%) and rule violations (10%), which together accounted for nearly 50% of the total errors.
- Slips and memory lapses (9%) and ten other causes of errors were in the range 2–9%.
- At the physician prescribing stage, lack of knowledge of the drug accounted for 36% of all errors, and lack of information about the patient accounted for 24% (i.e. 60% of all errors at the prescribing stage were due to these two factors alone).

It is much easier to find error than to find truth; the former lies on the surface, this is quite manageable. The latter resides in the depth, and this quest is not everyone's business.
Johann Wolfgang von Goethe, *Maxims and Reflections*

The previous chapter identified the stages at which medication errors occur. This chapter investigates the actual types of errors that are made and the attempts to assess their causation.

The nature of adverse events in hospitalised patients: results of the Harvard Medical Practice Study II[1]

This study further analysed the Harvard Medical Practice data which identified 1133 adverse events. The analysis was performed on the events caused not only by physicians but also by nurses and other supportive personnel. The types of adverse events are shown in Figure 5.1. Operative-related adverse events accounted for about 50% of all events, with wound infections and technical complications being the most common. Of the non-operative types of adverse events, drug-related events were the most frequent, and indeed the commonest single adverse event was drug related ($n = 178$), accounting for 19.4% of all adverse events.

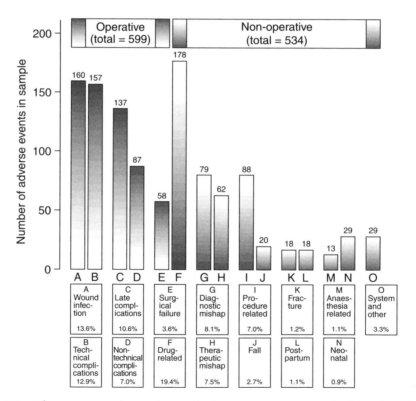

Figure 5.1: The types and numbers of adverse events recorded in the Harvard Medical Practice Study from 30 195 hospital records. The number of adverse events identified in hospitalised patients ($n = 1133$) is shown for operative- and non-operative-related events. The percentage value for each type of event is indicated. Prepared from the data of Leape *et al.*[1]

Table 5.1: Categories and incidence of specific types of errors in a weighted sample[1]

Type of error	Number of errors	Percentage
Performance (697)*		
Inadequate preparation of patient before procedure	59	9
Technical error	559	76
Inadequate monitoring of patient after procedure	61	10
Use of inappropriate or outmoded form of delivery	24	3
Avoidable delay in treatment	41	7
Physician or other professional practising outside area of expertise	13	2
Other	75	14
Prevention (397)		
Failure to take precautions to prevent accidental injury	178	45
Failure to use indicated tests	79	23
Failure to act on results of tests or findings	80	21
Use of inappropriate or outmoded diagnostic tests	6	1
Avoidable delay in treatment	120	31
Physician or other professional practising outside area of expertise	16	4
Other	77	19
Diagnostic (265)		
Failure to use indicated tests	134	50
Failure to act on results of tests or findings	83	32
Use of inappropriate or outmoded diagnostic tests	3	1
Avoidable delay in diagnosis	149	55
Physician or other professional practising outside area of expertise	17	6
Other	24	10
Reason not apparent	16	6
Drug treatment (153)		
Error in dose or method of use	67	42
Failure to recognise possible antagonistic or complementary drug–drug interactions	10	8
Inadequate follow-up of therapy	65	45
Use of inappropriate drug	38	22
Avoidable delay in treatment	21	14
Physician or other professional practising outside area of expertise	8	5
Other	18	9
System (68)		
Defective equipment or supplies	8	8
Equipment or supplies not available	8	5
Inadequate monitoring system	8	10
Inadequate reporting or communications	11	26
Inadequate training or supervision of physician or other personnel	15	31
Delay in provision or scheduling of service	10	14
Inadequate staffing	5	6
Inadequate functioning of hospital service	7	8
Other	12	20

* Number in parentheses after each category of error is the number of errors found by the reviewers for that category. Since the reviewers were not limited to identifying a single reason for each error, the percentages may exceed 100.

An analysis of the drug-related adverse events according to class of drug involved and the types of drug-related complications revealed that antibiotic, antitumour, anticoagulant, cardiovascular and anticonvulsant drugs caused a significant number of ADEs. However, numerous other agents also contributed to the problem.

In this retrospective analysis of patient medical records, the authors also attempted to define the incidence of specific types of error that were related to performance, prevention, diagnostic, drug treatment and system defects (see Table 5.1). It was noted that:

- technical errors were by far the commonest class of error, but relatively few of these were judged to result from negligence
- errors of omission, failure or delay in making a diagnosis or instituting treatment, and failure to use indicated tests or to take precautions to prevent injury, were often classed as negligent
- when the errors of omission were combined, they were more common than the errors of commission.

Frequently recorded errors included the use of inappropriate or outmoded forms of delivery, diagnostic tests and drugs, and physicians or other health professionals acting outside their area of expertise.

Medication prescribing errors in a teaching hospital

The details of the study by Lesar and colleagues[2] involving an investigation of prescriber-only-induced medication errors during 1987 in a tertiary-care teaching hospital in north-eastern New York can be found on page 37. The overall detection rate of significant errors was 1.81 errors per 1000 medication orders.

The types of error that were reported in this study are shown in Table 5.2. They encompassed the full range of potential errors of wrong dose, form, route or patient, allergy, duplicate therapies and missing information that endangers safe prescribing. However, it was particularly noteworthy that errors of dose – underdose or more frequently overdose – accounted for no less than 65% of all the errors that were made.

Factors related to errors in medication prescribing

Lesar and colleagues[3] subsequently designed a further study to quantify the type and frequency of factors associated with prescribing errors. This was a

Table 5.2: The types of prescriber-related medication errors[2]

Error type	Total number of errors	Number of significant errors	Percentage of significant errors
Overdose	260	203	38.9
Missing information	202	0	0
Underdose	161	133	25.5
Wrong dose form	66	19	3.6
Allergy to drug	61	61	11.7
Duplicate therapies	50	30	5.7
Wrong drug	50	38	7.3
Wrong route	31	23	4.4
Wrong patient	10	10	1.9
Miscellaneous	14	5	1.0
Total	905	522	100

Note: 905 prescribing errors were detected in 289 411 medication orders in a tertiary-care teaching hospital in north-eastern New York (an overall detection rate of 3.13 errors per 1000 medication orders written). 'Significant errors' (1.81 errors per 1000 orders) were rated as potentially fatal, severe, serious or significant (*see* Appendix 3).

systematic evaluation of every third prescribing error detected and averted by pharmacists in a 631-bed tertiary-care teaching hospital in New York State between July 1994 and June 1995. Each error was retrospectively evaluated by a physician and two pharmacists who identified the factor(s) linked with the error.

A total of 2103 errors which were thought to have potential clinical importance were detected during the study. The overall error rate was 3.99 errors per 1000 medication orders. A total of 696 errors fulfilled the study criteria; 6.2% were rated as potentially fatal or severe, 13.8% were rated as potentially serious and 80% were rated as potentially clinically significant.

The most common specific factors associated with errors were as follows:

- a decline in renal or hepatic function requiring alteration of drug therapy (97 errors, 13.9%)
- patient history of allergy to the same medication class (84 errors, 12.1%)
- using the wrong drug name, dosage or form (79 errors, 11.4%)
- incorrect dosage calculations (79 errors, 11.4%)
- atypical or unusual and critical dosage frequency considerations (75 errors, 10.8%).

The resulting error types and the commonest groups of factors associated with the errors are shown in Figure 5.2. Knowledge of drug therapy and the application of that information, and knowledge of patient factors that affect drug therapy accounted for no less than 59.2% of all errors.

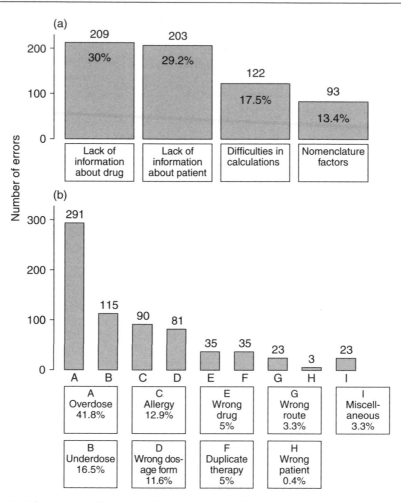

Figure 5.2: The quantification of the type and frequency of prescribing errors in a tertiary-care teaching hospital in New York between 1994 and 1995. (a) The commonest group of factors associated with the errors. (b) The resulting error types and the percentage values. Prepared from the data of Lesar *et al.*[3]

It was concluded that several easily identified factors are associated with a large proportion of medication-prescribing errors. The authors reached the following conclusions:

> *Our findings suggest that initiatives designed to prevent, detect and avert problems associated with a limited number of factors related to errors would address a large proportion of medication-prescribing problems.*
>
> *A large number of errors appeared to result from a lack of knowledge or appreciation of drug therapy issues – misapplication of drug therapy rules – as well as apparent mental lapses and mental*

slips. Many of these types of medication errors could be prevented by ensuring that prescribers have timely information, an adequate knowledge base to use the information, and a level appreciation for the many complexities of drug therapy . . . Whether errors are due to a lack of knowledge, inadequate access to patient information, or even slips, improved education and training of all medical professionals in the use of medications is likely to have a positive effect, primarily by increasing the level of appreciation for applying the information in practice and increasing the chance of error detection. However, given the number of new medicines available and the amount of new information regarding use of older agents, it is unlikely that achieving the level of expertise and experience through education needed to dramatically reduce errors is possible. Instead, redesigning the medication ordering and use system to reduce errors and improve outcomes is necessary.

Systems analysis of adverse drug events

In this important study, Leape and colleagues[4] attempted to identify and evaluate the proximal causes that underlie errors (ADEs and potential ADEs).

The investigators used a prospective cohort study of all admissions to 11 medical and surgical units in two tertiary-care hospitals in the USA over a 6-month period. Errors were detected by interviewing those involved and by daily review of each patient's hospital record.

Each ADE was first ascribed to one or more failures in the physicians' ordering of the drug, transcription and verification, pharmacy dispensing and delivery, or nurse administration of the drug to the patient.

Each error was then classified according to its 'proximal cause', which was defined as the apparent 'reason' for the error. The authors emphasised that the proximal 'causes' should be considered as broad 'categories' or 'domains' useful for further investigation to determine the underlying problems.

A total of 13 proximal causes of errors were described. For example, the first proximal cause was described as 'lack of knowledge of the drug' and defined as 'inadequate knowledge of indications for use, available forms, appropriate doses, routes and compatibilities'. In total, 334 errors were detected as the cause of 264 preventable ADEs.

The stages and distribution of the 334 errors (i.e. preventable plus potential adverse drug events) in the drug ordering and distribution process are shown in Figure 5.3. In total, 77% of all the errors occurred at the prescribing and drug administration stages.

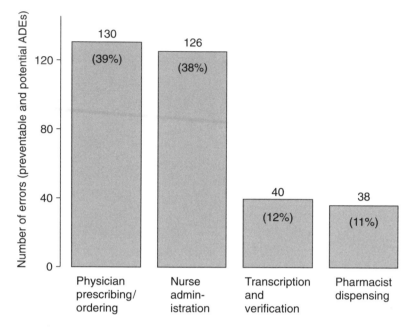

Figure 5.3: The distribution of 334 medication errors (as the cause of 264 preventable ADEs and potential ADEs) between the stages of prescribing, administration, transcription and dispensing of drugs in two tertiary-care hospitals in the USA over a 6-month period in 1993. Percentage values are also shown. Prepared from the data of Leape *et al.*[4]

The three main causes of error

These are as follows:

1 lack of knowledge of the drug
2 lack of information about the patient
3 rule violations.

The first two factors accounted for 36% of the total errors made. If taken together with 'rule violations' (10%), just three factors accounted for 46% of the total errors made by medical management (*see* Figure 5.4). Other causes (e.g. 'faulty dose checking' and 'preparation errors') were considerably less frequent. In particular, it should be noted that a transient 'slip or memory lapse' accounted for only a small proportion (9%) of the total errors.

If the errors are subdivided into the various stages of drug ordering and delivery, it can be seen that with respect to the physician ordering, nurse administration, transcription/verification and pharmacist dispensing, lack of knowledge of the drug plus lack of information about the patient were responsible for 60%, 25%, 25% and 0% of the errors, respectively. Lack of

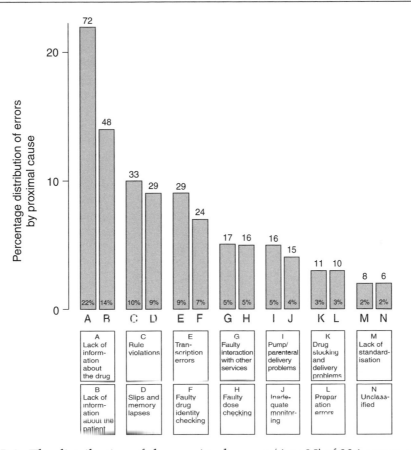

Figure 5.4: The distribution of the proximal causes (A to N) of 334 errors within the medication process from prescribing to administration of the drug to the patient in two tertiary-care hospitals in the USA. The percentage as well as the number of errors attributed to each cause are shown. Cause B includes 24 errors in which the patients received medication to which they were known to be allergic. Cause F includes 10 cases involving errors due to name confusion. Prepared from the data of Leape *et al.*[4]

knowledge of the drug plus rule violations were responsible for 55%, 17%, 15% and 16% of the errors, respectively (*see* Figure 5.5). (Failures with regard to drug identity, checking and stocking/delivery were proximal causes of error in pharmacy.)

Lack of knowledge of the drug caused important errors, including wrong dose, wrong choice, wrong technique, wrong drug and drug–drug interactions, as well as other consequences (*see* Figure 5.6). However, these errors were not solely the result of lack of knowledge, and taking 'wrong dose' as an example, other causes of error relate to rule violation, faulty dose checking, mental slips and other factors (*see* Figure 5.6 inset).

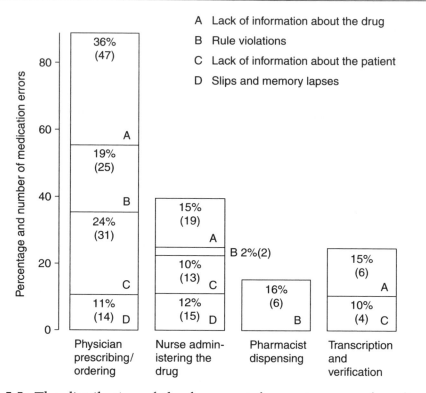

Figure 5.5: The distribution of the four most frequent causes of medication errors (lack of information about the drug, rule violations, lack of information about the patient, and slips and memory lapses) between the stages of drug ordering and delivery in two tertiary-care hospitals in the USA. The percentage errors as well as the number of errors (in parentheses) are shown. Prepared from the data of Leape *et al.*[4]

Nevertheless it remains clear that lack of knowledge is still the single most frequent cause of error.

A systems analysis

Within the study a systems analysis group identified 16 major systems failures underlying the errors and proximal causes that were recognised (*see* Appendix 5). The systems described are broadly defined. For example, 'lack of drug knowledge' as causing the largest number of errors was found within the first system entitled 'Drug Knowledge Dissemination', and was described by Leape and colleagues as follows:

> '*System 1. Drug knowledge dissemination*' (responsible for 98 errors out of 322). Physicians made major prescribing errors that appeared

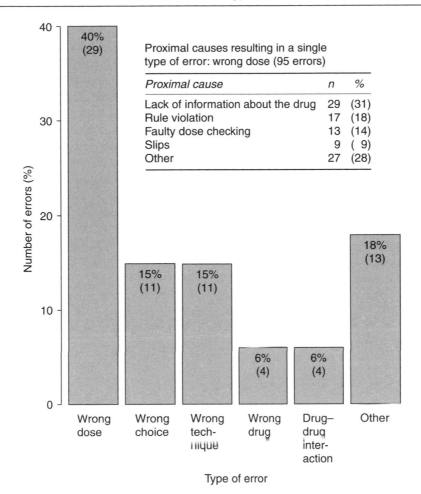

Figure 5.6: The types of error resulting from a single cause, namely lack of information about the drug. There were 72 errors in total, and the percentage values and numbers (in parentheses) are shown. Inset shows additional and different causes that give rise to the error 'wrong dose'. Prepared from the data of Leape *et al.*[4]

to be due to deficiencies of knowledge of the drug and how it should be used. They included incorrect doses, forms, frequencies, and routes of administration, as well as errors in the choice of drug . . . Nurses also made errors related to lack of understanding of the drug, but these were less frequent and less likely to lead to an ADE.

In the accompanying text, the authors indicated that the 'systems' are broadly defined. For example:

> drug knowledge dissemination is typically viewed as drug educa-
> tion, whether in medical school, during residency, at hospital
> conferences, at a postgraduate course, or by continuing self-
> education, but it can also be usefully considered as the sum of the
> methods that are used to make information available to physicians,
> nurses and pharmacists at the time of use.

The authors were clear that a systems approach is based on the concept that 'although individuals make errors, characteristics of the systems in which they work can make errors more likely and also more difficult to detect and correct'.

Furthermore, it takes the position that while 'individuals must be responsible for the quality of their work, more errors will be eliminated by focusing on systems than on individuals'.

The study was based in two hospitals at large urban academic medical centres where the rates and types of adverse drug events may differ from those which occur in community hospitals. However, the events which were identified are common errors that are easily recognised by physicians, nurses and pharmacists everywhere. Although the precise rates may differ, and it is less than certain whether smaller hospitals have a lower incidence of adverse events (*see* page 66), the findings are probably qualitatively applicable to most hospitals.

Preliminary analysis of the causes of prescribing errors in the UK

Dean and colleagues[5] asked pharmacists to give the researcher details of potentially serious prescribing errors during an 8-week period. Prescribers were then contacted and invited to participate in a non-disciplinary study. Semi-structured interviews were conducted with the help of a questionnaire to explore the factors that influenced performance.

A total of 88 potentially serious prescribing errors were reported, and it was possible to contact 53 of the prescribers, of whom 83% agreed to participate. These represented a wide range of grades and clinical specialities, and contributed to a wide range of error types.

Failures included gaps in medical school training (some interviewees reported no training in drug dosing or in the practicalities of prescribing), staff shortages, misunderstandings of responsibilities when one doctor asked another to write a prescription, and also frequently fatigue, interruptions, time pressures and the need to cover other doctors' patients with whom the prescriber was unfamiliar.

Several interviewees regarded writing discharge prescriptions as a transcription rather than as prescribing, with little thought being given to the process. Many also viewed the pharmacist as having an important role in preventing prescribing errors, and indicated that they themselves might be more careful if there was no pharmacy check. Doctors varied in their attitude to errors. Some were very concerned about the problem and were keen to reflect on and change their practice. Others felt that errors were inevitable and were relatively unconcerned about the issue. It was concluded that error reduction strategies should focus on medical school training, teamwork and hospital culture, rather than being implemented at the level of the individual.

Chapter 6

Risk factors predisposing to adverse drug events and medication errors

Summary: Risk factors involved in adverse drug events and errors

A number of factors may be interdependent:

- patient age (especially those who are 65 years or older) is a particularly important factor
- increasing numbers of medical treatments or time spent in hospital
- inexperienced staff
- staff working outside their area of expertise
- failure to acknowledge fatigue and stress
- hospital characteristics (teaching or otherwise)
- increasing workloads

A number of factors have been identified which may predispose patients to adverse events and medication errors.

Age

Patients over 65 years of age with changes in pharmacokinetics, a possible higher incidence of co-morbid illness and frailty have a notably increased risk of serious injury and death from adverse events compared with younger patients.[1-3] The data obtained from the Quality in Australian Health Care Study is particularly revealing (*see* Figure 6.1). The total number of adverse events and preventable adverse events increased by approximately 400% in patients 65 years of age and older. The number of adverse events resulting in permanent disability was even higher, with a 1700% increase. The same study also showed that the risk of adverse events resulting in death increases dramatically by 2300% in patients 65 years of age and older (*see* Figure 6.2).

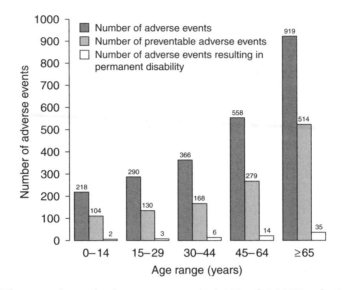

Figure 6.1: The number of adverse events (16.6% of 14 179 admissions to 28 hospitals in New South Wales and South Australia in 1992), the number of preventable adverse events and the number of adverse events resulting in permanent disability related to age. Prepared from the Quality in Australian Health Care Study (Wilson et al.[2]). © Med J Aust. Reproduced with permission.

One in five people in England is over 60 years of age, and between 1995 and 2025 the number of people over the age of 80 years will increase by almost 50% (see Figure 6.3).[4] At any one time older people occupy about two-thirds of hospital beds and people over 60 years of age receive 52% of all prescriptions.[5] Older people frequently take more drugs for a variety of conditions, and 36% of the population over 75 years of age are taking four or more drugs.[6] Polypharmacy and age-related changes in drug pharmacology place older people at an increased risk of adverse drug reactions, which is around 300% higher in patients 65 years of age and older than in those under 30 years,[7] and they are a factor implicated in 5–17% of hospital admissions.[8–10] In an analysis of all prescriptions dispensed over a 1-month period in Sweden in 1999 ($n = 962\,013$), the prevalence of drug interactions was correlated with the number of drugs dispensed per patient (see Figure 6.4),[11] a proportion of these interactions were of serious clinical concern (see Figure 3.1),[12] and the prevalence of interactions was proportionally far higher in patients 65 years of age and older, with some evidence of differences in gender prevalence (see Figures 6.4 and 6.5).[11]

A medication review by community pharmacists involving 205 patients with a mean age of 64 years showed that 12% of review problems frequently involved psychoactive drugs, NSAIDs and beta-blockers in such a way that the potential outcome could have been hospital admission.[13] As many as 50% of all older people may not be taking their medicines as intended.[14]

In the National Sentinel Clinical Audit of Evidence-Based Prescribing for

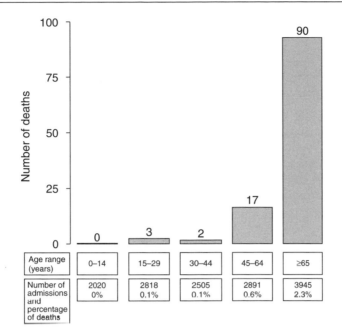

Figure 6.2: The number and percentage of deaths recorded in a total of 14 179 admissions to 28 hospitals in New South Wales and South Australia in 1992, related to age. In total, 16.6% of admissions were associated with an adverse event, and 4.9% of these were the cause of death; 69.6% of deaths were judged to have had a high preventability. Prepared from the Quality in Australian Health Care Study (Wilson *et al.*[2]). © *Med J Aust*. Reproduced with permission.

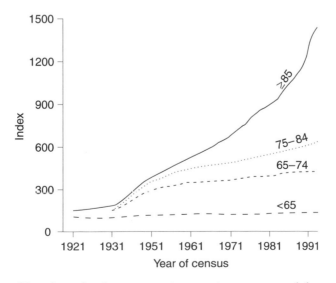

Figure 6.3: Profile of England as an ageing society, prepared from census data (Department of Health[4]).

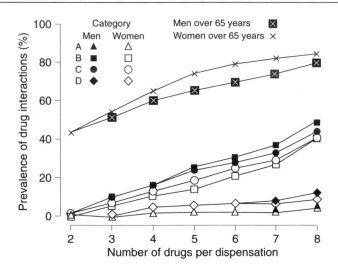

Figure 6.4: The prevalence of drug interactions in relation to the percentage of patients over 65 years of age, by gender and by the number of drugs dispensed per patient, from a total of 962 013 dispensations at all pharmacies in Sweden in January 1999 for a population of 7 214 509 individuals aged between 15 and 95 years.[11] The potential drug interactions were categorised according to clinical relevance as follows: A, probably no clinical relevance; B, clinical relevance not completely assessed; C, clinical relevance – interaction may modify the effect of the drug, but this is susceptible to control by dose adjustment (includes both beneficial and adverse drug interactions); D, clinically relevant – interaction may have serious clinical consequences, or may suppress a drug effect, or the effect modification is difficult to control by dose adjustment.

Older People conducted by the Royal College of Physicians,[15] the project evaluated and promoted the quality of prescribing for people aged 65 years or over. Data were collected from over 23 000 patients and 140 000 prescriptions from hospitals ($n = 62$), general practices ($n = 8$) and nursing ($n = 6$) and residential homes in England, Wales and Northern Ireland in 1999, with a re-audit in 2000. The results of the study for documentation of allergy/ sensitivity information, 'as required' prescriptions for a maximum number of doses per day, and for appropriateness of prescribing of benzodiazepines showed variation between sites. The data are relevant to a quality improvement strategy, the design of effective interventions and the progress that has yet to be made in order to ensure a standard level of decent treatment for a group of patients who are at particular risk.

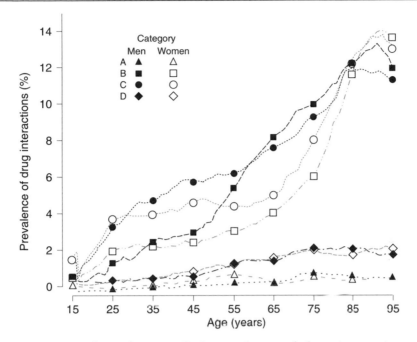

Figure 6.5: Age- and gender-stratified prevalence of drug interaction among the 962 013 dispensations at all pharmacies in Sweden in January 1999 for a population of 7 214 509 individuals aged between 15 and 95 years.[11] The potential drug interactions were classified according to clinical relevance as follows: A, probably no clinical relevance; B, clinical relevance not completely assessed; C, clinical relevance – interaction may modify the effect of the drug, but this is susceptible to control by dose adjustment (includes both beneficial and adverse drug interactions); D, clinically relevant – interaction may have serious clinical consequences, or may suppress a drug effect, or the effect modification is difficult to control by dose adjustment.

Time spent in hospital and intensity of treatment

Andrews and colleagues[16] have reported that the likelihood of experiencing an adverse event increases by 6% for each day spent in hospital. Several factors may contribute to the many preventable adverse events that also occur in the emergency department. This is because this department is the point of entry for acutely ill patients, fluctuating demand causes uneven and possibly abbreviated care, there is limited time to make a diagnosis, and junior staff are extensively used, among other factors.

It is also pertinent that in paediatric patients admitted to a UK hospital, drug errors were 700% more likely to occur in the intensive-care unit (ICU) than elsewhere in the hospital.[17] Similarly, using data collected via incident reports, staff interviews and daily chart reviews, where all data were analysed independently by two physician reviews, ADEs were shown to occur more often among adult patients in medical ICUs than in surgical ICUs, with a modest but similar trend in the general medical or surgical wards[18] (*see* Figure 6.6).

The number of drugs received by non-ICU and ICU patients during the 24-hour period prior to an adverse event was assessed by Cullen and colleagues[18] (*see* Figure 6.7). Such extremes of polypharmacy, when the patients are routinely taking an *average* of 9 to 15 different medications, increases the likelihood of error in drug selection, dosing schedules and monitoring and the risk of drug–drug interactions.

Bates and colleagues[3] performed a similar analysis but were careful to state that when the number of drug doses dispensed within the different units was adjusted for, the differences were not significant. This provides evidence to support the hypothesis that it is not a unique feature of the ICU that is a major determinant of the increased ADEs, but rather it is a reflection of the fact that the patients simply receive more treatments.

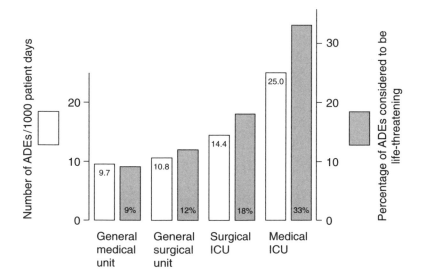

Figure 6.6: A comparison of the number of adverse drug events (preventable and potential ADEs) and the percentage of adverse drug events considered to be life-threatening in intensive-care and non-intensive-care units, recorded at Massachusetts Hospital and Brigham and Women's Hospital over a 6-month period (n = 264 from 4031 admissions). Prepared from the data of Cullen *et al.*[18]

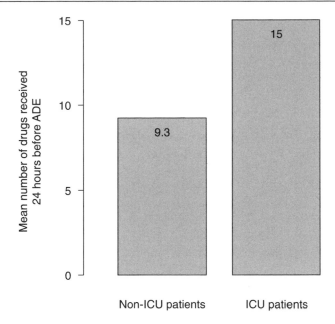

Figure 6.7: The mean number of drugs received by patients in intensive-care and in non-intensive-care units during the 24-hour period before the occurrence of an adverse drug event. Prepared from the data of Cullen *et al.*[18]

An investigation of mortality with workloads in an ICU

It is not the purpose of this chapter to review the influence of workloads on healthcare provision. Indeed, there is little quantitative evidence available to relate this to the quality of care. Yet there is a fine balance between efficient work practices and the well-accepted negative influence of inappropriate stress on cognitive performance, including memory and judgement.

Tarnow-Mordi and colleagues[19] investigated whether patients who were admitted to the ICU at Ninewells Hospital in Dundee would be at greater risk when nursing or medical staff workloads were high than during periods of lower workload. Under these circumstances the risks of adverse events involving human errors, delayed weaning from mechanical ventilators and hospital-acquired infections could increase. These researchers investigated whether ICU mortality is independently related to nursing requirements and other measures of workload, after adjusting for risk by use of the APACHE II (Acute Physiology Chronic Health Evaluation) equation. The results of the study analysing data from January 1992 to December 1995 ($n = 1050$) are shown in Figure 6.8.

The outcome was that there were 337 deaths, which is 49 more deaths (95% CI, 34–65) than predicted by the APACHE II equation. On multiple logistic regression analysis, adjusted mortality was more than twofold higher (odds ratio

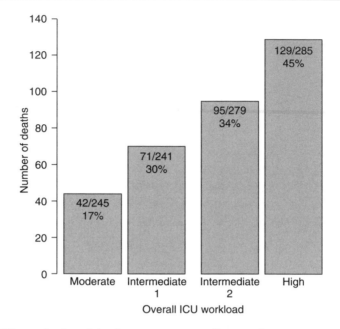

Figure 6.8: The relationship between mortality and measures of workload (described as moderate, intermediate 1, intermediate 2 or high) in an intensive-care unit. Data were analysed over a 3-year period at Ninewells Hospital, Dundee. The mortality rate is expressed both as the number of deaths (42–129)/population (245–285) and as a percentage. Prepared from the data of Tarnow-Mordi et al.[19]

3.1; 1.9–5.0) in patients who were exposed to high rather than low ICU workloads. The adjusted odds ratio for this comparison was 4.0 (2.6–6.2). Assuming that the APACHE II equation adjusted adequately for risk, it was concluded that variations in ICU mortality may be partly explained by excess ICU workload. This excess could reflect inadequate numbers of nursing and medical staff, training, supervision or equipment. The study is relevant to the report that the NHS workload is rising by 4.4% a year.[20]

Fatigue and stress

In an important analysis and comparison of staff attitudes with regard to error, stress and related issues, major differences were revealed between aviation and medical staff.[21] Both passengers and patients hope that the pilot or doctor is alert and in complete physical and mental control, yet aviation companies have strict rules about the hours that their staff may work and the use of recreational drugs and alcohol, whereas medicine does not.

With regard to different attitudes, in response to the statement 'Even when fatigued I perform effectively during critical times', 60% of all medical respondents agreed, whereas only 26% of pilots agreed. Pilots, anaesthesia consultants, residents and nurses (53–59%) were also less likely to deny the possibility that personal problems could affect their work than were surgeons (82%).

In general, only a minority of medical respondents openly acknowledged the effects of stress on performance. Yet 90% of intensive-care staff believed that a 'confidential reporting system that documents medical errors is important for patient safety', whilst reporting that many errors are neither acknowledged nor discussed. Indeed, one-third of the intensive-care staff did not acknowledge that they make errors. The authors concluded that medical staff seem to deny the effects of stress and fatigue on performance.[21]

Stress can also seriously affect communication between healthcare staff and their patients, which may influence treatment outcomes. In a survey of cancer patients and the consultants with up to 30 years' experience who were responsible for their treatment, many of the physicians did not know how to relay basic information to patients who were emotional, withdrawn or in denial. Research involving 178 of the UK's most senior doctors found that 43% of them considered it very difficult to communicate with members of ethnic minorities, 38% found it more difficult to relate to people much older or younger than themselves, and 29% struggled to talk to emotional patients. Similarly, among senior cancer nurses, 46% found it very difficult to give full information to emotional or withdrawn patients, and 39% admitted experiencing communication problems with ethnic minorities. An analysis of the medical staff members' own mental states showed that they were as stressed as patients who had recently been found to have cancer. In a survey of 2500 cancer patients in the UK, 87% said that they wanted as much information as possible, whether it was good or bad news. However, most of the senior doctors who were seeing such patients were seriously underestimating this need (see Fallowfield et al.[22–24] and Jenkins et al.[25]). Professor Fallowfield, Director of the Cancer Research Campaign's psychosocial oncology group, was reported as saying:[26]

> Many doctors simply lack the skills to communicate with someone who is withdrawn, depressed or highly anxious. The doctors had similar health questionnaire scores to their patients – they were in a mess as well. You can hardly expect them to get near the emotional and psychological needs of their patients if they are too burnt out with stress themselves.

In a recent report on intrathecal medication errors in the UK, the following comment was made:[27]

> Latent conditions have contributed to past cases of intrathecal injection error. Fatigue, distraction and stress are well recognised contributions to human error in general. They are endemic to NHS practice and will remain so, at least until capacity and manpower

*problems have been alleviated by the measures now being
implemented under the NHS Plan.*

*England has too few hospital beds per head of population com-
pared with most other healthcare systems. The NHS lacks sufficient
doctors, nurses, and other skilled staff. There are 1.8 practising
doctors per 1000 people compared with a European Union average
of 3.1 per 1000 population.*[28]

Newly qualified junior doctors in hospital face particularly long working hours.
Almost half (48%) of the UK's 39 000 junior doctors are working more than 56
hours a week, and the preregistration house officers are working even longer
hours (*see* Figure 6.9).[29] However, from the 1 August 2001 it has become illegal
for newly qualified doctors to be working more than 56 hours a week (or 72
hours on call), and this will also apply to all other doctors from August 2003.[29]

Staff inexperience

Trainees often make errors in all aspects of healthcare. In an analysis of 289 411
medication orders, it was found that first-year postgraduate residents made
more than four times more errors than fourth-year residents, which would

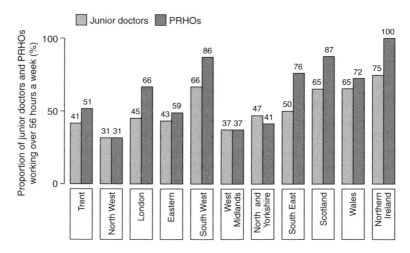

Figure 6.9: The percentage of newly qualified junior doctors and preregistration
house officers (PRHOs, the first junior post after qualification from medical
school) ($n = 39\,000$) in the UK who are working more than the maximum agreed
standard of 56 hours per week. The data are presented for the eight regions
within England (where the average values for all junior doctors and PRHOs are
44 and 56%, respectively) and for Scotland, Wales and Northern Ireland. The
figures are based on returns for 30 March 2000.[29]

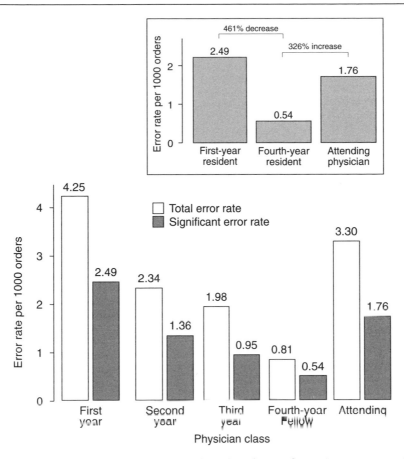

Figure 6.10: Order (prescription) errors (total and significant) per 1000 orders for each class of physician in a tertiary-care teaching hospital in New York State. In total, 905 prescribing errors were detected from a total of 289 411 medication orders. Inset indicates the percentage decrease in errors for the junior physicians during the 4-year period, and the higher error rate of the attending physician compared to the fourth-year Fellow. Prepared from the data of Lesar et al.[30]

indicate that knowledge and experience are important factors in physician performance[30] (see Figure 6.10). It was an interesting observation that attending physicians, who wrote only 4% of the medication orders, were three times more likely than the experienced residents to make errors, indicating that the knowledge base or skills are eroded over time.

In total, 45% of medical house officers reported making at least one error during training programmes, 31% of which resulted in the patient's death.[31] Similarly, internists were responsible for twice as many negligent adverse events (perhaps the cause could have been more accurately described as

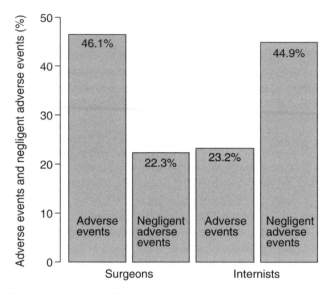

Figure 6.11: The differing profiles of experienced surgeons and inexperienced staff (internists) as causes of adverse events and negligent adverse events in hospitalised patients in the USA. Prepared from the data of Thomas et al.[32]

ignorance), leading to permanent disability or death in 9–10% of patients, as their senior colleagues[32] (see Figure 6.11).

The nature of the intervention

This may signal a higher risk (e.g. vascular and cardiothoracic surgery, neurosurgery and interventions considered to be life-saving, where the severity of the patient's illness may interact to increase the likelihood of a poor outcome).[2]

Hospital characteristics

The relationship between hospital characteristics and adverse events and substandard care was studied in a sample of 31 000 medical records drawn from 51 hospitals in New York State.[33] There were substantial variations in both adverse event rates (range 0.2–7.9%, mean 3.2%) and the percentage of adverse events due to negligence (range 1–60%, mean 24.9%) (also see Figure 2.4). Primary teaching hospitals had significantly higher rates (4.1%)

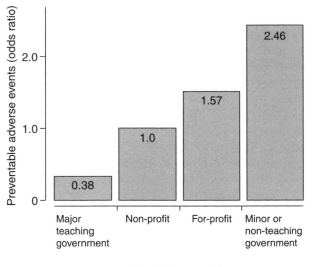

Figure 6.12: The relationship between preventable adverse events and hospital ownership in the USA. The data are presented as an odds ratio which allocates a value of 1.0 to non-profit hospital ownership. Prepared from the data of Thomas *et al.*[34]

than rural hospitals (1.0%). The percentage of adverse events due to negligence was significantly lower in primary teaching hospitals (10.7%) and for-profit hospitals (9.5%) than in hospitals with predominantly minority patients who had been discharged (37%). The authors concluded that adverse events and injury are not randomly distributed, and that certain types of hospitals have higher rates of injury because of substandard care.

Preventable adverse events were also compared in four categories of major/teaching/government, non-profit, for-profit and minor/non-teaching government hospitals in Utah and Colorado.[34] In these categories, preventable adverse events occurred least often in the major/teaching hospitals, and were 647% more common in the minor or non-teaching government hospitals (*see* Figure 6.12).

In an investigation of the relationship between hospital teaching status, quality of care and mortality, Allison and colleagues[35] examined the Cooperative Cardiovascular Project database for elderly patients with an acute myocardial infarct (MI) in 'major teaching', 'minor teaching' and 'non-teaching' hospitals. Their study involved an analysis of 114 411 patients in 4361 hospitals.

It was found that for non-teaching, minor teaching and major teaching hospitals:

- medication rates for aspirin were 81.4%, 86.4% and 91.2%, respectively ($P < 0.001$) and for beta-blockers the values were 36.4%, 40.3% and 48.8%, respectively ($P < 0.001$)

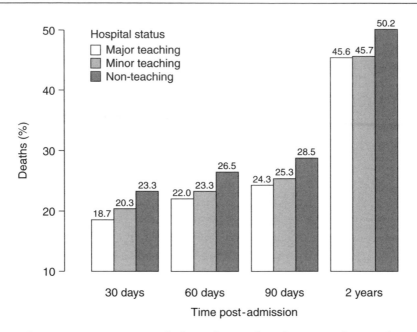

Figure 6.13: An investigation of the relationship between hospital teaching status and quality of care and mortality. The data indicate the mortality for acute myocardial infarction and hospital teaching status at the four post-admission dates. Comparisons within the four post-admission time intervals were significant at $P < 0.001$. Prepared from the data of Allison *et al.*[35]

- this 'gradient effect' of increasing quality of care was accompanied by a corresponding survival gradient suggesting a dose–response effect for differences in unadjusted 30-day, 60-day, 90-day and 2-year mortality between hospitals ($P < 0.001$ for all time periods) (*see* Figure 6.13).

Multivariate analyses suggested a strong relationship between the processes of care measure used and mortality. The authors emphasised that there was substantial room for improvement by all hospitals in the treatment of MI (where the medication error is one of underprescribing of drugs, leading to premature death) and they also highlighted the role that teaching hospitals may play in improving healthcare quality.

Clinical guidelines

Three examples have been selected to illustrate the possibility that author-itative clinical guidelines may perpetuate, reveal or fail to prevent adverse events or medication errors.

The first example is taken from the MeReC Bulletin, National Prescribing Centre,[36] which provides guidance on antischizophrenic medication.

All schizophrenic patients who are treated with traditional neuroleptic drugs will, to a greater or lesser extent develop a serious litany of adverse reactions (extrapyramidal side-effects) that include greatly reduced movements and muscle rigidity (Parkinson-like symptoms), dystonias (muscle spasm) (in around 70–90% of patients) and abnormal involuntary movement disorders or tardive dyskinesias (in around 5–50% of patients). The latter reflect long-term or permanent brain damage (*see* reviews by Hummer and Fleischhacker,[37] Buchanan and Carpenter[38] and Jann and Cohen[39]). The 'side-effects' of neuroleptic therapy are predictable, dose related and intractable. They have been related to compromised compliance, poor outcome, secondary negative symptoms and depression.[40]

However, the recent introduction of clozapine and other atypical antipsychotic agents provides an excellent opportunity to investigate a new group of drugs that may avoid or reduce the serious adverse drug reactions associated with current treatment and improve compliance in schizophrenic patients (*see* Kane *et al.*,[41] reviews by Taylor[42] and Geddes *et al.*[43]). However, this is not facilitated by the guidelines of the MeReC bulletin:

> *Although many patients are well controlled on a typical antipsychotic agent, the atypicals may provide a useful alternative in those who develop intolerable extrapyramidal side-effects . . . . A therapeutic trial of one of these agents may also be indicated in those with profound negative symptoms which are unresponsive to typical agents.*

The reader may consider that to allow patients to develop *intolerable* drug-induced reactions or *profound* negative symptoms represents most regrettable guidance in attempts to improve patient care and reduce serious adverse drug-induced events and reactions. Indeed, could this be perceived as a breach of care? In the USA, three out of four new antipsychotic prescriptions are for atypical agents.[44] Furthermore, the future involvement of patients in their recording of adverse events and errors (*see* page 108) should provide a fascinating insight into whether or not they consider that 'many patients are well controlled on a typical antipsychotic agent'.

The second example is taken from the National Institute for Clinical Excellence (NICE) guidance on proton-pump inhibitors (PPI) for dyspepsia.[45]

In a detailed statement on dyspepsia and its treatment, NICE issued the following guidance:

> *Patients who have severe gastro-oesophageal reflux disorder (GORD) or who have a proven pathology (e.g. oesophageal ulceration, Barrett's oesophagus) should be treated with a healing dose of a proton-pump inhibitor until the symptoms have been controlled. After that has been achieved, the dose should be stepped down to the lowest dose that maintains control of symptoms. A regular*

maintenance low dose of most PPIs will prevent recurrent GORD symptoms in 70–80% of patients and should be used in preference to the higher healing dose. Where necessary, should symptoms reappear, the higher dose should be recommenced. In complicated oesophagitis (stricture, ulcer, haemorrhage), the full dose should be maintained.

The Institute's Chief Executive noted (for the entire guidance) that 'This advice, if implemented fully, will have real benefits to patients because there is no advantage in having more of a drug than needed'.

It is perceived that the reason for exposing 20–30% of the patients (and possibly more)[46] to a lower dose, and one which was subsequently shown to be an inadequate dose regimen, and the consequent injury (a recurrence of painful symptoms and pathology),[47,48] was to reduce inappropriate drug use and costs.

In this case the patients experienced an adverse event as a consequence of the reduction in dose of an appropriate treatment. The error was one of omission, which is generally regarded as a failure or delay in making a diagnosis or instituting a treatment, or in using indicated tests or taking precautions to prevent injury.[49] Thus it becomes difficult to distinguish the consequences of the advice offered by NICE from an inevitable medication error and an adverse event in around 20–30% of the patient population referred to, and whose future views on medication errors will be sought.

The third example comes from the Perugia Consensus Conference: Antiemetic Subcommittee of the Multinational Association of Supportive Care in Cancer.[50]

Specialists in cancer care attempted to define the cytotoxic drugs in terms of their emetogenic potential (high, moderate to high, low to moderate, or low) in order to identify or justify the appropriate use of new antiemetic drugs such as ondansetron. Treatment could then be directed towards those patients who had the greatest need (while other patients may be offered traditional and cheaper antiemetics whose efficacy, or lack of it, can cause problems in use). However, the emetogenic potential of cytotoxic treatments can be markedly influenced by drug combinations, dose, schedule and route of administration, as well as by the sex, age and psychogenic profile of the patient, and any previous experience of chemotherapy or radiation.[51] Unfortunately, it is not possible to predict with any degree of confidence which patients will respond with intense and intractable nausea and emesis.[51] Thus some patients will inevitably continue to develop a serious adverse reaction to the cytotoxic treatment in the absence of optimal antiemetic control, and some will also develop anticipatory emesis.[52,53]

The intense nausea, vomiting and retching induced by cytotoxic treatments are one of the most severe and feared by patients of all drug-induced adverse reactions.[54] The reason for the restriction and failure to prevent or adequately control a serious and distressing adverse drug reaction was one of drug cost. Again it is important to emphasise that the patient will move to centre-stage in the new NHS, and his or her views on adverse drug-induced events will be actively sought. Such views expressed by a patient who has been very sick for many days as a result of failure to provide effective antiemetic treatment should be instructive.

In summary, the above three examples illustrate the fact that economic constraints are setting new cost-effective endpoints for clinical practice *which do not appear to address the problem of reducing adverse drug events or enhancing patient safety.*

Genetic testing: induction or prevention of adverse events?

Adverse events can arise from diagnostic tests in two ways. First, the traditional false-positive results can result in needless and inappropriate therapy or surgery and potential injury, whereas a false-negative result can provide a false sense of security in the face of a developing disease. Both of these outcomes reflect a physical hazard. However, the consequences of taking a genetic test are far more complex.

Dr George Poste, previously Chief Science and Technology Officer at Smith Kline Beecham, had a major influence in directing pharmaceutical research into molecular biology and genomics. In his address entitled 'The pharmaceutical industry and the evolution of molecular medicine', presented on the occasion of his receiving the AstraZeneca Industrial Achievement Award 2000, he considered the future role of molecular diagnostic tests in identifying disease subtypes.[55] Dr Poste felt that safety would be the key driver in advancing our understanding of individual variation in responsiveness to drugs:

> *Adverse drug–drug reactions and the consequent morbidity and mortality were an enormous problem. At present drug therapy was routinely assessed for drug–drug interactions, but this would move to drug–patient interactions. Knowledge of a patient's genetic information would indicate whether patient–drug interactions might be problematic. The answer to the questions of what was different between people who had a disease and those who did not and why disease progression varied between individuals was in their genes. At present, medicine was reactive, with treatments only being sought when symptoms arose. In the future, individual genetic risk profiling could be used for disease prevention and preventative therapy. However, linking clinical outcomes to genetic variation was an enormous task, requiring both time and resources. Work in this field also had significant ethical, legal and social implications, including privacy, discrimination, eugenics and racism.*
>
> *If this proves possible, treatments could be targeted to patients with the genetic profile which correlated with drug efficacy and*

safety; ineffective treatments and adverse reactions could be avoided.

It is clear that if this could be achieved, it would represent an outstanding therapeutic advance.

However, Dr Poste also noted that: 'The immense amount of data that was now available had reached a crisis point which neither industry nor academia could handle. Linking genetics to medicine would require vast information technology support'. It is interesting to note that, with respect to gene therapy itself, it was believed that it had suffered 'from excessive hype and lack of realism, and its impact on clinical medicine was likely to be minimal in the coming years'.

Others have been more direct. Professor Holtzman has taken issue with those who exaggerate the clinical benefits that will accrue from the human genome project, believing that 'the application of knowledge from the project will, in time, materially benefit everyone in the world'[56] as ludicrous. With regard to pharmacogenetics and the question 'Isn't the industry predicated on the assumption that exploration of individual phenotypes will allow doctors to prescribe tailor-made therapy and avoid adverse drug reactions?' his response was equally brief: 'It is and it won't. Sure, there are a few cases where testing patients for certain enzymes involved in drug metabolism may help, but it's ridiculous to suggest that drug sensitivity and resistance are wholly determined by inherited genetic profiles'.

These are the views of the sceptic, and are compared with those of the 'enthusiast' and 'visionary' which are described elsewhere.[57,58] Also, it is not clear that healthcare professionals are prepared for genotyped prescribing in the near future, or indeed, whether or not it will actually occur.[59]

However, there is no doubt that linking clinical outcomes to genetic variation has major ethical, legal and social implications. The taking of some genetic tests with a positive outcome, notwithstanding the fact that the person concerned may be in excellent health and may remain so for many years, has the very real potential to create major difficulties in employment, personal relationships, insurance and subsequent financial protection. These are major adverse events which, although caused by sectional interests within society, are predictable and precipitated by a genetic test that is undertaken in a healthcare system. Their future recognition, recording, attribution and redress will be of considerable interest.

Chapter 7

The cost of medical errors

Summary: The cost of adverse events

- This first falls on the patient (and indirectly their family), who may be injured, disabled or die.
- The second victim is the healthcare team, with a serious conflict of loyalties to their patient, their colleagues and their institution.
- The third victim is the physician or healthcare worker, who makes a mistake and experiences guilt, remorse and possible litigation.
- The fourth victim is the reputation of the institution and the staff.
- The fifth victim is society and/or the healthcare system, which may have to redistribute its finances to meet the costs of litigation.
- In addition, medication-related problems cost millions of extra prescriptions, extra hospital visits, and extra emergency department visits.

The cost of adverse drug-induced events and medication errors has provided a major stimulus for their prevention. This cost relates to physical and psychological injury to the patients and also great distress to healthcare professionals, with major legal and financial implications.

The human cost

The initial and major burden falls on the patient (and/or their family), who may be injured, disabled or die. The emotional, social and financial implications of profound disability or death may resonate for years or decades. However, there are also many other victims. The second and generally innocent victim is the healthcare team, who face a desperate conflict of loyalties to their patient, their colleagues and their institution. A professional betrayal of the patient's trust can be a profoundly traumatic event which may remain with the practitioner(s) for the rest of their career(s). The physician or staff member who is in error becomes the third victim, with feelings of guilt, remorse and embarrassment as well as the possibility of recrimination, litigation and loss of employment. The fourth victim is the reputation both of the institution and of other staff within that institution who may be tainted by association. Whether the physician/staff or institution are 'innocent' victims is influenced by the nature of the error (mishap or negligence) and the systems in place to prevent errors. The fifth victim is society and/or the healthcare system, where finite resources have to be redistributed to meet the financial costs of litigation and additional healthcare treatments. Again, whether or not the fifth victim is 'innocent' or 'culpable' depends on whether or not the resourcing of the institution had been undertaken at a safe level.

The financial cost

To assess the additional resources associated with an adverse event, a study was undertaken in 11 medical and two surgical units in two tertiary-care hospitals in America over a 6-month period.[1] The cohort included 4108 admissions to a stratified random sampling. The control for each case was a patient on the same unit as the case with the most similar pre-event length of stay. Post-event length of stay and total costs were determined. The authors focused on 190 adverse events, of which 60 events were preventable. The additional length of stay associated with an adverse event was 2.2 days, with an associated cost of $3244. For preventable adverse events the increased length of stay and cost were 4.6 days and $5857, respectively. After adjusting for sampling strategy, the cost of all adverse drug events and preventable ADEs for a 700-bed teaching hospital was estimated to be $5.6 million and $2.8 million a year, respectively.

In a further study designed to investigate the effects of adverse drug events in a tertiary-care health institution in the USA, when the cases were compared with matched controls, the length of stay increased by 1.91 days at an increased cost of $2262 and an almost twofold increased risk of death.[2]

In a random selection of discharges from 28 hospitals in Utah and Colorado in 1992, which detected 459 adverse events, healthcare costs totalled $348 million for all adverse events and $159 million for the preventable adverse events. In total, 57% of the adverse event healthcare costs and 46% of the preventable adverse event costs were attributed to outpatient medical care.[3] From the latter study, the estimated total national costs of preventable adverse events (lost income, lost household production, disability and health-care costs) are seen to be between $17 and $29 billion, with the healthcare costs representing over 50%. Such costs may appear extreme, yet it has been estimated that $3.9 billion were spent in 1983 on the management of the preventable adverse gastrointestinal effects of non-steroidal anti-inflammatory drugs alone.[4] Similarly, it has been estimated that for every dollar which is spent on drugs in a nursing-home facility, $1.33 is spent on the treatment of drug-related morbidity and mortality, amounting to $7.6 billion for the nation as a whole.[5]

In the USA it has been calculated by Johnson and Bootman[6] that the cost of adverse outcomes which occur as a result of drug treatment accounts for:

- 116 million extra visits a year
- 76 million additional prescriptions
- 17 million emergency department visits
- 8 million admissions to hospital
- 3 million admissions to long-term care facilities
- 199 000 additional deaths.

The total cost was estimated to be over 70 billion dollars.

The cost of medication errors involving failures of treatment due to non-prescribing or non-compliance can be equally high. With regard to non-compliance with antipsychotic medication in schizophrenic patients alone, the total annual cost of short-term hospitalisations for relapsing patients was $2.3 billion.[7]

The Quality in Australian Health Care Study estimated that adverse events accounted for 8% of hospital bed days and cost the Australian healthcare system $4.7 billion a year.[8] Similarly, a French study estimated the cost of serious ADRs in a general medicine ward to be £4700 per bed per year, or around 5–9% of the total hospital costs.[9]

In the UK, failure to measure errors and adverse events formally has precluded accurate measurements of the costs involved. However, the cost to the NHS of adverse events has been estimated by the Department of Health to be £2 billion for the extra stay in hospital, with negligence costs running at around £400 million a year, plus a potential liability of around £2.4 billion for existing and expected claims. Hospital-acquired infections alone, about 15% of which may be avoidable, are estimated to cost the NHS nearly £1.0 billion a year.[10] In a recent study by Vincent and colleagues,[11] conducted in two acute hospitals in the Greater London area, the 119 adverse events resulted in a total of 999 extra bed days, 460 (46%) of which were judged to have been preventable. Each adverse event led to an average of 8.5 additional days in hospital (range 0–70 days), with additional costs of £290 268 to the Trusts concerned.

In the UK, the cost of legal aid involved in cases of clinical negligence is invariably ignored. During the decade from 1988 to 1998 the number of complaints notified to the medical defence organisations increased by more than tenfold. The UK legal aid bill increased from £166 million in 1990 to over £600 million in 1996, and the cost to the NHS of providing indemnity increased by over 300% during that period.[12]

Perhaps most worryingly of all, the studies by Localio and colleagues[13] and Andrews and colleagues[14] challenge the portrayal of the American patient as over-litigious. Despite patients experiencing a serious adverse event caused by medical negligence, only 2% or less made a claim for compensation. Localio and colleagues used the Harvard Medical Practice Database to analyse statewide estimates of adverse events due to negligence that did not lead to malpractice claims (see Figure 7.1).

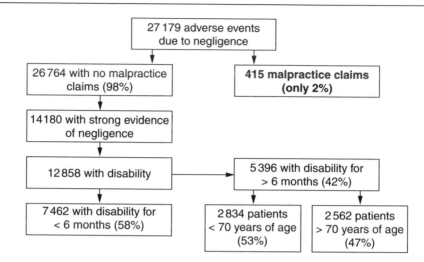

Figure 7.1: Statewide estimates of adverse events in the USA due to negligence that did not lead to malpractice claims. Prepared from the Harvard Medical Practice Study data (Localio *et al.*[13]).

The authors' conclusions were distressing:

> *The results of this study, in which malpractice claims were matched to inpatient medical records, demonstrate that the civil-justice system only infrequently compensates injured patients, and rarely identifies and holds healthcare providers accountable for substandard medical care.*

The reader is invited to consider the financial consequences of even a modest increase in compensation claims within the future perspective of transparency and the mandatory reporting and recording of errors by healthcare staff, and the invitation to patients to do the same (*see* pages 101 and 108). The financial consequences of this could be appreciable.

Chapter 8

Summary of the problem of adverse drug events, medication errors and their cost

The extent of adverse events, adverse drug reactions and medication errors

Adverse events and injuries to patients in hospital caused by medical mis-management (i.e. by physicians, nurses, pharmacists, physiotherapists or other supportive personnel) are revealed as a leading cause of impairment, disability and death. The events and injuries are recorded following surgery, medication, diagnostic testing or any other aspect of healthcare. They were identified in initial studies using retrospective medical record review, and their most serious limitation is probably the failure of the record charts to record faithfully all events and errors. Indeed, there is gross under-reporting. This is likely to lead to a substantial underestimate of the prevalence of injury, although this may be offset to some extent by hindsight bias. In any event, some of the major findings of the studies conducted in hospitals are as follows.

- Adverse events occurred in 3.7% of admissions, and 27.6% of these were attributed to negligence.[1]
- Adverse events occurred in 16.6% of admissions, and 51% of these were preventable.[2]
- Serious and fatal adverse drug reactions attributable to drugs that were properly prescribed and administered occurred in 6.7% and 0.32% of hospital patients, respectively. The overall incidence of adverse drug reactions of all severities was 15.1%.[3]

From retrospective studies, in which adverse events and errors may be under-reported, it could be cautiously concluded that at least one in ten patients who enters hospital may be injured by the treatment that they will receive. In the UK, the incidence of hospital-acquired infections was shown to be 7.8% in inpatients alone.[4] Similarly, Kirkland and colleagues,[5] who conducted a large controlled study in the USA, reported that the excess mortality rate of surgical site infections was 4.3%, equivalent to around 20 000 deaths per year from this cause alone. Such findings support the estimates by the Centers for Disease Control and Prevention in the USA that around 500 000 surgical site infections may occur each year.[6]

In prospective cohort studies using daily chart review and/or stimulated self-reports, computerised surveillance or observational methods, injury rates and errors are invariably higher. This has been apparent for many years. In an early study of 815 consecutive patients in a general medical service of a university hospital in the USA, it was determined that of 815 consecutive admissions, 36% had an iatrogenic illness.[7] In a review of the early literature, Davis and Cohen[8] reported a common error rate in medication of 12%. Dubois and Brook[9] found that 14–27% of all deaths in hospital due to myocardial infarction, pneumonia or cerebrovascular accident were preventable. The error rates reported by Bates and colleagues[10] and Classen and colleagues[11] are also higher than those recorded from patient chart records. Furthermore, Andrews and colleagues[12] reported that 45.8% of patients in an intensive-care unit had experienced an adverse event (mean value of 4.5 events per patient), and 17.7% of the patients had experienced at least one preventable serious adverse event.

It is still of considerable concern that there have been no large-scale studies to examine the extent of medically induced injuries that occur outside hospital. Yet the incidence of adverse drug reactions in patients admitted to hospital was at least twice that in patients from within the hospital.[3] Furthermore, in the USA more than 50% of surgical procedures now occur outside a hospital setting, with no measurement of adverse events or death rates.[13]

In the UK, around 75% of all medications are prescribed by a general practitioner, and there are no published figures to indicate the nature of the adverse event profile, yet major prescribing differences between practices and practitioners require explanation. For example, the apparent major under-prescribing of lipid-lowering drugs[14,15] may reveal a potential and serious medication error. Moreover, medication errors have accounted for 25% of litigation claims in general medical practice,[16] and the general failure of the patient to take medicines as prescribed may be a major factor in therapeutic failures.[17]

The stages at which adverse events and medication errors occur

In an initial study of drug-related incidents, it was shown that physicians were primarily responsible for 72% of the incidents, with the remaining incidents occurring as a consequence of the actions of clerical, nursing and pharmacy personnel.[18] In a subsequent detailed analysis of adverse drug-induced events, the errors made during prescribing, drug administration, transcribing of the prescription and dispensing were 49%, 26%, 11% and 14%, respectively. Errors that resulted in preventable adverse drug events occurred most often at the stages of prescribing (56%) and drug administration (34%). Errors of transcription (6%) and dispensing (4%) were much less frequent. Thus of the preventable adverse events, 90% of errors occurred at the prescribing and drug administration stages.[10] In a study of medication errors in paediatric practice, doctors accounted for 72% of the errors, nurses accounted for 22% and pharmacy staff accounted for 5%.[19]

Types and causes of medication errors

The commonest non-operative adverse events experienced by hospitalised patients are drug related. They are experienced as the wrong dose, wrong route, wrong choice, wrong drug, wrong technique, wrong frequency, wrong drug–drug interactions or drug allergies. The most important single cause of error was lack of knowledge or information, which accounted for 22% of all errors made by the healthcare team. Lack of information about the patient, rule violations or mental slips/memory lapses caused 14%, 10% and 9% of the errors, respectively. Ten other causes of errors (e.g. preparation errors) were less common.

Lack of knowledge as a cause of error was distributed unevenly between the four stages of medication. When expressed as a percentage of the total errors occurring at each stage, the lack of knowledge at the prescribing, drug administration, transcribing and dispensing stages accounted for 36%, 15%, 15% and 0% of the errors, respectively. For the physician prescribing the drug and the nurse administering it, the single most frequent cause of error was lack of knowledge of the drug. If the two most important causes of error, namely lack of knowledge of the drug and lack of information about the patient, are pooled together, then these can be seen to be the cause of 60%, 25%, 25% and 0% of the errors at the prescribing, drug administration, transcription and dispensing stages, respectively.[20,21]

Risk factors

The most important risk factors probably relate to the age of the patient,[2] the number of treatments received,[22] the nature of the intervention,[2] staff fatigue, stress and workloads,[23,24] staff inexperience[25] and the characteristics of the hospital.[26]

In the future, diagnostic and genetic tests that will predictably invade privacy, and which may cause serious discrimination, may induce adverse events whose recognition and attribution may create a new cause of medically induced social injury. Moreover, clinical guidelines that do not adequately control disease may contribute to the recording of a medication error.

The cost of medically induced injury

The major human cost is the distress of injury or death to the patient (and distress to their family), closely followed by the severe trauma to the healthcare team and their colleagues who have been involved in an error. The financial costs are profound, and are measured in billions of pounds to meet the additional length of time spent in hospital, subsequent treatments and the cost of litigation. It is a sobering thought that in two USA studies, only 1–2% of patients who had good reason to claim for compensation actually did so.[12,27] If this percentage was to increase to only 5% as a consequence of greater awareness of errors and encouragement to report errors, both by healthcare professionals and by patients, and also compensation successes, then there could be major financial implications for the healthcare system.

Reducing adverse events and medication errors

Our knowledge of the clinical staff who actually make errors is still in its infancy. Detailed reporting of the experience or inexperience of the staff and the nature of the causes and errors that are incurred are important for the rational design of error reduction systems.

Based on the available evidence, the reduction of preventable adverse drug-induced events (medication errors) should:

1 address both primary and secondary care
2 initially focus on the stages of prescribing and drug administration in hospitals
3 address the causes of error, in particular:
   • lack of knowledge of drugs and rule violations, which have a serious impact on individual responsibility, education and training
   • lack of information about the patient and other causes of errors, many of which frequently involve inadequate systems and procedures.

Chapter 9

Errors in healthcare: a major cause for concern

> **Summary:** Definitions of error
>
> - Errors may be defined as 'the failure of a planned sequence of mental or physical activities to achieve its intended outcome when these failures cannot be attributed to chance'.
> - A mistake occurs when an action proceeds as planned but fails to achieve its intended outcome. It is a failure of planning.
> - A slip or lapse occurs when the action performed is not what was intended. It is an error of execution. Slips are observable, whereas lapses are not.
> - Slips and lapses are not minor, lesser or more excusable events than a mistake. Patients are readily injured or die from all three causes.

Introduction

There is substantial evidence from the developed world that healthcare is unsafe and is a leading cause of patient injury and death.[1,2] The adverse events which occur are either preventable or non-preventable. The preventable events are due to errors of medical management, whereas the non-preventable events reflect the inherently dangerous nature of medical, surgical and other interventions.[3,4] Errors involving the use of drugs are the single commonest adverse event, and many of these incidents are preventable.[3–5]

The major findings of the previous chapters, based mainly on data obtained from hospital patients, are that adverse events caused by medical management are a serious and grossly under-reported public health problem. Over 50% of all medication errors were attributable to the prescribing stage of medication, and over 30% were attributed to the administration of the drug. The single most frequent cause of error was lack of knowledge of the drug, which gave rise to fundamental errors of wrong dose, wrong route, wrong frequency, wrong drug, wrong patient and drug allergy, among others. It was concluded that a lack of knowledge or ignorance of clinical staff with regard to some of the most elementary principles of pharmacology and therapeutics precluded the safe and effective use of medication. This simply should not happen, and it is difficult to distinguish such causes of error from potential negligence.

Other causes of error included inadequate information about the patient, rule violations, mental slips and lapses and additional causes which may be related to individual errors or faulty procedures and systems. Risk factors predisposing to errors included the nature and intensity of the medical intervention, the age of the patient, the inexperience of the staff and the characteristics of the hospital.

However, all such comments on hospitals and their patients reflect a modest estimate of the extent of the problem – they represent only a small proportion of the population at risk. Increasingly, more extensive and complex care is being provided in primary care or ambulatory settings in general practice, outpatient surgical centres and clinics. Nursing homes provide a service to some of the most vulnerable members of our society, and home care will increasingly require patients and their families to use sophisticated medications and complex equipment. Community pharmacies play a major role in dispensing medicines and an increasing role in educating patients in their use. Medical errors, patient errors and carer errors appear to represent a major problem in many settings which we have barely started to investigate. They are generally beyond the scope of this chapter.

Overview of medical errors

Types of errors

When asked about the main causes of medical mistakes, the public frequently (29% of respondents) cites the carelessness or negligence of healthcare professionals who are perceived to be overworked.[6] They hear about the latest medical mistake from a friend or relative (42%), the media (39%) or, perhaps most disconcertingly of all, from personal experience (12%), and they believe that an effective solution for preventing such mistakes is to ensure that healthcare professionals with bad track records receive improved training (69%) or are barred from providing care (75%).[6]

These reactions are understandable and not necessarily punitive – the public wishes the perceived source of harm to be removed and/or the person concerned to be retrained. Indeed, a common motive in claims for negligence is to attempt to reveal the truth in order to ensure that others may be spared the same fate. Not only are these beliefs understandable – they are also correct. *In any industry, the one factor which contributes most to accidents (around 60–80%) is human error,*[7] and this is probably equally true in healthcare. An analysis of accidents in anaesthesia revealed human error to be involved in 82% of cases.[8] However, attributing an accident to human error is not necessarily the same as assigning blame, since errors are committed for a variety of reasons.

Nevertheless, a common and emotive reaction to error is to blame an individual, notwithstanding the fact that the error may have arisen from an unfortunate series of events, which will predictably recur sooner or later.

Definitions of error

Reason[9] has defined errors as 'the failure of a planned sequence of mental or physical activities to achieve its intended outcome when these failures cannot be attributed to chance'. The critical feature of the definition relates to the intention. There can be no error without intent, because failures that relate to errors reflect either actions that do not go as intended, or an intended action that is not the correct one.

Slips, lapses and mistakes

Reason[9] defines these as follows. A slip or lapse occurs when the action that is performed is not what was intended – it is an error of execution. The difference between a slip and a lapse is that a slip is observable and a lapse is not. Slips are unintended acts that frequently involve skill-based errors where there is perhaps a break in the routine or diversion of attention. For example, turning the wrong dial on an infusion pump would be a slip. Failure to recall accurately from memory is a lapse. Factors which can divert attention, such as fatigue, sleep loss, illness, overwork, noise, heat and other environmental influences make both slips and lapses more likely, and some of these factors are endemic within the NHS.

Such errors of execution are known to everyone, and even catastrophic errors generally give rise to a sympathetic understanding. For example, a junior doctor who administered penicillin intracerebrally rather than intravenously, resulting in the death of his patient, was charged with manslaughter. However, the court heard that the doctor had been required to work 110 hours in the previous week and had already been on duty for 14 hours when the incident occurred. The doctor was acquitted and the patient's widow said that her husband 'had paid the price for the long hours demanded from untrained doctors'.[10]

A mistake (a euphemism for which could be 'unintended injury' or 'suboptimal prescribing') occurs when the action proceeds as planned but fails to achieve its intended outcome. This may be due to an incorrect diagnosis, selection of the wrong drug or lack of knowledge of the situation. In any case, the intention is inadequate and a failure of planning is involved. Such errors of planning also relate to associated issues of overuse, underuse and misuse of medication, and to personal responsibility, and they are less likely to lead to a sympathetic response.

It should be carefully noted that in therapeutics, surgery, diagnostics and other areas of healthcare, a slip or lapse is not a 'minor', 'lesser' or more 'excusable' event. It is quite as serious as a mistake, and patients die from all three causes. For example, the simple slip of the physician who wrote a prescription for methotrexate with the instruction for a daily dose instead of a weekly dose of 10 mg was subsequently shown to have instigated the events which caused the death of the patient (*see* page 147).

Active and latent errors

Summary: 'Latent' and 'active' errors and their reduction

- Healthcare services represent a highly complex technological industry which is readily prone to accidents.
- Human error is the single largest contributor to accidents, but to apportion blame to an individual on the basis of an error will only address a single retrospective incident, and may also be seriously misleading.
- Human error (i.e. an 'active' error) may result from a failure of the system in which the individual is working (e.g. inadequate training or facilities, or excessive workload) – that is a 'latent' or 'systems' error.
- Latent errors are present before the active error, they are inherent to and usually indiscernible within the system, and they are believed to be one of the greatest continuing threats to safety.
- The discovery and reduction of latent errors is a most effective way to reduce errors and improve safety.

The distinction between errors at either the 'sharp end' or the 'blunt end' have important implications for the understanding and reduction of errors. Active errors at the 'sharp end' in healthcare involve the frontline operator – the physician, nurse or other professional staff member or trainee – and their errors are noted almost immediately. Active errors are therefore related to an individual or individuals. Latent errors at the 'blunt end' are usually inherent in the design and maintenance of the workload and environment, facilities, equipment or management of the organisation and its culture. An example of a latent error would be the use of junior staff with limited experience working under limited supervision and with excessive workloads – it would represent an accident 'waiting to happen'.[11]

Cognitive psychology has greatly advanced our understanding of how errors may occur, and models based on skill-focused patterns of thought and action, rule-based solutions to familiar problems or knowledge-based situations requiring conscious analytical processing are crucial to our understanding of error reduction. Leape[12] has reviewed the theories and models of why humans make errors, but such detail and other essential reading[13–16] is beyond the scope of the present chapter.

The importance of the distinction between active and latent errors lies in both the attribution of blame and the reduction in errors. By their very nature, active errors are relatively easy to detect and relate to an individual, who is subsequently punished, removed, suspended or retrained in an attempt to prevent a recurrence of the error. However, removing an individual does little to address the latent errors, which may be more difficult to identify and which can result in a perpetuation of the active error.

Latent errors may be hidden within the normal work culture and, as such, pose one of the greatest threats to patient safety. Individuals may overlook, misinterpret or unknowingly learn to work around problems in the system in order to normalise deviant and error-inducing behaviour.[17] For these reasons, there is currently intense interest in finding ways to reduce errors in healthcare by focusing on the reduction of latent or systems errors rather than active errors, which are frequently depicted to address a single incident.

However, reducing medical errors is a very formidable challenge. It is deeply regrettable that for many years the medical and other healthcare professions and/or their employers were either ignorant of the serious level of substandard care, or chose to ignore it. The moral imperative has been seized by others.

To err is human: the Institute of Medicine (IOM) Report

In June 1998, the Institute of Medicine (IOM) Quality Of Health Care in America Committee was formed to develop a strategy that would result in a threshold improvement in quality over the next ten years. It was charged with the following tasks:[18]

- *review and synthesis of findings in the literature pertaining to the quality of care provided in the healthcare system*
- *development of a communications strategy for raising the awareness of the general public and the key stakeholders of quality-of-care concerns and opportunities for improvement*
- *articulation of a policy framework that will provide positive incentives to improve quality and foster accountability*
- *identification of key characteristics and factors that enable or encourage providers, healthcare organisations, health plans, and communities to continuously improve the quality of care and*
- *develop a research agenda in areas of continued uncertainty.*

The president of the IOM, Dr Kenneth Shine, concluded:

> *The IOM will continue to call for a comprehensive and strong response to this most urgent issue facing the American people. This current report on patient safety further reinforces our conviction that we cannot wait any longer.*

In November 1999, the publication of the first report entitled *To Err is Human:*

Building a Safer Health System, by the Institute of Medicine (IOM) of the National Academy of Sciences received unprecedented media coverage in the USA. The committee focused its initial attention on quality concerns that fall into the category of medical errors. The reasons for the report were described as fivefold.[18]

- *First, errors are responsible for an immense burden of patient injury, suffering and death.*
- *Second, errors in the provision of health services, whether they result in injury or expose the patient to the risk of injury, are events that everyone agrees just shouldn't happen.*
- *Third, errors are readily understandable to the American public.*
- *Fourth, there is a sizeable body of knowledge and a very successful experience in other industries to draw upon in tackling the safety problems of the healthcare industry.*
- *Fifth, the healthcare delivery system is rapidly evolving and undergoing substantial redesign, which may introduce improvements but also new hazards.*

It is hoped that the report can serve as a call to action that will illuminate a problem to which we are all vulnerable.

Preventing errors is a prerequisite for developing a safer healthcare system, and the goal of the IOM report in America was described as an attempt to:

break the cycle of inaction. The status quo is not acceptable and cannot be tolerated any longer. Despite the cost pressures, liability restraints, resistance to change and other seemingly insurmountable barriers, it is simply not acceptable for patients to be harmed by the same healthcare system that is supposed to offer healing and comfort. 'First do no harm' is an often quoted term from Hippocrates.[19] Everyone within the healthcare system is familiar with the term. At the very minimum, the healthcare system needs to offer that assurance and security to the public.

A comprehensive approach to improving patient safety is needed. This approach cannot focus on a single solution, since there is no 'magic bullet' that will solve this problem, and indeed no single recommendation in this report should be considered as the answer. Rather, large complex problems require thoughtful, multifaceted responses. The combined goal of the recommendations is for the external environment to create sufficient pressure to make errors costly to healthcare organisations and providers, so they are compelled to take action to improve safety. At the same time there is a need to enhance knowledge and tools to improve safety and break down legal and cultural barriers that impede safety improvement. Given the magnitude of the problem, the committee believes it would be irresponsible to expect anything less than a 50% reduction in errors over five years.[20]

The IOM report focused on a broad remit to:

- *establish a national focus to create leadership, research, tools and protocols to enhance the knowledge base about safety*
- *identify and learn from errors through immediate and strong mandatory reporting efforts, as well as the encouragement of voluntary efforts*
- *raise standards and expectations for improvements in safety through the actions of oversight organisations, group purchasers and professional groups and*
- *create safety systems inside healthcare organisations through the implementation of safe practices at the delivery level. This level is the ultimate target of all the recommendations.*[20]

In summary, the report focused on systems and procedures of the healthcare workplace to improve safety. It is axiomatic that if the workplace is unsafe, whatever the skills of the individual staff, the systems and procedures will inevitably predispose to the occurrence of errors. The IOM report emphasised that although almost all accidents result from human error, these are usually induced by faulty systems that 'set people up' to fail.

The report also recognised that some individuals may be incompetent, impaired or uncaring, or may even have criminal intent, and that these individuals were unlikely to be amenable to the types of approach described. However, the report made no recommendations on the professional competence of individuals. In brief, the IOM report focused on latent or systems errors.

Although some of the data that were presented had been available for nearly 10 years,[21] the American public finally became fully aware that around 44 000–98 000 patients a year in hospitals in the USA were dying, with over a million injured, due to medical error. The response was fascinating.

Within two weeks Congress began hearings and the President ordered a feasibility study to implement the report's recommendations. The IOM had called for a broad national effort to improve patient safety to include the following:

1 *a center for patient safety within the Agency for Health Care Research and Quality*
2 *an expanded confidential and voluntary reporting of adverse events and errors and some federally mandated*
3 *the development of safety programs in healthcare organisations*
4 *intensified efforts by regulators, healthcare purchasers and professional societies.*

On 22 February 2000 the President introduced measures requiring hospitals to report mistakes that kill or seriously injure patients. The aim was to reduce medical errors by 50% in the next five years. Scepticism was voiced by Nancy Dickey, past president of the American Medical Association, who was reported as saying 'our fear is that mandatory reporting will drive information about errors underground. Doctors will be worried that after reports are turned in, the next person they will hear from is the patient's lawyer'.[22]

McDonald and colleagues of the Regenstrief Institute suggested that the IOM report contained two different messages:

> One is cool and measured, a call for understanding the cause of errors and for developing an approach using computerised and other mechanical support systems to decrease error rates . . . . The other message in the IOM report is hot and shrill. It shouts about death and disability in US hospitals . . . and claimed that the figures were exaggerated . . . more study with careful attention to risk levels is needed to determine the true impact of adverse events on death rates among hospitalised patients. Until those are available, the design of regulatory systems is premature.[23]

Leape[24] refuted these allegations and emphasised that the long-term impact of the IOM report will result from the validity of its message that errors can be prevented by redesigning medical work. Brennan[25] was less sanguine, noting that with current fiscal constraints to fund innovations (computer systems) in safety, the cost of preventative systems must be addressed. Noting the opportunity to do much more, it was suggested that medical leaders should also take the next step by addressing liability reform as part of the overall solution to the problem of medical errors.

The understanding of errors in the UK

Summary: Learning from errors to prevent their recurrence

- The greatest barrier to improving patient safety is a lack of awareness of the extent to which errors occur in all healthcare organisations.
- It is difficult to remedy problems that are not known to exist.
- This lack of awareness occurs because, in most cases, errors are not reported.
- Reporting of errors should be developed in six stages as a culture for their recognition, acknowledgement, recording, reporting, analysis and a reflective response within a just and flexible learning environment.

In the UK, the picture could not have been more different. Media stories of medical and surgical errors focusing on the catastrophic, criminal or bizarre were creating populist entertainment that seriously obscured the real nature and magnitude of clinical error. This is a crucial issue which can be exemplified as follows. On 19 December 1999, *The Sunday Times* ran a headline and article entitled 'Blunders by doctors kill 40 000 a year'. The report stated that medical error in the UK is the third most frequent cause of death. A pilot study by Vincent and colleagues in the Clinical Risk Unit at University College London had shown that one in 14 patients suffer some type of adverse event. In a classic juxtaposition, this very important article (although briefly reported) was obscured by another of equal size and with larger graphics, entitled 'Heart surgeon suspended over threats claims', which informed the reader that a top children's heart surgeon had been suspended from duty following accusations of drunkenness at work and threats to nurses.

With the media trivialising a major public health problem, it is likely that most clinical practitioners, patients, policy makers and educators have for many years seriously underestimated the real extent of the risk of harm to patients in healthcare.

In December 1997, the UK Government published a White Paper, *The New NHS: Modern, Dependable*, which set out a ten-year modernisation strategy for the NHS:[26]

One of the main aims of the proposals set out in the White Paper is to bring about a major improvement in the quality of clinical care delivered to patients in the NHS. As part of these changes, a formal responsibility for quality has been placed on every health organisation in the country through arrangements for clinical governance (defined as 'A framework through which NHS organisations are accountable for continuously improving the quality of their services and safeguarding high standards of care by creating an environment in which excellence in clinical care will flourish') at local level.[27] This responsibility is underpinned by a new statutory duty of quality on NHS providers. Clinical governance is thus an organisational concept. It requires the creation of a culture as well as systems and methods of working which will ensure that opportunities for quality improvement are identified in all the organisation's services and that over time there is a major step up in the quality of care provided throughout the NHS. Under these new policies local clinical governance is reinforced by new national structures: National Service Frameworks and the National Institute for Clinical Excellence (NICE) will set standards, a new NHS Performance Assessment Framework will provide a better-balanced means of gauging NHS performance, and the Commission for Health Improvement (CHI) will review local clinical governance arrangements. The Commission will also have a 'trouble-shooting' role to help individual NHS organisations identify the root causes of serious difficulties and advise on the measures needed to resolve them.

The above comments were taken from the report entitled *An Organisation With a Memory* which was published in the year 2000 by an expert group on learning from adverse events in the NHS.

An Organisation With a Memory[1]

The tenor of this report was similar to that of the IOM report. The executive summary noted the following:

> 1 *The great majority of NHS care is of a very high clinical standard, and serious failures are uncommon in relation to the high volume of care provided every day in hospitals and in the community. Yet where serious failures in care do occur they can have devastating consequences for individual patients and their families, cause distress to the usually very committed healthcare staff involved and undermine public confidence in the services the NHS provides. In addition, the cumulative financial cost of adverse events to the NHS and to the economy is huge. Most distressing of all, such failures often have a familiar ring, displaying strong similarities to incidents which have occurred before and in some cases almost exactly replicating them. Many could be avoided if only the lessons of experience were properly learned.*

> 2 *The introduction of clinical governance provides NHS organ-isations with a powerful imperative to focus on tackling adverse healthcare events. This report, commissioned by Health Ministers from an expert group under the chairmanship of the Chief Medical Officer, sets out to review what we know about the scale and nature of serious failures in NHS healthcare, to examine the extent to which the NHS has the capacity to learn from such failures when they do occur, and to recommend measures which could help to ensure that the likelihood of repeated failures is minimised in the future. The work of the group was informed by evidence and experience from a range of sectors other than health, including industry, aviation and academic research . . .*

> 20 *We believe that, if the NHS is successfully to modernise its approach to learning from failure, there are four key areas that must be addressed. In summary, the NHS needs to develop:*

> - *unified mechanisms for reporting and analysis when things go wrong*
> - *a more open culture, in which errors or service failures can be reported and discussed* *
> - *mechanisms for ensuring that, where lessons are identified, the necessary changes are put into practice*
> - *a much wider appreciation of the value of the systems approach in preventing, analysing and learning from errors.*

> 21 *Only if these four conditions are met can the NHS hope to develop the modern and effective approach to learning from failures that it so badly needs. It is the specific action needed to create these*

conditions that our conclusions and recommendations seek to address in detail.*

(*Openness applies throughout the system and not least to the Secretary of State for Health, who lost a valuable opportunity in affirming the importance of openness in attempting to hold the Shipman Inquiry in private. It is particularly regrettable that 113 relatives of 55 alleged victims had to apply for judicial review proceedings against Mr Milburn, who had argued that holding an inquiry in private would be speedier, allow individuals to speak more freely and cause less distress to the relatives. However, Lord Justice Kennedy and Mr Justice Jackson agreed with the relatives; a private inquiry would limit the ability to test one piece of evidence against another and the totality of the information would be reduced. The court decided on using strong language in favour of a public inquiry, citing the scale of the tragedy, the worry about why the murders were not detected sooner, the uncertainty as to who the victims were and other concerns. In brief, the inquiry should restore confidence in the NHS and trust in general practitioners, which was a matter of national importance).[28,29]

In this landmark report, the setting up of a national system for reporting medical accidents and 'near misses' in the UK was announced by Professor Liam Donaldson, the Chief Medical Officer, on 13 June 2000. The latest analysis of incidents had suggested that between 314 000 and 1 400 000 NHS patients are harmed every year.[1] The incident reporting and some of the events described in the report are shown in Table 9.1.

It is striking that much of the data was obtained from a 'Confidential Enquiry', which provides an eloquent testimony to the nature of the proceedings and secrecy governing previous investigations of serious incidents in the NHS.

In an analysis of the incident-reporting systems in NHS trusts, the report concluded as follows:

> *4.14   The evidence suggests that historically incident reporting has been rather haphazard. Today, although the great majority of NHS trusts have some form of incident-reporting system in place, there is substantial variation in the coverage and sophistication of these systems.*
>
> *Status of incident reporting in NHS trusts:*
>
> - *a fifth do not have reporting systems covering the whole organisation*
> - *less than half provide specific training on risk management or incident reporting*
> - *less than a third provide guidance to staff on what to report*
> - *a third do not require clinicians to report unexpected operational complications or unexpected events*
> - *rates of reporting vary widely.*[30]

Table 9.1: Information from NHS incident reporting and recording systems, prepared from *An Organisation With a Memory*[1]

Source	Event	Estimated number
Confidential Inquiry (Suicides and homicides)	Suicides by people in recent contact with mental health services (in the 12 months prior to the event)	1150*
	Homicides by people in contact with mental health services (in the 12 months prior to the event)	40*
Confidential Inquiry (Maternal deaths)	Deaths of women during pregnancy or within one year of giving birth	125†
Confidential Inquiry (Peri-operative deaths)	Deaths within 30 days of surgery	20 000
Confidential Inquiry (Stillbirths and deaths in infancy)	Stillbirths and infant deaths	7800†
Complaints data	Written complaints about aspects of clinical treatment in hospitals	27 949*
	Written complaints about all aspects of treatment in primary care	38 857*
NHS Litigation Authority claims data	Clinical negligence claims settled by the Authority above local excess levels	810†
Regional Serious Untoward Incident Reporting Systems	Serious untoward incidents (as variously defined)	2500‡
Medical Devices Agency	Adverse incidents involving medical devices (including 87 deaths and 345 serious injuries)	6610
Medicines Control Agency	Reported adverse drug reactions (ADRs)	18 196 (9819 serious)

* Most recent year for which information is available.
† Average of several years.
‡ Extrapolated from the best-developed regional system.

It was also noted that:

> *4.64 NHS activity. Adverse event reporting is least developed in sectors where most patients are seen: figures quoted are for 1998–99.[31]*
>
> *Primary care:*
> * *251 million GP consultations*
> * *26 million courses of dental treatment.*

Community healthcare:
- *16 million new episodes.*

Hospital care:
- *8.6 million hospital admissions*
- *11.8 million new outpatients*
- *12.8 million attendances at Accident and Emergency depart-ments.*[32]

However, it remains clear that Confidential Enquiries can effect change:

> *4.60   Further evidence of the ability of the Confidential Inquiries to bring about change, and of the variable pace with which that change comes about, is provided by the Report of the National Confidential Enquiry into Perioperative Deaths (NCEPOD) 1997/1998.*[33]

The NCEPOD report returned to a study of 1989 and assessed the degree of change in practice in relation to surgery and anaesthesia in children.

The 1989 report stated that 'surgeons and anaesthetists should not undertake occasional paediatric practice'. Comparison between the data for 1989 and 1997/98 shows evidence of a number of positive changes in practice:

> *Meaningful improvements have occurred in paediatric surgery, but they have taken a number of years to come about, and in some cases recommendations have not been universally adopted.*
>
> - *The proportion of anaesthetists who did not anaesthetise infants of less than six months had increased from 16% (1989) to 58% (1997/98).*
> - *The proportion of orthopaedic surgeons dealing with small numbers (1–9 cases per year) of infants has fallen from 41% to 19%, and of those dealing with 10–19 cases per year has fallen from 9% to 3%.*
> - *The proportion of anaesthetists dealing with small numbers (1–9 cases per year) of infants has fallen from 40% to 26%, and of those dealing with 10–19 cases per year has fallen from 22% to 7%.*
> - *The proportion of orthopaedic surgeons who do not operate on infants has increased from 39% (1989) to 74% (1997/98).*
> - *The figures for many of the other surgical specialties show similar trends, with more specialisation in children's surgery.*

(The NHS uses four National Confidential Enquiries, namely the Confidential Enquiry into Maternal Deaths (deaths of women during pregnancy or within one year of childbirth), the Confidential Enquiry into Stillbirths and Deaths in Infancy (stillbirths and infant deaths), the Confidential Enquiry into Perioperative Deaths (hospital deaths within 30 days of surgery) and the Confidential Enquiry into Suicides and Homicides by People with Mental Illness (suicides within one year of contact with mental health services and homicides involving people who have been in contact with mental health services at any time). Each Enquiry takes anonymised information, on a comprehensive or sample basis, about deaths related to a particular condition or aspect of healthcare and analyses it to produce recommendations for improved practice.)

4.41   Key features of the confidential enquiries:[32]

- *aim to identify all deaths in a specific category*
- *confidential reporting (i.e. patient, staff and hospital not identified in reports)*
- *multidisciplinary review of deaths to discover avoidable factors*
- *results published in periodic reports*
- *key themes identified and recommendations made for improve-ment*
- *no mandatory compliance with recommendations*
- *no systematic monitoring of uptake of recommendations.*

The disadvantages relate to the voluntary nature of the recommendations and the failure to monitor uptake. In summary, some patients will remain exposed to suboptimal care, resulting in their injury or death. This was recognised in *An Organisation With a Memory:*[34]

> *4.7   It is important to recognise that the great majority of adverse events are not indicative of or attributable to deep-seated problems of poor performance on the part of individual clinicians. As we have already discussed, the causes of errors are manifold and complex, and can rarely be attributed solely to the actions of one individual. But there are inevitably some links between sub-standard profes-sional performance and adverse events. In particular, in healthcare, action to prevent recurrence may need to be directed at an indi-vidual or a team as well as at organisational systems.*

> *4.8   The Government published last year a consultation document setting out proposals for new ways of preventing, recognising and dealing with poor performance among doctors specifically.*[35] *That document emphasised the importance of exploring thoroughly apparent poor performance problems to ensure that the root causes of any problems can be accurately identified and dealt with, and it specifically recognised the likelihood that a systematic examination of some professional performance issues may well reveal deeper and more complex problems within organisations. Similarly, it is pos-sible that systems for detecting and analysing adverse events might provide indications of emerging problems with a particular clini-cian. Although poor professional performance and adverse clinical events are very distinct issues, it is therefore important that systems put in place for detecting and addressing each of these problems can link with and refer to the mechanisms for tackling the other.*

Within this perspective, the *An Organisation With a Memory* report stressed the following:

3.39   A focus on the individual makes it harder for systems to learn, to spread the impact of events or accidents beyond their immediate environment. Researchers have identified a number of 'barriers to learning' which contribute to this:

- *an undue focus on the immediate event rather than on the root causes of problems*
- *latching on to one superficial cause or learning point to the exclusion of more fundamental but sometimes less obvious lessons*
- *rigidity of core beliefs, values and assumptions, which may develop over time – learning is resisted if it contradicts these*
- *lack of corporate responsibility – it may be difficult, for example, to put into practice solutions which are sufficiently far-reaching*
- *ineffective communication and other information difficulties – including failure to disseminate information which is already available*
- *an incremental approach to issues of risk – attempting to resolve problems through tinkering rather than tackling more fundamental change*
- *pride in individual and organisational expertise can lead to denial and to a disregard of external sources of warning – particularly if a bearer of bad news lacks legitimacy in the eyes of the individuals, teams or organisations in question*
- *a tendency towards scapegoating and finding individuals to blame – rather than acknowledging and addressing deep-rooted organisational problems*
- *the difficulties faced by people in 'making sense' of complex events is compounded by changes among key personnel within organisations and teams*
- *human alliances lead people to 'forgive' other team members their mistakes and act defensively against ideas from outside the team*
- *people are often unwilling to learn from negative events, even when it would be to their advantage*
- *contradictory imperatives – for example, communication versus confidentiality*
- *high stress and low job satisfaction can have adverse effects on quality and can also engender a resistance to change*
- *inability to recognise the financial costs of failure, thus losing a powerful incentive for organisations to change.*[36–38]

It remained clear in the conclusions of the report[39] that:

- *awareness of the nature, causes and incidence of failures is a vital component of prevention ('you can't know what you don't know')*

- *analysis of failures needs to look at root causes, not just proximal events; human errors cannot sensibly be considered in isolation of wider processes and systems*
- *error reduction and error management systems can help to prevent or mitigate the effects of individual failures*
- *certain categories of high-risk, high-technology medicine might be regarded as special cases. In these areas the level of endemic risk is such that serious errors or complications will never be eradicated. The evidence suggests that here a focus on compensating for and recovering from adverse events might be an important part of the approach to improving safety and outcomes*
- *organisational learning is a cyclical process, and all the right components must be in place for effective, active learning to take place. Distilling appropriate lessons from failures is not enough: there is a need to embed this learning in practice, and it is at this stage that the 'learning loop' often fails*
- *it is possible to identify a number of important barriers to learning which must be overcome if the lessons of adverse incidents are to be translated into changes in practice*
- *culture is a crucial component in learning effectively from failures: cultural considerations are significant in all parts of the learning loop, from initial incident identification and reporting to embedding appropriate changes in practice. Safety cultures can have a positive and quantifiable impact on the performance of organisations*
- *sound safety information systems are a precondition for systematic learning from failures. They need to take account of the fact that low-level incidents or 'near misses' can provide a useful barometer of more serious risks, and can allow lessons to be learned before a major incident occurs*
- *given appropriate approaches to analysis, it is possible to identify common themes or characteristics in failures which should be of use in helping to predict and prevent future adverse events*
- *the NHS is not unique: other sectors have experience of learning from failures which is of relevance to the NHS.*

An Organisation With a Memory identified in Recommendation 10 that the Department of Health should establish groups to work urgently to achieve four specific aims:

- *by 2001, reduce to zero the number of patients dying or being paralysed by maladministered spinal injections (at least 13 such cases have occurred in the last 15 years)*
- *by 2005, reduce by 25% the number of instances of negligent harm in the field of obstetrics and gynaecology which result in litigation (currently these account for over 50% of the annual NHS litigation bill)*

- *by 2005, reduce by 40% the number of serious errors in the use of prescribed drugs (currently these account for 20% of all clinical negligence litigation)*
- *by 2005, reduce to zero the number of suicides by mental health inpatients as a result of hanging from non-collapsible bed or shower curtain rails on wards (currently hanging from these structures is the commonest method of suicide on mental health inpatient wards).*

Sound baselines will first need to be established for the second and third of these areas in particular, and it is important to recognise that in the short term the number of recorded events may rise as reporting and recording systems improve.

It was intended that every staff member would be obliged to report any mistake of which they were aware, whether it was their own or a colleague's error, and whether or not it led to harm. These data would then be collated in order to assess patterns of poor practice, and to seek ways of avoiding common faults. The aim is to establish a blame-free 'safety culture' within which the lessons of error are learned. The data will be of considerable value if resources are made available both to analyse the information and to produce a response. However, it is disappointing that six years after the tragedy at Bristol Royal Infirmary, there is still no satisfactory record of the children who survive or die after heart surgery,[40] and in the report entitled *Learning from Bristol*, it is emphasised that:

49 *We must learn the lessons of Bristol. Even today it is still not possible to say categorically that events similar to those which happened in Bristol could not happen again in the UK – indeed, are not happening at this moment.*

50 *That said, we must not lose a sense of proportion. Every day the NHS provides a service to hundreds of thousands of patients, with which patients are satisfied and of which healthcare professionals can be justifiably proud.*[41]

The establishment of the National Patient Safety Agency (*see* page 101) should assist in the prevention of future disappointments.

However, there is another important resource within the existing complaint/litigation literature that has been little investigated, and which could reduce errors further. In what has been described as:

4.39. *Wasted and lost opportunities for learning from litigation in the NHS, to date little or no systematic learning across the NHS has taken place from:*

- *a historical base of over 14 000 claims (relating to events stretching back many years) held by the NHS Litigation Authority*
- *an annual rate of around 800 new claims settled by the NHS Litigation Authority arising from incidents in NHS trusts*

- *a historical base of tens of thousands of claims from primary and secondary care held by organisations such as the Medical Defence Union and the Medical Protection Society**
- *an annual rate of around 700 new claims settled by the medical defence organisations, arising mainly from incidents in primary care.**

* The Medical Defence Union (MDU) and Medical Protection Society (MPS) publish analyses of their data for the benefit of their members, and have made it clear that they are willing to share information and experience to maximise the opportunities for collective learning.[42]

In the report chaired by the Chief Medical Officer it was reported in section 4.34, for example, that the average sum awarded to babies who sustained brain damage at birth was £1.5 million, with some awards as high as £4 million, such claims accounting for 50% of the NHS litigation bill every year. The evidence suggested that such risks could be substantially reduced by the following:

- improved staff supervision
- proper use of equipment to monitor labour
- better technique and diagnostic skills at delivery.

Similarly, in a Medical Defence Union (MDU) survey of 100 clinical negligence claims against consultant anaesthetists, in which the MDU paid the claims, it was found that every claim involved problems in at least one of the following key areas:

- inadequate or no preoperative assessment
- failure to use essential equipment
- medication issues (e.g. overdose of muscle relaxant)
- monitoring before, during or after the operation.

The Department of Health Report stated that 'many of the injuries to patients that resulted in litigation are judged in retrospect to have been potentially avoidable'. Further analysis of these failures would be very important with regard to identifying the primary causes of error and then their reduction.

Spink has summarised the situation as follows:[43]

> *Data from litigation claims represent a potentially rich source of learning from failure. Only a small proportion of potential negligence claims are pursued through to court. There is a tremendous amount of unutilised data, beyond high-profile court cases, which provides a further potential source of learning from failure. There are currently no systematic analyses of the litigation data on hospital cases held by the NHS Litigation Authority, and clinical data arising from negligence claims are not in general being used effectively to learn from failures in care. There is significant potential to extract valuable learning by focusing, speciality by speciality, on the main areas of practice which have resulted in litigation. Thus it*

is also important to note that extensive expert scrutiny has already been given to any individual clinical negligence claim to the question of the standard of care received by the claimant. Furthermore, and importantly, simply because the claimant lost the claim on the basis of a causation issue does not in any way affect the lessons to be learned from the medico-legal investigations; clinical negligence, a breach of a duty of care [see page 204], remains intact.

Although there are no systematic analyses of litigation data on hospital cases held by the NHS Litigation Authority, the medical defence organisations such as the Medical Protection Society and the Medical Defence Union (which cover against negligence in primary care and private practice) publish findings to their members in general practice. The profile of adverse events resulting in litigation claims in general medical practice is shown in Table 9.2. It is also possible to identify a number of recurrent problems in medication errors which account for around 25% of all litigation claims (*see* Table 9.3). In particular, incorrect or inappropriate dosage heads the list of errors.

Building a Safer NHS for Patients

The landmark report, *Building a Safer NHS for Patients*[32] sets out the UK Government's plans for promoting patient safety following the publication of the report, *An Organisation With a Memory*, and the commitment to implement it in the NHS Plan. *Central to the plan is the new mandatory, national reporting scheme for adverse healthcare events and 'near misses' within the NHS.*

Table 9.2: Adverse incidents resulting in litigation claims in general medical practice

Delays in diagnosis (55% of claims)*
    Missed malignancies
    Missed heart attacks
    Missed conditions requiring surgery
    Missed meningitis and pneumonia
Medication errors (25% of claims)
Management of pregnancy (10% of claims)
Other procedures and interventions (20% of claims)

* Approximate percentage of total indemnity paid out.
Total value of payments in the latest 2-year period is £16.9 million.
Source: Medical Defence Union.
Prepared from the report *An Organisation With a Memory*.[1]

Table 9.3: The identification of a number of recurrent problems or types of medication error resulting in litigation claims which account for approximately 25% of all litigation claims in general practice in the UK

Incorrect or inappropriate dosage
Wrong drug
Administration error (correct medication wrongly administered)
Contraindicated medication (e.g. patient given medication which reacts badly with another drug or condition)
Prescribing and dispensing errors (e.g. prescribing or dispensing an incorrect drug with a similar name to the intended medication)
Failure to monitor progress
Failure to warn about side-effects
Repeat prescribing without proper checks
Over-reliance on computerised prescribing
Prescribing unlicensed drugs

Source: Medical Protection Society and Medical Defence Union.
Prepared from *An Organisation With a Memory*.[1]

The principles and components of the new national system for learning from adverse events and 'near misses' were described as follows.

The new national reporting system is founded on the following principles:

- mandatory for individuals and organisations
- confidential but open and accessible
- generally blame-free and independent
- simple to use but comprehensive in coverage and data collection
- systems learning and change at local and national levels.

The system consists of five linked key components:

- identifying and recording reportable adverse events
- reporting by individuals to local sites and to the national system, and by institutions to the national system
- analysing incidents, including root cause analysis, and trends
- learning lessons from analysis, research and other sources of information, and disseminating them
- implementing change at local and national levels.

The report focuses on the action, both nationally and locally, that is necessary to establish a system which ensures that lessons from adverse events in one locality are learned across the NHS as a whole. The system will enable reporting from local to national level, and is based on extensive meetings and discussions at an international level.

> *These meetings have clearly demonstrated:*
> *Firstly, that the problems faced are very similar. For example, medication error accounts for around a quarter of the incidents*

which threaten patient safety in each country. The underlying causes of medication error are similar across health systems.

Secondly, that there is a major need for international standardisation of terminology in the definition of different types of adverse event and in reporting.

Thirdly, that there is enormous scope for collaboration in designing solutions for patient safety and finding effective ways of implementing them.

The plan will introduce a new integrated approach to learning from medical error, adverse events and near misses, and it will capture adverse event information from a wide variety of sources. Local reporting of adverse events and action to reduce risk within the organisation concerned is essential. On a selected basis, reports to national level will enable service-wide action where patterns, clusters or trends reveal the scope to reduce risk or prevent recurrence for future patients in other parts of the country.

The report describes the necessary steps to be taken in order to set up the linked components of the new system, including the following:

- *establishing agreed definitions of adverse events and near misses for the purposes of logging and reporting them within the NHS (moving gradually to agreed international standards); detailed guidance for organisations, staff and patients will be issued and pilot sites activated*
- *formalising a minimum data set for adverse events and near misses*
- *producing a standardised format for reporting (initially on paper as well as electronically, but gradually moving towards the latter exclusively)*
- *building expertise within the NHS in root cause analysis (the more in-depth approach to identifying causal or systems factors in more serious adverse events or near misses)*
- *ensuring that information from all other major existing adverse event reporting systems (e.g. medical devices, reactions to medicines, complaints to the Health Service Commissioner, serious accidents reported to the Health and Safety Executive) are fed into the new system*
- *promoting a culture of reporting and patient safety within NHS organisations, building on the transformation already under way as part of the clinical governance initiative.*

The National Patient Safety Agency

A new independent body, the National Patient Safety Agency, will be established within the NHS.[32] It will implement and operate the system with one core purpose – to improve patient safety by reducing the risk of harm through error.

The National Patient Safety Agency will:

- *collect and analyse information on adverse events from local NHS organisations, NHS staff, and patients and carers*
- *assimilate other safety-related information from a variety of existing reporting systems and other sources in this country and abroad*
- *learn lessons and ensure that they are fed back into practice, service organisation and delivery*
- *where risks are identified, produce solutions to prevent harm, specify national goals and establish mechanisms to track progress.*

Everyone involved in providing care and treatment to NHS patients will be included. This will include patients and carers who will play an important part in the adverse event reporting scheme. They will be entitled to report an incident that they see in their own care or in the care of another patient. If they believe that they have witnessed a 'near miss' they will also be encouraged to report this.

In developing a Patient Safety Research Agenda that may help to recognise, anticipate and prevent adverse events, examples of research questions posed were as follows.

- *What are the main types of error and adverse event in different healthcare settings?*
- *What methodologies would ensure effective patient and consumer involvement to enhance patient safety?*
- *What strategies would ensure early detection of new risks before they result in a rare but catastrophic event?*
- *How can organisational cultures be achieved that are safety conscious, reporting-friendly and free of blame?*
- *What methods can reduce error in particular specialist fields of healthcare (e.g. drug therapy)?*
- *How can equipment acquisition and management policies reduce risk?*
- *What automated methods of data capture could be developed to reduce reliance on human reporting?*
- *How can data collation, classification and analysis be enhanced to allow patterns of causation, presentation, detection and amelioration to be elucidated?*
- *What are the characteristics of good leadership of clinical teams that have a good performance on patient safety?*
- *Why does change to improve patient safety so often fail to be*

implemented despite widespread dissemination of strategies which have been shown to work?

Basic epidemiological research is now needed to establish the size, pattern and nature of medical error, adverse events and near misses in different kinds of healthcare settings. Information is needed about the size and nature of the problem at boundaries between healthcare settings, for example between primary and secondary care specialities, disciplines and organisations. Methodologies will have to transcend such boundaries.

Building a Safer NHS for Patients has set out an ambitious implementation timetable (*see* Table 9.4) which clearly identifies the seriousness of the Government's intention to improve patient safety.

Concomitant to the above developments, numerous international initiatives on patient safety are developing. These activities will play an increasingly important role, and most of them can be accessed via websites.

The Institute for Safe Medication Practices (ISMP)[44] in the USA is dedicated to making healthcare organisations as safe as possible for patients and staff. The ISMP runs educational programmes on medication safety and produces the ISMP Medication Safety Alert (www.ismp.org) and the USP-ISMP Medication Errors Reporting Program (MERP), which receives information about medication errors and through the Internet at www.usp.org for the dissemination of knowledge about circumstances and causes. For medication error reports outside the USA, ISMP can be contacted at ismpinfo@ismp.org. The site also provides excellent and detailed yet readable advice to patients on how to avoid medication errors.

The Institute for Healthcare Improvement (IHI)[45] in the USA is an organisation that runs courses, collaboratives, conferences, seminars and other activities to pursue perfection in healthcare. It is also the National Program Office for a major new $20 million initiative to help highly committed healthcare organisations to achieve improved performance (www.ihi.org).

Other sites include the Agency for Healthcare Research and Quality (AHRQ)[46] in the USA (www.ahcpr.gov/qual/errorsix.htm), the Joint Commission on the Accreditation of Healthcare Organizations (JCAHO)[47] (www.jcaho.org), the Australian Patient Safety Foundation (APSF)[48] (www.apsf.net.au), the European Foundation for the Advancement of Healthcare Practitioners[49] (www.efahp.org) and the Patient Safety Center, American Society of Health-System Pharmacists[50] (www.ashp.org/patient_ safety/index.html).

Clearly, programmes to enhance patient safety are developing very rapidly on a global scale.

Table 9.4: Targets and deadlines identified in *Building a Safer NHS for Patients*[32]

Implementation deadlines	Date
Headline targets	
60% of NHS trusts in a position to provide information to the national system; all NHS trusts will be working towards this goal	December 2001
All NHS trusts and a significant proportion of primary care providing information to the national system	December 2002
Levels of reporting in NHS doubled	December 2002
Supporting targets	
Establish the National Patient Safety Agency	July 2001
Develop and issue guidance:	
• on identifying and recording adverse events and near misses, including a glossary of standardised terms and associated definitions	August 2001
• to all organisations providing care to NHS patients on the reporting of adverse events and near misses, including potential for use of IT	August 2001
• on reporting by staff to the new national body	August 2001
• to patients and carers on adverse events and how to report them	November 2001
• on root cause analysis for individual events and analysis of patterns and trends across clusters of events and near misses	November 2001
• on procedure and criteria for establishing independent investigations and inquiries in the NHS	July 2001
Test the reporting system through selective pilots and other evaluations	from August 2001
Work closely with other national reporting agencies	from April 2001
Produce a strategy on building local capability	October 2001
Develop a strategy for learning lessons, disseminating them and implementing effective strategies for change	December 2001
Implement the system progressively	from December 2001
Work with key partners to establish methods for implementing solutions from investigations and inquiries across the NHS	from March 2001
Deliver the four specific targets identified in *An Organisation With a Memory*	
Maladministered spinal injections	end of 2001
Harm caused during obstetrics, gynaecology and midwifery care	end of 2005
Serious error in the use of medicines	end of 2005
Suicides by mental health patients as a result of hanging from non-collapsible bed or shower curtain rails	March 2002
Progress work to take early action to reduce risk in specific areas and by influencing specific processes onwards	April 2001
Liaise with key stakeholders to progress patient safety research agenda	April 2001
Fund a programme of patient safety research – issue a call for proposals	May 2001
Link with education and training bodies to increase content of curricula and training programmes in relation to understanding error, systems thinking and patient safety	September 2001

Prepared from *Building a Safer NHS for Patients*.[32]

'There but for the grace of God go I'

Summary: Reducing errors

Latent or systems errors
The introduction of modern electronic information systems can reduce errors in communication and provide patient information where it is required; this has implications for resourcing, privacy and confidentiality, ensuring that jobs are well designed, that work schedules are reasonable, that the appropriate facilities and equipment are available and that the workforce has the knowledge and skills necessary to do their jobs.

Active or individual errors
Almost all accidents result from human error, and a most unfortunate and rare slip, lapse or mistake is known to everyone. Their reduction is best approached by decreasing the likelihood of their occurrence through reducing systems errors. The individual then remains inherently 'safe'.

However, identification of the 'unsafe' professional is a major and quite different problem for all professions. In the absence of safety systems to identify and act on information about individuals at risk of error, they inevitably err. Within future error-reporting and active investigative systems, such staff may perhaps be more readily identified. Their identification may facilitate retraining programmes and identify alternative employment opportunities, suspension or dismissal.

Medical care cannot be provided without error. Yet errors in healthcare have been inextricably linked with shame, humiliation and damage to professional self-image, blame, punishment, fear, lawsuits and job loss. It is hardly surprising that healthcare workers would prefer to talk about almost any subject other than errors. This may reflect a cultural view that errors reflect a human failing of incompetence, inattention or laziness, and this is inevitably followed by blame and punishment. Some errors do indeed reflect inattention and some reflect negligence, as in any profession. However, in addition to personal mishaps, many errors are 'mistakes waiting to happen' (as thoroughly documented in previous chapters) arising from inadequately designed systems and processes of care.

Reason[51] has identified the critical elements of an effective safety culture as a reporting, just, flexible and learning culture.

The first essential requirement of the cultural change is for individuals to recognise, acknowledge, record and report errors for themselves and others in order to begin to understand the patterns of their occurrence so as to prevent their recurrence. The reporting of 'near misses' offers an easier and less threatening introduction to the new culture, with fewer barriers to data collection, to de-emphasise and defuse the culture of blame. However, irrespective of even the professional and legal imperatives, the moral imperative to reduce human suffering and death as quickly as possible dictates the approach of the IOM, *An Organisation With a Memory*, and *Building A Safer NHS For Patients*, in which all errors are fully reported in order to substantiate the total commitment to patient safety.

The objectives and consequences of reporting errors

Summary: The consequences of establishing an error reporting system

To ensure a safe duty of care to patients, reporting systems can fulfil three purposes:

1 to establish the causes of both human and systems errors, which may reveal the faulty systems and procedures that need revision to ensure safe and effective practices, which may then require the introduction of modern information systems, a reappraisal of the previous educational and clinical experience afforded to healthcare staff, an assessment of the continuing and formal provision of staff education and training to ensure future competency in post and a possible revision of work tasks
2 to facilitate the expectation for safety amongst healthcare providers and consumers, making it possible for patients to demand better care
3 for the setting and enforcing of standards of safety that can define minimum levels of performance for both health organisations and their professional staff.

Reporting systems can fulfil four broad purposes.

The first purpose is to report errors so that both the individual who was in error and the healthcare system can learn from the experience in order to reduce future errors. The purpose is to identify various trends or patterns in different types of adverse events. With the many thousands of adverse events that occur every year, this may be achieved quite quickly and establish the generic causes of errors to help the design of their reduction or elimination. *Based on such information, the goal is to attempt to design future systems that make it easier for individuals to do the right thing and more difficult for them to do the wrong thing.*

The disincentives for the individual to report will relate to the organisational culture, and include extra work, lack of trust and fear of reprisals. To ameliorate these genuine difficulties, reporting systems are being designed to offer the following:

- immunity as far as possible without compromising the patient's legal rights
- confidentiality or data de-identification, making data untraceable to care-givers, patients and institutions
- analysis of the incident by peer experts
- leadership support.

In a challenging editorial in the *British Medical Journal*, Reinertsen[52] emphasised the importance of the leadership role:

> If 'attention is the currency of leadership',[53] all of us who have leadership roles have a responsibility to direct the attention of our fellow physicians, healthcare professionals and communities to this problem and to keep attention on the problem until it is satisfactorily resolved. Rather than assigning blame to the unfortunate individuals who find themselves at the sharp end of an error, leaders would take personal responsibility for the safety of the processes and systems in which those individuals work.

The second purpose is to create sufficient pressure to ensure that healthcare organisations are compelled to take action to improve patient safety. The identification of characteristics and factors that cause errors enables or encourages the providers of healthcare to monitor and improve the quality of care continuously. For example, the information gained from the monitoring of serious and fatal events could be used to hold healthcare organisations to account for their performance.[21] The setting and enforcing of explicit safety standards would also then enable the healthcare systems to engage in discussions with the accreditation bodies and the educational system to define the minimum levels of acceptable educational and professional performance for those entering the professions (*see* page 180).

The third purpose is for the healthcare professional to be aware of error reporting by colleagues and patients, and to act as a gentle but positive reminder of the importance of good practice.

The fourth purpose is to identify potential clinical negligence claims.

To achieve these four objectives, a standardised approach to reporting errors is required. This is defined in *Building a Safer NHS for Patients* as follows.

Summary: Strategies to reduce medication errors caused by latent or systems errors

- Make all information relevant to medication available at the point of patient care to support the knowledge base.
- Implement standard processes for medication doses, dose timing and routes of administration in a given patient care unit wherever possible.
- Implement unit dosing where appropriate.

- Information on new or non-formulary drugs should be made accessible to clinicians prior to ordering, dispensing and administering medications.
- Use computerised physician order/prescriber technology to ensure the electronic recording of the prescription for dispensing (to automatically alert to an inappropriate dose for patient/weight, timing, doses, route of administration, duplicate drug therapies, drug–drug interactions or drug allergy) and then administration of the drug.
- Ensure the availability of pharmaceutical decision support.
- Include a pharmacist on ward rounds.
- Pharmacy should supply high-risk intravenous medications.
- Improve the patient's knowledge about their treatment.

Minimum data set for adverse event and near-miss reporting

- *What happened? (event/near miss description, severity of actual or potential harm, individuals and equipment involved)*
- *Where did it happen? (location/speciality)*
- *When did it happen? (date and time)*
- *How did it happen? (immediate or proximate cause(s))*
- *Why did it happen? (underlying or root causes(s))*
- *What action was taken or proposed? (immediate and longer term)*
- *What impact did the event have? (harm to the organisation, the patient or others)*
- *What factors minimised or could have minimised the impact of the event?*

In addition to the provision of data on errors by healthcare staff, *Building a Safer NHS for Patients* requires that information is also provided by patients and carers. *This is clearly a landmark in the history of patient safety* and reflects developments in the USA. It is described as follows:

Using information provided by patients and carers

18 Patients and carers are a potentially valuable source of information on adverse events and near misses outwith the complaints procedure which will continue as a strong feature of the NHS. As a first step, current work is focusing on devising reporting routes that patients and carers find accessible with a view to piloting detailed and comprehensive information. Distinguishing these routes from the complaints process is very important. Work to establish the routes for patient and carer reporting will:

- *raise patient and carer awareness about safety, error and the benefits of learning from adverse events and near misses*
- *provide information or 'tips' for patients on what to look for so as to specifically engage them in promoting patient safety*
- *involve the new Patient Advocacy Liaison Schemes (PALS), introduced under the NHS Plan, as a reporting vehicle that will also offer patients and carers assistance with the reporting process.*[54]

Clearly, the reporting of errors has consequences that extend considerably beyond the reduction of medical errors to influence standards of practice, training and education. Moreover, in the UK this has been supported by the most significant reforms in civil litigation since 1875. *These reforms directly address the reporting of complaints, substandard care and errors and their redress.* These changes will affect the entire spectrum of healthcare and are described in the next chapter.

Chapter 10

The UK litigation process as a potent tool to influence errors and complaints

Summary: Changes in UK litigation to reduce errors and complaints

- Complaints are caused by misdiagnosis and substandard care.
- The three commonest complaints against doctors are that they do not listen to the patient, explain the diagnosis and treatment or discuss a disappointing result.
- The patient requires an explanation, an apology and reassurance that the error will not occur again. Previous litigation was expensive, laborious and highly unsatisfactory.
- The new Civil Procedure Rules are an entirely new approach to settle complaints.
- A Clinical Disputes Forum established in 1997 a Pre-Action Protocol for the resolution of clinical disputes. It applies to general practitioners, NHS trusts and private practice.
- This forum aims to maintain or restore the patient–healthcare relationship and to resolve as many disputes as possible without litigation.
- The culture of negligence may change. The historical perspective is that the patient had to prove their case against a doctor for clinical negligence on the balance of probabilities. In future, the defendant healthcare professional may have to show excellence of conduct and competence, whilst the patient has to show injury.

Introduction

Complaints are caused by misdiagnosis and substandard care. However, most complaints are about communication with and the behaviour of doctors. Patients appear to be more willing to bring a complaint against doctors who are perceived to be rude and arrogant than against those who are polite and have good communication skills, regardless of the standard of medical care involved.[1]

The three commonest complaints by patients are that doctors fail to:

- listen to what the patient is saying about their personal circumstances and illness
- explain in simple and clear language the diagnosis, treatment and associated risks
- discuss an unsatisfactory result.

The patient needs to know what happened, to seek an apology for what happened, and to seek reassurance that it will not happen again.[2,3] A defensive attitude by the doctor leads to resentment, and this as much as any other factor leads to litigation.[4] Perhaps half of all complaints against general practitioners are due to systems failures rather than to clinical error. A timely and comprehensive response reduces the likelihood of litigation.[5]

For many years the NHS complaints procedures were regarded by both doctors and patients as obscure, difficult and unfair. One of their achievements was described as being 'to unite demoralised adversaries in a sense of frustration and exhaustion'.[4]

However, the impetus to improve the complaint procedures was more than an attempt to satisfy customers, and was understood to have the potential to improve the quality of the service. This was apparent in 1983 with the Griffiths Report,[6] which was accepted by the government in the White Paper entitled *Working for Patients*.[7] Notwithstanding a diffident national character, complaints between 1980 and 1992 had risen by an alarming 1000%, and 30% of these complaints had been shown to be justified.[4] Thus:

> *From 1988 to 1998 the number of complaints notified to the medical defence organisations increased more than tenfold. And the average cost of compensation doubled. The highest award increased from £132 000 in 1977 to £1.6 million in 1998 (awarded to a family of a child who died after the general practitioner failed to diagnose meningitis). Between 1988 and 1997 the number of complaints about doctors received by the GMC more than tripled, and the number in which action was taken more than doubled. The UK legal aid bill increased from £166 million in 1990 to over £600 million in 1996, and during that period the cost to the NHS of providing indemnity rose by over 300%.[8]*
>
> *Although the number of complaints and the size of the awards has increased, the proportion of successful claims in the courts has not increased. Less than 2% of the cases in which legal action is commenced actually reach court, and of those that do, only 17% of cases secure a judgement against the doctor. There are probably more patients with a genuine cause for grievance who do not sue than there are patients with spurious claims who do. One in four complaints against general practitioners follows a patient's death.*
>
> *The rise in the number of complaints has occurred in many countries and against all professions – lawyers, accountants and*

others – and the causes of complaints are complex. Patients have a better knowledge of medicine and greater expectations, expectations which may be hyped by the medical staff and the media. There may be less tolerance and patience with anything less than best practice, and fewer barriers to making the complaint known. If something has gone wrong there is a widespread belief that someone is to blame. There is also a widespread feeling that doctors and other professionals have been insufficiently regulated for too long.[8]

The new Civil Procedure Rules (CPR)

Within the above perspective, in 1994 Lord Woolf was appointed to review the rules and procedures of the civil courts in England and Wales with respect to negligence.[9]

The major aims were as follows:

- to improve justice and reduce the costs of litigation
- to reduce the complexity of the rules and simplify terminology ('medical negligence' has been replaced by 'clinical negligence')
- to remove unnecessary distinctions of practice and procedure.

The reforms which are embodied in the Civil Procedure Rules 1998 (CPR) came into effect in April 1999 and provided an entirely new procedural code to address defects in the old system, which were identified as:

- expensive in many cases, with costs exceeding the value of the claims
- too slow in bringing cases to a conclusion
- showing lack of equality between wealthy and poor litigants
- giving cause for concern about the duration and fragmentation of the procedure.

CPR Rule 1.1(1) describes the Overriding Objective as follows: 'these rules are a new procedural code with the overriding objective of enabling the court to deal with cases justly'.

This includes in CPR 1.1.(2):

1   ensuring that the parties are on an equal footing
2   saving expense
3   dealing with a case in ways which are proportionate to:
    - the amount of money involved
    - the importance of the case
    - the complexity of the issues
    - the financial position of each party
4   ensuring that it is dealt with expeditiously and fairly
5   allotting to it an appropriate share of the court's resources, whilst taking into account the need to allocate resources to other cases.

CPR 1.3 states that 'the parties are required to help the court to further the overriding objective' with a clear obligation imposed on the parties and, equally important, a clear role for the court in terms of case management. In summary, the court will actively participate in the management of the case to ensure that it runs smoothly and that a resolution to the dispute is brought about as quickly and effectively as possible.

So fundamental is this reform process that, in interpreting the rules, no regard will be given to the previous rules and their associated case law.

Healthcare workers should understand the key procedural stages that will be followed with regard to a case of clinical negligence. It recognises the need to address every aspect, from the moment of identifying the adverse event to the commencement of litigation in the courts. The fundamental premise of Lord Woolf's thinking is the desire to reduce litigation by fostering a less adversarial culture. A difficulty in clinical negligence cases had been identified in the Access to Justice Report in 1996, where costs and delays at the prelitigation stage were particularly problematic. *This included inadequate incident reporting and record keeping, delays in making a claim, inadequate resources for investigation and a reluctance of the healthcare professionals to admit negligence, provide an explanation or apologise.*[9]

A Clinical Disputes Forum whose membership included patients and patients' representatives (e.g. Action for Victims of Medical Accidents, The National Consumer Council) and the clinical professions (e.g. the Academy of Royal Medical Colleges), the NHS Confederation Statutory Regulators (e.g. the General Medical Council) and members of the legal professions was established in 1997 and produced a Pre-Action Protocol for the Resolution of Clinical Disputes. It is embodied within the CPR and supported by a Practice Direction.

The protocol applies to every area of clinical dispute – general practitioners, NHS trusts and private practice.

It aims to:

- maintain or restore the patient–healthcare relationship
- resolve as many disputes as possible without litigation.

The protocol attempts to set out a code of good practice and commitments on both sides.

The requirements expected of the healthcare professional

- Ensure that key staff are appropriately trained (i.e. have a working knowledge of the relevant healthcare law, complaints procedures, civil litigation practice, etc.).

- Develop appropriate approaches to clinical governance consistent with good standards of practice within their specific area.
- Create adverse-outcome-reporting systems which will also facilitate the speedy gathering of evidence.
- Apply the results of adverse incidents and complaints positively (i.e. learn from poor performance and try to correct practice).
- Ensure that patients receive clear and comprehensible information.
- Establish proper systems for recording and storing patient notes and records.
- Advise patients of serious adverse outcomes and provide an oral or written explanation upon request.

The last requirement is particularly important because it recognises the obligation of the healthcare provider to advise the patient pro-actively of the serious adverse outcome and to provide a suitable explanation, apology, offers of further treatment, etc., so as to ensure that the patient's concerns are properly dealt with. It is claimed that 'There is a strong argument that a proper adoption of the commitments and underlying philosophy embodied in the protocol may reduce the number of errors and the claims actually proceeding to litigation'.[9]

The requirements expected of patients

- Report any concern and dissatisfactions as soon as is reasonably possible, thereby giving the provider an opportunity to investigate and take appropriate action.
- To consider the full range of options available. The intention is that the patient should not simply focus on pursuing litigation, but should look at the full range of possibilities available, including requests for an explanation and meeting, use of the complaints procedure and other alternative dispute resolution methods. Of particular importance is the obligation of the adviser of the patient to have this breadth of approach when considering how best to advise the patient. In many respects litigation is an option of last resort.
- Inform the healthcare provider when the patient is satisfied that the matter has been concluded.

In operation there are effectively two stages to the proceedings (*see* Figure 10.1). The initial stages assume that a responsible attitude will be adopted by all parties and that many disputes can be resolved without the need for professional advisers to become involved. Sensible 'patient-handling attitudes' should be encouraged and a defensive attitude discouraged. The protocol stages become effective when a satisfactory solution has not been worked out between patient and doctor, and they are described by Pickering:[9]

> *It should be noted that the legal profession itself through the Law Society is also anxious to improve its competence in the handling of clinical negligence claims. In 1995 the Law Society responded to*

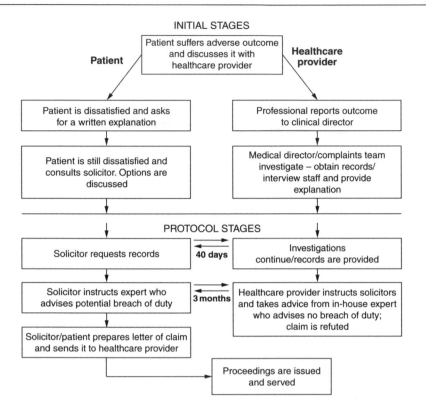

Figure 10.1: Illustrative flowchart of the initial stages and protocol for the resolution of clinical disputes within the new Civil Procedure Rules. Reproduced from the Procedure Rules (1999) with permission from the Clinical Disputes Forum.[9]

concerns of incompetent practitioners [see Blackburn v Newcastle Health Authority[10]] by establishing the medical negligence panel. Since 1 August 1999, legal aid for clinical negligence cases has only been granted to practitioners operating within franchised firms who have demonstrated competence within the area. Membership of either or both the Action for Victims of Medical Accidents and Law Society panels is mandatory. In the year 1996/97, of 11 400 civil medical negligence legal aid cases billed to the Legal Aid Board, only 2632 were dealt with by a firm with at least one panel member. Hence the majority of cases were dealt with by seemingly less experienced practitioners. There was a very significant difference in the success rate, with panel members producing virtually double the number of successful cases, with a correspondingly higher recovery of compensation. The Legal Aid Board publicly expressed the view that one of the main reasons for this was that people were represented by lawyers who were not experts in clinical negligence law.[9]

Such views reflect the strident criticisms by Lord Woolf in his report *Access to Justice* in the mid-1990s. On medical negligence he denounced the costs of medical negligence litigation compared with other personal injury work, the number of dubious claims that were being pursued and the dubious nature of many defences. Mr Steve Walker, the Chief Executive of the NHS Litigation Authority, which was also established at this time, was even more blunt:

> *We found expressly that all these complaints were justified. Now this criticism is addressed primarily to the legal profession, although one of the major features which is directed against the medical profession is that both Woolf and we found that there were excessive sums of money being effectively wasted on poor quality medical evidence from medical experts on both sides. Medical experts were setting up cases which couldn't be run or which, if they were acting for the defence, couldn't be defended . . . . We were probably the first defence organisation to address those issues . . . . Notwithstanding the changes we began to make, we decided that we couldn't manage 100 practices. We didn't think there were 100 good practitioners, never mind 100 good practices in the country. Before the Civil Procedure Rules came into effect . . . we reduced the panel of solicitors we instruct to 18 firms . . . and that number will fall.*[11]

In summary, patients who had been injured by medical care were then disadvantaged by their legal representation – a devastating indictment of the system. Consistent with the philosophy of the protocol, future cases should be properly scrutinised by those with expert knowledge. The incidence of mischievous claims (and their perceived encouragement by certain legal practitioners, which has caused understandable and widespread bitter resentment among the medical profession) should be reduced, and the remainder should be dealt with more speedily and at reduced cost. It would appear that the Lord Chancellor and the Judiciary may be achieving success in moving 'litigation to mediation'.

Two years after Lord Woolf's civil justice reforms, it is reported that litigation has decreased by 37%, and in the first 18 months claims issued in the civil courts fell from 220 000 to 175 000.[12] The culture shift has led Ince & Co. and others to forms of 'alternative dispute resolution' involving mediation which have achieved a very high success rate (85%) in settlement.[13] The mechanisms involved in assessing costs in civil justice may take longer to resolve.[14] However, resolution remains an important subject. In the period 1999–2000, there were 86 536 written complaints about hospital and community health services. The majority of these were settled by local resolution, but no less than 2061 cases requested an independent review.[15] That is the nature of the problem and we cannot be complacent.

Complaints should be treated with courtesy and respect. Yet as a patient, Elizabeth Evans describes an experience that shows this is just not happening, suggesting that patients are not treated as valued customers but as an annoying nuisance. After being referred by her consultant to a hospital, the required treatment was not obtained; appropriate treatment was then received at another hospital. Two years later, and in the interest of good clinical governance, she decided to find out why things had gone wrong and requested to see her notes. She emphasised that she had no intention of filing a complaint, and that she would like a clinician to look at the case for interest, to see whether anything could be learnt to improve matters for patients in the future. No effective response was forthcoming. The real value of this particular experience is the fact that the patient is also a general practitioner and a clinical governance lead for an area whose patients were regularly referred to the hospital.[16]

Perhaps most important in terms of reducing errors, and therefore claims, is the extensive knowledge of the Litigation Authority database on the causes of errors. Access to this database would reveal a wealth of experience for preventing or reducing future errors.

Summary

The historical perspective is that patients have had to prove their case against a doctor for clinical negligence on the 'balance of probabilities'. *Increasingly, the defendant healthcare professional may have to show excellence of conduct and competence, while the patient has to show injury rather than demonstrate through expert testimony the presence of a lapse.* Changes in complaint procedures and court rules, commercial pressures, and a society which requires that all damaged patients are compensated may begin to change the perception or culture of negligence.[17]

Chapter 11

Reducing medical errors

Summary: Reducing medical errors

- Approximately one million people a day visit their doctor or hospital and interact with 700 000 healthcare staff – a quite remarkable enterprise. If each staff member interacts with just 10 patients a day with a (unattainable?) low error rate of 0.0001%, this would still result in a hazard to around 255 000 patients a year. This reflects the scale of the problem of error reduction in the UK.
- An initial increase in reported errors may arise due to: (a) improved reporting requirements that will include patients and carers; (b) a litigious culture; (c) a dramatic growth in the NHS: 100 new hospitals and thousands of extra beds, doctors and other healthcare staff; (d) difficulties in attracting new staff; (e) an increasingly aged population at high risk from errors.
- Conditions which may act to reduce medication errors are: (a) computerised technology in prescribing, transmission of prescriptions, dispensing and making patient information available at the point of use; (b) improvement in pharmaceutical support services to ensure the correct medication and dose; (c) standardisation of processes and equipment; (d) using the patient and carer as a valuable resource to provide the final safety check.
- To facilitate a reduction in medication errors requires that: (a) first and foremost the workforce has a known knowledge and skills base and is competent in post; (b) there are opportunities for continued staff training for both knowledge and skills; (c) jobs are well designed; (d) work schedules are reasonable; (e) the correct equipment is available, serviced and maintained; (f) cleanliness and other facilities are appropriate for safe practice. These all have major resource implications.

Will an increase precede a reduction in future adverse drug-induced events and medication errors?

It is almost inevitable that reported error rates in the USA would initially increase, due to their current gross under-reporting. This would probably also happen in the UK, but for different reasons – there are no accurate base rates. However, these would quickly be established with the above attempts to improve clinical practice and yet pro-actively report errors. There are also a number of additional factors that could act to appear to increase the incidence of adverse events and medication errors or to cause a genuine increase. This is presented within the perspective that the NHS has been under-funded for decades and that criticism of the NHS has been endemic. The state of under-resourcing for the NHS was perhaps most succinctly expressed by a judge of the Court of Appeal in 1980.[1] In a case concerning a decision to withhold resources from an orthopaedic unit in Birmingham, he stated that it was a matter of common knowledge that:

> . . . the Health Service currently falls far short of what everyone would regard as the optimum desirable standard. This is very largely a situation brought about by lack of resources, lack of suitable equipment, lack of suitably qualified personnel and, above all, lack of adequate finance.

In a survey of skeletal trauma treatment following serious accident, the British Orthopaedic Association studied 800 patients selected at random. Assessors were asked to decide how many patients suffered morbidity following treatment and whether the use of proper treatment methods could have prevented this. Morbidity that was of significant proportions to affect the quality of life occurred in 12% of patients. It is not surprising to read that the major causes of failure were inadequacies with respect to staffing, workload, facilities and organisation.[2]

Within this demoralising perspective, the dedication of the healthcare staff has been quite remarkable.

The scale of the enterprise in the UK – The NHS Plan: a plan for investment, a plan for reform[3]

Within a typical day:

- almost a million people visit their family doctor
- 130 000 people go the dentist
- 33 000 people receive the care that they need in Accident and Emergency departments

- 8000 people are transported by ambulance
- 1.5 million prescriptions are dispensed
- 2000 babies are delivered
- 25 000 operations are performed
- 30 000 people receive a free eye test
- district nurses make 100 000 visits.

These activities occur due to the united efforts of 90 000 doctors, 150 000 healthcare assistants, 10 000 health visitors, 24 000 managers, 22 000 midwives, 300 000 nurses, 15 000 occupational nurses, 7500 opticians, 6500 paramedics, 11 000 pharmacists, 19 000 physiotherapists, 90 000 porters, cleaners and other support staff, 105 000 practice staff in GP surgeries and 13 500 radiographers.

The scale of the enterprise is quite extraordinary. If the approximately 700 000 staff who interact with patients do so with just 10 patients each per day, and one reduces errors to a low (unattainable?) figure of, say, 0.0001%, this would still result in 700 errors or 700 patients a day or around 255 000 patients a year being exposed to a hazard. This is the scale of the problem, which should be made transparent to healthcare staff, patients, the media and society.

Factors which may conspire to increase the numbers of reported adverse events and errors

1 The report *Building a Safer NHS for Patients* specifically recognised patients and carers as valuable sources of information on adverse events and 'near misses'. Indeed, patients and carers will be provided with information and 'tips' on what to look for in order to specifically engage them in patient safety. The new Patient Advocacy Liaison Schemes will offer patients and carers assistance with the reporting process. It is difficult to think of a more effective way to reveal the reality of the occurrence of adverse events and errors, which has previously probably been under-reported by healthcare staff.

2 In addition, public recognition of error-reporting systems and frequent media reports of errors may synergise with a litigious culture that is driven by certain factions within the legal profession and other pressure groups (e.g. the Association of Personal Injury Lawyers) to register an increasing number of errors. For example, it was reported that a total of 4470 grievances against doctors alone (a rate of 86 cases a week) were lodged with the General Medical Council during the year 2000, compared with 3000 complaints in 1999. The figures continue a five-year trend.[4]

3 The cost of clinical negligence claims has focused attention on alternative methods of resolving disputes. The government, for *financial* reasons, has called for 'no-fault' compensation as one such method. It is based on the resolution of a medical accident through a non-adversarial dispute and with a tariff that would pay a certain amount for different injuries, whatever the circumstances and cause of blame. In summary, the advantages are

perceived to be that the costs will be less, the money spent on establishing negligence could be saved, and the doctor's reputation would not be tarnished, at least in the public arena. The BMA strongly supports the scheme.

In the Report of the Public Inquiry into Children's Heart Surgery at the Bristol Royal Infirmary during 1984–1995, conducted between October 1998 and July 2001, which was the most detailed inquiry ever undertaken into the failings of the NHS, a consideration of clinical negligence litigation was developed even further, but as *an actual barrier to openness and reporting errors*, and therefore safety:

> *14   Safety. For the future, the NHS must root out unsafe practices. It must remove barriers to safe care. In particular, it must promote openness and the preparedness to acknowledge errors and learn lessons. Healthcare professionals should have a duty of candour to patients. Clinical negligence litigation, as a barrier to openness, should be abolished.*[5]

And:

> *86   The culture of blame is a major barrier to the openness required if sentinel events (defined as 'any unexplained occurrence involving death or psychological injury, or the risk thereof') are to be reported, lessons learned and safety improved. The system of clinical negligence is part of this culture of blame. It should be abolished. It should be replaced by effective systems for identifying, analysing, learning from and preventing errors and other sentinel events. An expert group should consider alternatives to clinical negligence, including an alternative administrative system of compensating those who suffer harm arising from medical care.*

> *87   Incentives for reporting sentinel events should be introduced, whereby healthcare professionals' contracts would provide that they would be immune from disciplinary action from their employer or professional regulatory body if they were to report a sentinel event within 48 hours. Confidential reporting should be provided for. Failure to report would attract disciplinary action.*[6]

It would be of some interest to observe the response of the legal system to an attempt to abolish (clinical) negligence in a confusion or obfuscation with blame. Such dissembling appears ingenuous. The disadvantages of 'alternate administrative systems' are also obvious. As long as the NHS Litigation Authority continues to pay claimants to 'go away' rather than defending mischievous and spurious claims, these claims will continue or perhaps increase. If 'no-fault' compensation was introduced for clinical negligence, then justice could dictate that it should be introduced for injury or accidents while playing sport, in the workplace, on the highway and elsewhere. For example, it might be argued that negligence litigation arising outside the healthcare system as a 'barrier to openness' should also be abolished. As important, the no-fault system and the abolition of clinical negligence litigation would lead to more autonomy for healthcare professionals, less clinical accountability, and might cause an even further worsening of trust in the system. It would also lead to a poorer standard of reporting, and there would be no purpose in attempting to investigate the causative fault. Thus there would be no or only minimal attempts to learn from the experience, and errors would be perpetuated.[7] It is difficult to perceive how this would encourage good practice and enhance standards of healthcare and safety.

4 The new NHS Plan[3] aims to increase the following:
   • the number of patients treated – there will be 100 new hospitals, 7000 extra beds, 5000 extra intermediate beds, 1700 extra non-residential intermediate-care places and a 30% increase in adult critical care beds
   • the number of healthcare workers – there will be 7500 more consultants, 2000 more general practitioners, 20000 more nurses, and 6500 more therapists and other healthcare professionals
   • as a consequence, the number of staff who will have a prescriber's role and who will have made most of the medication errors.

5 The new NHS Plan aims to reduce long working hours in order to relieve fatigue. In the medium to long term this should act to reduce errors. However, in the recent report on prevention of intrathecal medication errors[8] it was considered that:

> In the short term, reductions in working hours will relieve fatigue but at the expense of:
>
> • increased work intensity for staff when on duty
> • increased cross-cover between specialities
> • reduced formal supervision of inexperienced by more experienced staff
> • less opportunity for more formal training (induction courses, speciality tutorials and audit meetings).

In brief, there will be increased opportunities for errors. Furthermore, attempts by the NHS to develop safe systems will occur in:

> an environment which, for historical reasons, is ill-suited to the human factors approach. The unpropitious starting point makes it even more important that system safety is urgently addressed. Risk management strategy must however:
>
> • be parsimonious in the use of stretched resources, notably staff time
> • be efficient, by implementing first those changes which will yield most

- *seek, where possible, to develop design solutions which will prevent human error in preference to human factor solutions which only reduce the likelihood of error*
- *be system wide, with careful consideration of all the consequences of change.*[8]

In addition, the components of clinical governance set out in a *A First-Class Service: Quality in the New NHS*[9] include the following:

Clear policies aimed at managing risks:

- *controls assurance which promotes self-assessment to identify and manage risks*
- *clinical risk systematically assessed with programmes in place to reduce risk.*

High risk means either that there is a high probability of error or that the consequences would be severe, or both. Effective local governance therefore requires that there is an explicit local strategy to contain that risk. Thus intrathecal chemotherapy has a high risk and is a highly damaging public event, although it is a rare event (*see* Appendix 8). Addressing the problem will prevent inordinate adverse publicity, although it will not noticeably affect the number of errors.

6 The NHS Plan intends to change roles. Will the retraining of staff to perform minor surgery and other duties lead to more or less errors? Clearly, these and related issues will be decided by training and the measurement of outcomes.

7 With regard to the trend towards increasing outpatient provision, is the trend reported by Phillips and colleagues[10] for medication errors to increase more with outpatients than inpatients a universal problem? Will the trend for surgical procedures to be performed outside hospitals be associated with greater risks?[11]

8 Will the increasing use of minor hospitals give rise to higher error rates than those recorded in larger and better equipped hospitals with a broader range of facilities and skills?[12–14]

9 Will the increasing numbers of patients over 65 years of age, who are at much greater risk of adverse events, contribute to a higher error rate?[12,15]

10 Will the incessant pressures within the NHS to move patients out of hospital or out of specialist units as quickly as possible contribute to unnecessary and increasing mortality? A recent study using computer modelling has shown, after analysis of almost 14 000 cases, that no less than 39% of patients who were moved out of intensive care onto the wards would have survived if they had remained in the ICU for a further two days.[16] All such deaths would be regarded as an omission of treatment and therefore as an adverse event. The problem is one of resource.

11 Will the rapidly increasing use of 'alternative medicines' contribute to an increasing number of adverse events? The frequent absence of proven efficacy, possible contamination with toxic substances, adverse drug interactions with other herbal or conventional medicines and, perhaps most

important of all, the failure of patients to inform their practitioner or pharmacist about their use of 'alternative medicines' is a cause of considerable, if not major, concern (*see* page 236).

12 Perhaps most importantly, will the government succeed in attracting the additional staff that are needed to treat the increasing number of patients? The focus of media attention on the challenges of attracting new staff from overseas has been extensive, and the issue is of serious concern.[17] It is reported that only 8703 new doctors registered to work in the UK in the year 2000, the lowest number since 1992.[18] The number of unfilled posts for nurses and consultants in the NHS is reported to have risen by up to 43%,[19] and there are shortages of community pharmacists.[20]

In summary, a scenario is being developed in which errors may initially increase, although this may be attenuated by some improvements aimed at reducing errors in systems and procedures. The possibility that NHS patients may be allowed to seek treatments abroad has also been welcomed.[21]

The role of the media

It will remain essential to fully involve and engage with the public and the media in the determined attempts of the healthcare system to reduce errors.

For example, new services such as NHS Direct remain exposed to covert enquiries as recently reported by the consumer association *Health Which.*[22] Failure to offer the correct advice would be an error. Covert studies do not reveal the relative strengths and weaknesses of service provision. Indeed, in a substantial and controlled trial the service offered by NHS Direct was found to be as effective as the normal GP service.[23]

An understandably critical but hostile and incessant reporting of error rates could fatally hinder the new approach. It is imperative that this does not occur. The media should be encouraged to develop a creative and understanding partnership with healthcare services, society and patients in a united contribution to a safer healthcare system (*see* Figure 11.1). This would not detract from the media's duty to seek out and report wrongdoing. However, it would provide a balanced view and provide vital encouragement to the beleaguered army of dedicated, skilled and well-meaning healthcare staff whose morale must be maintained.

Reducing adverse events and medication errors

An understanding of errors and their reduction in any system is inevitably linked to an understanding of active and latent errors, accidents and concepts of safety. The key features of a detailed 'root cause' analysis of an adverse event have been described by the Joint Commission on the Accreditation of Healthcare Organizations in the USA as follows:

- *determination of the human and other factors most directly associated with the event, and the processes and systems related to its occurrence*
- *analysis of the underlying systems and processes through a series of 'why' questions to determine where redesign might reduce risk*
- *identification of risk points and their potential contributions to the event*
- *determination of potential improvements in processes or systems that would tend to decrease the likelihood of such events in the future, or a determination, after analysis, that no such improvement opportunities exist.*[24]

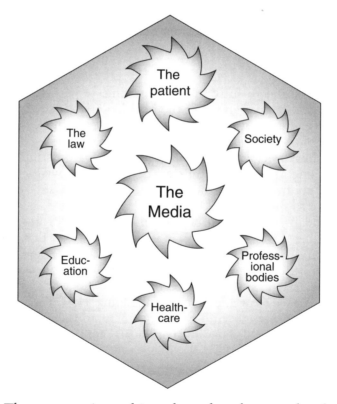

Figure 11.1: The seven major and interdependent factors related to healthcare that will influence future perceptions of the success or otherwise of the reduction in adverse events caused by medical management for a safer healthcare system. The encouragement of a dynamic, critical yet supportive interaction between the various influences is essential, with the media playing a pivotal role.

The importance of systems errors

The fundamental concept is that focusing on active (individual) errors allows the latent errors to remain within the system. Over time, the latent errors will inevitably increase, making the system ever more prone to the occurrence of accidents and failures.[25] Therefore, by focusing on latent errors there is a greater likelihood of building safer systems for the future.

In the USA, the influential National Patient Safety Foundation has defined patient safety as the avoidance, prevention and amelioration of adverse outcomes or injuries resulting from the processes of healthcare.[26] This adds emphasis to the understanding that safety does not reside in any one individual, but rather it results from complex interactions between people, equipment and processes within a highly sophisticated technological system. Although safety is inevitably a relative concept, and in healthcare benefit relates to risk (the seriousness of the illness), the focus should remain fixed on the ability of the system to deliver care safely.

Moreover, safety involves more than reducing errors – it is about minimising risk or hazard. It has been defined as freedom from accidental injury. This involves the establishment of operational systems and processes that increase the reliability of patient care.[27]

Preconditions which create systems errors

Factors which can disrupt the design of a system to facilitate the production of errors have been described by Reason as 'preconditions'.[10] For example, the system will fail if:

- the workforce is not knowledgeable and skilled
- opportunities for continued training and updating of staff skills and knowledge are not available
- the jobs are not well designed
- the work schedules are not reasonable
- the right equipment is not available
- the equipment is not properly serviced and maintained
- management is inadequate
- heating, lighting, cleanliness and other facilities are poor.

All of these factors are vital elements in the design of safe procedures, and all of them will finally be revealed as a latent failure if they are not addressed.

Conditions which reduce errors

Perhaps the single most important failure in any organisation is human error, which accounts for around 80% or more of all errors.[28] This has created the impression that humans are inefficient, if not unreliable. One response to this perception has been to automate processes in order to reduce the opportunities for human error.

Computer technology

Within the UK, plans for the electronic patient record and transmission of prescriptions from general medical practitioners to pharmacies and the Prescription Pricing Authority (PPA) by the year 2004 are in place.[29,30] It is hoped that cryptography will secure the transmission of patients' data. It will immediately reduce the errors associated with handwriting of prescriptions and the errors in transcription, as has already been shown by the US experience.[31]

Computerised robotic dispensing, as has been installed at St Thomas's hospital in London, enables some medicinal products to be delivered directly to the place where the pharmacy staff are working. The robot uses laser-scanned barcodes which have errors of only one in one million – the drawback to this technology is one of cost.[32]

However, one of the greatest advantages of computer technology is that it can enhance human performance by questioning the actions of the operator and providing advice through different alternative possibilities which are beyond the scope of human memory.[33,34]

The American experience of the use of such technology in drug ordering/prescribing for over a decade in reducing errors provides one of the best examples. Computerised order entry as pioneered by the Brigham and Women's Hospital[35] has shown a meaningful reduction in serious medication errors as well as a reduction in other errors (see Figure 11.2). However, the technology did not abolish errors, although computerised order entry was effective in dramatically reducing or virtually abolishing the documented and serious drug-induced allergy events (see Figure 11.3).[35] The computer-based ordering algorithms can also be used to guide physicians to the most appropriate therapies and warn about drug–drug interactions and other suboptimal prescribing patterns.[36,37]

The implementation and assessment of a rules-based computerised prescribing system at the Queen Elizabeth Medical Centre in Birmingham between October 1998 and August 1999 was undertaken using 14 doctors and 24 nurses.[38] It was designed to improve the safety of prescriptions and administration of drugs. The system contained integrated patient-specific data including demographics, main diagnoses, drug allergies and other medical conditions, current drug treatment, previous treatment, laboratory results, radiology reports and body weight, and also calculated the creatinine clearance.

The prescription warning messages generated by the system are shown in Table 11.1, and the staff views on the computerised system are shown in Table 11.2. The system cancelled 58 (0.07%) out of 87 789 prescriptions on the grounds of clinical safety; either the patient had been prescribed a drug to

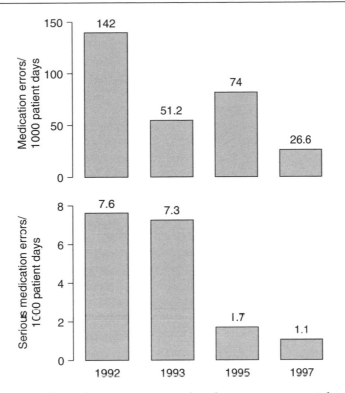

Figure 11.2: The effect of a 'computerised order entry system' for preventing medication and serious medication (preventable and non-intercepted potential adverse drug events combined) errors at the prescribing stage, introduced at the Brigham and Women's Hospital in 1993. In 1992 all orders were written on paper. In 1995 the programme received an improved drug allergy checking, and in 1997 it received an improved potassium and drug–drug interaction addition. Prepared from the data of Bates *et al.*[35]

which they were allergic ($n = 37$) or there was a potentially serious interaction ($n = 21$). In addition, the system generated 427 high-level warnings and 1257 low-level warnings. Overall, the system was well received by 82% of doctors, nurses and also pharmacists.

'PRODIGY', the computer-based decision-support system for UK general practices, is now in its fifth year and embraces evidence-based healthcare, improving patient care, clinical audit, risk management and lifelong learning. It is supported by a full training and education programme. In total, 94% of practices using the system found its clinical guidance useful, and Phase 3 involves building on the area of chronic disease management. The programme is not intended to interfere with the GP's clinical freedom or to impair the doctor–patient relationship.[39]

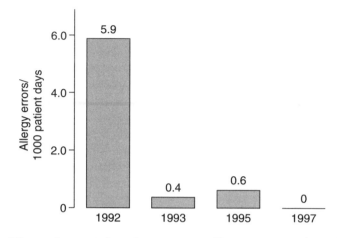

Figure 11.3: The substantial reduction in allergy errors that followed the introduction of computerised physician order entry of patient information at the Brigham and Women's Hospital in 1993. Prepared from the data of Bates *et al.*[35]

In an American study, a comparison of the performance of emergency 'medical faculty' against an 'expert' emergency physician and a 'standard computer database' was used to identify potential drug interactions. The difference in performance between the three groups demonstrated the value of the computer in aiding decisions in a high-technology rapid-response environment (*see* Figure 11.4).[40]

However, it remains the case that the introduction of all such technology is not necessarily beneficial. The machine operator may become less practised in basic skills and lose skills or knowledge in precisely those areas where they are immediately required when the machinery fails, as it rarely but inevitably will.

Of greater concern are the observations that automation can also 'distance' people or make them more 'opaque' to the systems that they operate.[41] The automative intervention ensures that the processes become less visible as people have less hands-on contact. Furthermore, information is frequently being filtered, and this causes increasing concern that the operator either is being deluged with too much information or fails to obtain the correct information. In addition, the operator must retain competence in those tasks which cannot be automated, and in the distinctive tasks with which the automated systems cannot cope (patient variability is the most obvious example within the healthcare system).

Human factor analysis

Research in the area of 'human factor analysis' involves the study of the interrelationships between humans, the tools that they use and the environ-

Table 11.1: Prescription warning messages generated by a computerised system at the Queen Elizabeth Medical Centre, Birmingham from October 1998 to August 1999[38]

Category	Number of warning messages	Number and percentage of prescriptions completed
Disallowed	58	0
Contraindications	37	0
Interactions	21	0
Password-level warnings	749	322 (43)
Contraindications	141	103 (73)
Interactions	99	84 (85)
Maximum recommended single dose exceeded	206	89 (43)
Maximum recommended daily dose exceeded	30	46 (15)
Low-level warnings	16 607	15 350 (92)
Contraindications	793	677 (85)
Interactions	15 743	14 635 (93)
Maximum recommended single dose exceeded	46	25 (54)
Maximum recommended daily dose exceeded	25	13 (52)

Percentage values are shown in parentheses.

ment in which they work.[1] It is being increasingly used to understand the causes, circumstances and procedures associated with errors. It uses critical decision analysis, which focuses on specific or pivotal events (e.g. it revealed that 82% of preventable incidents in anaesthesia are caused by human error) or 'naturalistic decision making',[43] which examines the way in which people actually make decisions in their natural work environment. The application of 'human factors' has successfully reduced errors in many industries, and its strengths are now being applied to healthcare.

Strategies to reduce medication errors

No less than six organisations in the USA, including the American Society for Health-System Pharmacists, have focused attention on medication errors.[44] The IOM committee[45] joined with these groups in calling for an implementation of the following proven medication safety practices:

1 *The adoption of a system-oriented approach that identifies and prevents errors or minimises patient harm from those errors that do occur.* It involves anticipating problems, tracking and analysing data as errors or

Table 11.2: Doctors' and nurses' views (at the Queen Elizabeth Medical Centre, Birmingham) on the computerised prescribing system compared with normal prescribing and administration procedures[38]

View sought	Number and percentage responding		
	System better	No difference	System worse
Doctors (n = 14)			
Prescribing on ward rounds	9 (64)	4 (29)	1 (7)
Prescribing discharge rates	14 (100)	0	0
Other prescribing	9 (69)	3 (23)	1 (8)
Time taken on ward rounds	9 (64)	4 (29)	1 (7)
Messages from nurses and pharmacists	4 (29)	5 (36)	5 (36)
Nurses (n = 24)			
Administration on drug rounds	17 (74)	6 (26)	0
Other administration	11 (46)	7 (29)	6 (25)
Nurse prescribing	6 (25)	3 (13)	15 (63)
Nurse taken on drug rounds	8 (35)	9 (39)	6 (26)
Messages to doctors	10 (42)	8 (33)	6 (25)
Doctors and nurses (n = 38)			
Availability of data	37 (97)	1 (3)	0
Legibility	36 (95)	2 (5)	0
Convenience	22 (58)	13 (34)	3 (8)
Safety	26 (68)	2 (21)	4 (11)
Overall opinion	31 (82)	7 (18)	0

Percentage values are shown in parentheses.

'near misses' occur, and modifying processes on the basis of the data to prevent recurrence.

2 *Implementation of physician order entry.* The transmission of medication orders on-line prevents misinterpretation of handwritten orders and should ensure that the dose, form and timings are correct and in line with the prescriber's intention. It can also alert to drug–drug and drug allergy interactions and patient conditions that may affect medication. Such systems have the potential to provide relevant patient or drug information to anyone who needs it. Serious medication errors decreased by more than 50% and the system has been shown to identify more than 80% of adverse events.[46,47] Computer installation costs are substantial, there are recurrent costs, and the system cannot eliminate all errors (*see* page 130). Issues of privacy and confidentiality are important factors that will need to be resolved before the successful introduction of the technique.

3 *The availability of pharmaceutical decision support.* Although it is not possible for pharmacists to be physically present at all times, there must be

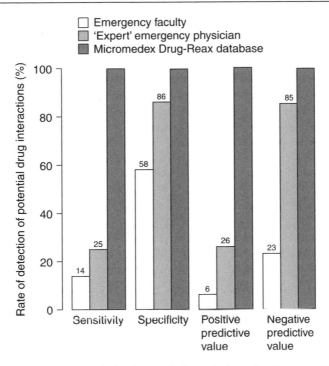

Figure 11.4: A comparison of the knowledge of the physician with that of the computer with regard to potential drug interactions in patients in an emergency department. In a retrospective review of 276 emergency department charts for drug, alcohol, laboratory and medical history, an evaluation of the performance of emergency 'medical faculty', 'expert emergency physician' and the Micro-medex Drug-Reax database was conducted. In total, 17% of patients had potential drug–drug interactions, of which 25% were judged to be clinically significant. The 'expert physician' was statistically significantly better than the 'medical faculty', but was still less sensitive and accurately predictive than the computer. Prepared from the data of Langdorf et al.[40]

access to pharmaceutical services as an essential resource support. The huge variety and complexity of medications and dosage calculations now available makes it difficult for physicians and nurses to keep up to date with the breadth of preparations available.

4 *Making relevant information with regard to the patient, medication and other relevant details available at the point of patient care.* Coloured wrist bands or a similar device have been used to alert clinical staff to allergies or other problems. Barcoding and a laser scanner offer a more sophisticated means of ensuring that the correct drug is administered to the correct patient at the correct dose at the correct time, thereby reducing medication error rates by around 70%.[44,48]

5 *Standardising processes.* This is one of the most effective ways of reducing errors, making it easier for personnel to remember doses, times, etc.

6 *Limiting the choice of equipment or standardising equipment* (e.g. infusion pumps). This reduces errors related to drug preparation and infusion rates. Errors associated with the use of different equipment can frequently cause serious errors.

7 *Implementing unit dosing in the pharmacy.* This reduces errors of calculation, measurement, mixing and handling on the nursing unit. It has significantly reduced dosing errors over a 20-year period, although its use incurs a financial cost.

8 *The supplying of high-risk intravenous medications by pharmacy.* This reduces the risks involved in calculation and preparation of medications on patient care units.[49]

9 *Concentrated potassium chloride solutions should not be stored in patient care units but in the pharmacy.* Potassium chloride has been described as the most potentially lethal chemical used in medicine.[50] Because it is never intentionally used undiluted, appropriate diluted solutions can be prepared by pharmacy and stored on the unit for use. The lethal accidents which have been caused with this chemical are legion, and reflect a lack of knowledge of the actions of potassium as well as confusion with other medications.[51]

10 *Antibiotics.* These are associated with a high proportion of medication errors (*see* Figure 11.5), involving over 50% of all dosing errors.[52] The once-daily dosing with the aminoglycosides poses a particular challenge with regard to the narrow therapeutic window and risk of nephrotoxicity, especially in elderly patients.[53] Pharmacy-managed protocols of dosage and frequency, calculated by patient weight and renal function by specially trained staff, have shown convincing reductions in cost (*see* Figure 11.5)[54] and nephrotoxicity.[55]

11 *The patient.* The patient as an important resource for reducing medication errors has received relatively little attention (*see* page 36), yet patients or their carers may provide the final safety check. Patients should be aware of their previous allergies and adverse drug experiences, the nature of their present medication and the reason for taking it as suggested, and they should clearly understand the importance of contacting their doctor immediately if they perceive a discrepancy in their medicines or if they experience unexpected effects. The National Patient Safety Partnership[56] recommends that patients ask the following questions before accepting a newly prescribed medicine.

- Is this the drug my doctor or other healthcare provider ordered? What are the trade and generic names of the medicine?
- What is the drug for? What is it supposed to do?
- How and when am I supposed to take it and for how long?
- What are the likely side-effects? What do I do if they occur?
- Is this new medication safe to take with other over-the-counter or prescription medication or with dietary supplements that I am already taking? What food, drink, dietary supplements or other medication should be avoided while taking this medicine?

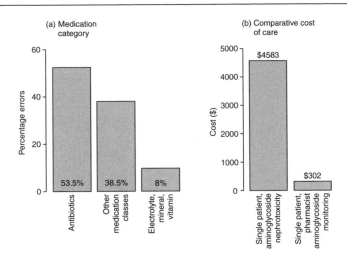

Figure 11.5: (a) Analysis of the medication category of errors by the prescriber in the use of medication dosing equations; over half of all dosing calculation errors involved antibiotics (Lesar *et al.*[52]). (b) Economic impact of aminoglycoside nephrotoxicity and the comparative cost of a pharmacist monitoring the aminoglycoside (gentamycin or tobramycin) treatment per single patient (Slaughter *et al.*[54]).

These strategies to improve patient safety range from the simple and elementary to the sophisticated and costly, yet all of them will reduce patient injury, and some will prevent fatalities.

Pharmacist involvement with medication management

A highly effective intervention for reducing medication errors has been the increasing involvement of the pharmacist with the management of medication. Two literature reviews have documented the value of clinical pharmacy services.[57,58] Of 104 studies that were published between 1988 and 1995, 89% recorded positive financial benefits of pharmacy services. There are increasing numbers of examples which have shown that pharmacist involvement with the medication team can substantially reduce medication errors and also improve the quality of treatment.

Medication management in secondary care

In the USA, which has established clinical pharmacy services in many hospitals, an evaluation of the associations between clinical pharmacy services and hospital mortality rates was investigated by Bond and colleagues.[59] Data for 14 clinical pharmacy services were obtained from the 1992 National Clinical Pharmacy Services (NCPS) database, which is the largest hospital-based pharmacy database in the USA.[60] The authors used clinical pharmacy services specifically to indicate the active participation of pharmacists in patient care. These were 'clinical pharmacy services' (drug use evaluation, in-service education, drug information, poison information, clinical research) and 'patient-specific clinical pharmacy services' (adverse drug reaction monitoring, pharmacokinetic consultations, drug therapy monitoring, drug protocol monitoring, total parenteral nutrition (TPN) team participation, drug counselling, cardiopulmonary resuscitation team participation (CPR), medical rounds participation and admission drug histories). Medicare mortality rates for 1992 were obtained from the Health Care Financing Administration (HCFA) for 5505 hospitals, and only general medical–surgical hospitals were used in order to provide more homogeneous hospital and patient populations. Data were finally matched for 1029 hospitals. The data were controlled for severity of illness and the results were assessed using both simple and multiple regression analysis.

Four services were associated with significant reductions in mortality rates, namely clinical research, drug information, taking drug admission histories and participating in a CPR team (see Figure 11.6) The study was the first to show that centrally based and patient-specific pharmacy services were associated with saving a significant number of lives in the nation's hospitals. Since mortality rates are associated with quality of care, it was concluded that the services may reflect quality of care indicators for both hospitals and pharmacies. The reasons for the associations have yet to be determined, since the study was not designed to show cause and effect. In particular, information about the services of physicians, nurses and other healthcare professionals could not be obtained. The authors emphasised that caution should be exercised when applying the findings to individual hospitals. However, the hospitals which provided these services had up to 40 478 fewer deaths per year than those without them. In these services and others, such as drug use evaluation and drug protocol management, there were also major financial savings, with lower total costs (see Figure 11.7).[61] Clinical research was associated with an increased total cost (see Figure 11.7) and with the greatest reduction in mortality (see Figure 11.6).

In other studies, in addition to reducing mortality rates, a senior pharmacist participating as a full member of the ICU team on medical rounds and making recommendations related to prescribing decreased the prescribing-related adverse drug events by 66% (see Figure 11.8).[62] Similarly, the addition to a heart failure management team of a clinical pharmacist evaluation which included medication review, therapeutic recommendations, patient education and follow-up monitoring significantly reduced all-cause mortality and heart failure events compared with the control group.[63] In addition, prospective interventions by a medical-team-based pharmacist in the medical unit of a district general hospital in the UK caused a significant reduction in medication errors, omissions and alterations on discharge prescriptions, from 32% to 8%.[64]

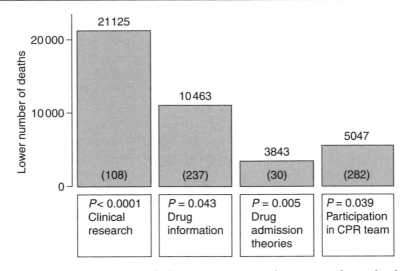

Figure 11.6: An evaluation of the associations between clinical pharmacy services and hospital mortality rates in 1029 hospitals in the USA. A database was constructed (from Medicare mortality rates from the Health Care Financing Administration and the National Clinical Pharmacy Services database), and a multivariate regression analysis controlling for severity of illness was used to determine the associations. The four clinical services which were associated with significantly lower mortality rates (*P*-values are shown), (i.e. clinical research and other categories), are shown together with the actual number of deaths (lower) in hospitals associated with the services. The number of hospitals is shown in parentheses. CPR, cardiopulmonary resuscitation team. Prepared from the data of Bond *et al.*[59]

All such studies attest to the improvement of prescribing practises and medicines management by pharmacists working closely with the medical team. Bond and colleagues[61] referenced 26 such studies that had been performed in the USA.

In the Noel Hall Report of the UK Hospital Pharmaceutical Service published in 1970, it was noted that a previous report of a Joint Subcommittee of the Standing Medical, Nursing and Pharmaceutical Advisory Committees of the Central Health Services Council drew attention to the high incidence of error in the administration of drugs to inpatients. It was suggested that in order to avoid errors, prescribers should have easier access to the pharmacist with his or her expertise, and that the pharmacist should have an opportunity to co-operate with the physician. The Subcommittee also commended the development of ward pharmacy systems to enable the pharmacist to check the pharmaceutical aspects and advise on the pharmacological anomalies of prescriptions, to be available for consultation by doctors and nurses, and to ensure a more rational and economical use of medicines. The Noel Hall Report also noted that a number of schemes were being developed which

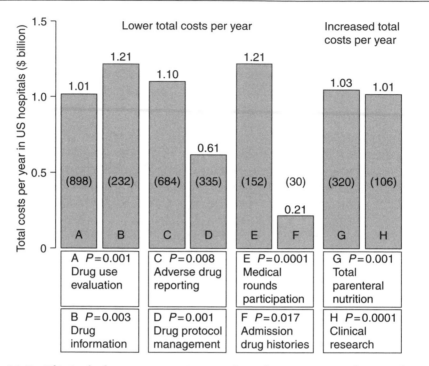

Figure 11.7: Clinical pharmacy services and total care costs in hospitals in the USA. A database was constructed from the 1992 American Hospital Associations Abridged Guide to the Health Care Field and the 1992 National Clinical Pharmacy Services database. Multiple regression analysis, controlling for severity of illness, was used to determine the relationships and associations in 1016 hospitals. Data are shown for the six clinical services that were identified which were associated with significantly lower total costs of care per year (P values are shown) both for the total number of hospitals using the service (shown in parentheses) and two services (G and H) with higher costs. Prepared from the data of Bond et al.[61]

sought to eliminate errors in the prescribing and administration of drugs.[65] Similarly, the Zuckerman Committee had reported in 1968 that 'there would seem to be a need in hospital for graduates (medical and non-medical) specialising in drugs and their effects in order to advise clinicians'.[66] It is highly regrettable that the above initiatives required a gestation period of more than three decades, so delaying progress and involving unnecessary harm to millions of patients.

Medication management in primary care

In the UK, a number of primary care groups (PCGs) now have full-time practice pharmacist posts to provide prescribing support. Experience had

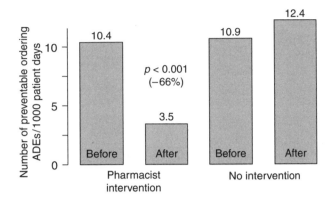

Figure 11.8: Pharmacist participation in intensive-care-unit ward rounds to reduce ordering/prescribing adverse drug-induced events and a non-intervention control. Prepared from the data of Leape *et al.*[62]

already been gained in GP commissioning groups where a prescribing adviser appeared to be an essential post to ensure that prescribing issues were addressed by the entire health team in developing and implementing safe and effective medication. Evidence of success in rational prescribing interventions,[67] in the structured delivery and monitoring of pharmaceutical care[68] and in educational outreach visits as a method of providing prescribing information[69] have been reported.

Professor Pringle, President of the Royal College of General Practitioners,[70] has emphasised that general practitioners want and need access to the knowledge of the pharmacy profession, and that pharmacists had already started to make a huge difference. A number of types of practice-attached pharmacists were envisaged, the defining feature being that the distinctive skills of doctors, pharmacists and nurses should be synergistic in the workplace for the improvement of patient care. The role of the pharmacist in primary care and prescribing is discussed on page 230.

The importance of 'active' errors

Correct systems and procedures cannot compensate for incompetent staff – they simply reduce the likelihood of error. It is not possible to 'dial out' all potential sources of error. If the staff employed in healthcare do not have the knowledge and skills to perform their roles, then errors and litigation are inevitable. The problem can be approached in two ways, focusing on two distinct groups of practitioners, namely healthcare professionals who are already in post, and future staff or trainees.

First, the inception in April 2001 of the National Clinical Assessment Authority (NCAA) proposed scrutiny of doctors in the UK.[24] It is to be innovatory in involving an active investigative role to provide a support service to health authorities and hospital and community trusts faced with concerns about the performance of individual doctors. The involvement of lay people, patient groups and others in the work of the authority is an important feature of the service.[71]

The direct encouragement and guidance of patients and carers in reporting errors and 'near misses', to themselves or to others, provides a powerful opportunity to detect overtly substandard practice at an early stage (see page 182). If successful, this would be preventative rather than corrective, and would afford a unique opportunity for the stimulus to professional development. This could also provide a role model for all other healthcare professions in their own attempts to improve the quality of care. Such developments would have major resourcing implications, although their cost would be offset against the savings made in reducing litigation claims and the additional costs of medical error to the healthcare system. However, such issues are beyond the scope of this chapter.

Secondly, an attempt to understand and reduce active errors caused by lack of knowledge and skills relates directly to the education and training of professional staff where the process begins (and to their 'continuing professional development'). These very important issues, which were only briefly mentioned in the context of the IOM report, *An Organisation With a Memory* and *Building a Safer NHS for Patients*, are discussed in more detail in the next chapter.

Chapter 12

Implications of error reduction for undergraduate teaching

Summary: Undergraduate education and improvement of patient safety

- A major cause of patient injury, disability and death identified in studies in the USA is a lack of knowledge of the healthcare professional.
- Government and other inquiries conducted into the cause of patient deaths in the UK reach similar conclusions.
- They reveal a profound cultural dysfunction involving a lack of understanding either by the healthcare and educational systems or by clinical training in the causes of error.
- Medication errors are particularly prevalent, and frequently betray gross ignorance of simple pharmacological principles and understanding.
- The educational imperative is to address these problems urgently, and also to introduce at the undergraduate level a culture of reporting errors as a normal and accepted procedure.

The introduction of a cultural change of reporting errors

First, the most effective way of introducing a 'cultural change' is at the undergraduate level. Indeed, there is no challenge of change, since the students are simply introduced to the routine reporting of errors as part of a safety culture as the norm.

The IOM report[1] emphasised that:

> Clinical training and education is a key mechanism for cultural change. Colleges of medicine, nursing, pharmacy, healthcare administration and their related associations should build more instruction into their curriculum on patient safety and its relationship to

quality improvement. One of the challenges in accomplishing this is the pressure on clinical education programs to incorporate a broadening array of topics. Many believe that initial exposure to patient safety should occur early in undergraduate and graduate training programs, as well as through continuing education.

Similarly, in their detailed analysis of the reporting and prevention of medical mishaps, Barach and Small[2] emphasised the essential task of introducing norms that 'inculcate a learning, non-punitive safety-reporting culture in professional schools and graduate training programmes, with support from consumers, patient advocacy groups and others'.

Clinical training programmes also need to ensure that teaching opportunities are safe for patients and ethically acceptable to students. There are examples of divergence between the standards established in ethico-legal teaching and clinical behaviour involving patient or student abuse.[3,4] A recent policy statement which identifies the rights of patients and students in medical education/practice can be found in Appendix 6.[5]

The following key points relate to professional and personal ethics of students.

- Patients must understand that medical students are not qualified doctors (and not 'young doctors', 'my colleagues' or 'assistants').
- Procedures that do not require immediate supervision should only be undertaken if there is recorded evidence of competence.
- If students are asked by anyone to do anything contrary to the guidelines, they must politely refuse.

Acceptance and adherence to these simple principles would act to reduce errors, and students or trainee/new doctors clearly require immediate assistance and advice when prescribing medication. In a UK paediatric unit, prescription errors doubled when new doctors joined the rotation, and Wilson and colleagues described their response as follows:[6]

Inexperience of medical and nursing staff and poor training contributed to recurrent medication errors in this and other studies.[7] Nurses undergo formal training in the administration of medications. Doctors are taught pharmacology and therapeutics, but seldom receive practical training on how to prescribe safely. Moreover, many problems are encountered when junior doctors make the transition from general medical practice to paediatrics, or even when more experienced trainee paediatricians rotate through the subspecialities. This was manifested by the increase in prescribing errors during months when a new doctor joined the rotation. Having identified training deficiencies, the Medication Error Committee set up regular multidisciplinary tutorials to train junior medical staff on the pitfalls of prescribing. Examples of drug charts were issued to reinforce safe practices. Specific practice was given to address the problem of wrong-dose errors, which often result from

miscalculation, misplaced decimal points, and the use of abbrevia-
tions which are misinterpreted by nursing staff . . . . Poor commun-
ication was an important factor in a number of medication errors in
this study. Examples include failure to communicate changes to the
medication chart, failure to communicate vital information during
transfer of patients between clinical areas, and failure to seek advice
when unfamiliar drugs were used . . . . Medication errors occurred
frequently in this study, but adverse consequences were rare, often
due to the vigilance of nurses and pharmacists. The adverse incident
scheme described was inexpensive to operate, and its non-punitive,
multidisciplinary approach enabled the detection of deficiencies
covering virtually every aspect of medication use in a hospital
setting. Following changes in practice, a reduction in certain types
of medication error was obtained. We believe this approach
improved the safety and quality of care for our patients.

However, not all inexperienced medical staff in the UK benefit from the best
practice shown in the above study, and this may lead to tragedy for both them
and their patients. A review of serious medication errors resulting in the death
of the patient and a manslaughter charge against the physician revealed that
over 50% of those prosecuted were junior doctors.[8] This figure is entirely
disproportionate to the number of junior medical staff on the Register.

Similarly, an analysis by Lesar and colleagues[9] of the error rates of junior
physicians in their early years of training at an American teaching hospital is at
least as disturbing as the results found in the UK (*see* Figure 6.10). First-year
trainees had significantly higher error rates (around 400%) than other
physicians. They appeared to learn gradually and at the expense of their
patients. In a follow-up study, Lesar and colleagues[9] reported that the risk of
errors was widespread among prescribers and not the result of a small number of
individuals. The authors discussed their findings as follows:

The inadequacy of physician training in pharmacotherapeutics has
been recognised by the American College of Physicians for some
years.[10] Errant medication prescribing may be one result of this
deficiency in training of physicians. Increased emphasis on and
monitoring of therapeutic and prescribing practices in physician
training programs may both improve the use of medications and
reduce the frequency of prescribing errors. Linking quality-assurance
programs such as the one described in this study with educational
programs at continuing education and graduate education levels
could decrease the risk to patients for drug-related iatrogenic illness.
The availability of such data also allows the performance evaluation
of physicians for accreditation and quality-assurance purposes, and
allows outcome analysis of educational programs to be based on
objective criteria.

The specific findings of this investigation are primarily applicable
to teaching institutions similar to the one studied; however,

prescribing errors may be committed in any patient-care setting. The findings of this study have important implications for the functional design, risk-management and quality-assurance procedures, educational priorities, and performance evaluation within healthcare systems. As a result of this study, an ongoing monitoring program of prescribing errors was implemented in the study hospital as part of the quality assurance program. All detected errors are currently evaluated, summarised and recorded. A monthly report of prescribing errors is generated. A report of errors detected for each department is forwarded to the respective department's quality-assurance committee for review. Potential causes of error are identified and solutions developed. Data collected by the described monitoring program are utilised to identify specific institutional and individual deficiencies in prescribing and allow targeting of educational programs and implementation of procedures designed to limit patient risks from prescribing errors. The impact of providing such feedback on specific errors to individual prescribers, and general information on common errors to prescribers as a group, will be evaluated through continued monitoring of error rates within the institution. The knowledge of how and why errors occur will hopefully reduce the hazards of hospitalization.

Addressing the pivotal causes of medication errors

Within the many articles reported in an issue of the *British Medical Journal* that was largely devoted to medical error, the major response to error can be summarised as a need to 'redesign systems so that latent errors are acknowledged, detected, intercepted and mitigated'.[2,11–13] It is emphasised that the importance of this approach to reducing latent errors is unquestioned and is fully documented in the IOM report[1] and *An Organisation With a Memory*.[14] The redesign of systems to enable the healthcare staff to have access to proper and complete information about all relevant circumstances of their patient must be a major goal. However, this must be in context. In *Promoting Patient Safety in Primary Care*[15] it was stated that 'Leaders need to emphasise that it is not individuals who make mistakes, but systems that fail', but this is ambiguous and unfortunate, for there remains an additional and so far largely unmentioned factor relating to active errors which must be urgently addressed. It is described below.

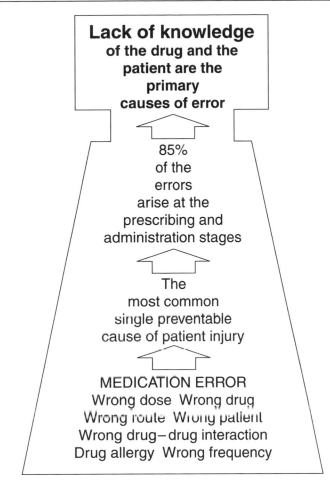

Figure 12.1: A pivotal cause of medication error; lack of knowledge by the healthcare professional.

The single most frequent cause of medication error: lack of knowledge by the healthcare professional

Lack of knowledge is of fundamental importance and can be determined from the data shown in Figures 5.2–5.6 and within the definition and observations by Leape and colleagues[16] relating to a 'systems failure' described as 'drug knowledge dissemination'. It is also apparent from the study by Lesar and colleagues,[17] where the commonest group of factors associated with errors were those related to drug knowledge and the application of knowledge about drug therapy and patient factors that affect drug therapy. The authors concluded that:

Many of these types of errors, totalling some 76% of all errors, could be prevented by ensuring that prescribers have timely information, an adequate knowledge base to use the information, and a level appreciation for the many complexities of drug therapy.

It is also clear from the study by Wilson and colleagues,[6] where a Medication Error Committee set up tutorials to train junior medical staff. Dean and colleagues,[18] also within the UK, in an analysis of prescriber errors mentioned that some interviewees reported no training in drug dosing or the practicalities of prescribing. It was concluded that error reduction strategies should focus on medical school training, teamwork and hospital culture, rather than on the individual.

In an analysis of the types of errors made by graduate medical trainees in the UK and the USA in hospital-based near-miss reporting systems, classified using the Eindhoven Classification Model, lack of knowledge was found to have contributed to the incidents in all cases.[19] The authors noted that inadequate educational preparation had the potential for causing significant harm.

A lack of knowledge among junior medical staff is also most potently expressed in the report by the Director of the NHS Technology Assessment Programme to the Chief Medical Officer on the prevention of intrathecal medication errors (*see* page 169).

In summary, it would appear that the prescriber (or administrator) of the drug who committed errors was unaware of some of the most basic and elementary principles of pharmacology and therapeutics that are required to ensure the rational and safe use of a drug. *This lack of knowledge or ignorance effectively precluded the safe and effective use of a drug and inevitably placed the patient at serious risk, as the medication errors so clearly and regrettably revealed.*

This must raise serious questions of *individual responsibility* (active errors) as distinct from *systems failure* (latent errors).

Leape and colleagues,[20] in their analysis of adverse events and negligence, reached the following conclusions:

> *The reduction of adverse events involving negligence will also require an increased emphasis on education. To the extent that failure to meet the standard of practice is due to ignorance, improved dissemination and enforcement of practice guidelines might be effective. The development of better mechanisms of identifying negligent behaviour and instituting appropriate corrective or disciplinary action is equally important.*

Leape and colleagues[16] in their analysis of medication errors and their development of a systems approach were clear that individuals must be responsible for the quality of their work, although the systems approach is likely to eliminate more errors. However, comment on either the prescriber or the administrator of a drug is placed within the context of a systems failure where the hospital or medical practice has exposed the patients to such dangerous incompetence.

The prescriber, dispenser or administrator of a therapeutic agent who wilfully advances on a patient armed with a drug in the absence of a knowledge of its use is grossly irresponsible. It is difficult to see how the patient, healthcare colleagues, the institution, society and the legal system could distinguish this behaviour from potential negligence.

Consider the case of a surgeon advancing on a patient with a scalpel and no knowledge or experience of the operation in hand, an airline pilot about to fly a Boeing 747 whose previous experience is limited to a two-seater Cessna, or a mechanic about to service the braking systems of a car who has no knowledge or skills relating to the systems involved. These examples would immediately be recognised as absurd, very dangerous and negligent. Yet in all four examples – the drug prescriber/dispenser/administrator, the surgeon, the pilot and the mechanic – lives are continually at risk. This suggests a cultural difficulty that has profound implications for the drug prescriber, dispenser or administrator, which will be explored further in the next section.

The Cambridgeshire Health Authority inquiry into methotrexate toxicity[21]

Important insights into the nature of medication error have been obtained from the recent account of the inquiry into the death of a Cambridgeshire patient following methotrexate treatment. The inquiry by the Cambridgeshire Health Authority is a remarkable milestone in reporting and learning from a tragic error. The authority has shown courage in reporting the full inquiry online at www.cambs-ha.nhs.uk/publications to enable a global learning and prevention experience. It presents a series of failures or misunderstandings in the care and treatment of the patient throughout that patient's whole care pathway. A synopsis of some of the key events is given below.

> The patient was commenced on methotrexate for rheumatoid arthritis by a consultant. Shared care arrangements with general practice were put in place to incrementally increase the dose to 17.5 mg once a week.
>
> Some three years later, the patient and her daughter ask the GP to prescribe methotrexate in a way that involves taking fewer tablets. The GP inadvertently writes a prescription for 10 mg tablets to be taken once daily without withdrawing the previously prescribed 2.5 mg tablets.
>
> A locum community pharmacist then dispenses methotrexate, 10 mg once daily, a total weekly dose of 70 mg.
>
> A few days later a second GP identifies the prescription error on a repeat-prescription request and crosses it off; the error remains unrectified on the computer-held record. The patient begins to feel unwell and continues to deteriorate.

After five days the patient is admitted to hospital with her own drugs and blood tests ordered; successive samples are inadequate for blood counts and are not followed through. The patient's drug chart indicates 100 mg daily of methotrexate.

The following day a staff nurse identifies the incorrect dosage of 100 mg and confirms with the patient that this should be 10 mg which was administered; the drug chart is not changed.

The following day the hospital pharmacy queries the methotrexate dose on the patient's drug chart and asks the nurse to tell the doctor to check the dose. The doctor phones the GP's surgery and gets confirmation from a non-medical member of staff that the 10 mg daily dose is correct. This is accepted and methotrexate is administered at 10 mg.

The next day the patient's condition is deteriorating; methotrexate is administered at 10 mg.

On the following day a nurse suggests that methotrexate could be the cause of the problem and the doctor chases the blood count results to finally reveal the serious problem. The patient is then transferred to the care of the haematology team.

Eight days later the patient dies.

Death certificates record the causes of death as gastrointestinal haemorrhage, pancytopenia and methotrexate toxicity.

The 31-page report reveals numerous errors of communication throughout the system, 28 detailed recommendations by the inquiry team and 17 actions either already taken or being taken by those involved in order to prevent future adverse events. The main focus of these various directives and improvements to practice was on reducing systems errors and poor communication.

However, the patient had responded over three years without untoward effect to a potentially toxic drug when it was administered at the correct dose. The patient died because of a drug overdose which was not corrected until it was too late. A major and continuing cause of error appeared to be a lack of knowledge of the effects of the drug, of its dose and frequency of administration, or of the patient. This was evident at all the stages of medication, and the situation was then exacerbated by a whole series of system and procedural errors.

In the recommendations it is only within recommendation number 23 that a lack of knowledge is considered to be relevant to the tragedy and is directed at the training of medical staff:

Drug side-effects need to be more prominent in junior doctor training and considered as a possibility in those with chronic diseases on multiple drug therapies . . . [with action by] . . . . Those responsible for clinical training, including the training of junior doctors, which should provide training on drugs and their side-effects.

There is no mention of individual responsibility.

However, the first item in 16 actions either already taken or in the process of being taken by the hospital to prevent future errors is highly instructive:

> 1 *The induction programme for SHOs will be reviewed with a view to ensuring that the importance of junior staff familiarising themselves with drugs before prescribing is emphasised, including the reaffirmation of the importance of the* British National Formulary (BNF). *This will include raising awareness of the pharmacy advice and information line for staff. A check will be made of all wards to ensure the availability of* BNF *books. The* BNF *is already available on the hospital's internal intranet.*

The Cambridge Health Authority is an archetypal health authority, and the comments of the inquiry may have applied to many if not most cases of methotrexate toxicity.

Learning from the Cambridge experience and others

The learning experience to discover the causes of errors could usefully debate three points.

First, a very strong case can be made that methotrexate and other cytotoxic agents are among some of the most dangerous drugs used in medicine. Even in specialist hands and at therapeutic doses they are problematic, with a serious and potentially fatal adverse-event profile which is one of the most thoroughly documented in medicine. Their inexpert use is an open invitation to disaster and litigation. There can be no justification for the initiation of their use other than by specialist care or their continued supervision other than by competent and specially trained staff. In the studies by Leape and colleagues,[20] cytotoxic treatments caused one of the two most frequent drug-related adverse events. Bone-marrow suppression and bleeding were the most frequent of all types of drug-related complications (*see* Tables 12.1 and 12.2). The fact that the majority of these complications are non-preventable adds to the urgency of the problem.[22]

Secondly, if junior medical staff have to be persuaded to 'familiarise themselves' with drugs just before prescribing them there is a further cultural difficulty of fundamental proportions. It inevitably gives rise to the most serious doubts about their personal knowledge and competence. In turn, this creates major problems for other members of the healthcare team and the institution in terms of a duty of care to the patient. Moreover, prescribing a cytotoxic drug based on a hasty perusal of a synopsis of drug action that is afforded by a pocketbook such as the *BNF* is difficult to understand. It was never intended that this most useful *aide-mémoire* would constitute the sole authority necessary to prescribe, dispense or administer drugs. Such comments are even more pertinent to cytotoxic agents that have a serious and predictable adverse-event profile.

For example, in the 1999 edition of the *BNF*[23] the comments on the use of

Table 12.1: Drug-related adverse events according to the class of drug involved[20]

Drug class	Number of events	Weighted percentage
Antibiotic	29	16.2
Antitumor	31	15.5
Anticoagulant	20	11.2
Cardiovascular	13	8.5
Antiseizure	15	8.1
Diabetes	8	5.5
Antihypertensive	10	5.0
Analgesic	6	3.5
Anti-asthmatic	5	2.8
Sedative/hypnotic	4	2.3
Antidepressant	1	0.9
Antipsychotic	2	0.7
Peptic ulcer	1	0.5
Other	33	19.3
Total	178	100.0

Note: Disabling injuries caused by medical treatment were identified in 1133 patients (3.7%) from a sample of 30195 randomly selected hospital records in New York State. Of the drug-related adverse events ($n = 178$, 19.4%), 17.7% involved negligence.

methotrexate in rheumatoid arthritis (under the heading of immunosupressants) are as shown in Box 12.1 (*see* page 152).

It is accepted that if the physician prescriber, the pharmacist dispenser or the nurse administrator of the drug had acted in accordance with these instructions, then the patient might not have died. It is also accepted that pocket-sized formulary manuals are prepared by many hospitals to assist physicians in medication ordering. *But is this a solution to a problem or a contributory cause of serious latent errors? Does this well-intentioned advice seriously mislead the prescriber into genuinely believing that a formulary is an adequate source to ensure safety in prescribing medication?* A formulary provides perfunctory information – there is not even the pretence of a provision of knowledge and understanding.

For example, the section on the vinca alkaloids in the *BNF* is very brief, although it indicates that the intrathecal route for these agents is contra-indicated (*see* Box 12.2). Indeed, the misuse of vincristine and vinblastine has caused catastrophic errors. However, the brevity of comment in the *BNF* compared with the detailed information provided in the manufacturer's data sheet is marked. For example, a brief extraction of crucial information is shown in Box 12.3 (*see* page 153).

Table 12.2: Types of drug-related complications induced by the medications identified in Table 12.1[20]

Type of complication	Number of events	Weighted percentage
Bone-marrow suppression	29	16.3
Bleeding	26	14.6
Central nervous system	26	14.6
Allergic/cutaneous	25	14.0
Metabolic	18	10.1
Cardiac	17	9.6
Gastrointestinal	14	7.9
Renal	12	6.7
Respiratory	5	2.8
Miscellaneous	6	3.4
Total	178	100

Note: The events covered a broad spectrum of adverse events, such as those which were unpredictable and unpreventable (including allergic reactions for which the patient had no known previous history), those that might have been unavoidable (such as bone-marrow suppression by antitumor drugs) and those that resulted from errors in administration or monitoring (such as bleeding with the use of anticoagulant drugs).

The manufacturer introduced the medication with a warning that the product is NOT FOR INTRATHECAL USE and then repeated this warning a further five times, clearly indicating the catastrophic or fatal nature of such an intervention. Finally, the syringe itself is prominently labelled NOT FOR INTRATHECAL USE.[24]

Thirdly, and most disturbing of all, if this approach reflects the professional culture of the prescriber, the dispenser or the administrator of the drug to treatments in general, it may reveal a major or perhaps even the main single cause of preventable adverse drug events and medication errors, namely a lack of knowledge of the elementary and most basic principles of pharmacology.

Fully one-third of physician-ordering errors are attributed to physicians' unfamiliarity with the medication.[17,25] Lesar and colleagues[17] related such difficulties to the unrealistic expectations of physicians:

> It is difficult, if not impossible, for physicians to maintain a working knowledge of all the medications they will prescribe and monitor in hospitalised patients. Errors, originating from any cause, are also more likely to go unrecognised by prescribers because of a lack of knowledge required to recognise an errant order as being wrong, or the presence of an adverse drug event.

Box 12.1: The description of methotrexate as it appears in the *British National Formulary*[23]

Methotrexate has also been shown to be effective. It is usually given in an initial dose of 2.5 mg by mouth once a week, increased slowly to a maximum of 15 mg once a week (occasionally 20 mg), subject to regular full blood counts (including differential white cell count and platelet count), renal and liver function tests.

METHOTREXATE

Indications: severe active rheumatoid arthritis unresponsive to conventional therapy: malignant disease (section 8.1.3); psoriasis (section 13.5.2).

Cautions: see section 13.5.2.

Pulmonary toxicity. Pulmonary toxicity may be a special problem in rheumatoid arthritis (patient to contact the doctor immediately if dyspnoea or cough). For other special warnings, including CSM advice and counselling advice relating to interaction with aspirin and NSAIDs, see Methotrexate, section 13.5.2.

Contraindications: see section 13.5.2.

Side-effects: see section 13.5.2.

Dose: by mouth, 7.5 mg once weekly (as a single dose or divided into 3 doses of 2.5 mg given at intervals of 12 hours), adjusted according to response; maximum total weekly dose 20 mg

Important: Note that the above dose is a ***weekly dose***.

Box 12.2: The description of vincristine as it appears in the *British National Formulary*[23]

VINCRISTINE SULPHATE

Indications: see notes above . . . *where it is stated . . . that . . .*

Vinblastine, vincristine, vindesine and vinorelbine are for ***intravenous administration only***. They are ***not*** for intrathecal administration because of severe neurotoxicity which is usually fatal.

Cautions: see section 8.1 and notes above; hepatic impairment (Appendix 2); caution in handling.

Contraindications: see section 8.1 and notes above.

IMPORTANT: Intrathecal injection ***contraindicated***.

Side-effects: see section 8.1 and notes above: irritant to tissues.

'Sections' and 'Appendix' refer to those in the *BNF*.

Box 12.3: A synopsis of the cautions to the use of vincristine emphasised on the manufacturer's data sheet[24]

ONCOVIN (Vincristine)

WARNING
THIS PRODUCT IS **NOT**
FOR INTRATHECAL USE

Dosage and administration
This preparation is for intravenous use only. It should be administered only by individuals experienced in vincristine administration.

FATAL IF GIVEN INTRATHECALLY
FOR INTRAVENOUS USE ONLY
See 'Warnings' section for the treatment of patients
given intrathecal vincristine sulphate

Extreme care must be used in calculating and administering the dose of vincristine, since overdosage may have a very serious or fatal outcome.

Contraindications, warnings, etc.
Contraindications:

FATAL IF GIVEN INTRATHECALLY
FOR INTRAVENOUS USE ONLY
See 'Warnings' section for the treatment of patients
given intrathecal vincristine sulphate

Warnings: This preparation is for intravenous use only. It should be administered by individuals experienced in the administration of vincristine sulphate. The intrathecal administration of vincristine sulphate usually results in death. Syringes containing this product should be labelled, using the auxillary sticker provided, to state 'FATAL IF GIVEN INTRATHECALLY. FOR INTRAVENOUS USE ONLY'.

Extemporaneously prepared syringes containing this product must be packaged in an overwrap which is labelled 'DO NOT REMOVE COVERING UNTIL MOMENT OF INJECTION. FATAL IF GIVEN INTRATHECALLY. FOR INTRAVENOUS USE ONLY'.

After inadvertent intrathecal administration, immediate neurosurgical intervention is required in order to prevent ascending paralysis leading to death. In a very small number of patients, life-threatening paralysis and subsequent death were averted but resulted in devastating sequelae, with limited recovery afterwards.

Pharmaceutical precautions
Special dispensing information: When dispensing vincristine sulphate in other than the original container, it is imperative that it be packaged in an overwrap bearing the statement 'DO NOT REMOVE COVERING UNTIL MOMENT OF INJECTION. FATAL IF GIVEN INTRATHECALLY. FOR INTRAVENOUS USE ONLY'. A syringe containing a specific dose must be labelled, using the auxillary sticker provided in the pack, with this warning.

Lack of pharmacological knowledge precludes the safe practice of therapeutics

The lack of knowledge of drugs with regard to medication error must be a cause for grave concern among all pharmacologists who have taught undergraduate and postgraduate students in pharmacy, medicine and other courses. Could the comments on the training of doctors by the Cambridge Health Authority be correct? And could these comments be extended to the training of nurses, pharmacists and other members of the healthcare team?

Huxley[26] and Ehrlich[27] would be mortified, as both of these eminent scientists envisaged that one day the pharmacologist would learn to aim with chemical substances to supply the clinician with drugs described as 'cunningly contrived torpedoes' or 'magic bullets', to selectively strike the illness or parasite, leaving the rest of the body untouched. It would appear that our aim has faltered or that some of the troops are uninformed – magic bullets have metamorphosed into potentially lethal bullets. How has this occurred?

In truth, the 'drug' treatment of disease has had a colourful history. Perusal of *The Extra Pharmacopoeia* by Martindale and Wescott (4th edition of 1858)[28] reveals an enthusiastic recommendation of the use of a handful of drugs and natural products, including powdered cockroach, phosphorus, antimony, arsenic, strychnine, morphine and similar agents for a diverse range of illnesses. By the year 1999, in Martindale's *The Extra Pharmacopoeia* (32nd edition)[29] the index alone is 1222 pages long, with a listing of around 400 000 items. Similarly, the *British National Formulary* of 1960 indexed 3200 items, whereas in 1999 it indexed around 6700 items, equivalent to about seven new items per month for 39 years.

The systems and procedures that are in place to accommodate and use this increase in medical preparations have in some ways barely changed in 40 years. Indeed, there is little if any evidence that this increase has been recognised or acknowledged in terms of the development of the knowledge and skills base required for the safe use of drugs in medicine. However, it should be noted that although the 'medical preparations' or 'items' identified above may reflect entirely new drugs with different pharmacological mechanisms and different therapeutic applications, which will require considerable time, experience and understanding to secure their optimal use, frequently they do not. For example, the 14 new drugs approved by the Food and Drugs Administration (FDA) between May and November 1997 included Toremifine (another anti-oestrogen), Tazarotene (another retinoid), Mibefradil (a calcium-channel antagonist which blocks both L- and D-type channels), Cerivastatin (the sixth HMG-CoA reductase inhibitor approved for use in the USA), Pramipexole (another dopamine receptor agonist), Bromfenac (another NSAID), Ropinerole (another dopamine receptor agonist), Dolasetron (another 5-HT$_3$ receptor antagonist), Quetiapine (another atypical antipsychotic agent) and Irbesarten (another angiotensin II inhibitor).[30]

Similar comments could be made about the launch of 32 new molecular

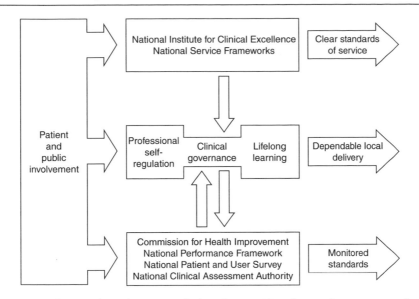

Figure 12.2: The quality framework for the NHS, where the system of profes sional self-regulation at a national level relates to clinical governance and professional responsibilities at a local level. Modified from *Supporting Doctors, Protecting Patients.*[32]

entities in the year 2000, which was the lowest number since at least 1979.[31] This is not an attempt to disparage the drugs or their introduction, where some may or have already been shown to have additional and major clinical advantages. However, the learning curve for understanding their pharmacology and therapeutic applications is clearly abbreviated.

Yet it is clear that many of the above and other drugs may have a greater potency or effect, or are increasingly used in combination, and do require a greater knowledge and skill to ensure their safe use.

It is emphasised that medical management is paying a heavy price for a lack of recognition, reporting and understanding of medication errors. The investigations reported in this chapter provide an understanding of the stages at which medication errors occur and also the beginnings of a bleak understanding of the reasons for their occurrence. They have major implications for the approach to and correction of the problems of medication errors and patient safety. However, it remains a simplistic understanding. Lesar and colleagues[9] reported (anecdotally) in the discussion of their study of follow-up data on 580 errors described over a 6-month period:

> the risk of errors to be widespread among prescribers and not the result of a small fraction of individuals writing a majority of the errant orders. The 580 detected errors were committed by 170 different prescribers. The range of errors per prescriber who committed errors was 1 to 12 errors, with a mode of 1 and a mean of 3.4.

> *One hundred and thirty-three prescribers committed 5 or fewer errors over the 6 months, 24 committed 6 to 10 errors and only 3 committed over 10 errors.*

No references could be found for a detailed study or for comparable investigations of nurses, pharmacists and other healthcare professionals.

Bearing such factors in mind, the present analysis distinguishes between experienced healthcare professionals and trainee/junior staff in terms of errors committed related to an inadequate knowledge base. It is considered that the lack of knowledge or skills of qualified or experienced staff requires individual recognition and resolution with the assistance of professional development, continuing postgraduate educational programmes, lifelong learning and the setting of clear standards of service which are monitored as shown in Figure 12.2. This is covered in *Supporting Doctors, Protecting Patients*[32] and *Assuring the Quality of Medical Practice*,[33] and is beyond the scope of this chapter.

Instead, this account focuses on the challenges of ensuring that the trainee healthcare professional has both an appropriate undergraduate experience and a sound ethical code of conduct (*see* Appendices 6 and 7) to ensure the safety of patients and the safe and effective use of medicines. In summary, a pharmacologist questions whether adverse drug events and medication errors relating to a lack of knowledge reflect limitations in the courses or teaching of pharmacology and therapeutics to our students.

Chapter 13

Have undergraduate courses failed to deliver students knowledgeable in pharmacology and therapeutics?

Summary: Error reduction relating to undergraduate teaching of healthcare professionals and the preregistration clinical tuition in the UK

- The first educational challenge for universities is to deliver the increase in student numbers required in medicine, nursing and other healthcare professions against complex quality assurance arrangements, changing funding regimes and the tripartite mission of education, research and service or patient care. It will take years to establish whether or not improvements in academic and clinical standards can be or have been attained.
- The incessant pressures to increase or broaden curricula content within finite programmes should be urgently addressed to prioritise the skills and knowledge base required for preregistration training. This should involve an increasing input from the accreditation bodies, future clinical tutors and employers.
- The knowledge and skills base (competence) of all healthcare graduates should be immediately obvious to clinical tutors and employers. This relates directly to a safe duty of care to the patient, and may involve formal testing or examinations at the commencement and conclusion of clinical training.
- Recent changes in undergraduate medical education which have involved increasing emphasis on problem-based learning, the cleansing of traditional disciplines such as pharmacology, a reduction in the factual content of the courses and basic sciences, and assessments that are directed at understanding and not recall have given rise to serious concerns.

- In particular, since therapeutics provides the bedrock of medical practice, the number of serious medication errors arising through ignorance of the most basic principles of pharmacology (e.g. lack of drug dose) must be addressed.
- The 'learning curve' shown by medical students is totally unacceptable. It poses serious risks to the patient, with severe legal consequences, and major embarrassment to other members of the healthcare team. It appears to reflect limitations in their academic and/or clinical tuition.

Academic background in the UK

The university–NHS interface

In the UK, an understanding of the academic background to subjects allied to medicine requires an appreciation of the very close relationship that now exists between higher education and the National Health Service. Indeed, the eventual success of the NHS Plan published in July 2000[1] will depend on the universities educating the greatly increased numbers of healthcare staff that will be required. Also, however, many universities are now dependent on the NHS. Sir Martin Harris, Chairman of the Universities UK Health Strategy Group, has reported that the NHS is the largest single employer of graduates and the second largest funder of universities after the funding councils. The MPET Levy (was NMET, Non-Medical Education and Training Levy) plus MDEL (Medical and Dental Education Levy) + SIFT (Service Increment for Teaching) is now £2.1 billion per annum. For some universities, as much as one-third of their funding comes from the NHS,[2] yet there is only limited evidence that this symbiotic relationship is appreciated. It is reported that it was as late as March 2001 that the Secretaries of State for Health and Education actually met for the first time to discuss the relationship.[2]

Medical schools alone have increased their intake by around 50% since 1998, and the Council of Heads of Medical Schools is confident that they can deliver on the numbers, provided that they receive sufficient applications.[2] The proviso is important, since applications to medical schools have fallen by about 20% over the last six years, although acceptances continue to rise (*see* Figure 13.1). The recent fall may be even greater[3] and is a cause for concern for medical and other healthcare students if the acceptance of a lower number of A-level points on entry[4] correlates with academic difficulties or course completion.[5] The increases in student acceptance numbers for pharmacy, nursing and the other healthcare professions are also shown in Figure 13.1.[6] There remains some concern that 'growth' within the system may contribute to a fall in academic standards.[7] Applications to medical schools in the USA are also reported to have

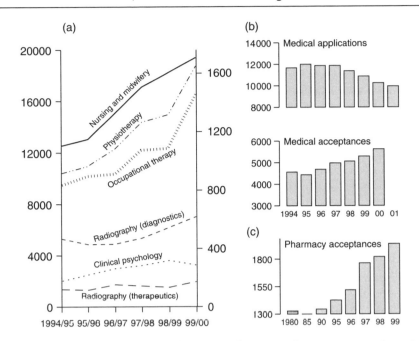

Figure 13.1: The increase in healthcare student numbers in UK universities to meet the future needs of the NHS. (a) The nursing and midwifery student numbers refer to the left-hand scale, whereas the other disciplines refer to the right-hand scale. (b) The number of student applications (home, EU and other applications are combined) to medical schools decreases, while the number of acceptances increases. Prepared from Department of Health data and UCAS (see Sanders[2]). (c) Increase in pharmacy student intake. Prepared from Pharmacy Student Analysis, RPSGB, 1999–2000.[6]

fallen by 20%, and the new career opportunities for young and upwardly mobile people afforded by the Internet and other new industries have been regarded as contributory factors.[8] Similarly, pharmacy school applications in the USA fell by 33% between 1994 and 1999.[9]

The second challenge is to maintain and enhance academic standards in the face of a potentially more diverse student entry (e.g. widening participation and changes in secondary education). For example, broadening the curriculum in sixth form A-level studies through the introduction of AS-levels has proved controversial. In a remarkable volte-face, the Chairman of the Qualification and Curriculum Authority, who advised the government on the AS-levels, on leaving his appointment and becoming Head of Winchester College is reported as saying 'We got it wrong, but I didn't think it was wrong until I came to take over a school, I don't think we fully thought out all the available options. I did think it was the right approach but it looks different when you are on this side of the fence'.[10] It would appear that the AS-levels are to be reformed yet again.

Heads of some schools are also rejecting the new key skills tests, and there is reported concern about the failure rate among students who have done the first papers for the new vocational A-levels.[10] Many universities, in response to such difficulties, have put in place remedial courses and procedures to help students in their transition from secondary to higher education. Inevitably such activities are incorporated within a course of finite length, but are essential in order to allay concerns of a slippage in academic standards in higher education.[11]

The third challenge is to progress even further the students' understanding of ethical issues and standards of professional behaviour. This is a top priority for all professional bodies who, together with academia and students, are addressing important contemporary issues of conduct and standards of professional behaviour – care for patients and others, the importance of respect and empathy towards others, the importance of good communication skills and the ability to reflect on one's own professional behaviour.[12–18]

Curricula development

There are many factors which have influenced curricula development to ensure relevant course structure and design, including the changing roles of healthcare professionals, the changing expectations of patients, the changing expectations of those who fund the healthcare systems, the incessant pressures to expand the curricula to include social and humanistic studies, ethics, genetics, safety and risk management, molecular biology, information technology and numerous clinical and scientific disciplines that were barely evident 20 years ago. Yet in most cases these additions have to be considered within a course of finite length.

Many of these factors may finally be seen to influence the learning, understanding and information retention of pharmacology and therapeutics by the undergraduate student. The teaching of pharmacology and therapeutics to medical and pharmacy students is taken to provide examples of contemporary academic practice.

Pharmacology teaching to medical students

The new medical degree

Predicted changes in the organisation of healthcare, the changing roles of physicians and the growth and change in the content of medicine, together with a progressive educational philosophy, have helped to redefine medical courses. In medicine there have been immense pressures to enhance the social and humanistic content of the degree to allow doctors to better understand and interact with their patients.[19] The President of the General Medical Council (GMC), Sir Donald Irvine, noted that patients want their doctors to be clinically competent, caring and kind, honest, communicative, respectful and generally trustworthy. However, he suggested that the profession has been distracted by technology at the expense of relationships with patients and basic humanity. He noted the criticisms made against doctors as being poor communicators, patronising and arrogant, lacking the knowledge and skills required, and unwilling to admit to error.[20] He indicated that:

> The key to closing the gap between professional and public expectation lies in the training of doctors and students. They must be engaged in understanding the values and behaviours essential for the profession. We are lucky that young people with good academic qualifications and the right personal qualities want to be doctors. . . . The secret of what goes wrong lies in how doctors are trained and conduct their practice, and not in the young people themselves. Good medical practice is essential to provide examples and role models for students and trainees. The profession is divided about its attitudes to patients and the changes the GMC is introducing. In a recent survey of doctors, 40% thought that relating to patients was not sufficiently important to warrant GMC action if deficient. 40% is 60 000 doctors in the NHS – this is a culture divide which must be addressed. Medical schools, Senior Consultants and teaching general practitioners must give leadership. Curricula in medical schools are becoming more sensitive to these issues . . . . Time is short as modern medicine is becoming increasingly more complex. The profession needs to be clear about what it can and can't do, and be open about this with members of the public and patients In the USA, in Managed Care Plans, doctors and patients work more closely together to identify what is needed and achievable. We need to have approaches which bring together the professions, patients and NHS organisations . . . . Through the GMC's proposals for revalidation, doctors must be able to demonstrate regularly that they remain fit to practice in their chosen field.

This new professionalism needs:

- a change in culture
- doctors' commitment to quality improvement
- stronger patient involvement
- an emphasis on attitudes and behaviours in medical education
- professional standards
- clinical guidelines.

Medical schools have responded vigorously to the challenge with innovative changes to the curriculum – the debate has been endless within a curriculum of finite length. There appear to be four dilemmas.

The first dilemma

This relates to the inclusion of new material in a fixed-length course which is inevitably at the cost of exclusion of existing material. This may have been exacerbated in some medical schools by the switch to problem-based learning, which may have reduced the opportunity to teach the basic concepts of various specialisms on which so much informed knowledge and understanding depends.

Following the General Medical Council's publication of *Tomorrow's Doctors* in 1993,[21] the UK medical schools began revising existing courses or developing new curricula. The main recommendations included the following:

- a reduction in overall factual content
- the encouragement of self-directed learning through curiosity
- the integration of basic and clinical sciences
- the promotion of a core plus options approach to curriculum design
- assessments that should be developed for understanding, not recall
- the use of a systems-based approach to curriculum design.

It was recommended that the core curriculum (that is not speciality or departmentally based) should account for about two-thirds of the course, with options of special study modules providing the remaining third. It is particularly regrettable that individual institutions were left to define the core content, since the GMC was clearly expecting that a broad national consensus would emerge. In summary, in medical schools education was to become driven towards problem-based learning. This is a major shift *away from teaching and content* to an emphasis on *student self-directed learning and educational process*.[22]

This was a particularly interesting initiative, since the problem-based learning orthodoxy was developed on the 'McMaster Philosophy' which was established for an adult graduate programme.[23] In retrospect, to introduce the new initiative into some schools while allowing the remainder to proceed as before would have provided a valuable educational experiment. There was no evidence base to support the use of the McMaster Philosophy in an undergraduate programme where some weeks earlier the first-year students had been in secondary education. However, medical students have always achieved excellent A-level grades and may have provided a resilient experimental group. What could not have been expected was a dramatic increase in medical student numbers in the subsequent years, and the possibility of a changing profile of A-level grades.

Many medical schools have adopted systems-based modules in the early years of the course, with some attempts to provide clinical problem solving and options for special study. Course descriptions are to be found in the review of student assessment in undergraduate medical education in the UK by Fowell and colleagues[24] and in the Subject Review Reports of the Quality Assurance Agency (QAA) for Higher Education of all the UK medical schools.[25,26]

Medical schools have achieved varying degrees of success in what for many schools has been a difficult and/or controversial transition. For example, the Subject Review Report of one medical school comments on curriculum design, content and organisation as follows:

> 11 *The reviewers consider that the current curriculum does not demonstrate a coherent overall strategy to guide development and change. There is continuing need to define and implement such a strategy because the curricular development has yet to eliminate all the long standing discipline and preclinical and clinical divisions. This has compromised the system-based approach and led to inconsistencies in the level, breadth and depth of study and to a lack of coherence. This is acknowledged in the self-assessment, but further modifications are required to ensure that integration consistent with the provider's aims is achieved.*

> 12 *There are clear lines of responsibility and accountability in the supervisory structure for the organisation of the curriculum, but the delegation of appropriate authority for ensuring that change is fully implemented is less well defined. This has compromised a primary aim of reducing factual content and limited the scope of both horizontal and vertical integration.*[27]

In the university's follow-up report to the subject review, the reader is informed that the: *overburden of factual content and lack of basic science is to be addressed* and that *the one or two remaining clinical specialities which have not yet accepted integration into a systems approach are revising their views.*[28]

It becomes clear that some clinical specialities have found the transition very difficult to accept.

(For the reader who is unaware of the philosophy of the QAA, it should be noted that the agency does not judge or comment on the actual respectability of the curriculum for a medical degree against a national norm. Their comments relate solely to whether or not the aims and objectives identified by the school in their own self-assessment submission have been achieved. This will change under Academic Review, where the Self-Evaluation Document has to be written against the Subject Benchmark Statement.)

This profound change in medical school teaching has been paralleled by the loss of individual departments of pharmacology and clinical pharmacology as these have amalgamated with other disciplines to form divisions of biomedical sciences and clinical sciences.[29] *Given that therapeutics remains the bedrock of medical practice such changes have given rise to deep concern – for all of the basic sciences.*[30,31]

These changes have had a dramatic effect on the teaching of pharmacology and therapeutics in most UK medical schools. Indeed, traditional 'teaching' in many schools has all but disappeared. Departmental courses in basic and clinical pharmacology and therapeutics (and other basic sciences) were replaced by integrated systems-based modules where neither the student nor the teacher (nor the future employer) could identify any pharmacology. In fact there was serious concern that 'pharmacology' and 'clinical pharmacology' would disappear from the medical student experience altogether. Certainly the word 'pharmacology' has all but disappeared from the curriculum, with the clinical pharmacologist remaining an endangered species.[29]

In an attempt to remedy this situation and extend the GMC recommendation that specialist organisations should establish the core content for specific subjects, the Clinical Section of the British Pharmacological Society has published its recommended core content of a course in clinical pharmacology.[32,33] This represented an advance in the teaching of clinical pharmacology to medical students, but provided no effective guidance on the teaching of the fundamental science of pharmacology on which successful clinical pharmacology is based. Similar concerns have been voiced about anatomy, biochemistry and physiology.

A useful perspective on the design of a drug formulary for medical students comes from the Newcastle medical school's *Student Formulary for Students Qualifying in 2003*. The 16-page formulary was introduced as follows:

> *This formulary has been produced to assist your learning of clinical pharmacology and therapeutics. It has been developed in consultation with all course directors, and lists the drugs of which you should have acquired 'core knowledge' by the end of your undergraduate training. We emphasise that the formulary is a minimum knowledge base. You should not restrict your reading and learning to these drugs alone, particularly if you encounter other drug therapy in patients you see. The formulary has the same structure as the* British National Formulary, *with drugs appearing in the same section and the same order. The order in which the drugs appear does not necessarily indicate the order of preference of use . . . .* Indicates drugs for which you are expected to have more detailed knowledge. This should encompass mechanisms of action, primary and secondary pharmacology, clinical pharmacology, therapeutic uses, adverse drug reaction profiles, monitoring requirements and toxicity in overdose. For other drugs, knowledge should encompass mechanism of action, therapeutic use and serious adverse drug reactions.*[34]

This formulary, which is similar to those used in other medical schools, usefully identifies for the student around 70 of the most important and frequently prescribed drugs used in medicine and required the student to have more detailed information/knowledge on about 50 of these drugs. In the section entitled 'Drugs used in the treatment of malignant disease and immunosuppression', the cytotoxic drugs cyclophosphamide, doxorubicin, methotrexate, vincristine and cisplatin are listed, and prednisolone and cyclosporin are included as agents that affect the immune system. Of all these drugs, only prednisolone was indicated as a drug for which the student was expected to have more detailed knowledge. Methotrexate was also included in the section entitled 'Drugs used in rheumatic diseases and gout', and prednisolone, ibuprofen and allopurinol (but not methotrexate) were expected to be studied in greater depth.

This is not intended to be a criticism of the formulary, since the construction of any formulary is a most unenviable and thankless task – the inclusion and exclusion criteria are inevitably arbitrary. Clinical formularies like *aide-mémoires* are required either when the information/knowledge base has become so extensive as to preclude immediate recall, or when the information/knowledge base of the practitioner is inadequate.

Within a drug formulary, a further delineation in terms of the relative depth of knowledge of a drug that is required may give rise to an illusion of relative 'importance'. *Every drug when administered to a patient is important, and the patient will surely require, expect and deserve professional expertise in its use.* This applies just as importantly to cytotoxic medication such as methotrexate or vincristine.

The design of the traditional medical curriculum has reflected a distinctive culture of preclinical and clinical aims and objectives. McCrorie[35] provides an instructive perspective on the cultural problem:

> *The idea that pharmacology is something completely different from clinical pharmacology (often the departments are separate and at war with each other), that biochemistry is separate from clinical biochemistry, and that histology and histopathology are poles apart, makes no sense to me. The reason for the separation is the old clinical/preclinical divide, usually reflected in a division between those who are medically qualified and those who are not . . . . It is true that there is little teaching by basic scientists during the later years of the undergraduate medical course, although many immunologists, clinical biochemists and epidemiologists, for example, are non-clinical and are involved in pathology teaching. Most of the basic science is instead taught by clinicians. Surgeons constantly refer to anatomy, endocrinologists to biochemistry, general physicians to physiology, general practitioners to psychosocial issues, public health physicians to statistics. I'm being a bit stereotypical here, but the message is nevertheless clear – physicians do pick up the basic science mantle in the latter years of the undergraduate medical course.*
>
> *There is also a bit of pride involved. Just as basic scientists feel uncomfortable trying to put their teaching into a clinical context because of their lack of clinical knowledge, so clinicians feel uncomfortable teaching basic science aspects of their clinical cases, partly because they have forgotten much of the basic science they rote-learned the night before their exams, and partly because of the huge explosion of scientific knowledge that has taken place over the last 20 years. As a result, many staff choose to stay inside their cocoons and don't venture outside their area of expertise, rather than show their ignorance . . . . With the advent of the new integrated*

courses, such barriers are beginning to break down. Problem-based learning is a particularly good leveller and helps the clinical/preclinical divide to disappear.

The experience of developing the new medical degree course at Liverpool provides an illuminating insight into the processes involved.[36] Key topics are revisited and developed throughout the course with, for example, adverse drug reactions occurring initially in the first year in connection with antibiotic use and in the third year in prescribing for the elderly. This broad-based approach can be developed in a Special Study Module on adverse drug reactions and drug toxicity. The authors emphasise that the outcome of the integration of clinical pharmacology will require careful scrutiny over the next few years.

It is interesting to compare briefly the UK experience with attempts in the USA to 'marry' a traditional lecture-based first-year programme with a problem-based curriculum in the second year. Doig and Werner[37] reported on the decision to present the preclinical curriculum in a sequence that uses both lecture-based and problem-based elements which developed from a positive experience with problem-based learning, tempered by the broad range of student ability and background. Although the faculty agreed that content integration, case-based learning, independent learning and group learning skills should form part of the education of all preclinical students, they wanted the foundation of basic science education to be shared by all students prior to beginning problem-based learning. This was accomplished in the first year when the non-behavioural basic science courses are departmentally administered, discipline based and delivered in large lectures. The focus is on fundamental concepts and principles in all of the sciences basic to medicine. Each week the clinical relevance of the basic sciences is highlighted by the presentation of a patient case which emphasises content from at least one of the concurrent basic science courses. Faculty teams consist of a clinician and a basic scientist who present the case and discuss the pertinent basic science content with the intention of reinforcing what is being taught in the basic sciences courses. All of the advanced basic science content in the second year is learned in a problem-based format, which was described as more structured and faculty centred than the prototypical problem-based learning described by Barrows and Tamblyn,[38] emphasising independent rather than self-directed learning. An evaluation of the new curriculum showed that graduates reported increased satisfaction with their basic science teaching and also its integration with clinical science. It was:

> *hypothesised that the curriculum promotes solid knowledge construction by providing the introduction to each basic science discipline in the first year upon which integrated conceptions are more readily built during the second year . . . . This may be a way to help the PBL students construct the cognitive scaffolding necessary to easily assimilate new basic science information.*[39]

Four points are relevant to the many changes in medical education in the UK.

First, and probably most important, the overall reduction in factual content required for the development of knowledge, associated with assessments that focus on understanding and not recall, has given rise to serious concern about future competence. The fundamental basis of any profession must surely relate to its unique knowledge base – without knowledge and understanding there can be no rational interpretation or analysis. It is the distinctive or proprietary knowledge base (and skills) of medicine, pharmacy, nursing and other subjects, whether that knowledge is propositional or procedural,[40] that provides the academic and professional *raison d'être*. Without an authoritative knowledge base the subject is defunct. What is the evidence base to support the hypothesis that a *reduction in knowledge and its assessment* will actually enhance the competence of the future practitioner? For example, in their practical guide for students and teachers undertaking problem-based learning in medicine, David and colleagues,[41] commenting on the development of an effective clinical reasoning process, reached the following conclusions:

> There is often confusion between problem-based learning and learning about problem solving. It is important to differentiate between the two. Problem-solving skills appear to be content or knowledge specific. The more you know, the better you are at solving problems. There is no evidence for a problem-solving skill that is independent of knowledge. Thus problem-based learning helps the development of clinical reasoning solely by improving knowledge. There is no evidence that problem-based learning curricula (or any other curricula for that matter) are able to enhance students' problem-solving skills independent of their acquisition of knowledge.[42]

It is somewhat contradictory that the presence of *increasing* knowledge (or at least information), which is so important for problem solving, was a factor in *reducing* the knowledge content and its assessment in the new courses. The production of vast amounts of scientific information has little relevance to the practice of medicine in the immediate future. Genomics provides an excellent example of this. Sir David Weatherall, Regius Professor of Medicine at the University of Oxford, cautioned some years ago about the infamous hyping of genomics and the time required to translate exciting advances in science into a therapeutic opportunity.[43–45] Schmidt[46] has also cautioned that the initial medical training may be an adequate basis for practice for an extended period of time, in particular because physicians seem to learn from their practice as well. Family physicians' diagnostic accuracy was shown to more than double as a function of the number of years of practice.[47]

However, Sir David Weatherall went much further. In his presidential address to the British Association for the Advancement of Science in 1993, he stated:

> the public is becoming less enthusiastic about scientific approaches to disease and is turning to alternative approaches. The whole ethos of modern medicine is being challenged. Whilst much of this new

thinking stems from a genuine wish to improve the quality of patient care in the shortest possible time, there is a danger that it will undermine the role of the basic medical sciences, which have to take a longer-term view of the control of disease. Claims by molecular biologists that within the next five to ten years we will be able to identify the major genes involved and somehow alter our suscept-ibility to our common killers are naive and misleading, based as they are on a complete misunderstanding of the enormous complex-ity of these diseases and those who suffer from them. Each break-through in molecular sciences promises to revolutionize the treatment of a particular disease, but so far has had little impact on our daily lives. One result has been an enormous increase in the growth of alternative medicine. Another has been the increasing pressure on medical schools to increase their emphasis on commun-ication skills and social science at the expense of basic biological sciences. It is not surprising, therefore, that our university clinical and basic science research departments are feeling uneasy . . . . But because these changes are occurring at a time when society is disillusioned with science, and when support for medical research is so limited, there is a genuine danger that the pendulum may swing too far, and that, in our new customer-driven approach to medical research, the vital role of the basic medical sciences may be neglected.

It is even more obvious that the majority of basic knowledge is not subject to transitory change. For example, for at least four decades the need to acquire and retain factual knowledge, such as the doses of drugs, has always been a requirement in the paramedical areas. For some 200 commonly used drugs their daily use has reinforced the knowledge base, and the common drugs and their doses have remained constant for around 40 years. Knowledge of drug doses and other aspects of the most basic and elementary concepts of pharma-cology provides a reassuring authority for the use of medication, with or without *aide-mémoires*, and is essential in patients whose individual needs can vary widely.

It has been known for some years that a lack of knowledge of the drug and in particular the drug dose by the prescriber is the single most frequent cause of medication error.

Has medical education, in seriously reducing the fundamental knowledge base in pharmacology, increasingly compromised those competencies that are immediately required for present patient needs?

Could it be that the lacunae in safe practice, or medication error, will actually be shown to increase with a declining knowledge of pharmacology and therapeutics? It is emphasised yet again that therapeutics remains the bedrock of medical practice and that the knowledgeable physician plays *the* central role in the practice of medicine. It is of vital importance that the healthcare system, other healthcare professionals and patients have unreserved confidence in the abilities of the physician. Even degrees of reservation are sufficient to commence the erosion of trust and finally reputation.

The medical course has frequently been evaluated by the learner, where his or her stated satisfaction and motivation have served as an index of course success. This situation will change, particularly within the shadow of the reporting of medical errors, to include first and foremost the perspectives of the patient, whose safety is of paramount importance, and secondly, those who fund the healthcare system.[48] Relevant to such concerns is the detailed report, *The Prevention of Intrathecal Medication Errors*, published in April 2001 by Professor Wood, Director of the NHS Health Technology Assessment Programme, to the Chief Medical Officer,[49] which included the following comments on education and training to prevent errors:

> *21 Lack of knowledge has contributed to several incidents of intrathecal medication errors. In one case a Senior House Officer was not fully aware of the magnitude of the hazard of intrathecal vincristine injection (but had read that the drug had neurotoxic side-effects). In another case, intrathecal vincristine was given in theatre by an anaesthetist providing cross-cover for an oncology colleague who had gone off duty. As an anaesthetist, he was unfamiliar with the drug. In a third case, an enquiry expressed concern at a more general lack of knowledge among recent medical graduates of drug prescribing and administration; this point was taken up with the Dean of the Local Medical School, and the curriculum for teaching clinical pharmacology and therapeutics was revised.*

> *24 Reforms of the undergraduate medical curriculum set out in* Tomorrow's Doctors *have sought to reduce the burden of factual knowledge placed upon students. This change was necessary, but must be selectively applied. Patients are not placed at risk if new medical graduates are no longer expected to know all the branches of the carotid artery, each enzyme of the Krebs cycle, or the histological classification of lymphomas – such detailed knowledge is best acquired during postgraduate specialist training. However, every doctor from qualification will be prescribing and administering drugs. The undergraduate curriculum must therefore provide a thorough understanding of drugs and their potential hazards. The 'learning curve' seen in a US study is no more acceptable in pharmacology than it would be in surgical practice.*

> *25 Tomorrow's Doctors devotes fewer than a dozen words to this topic. It is reasonable (and proper) that details of doses should be looked up rather than committed to memory. However, prior awareness of contraindications, drug interactions and toxicities is essential for safe prescribing. These in turn require a thorough knowledge of the clinical pharmacology of all drugs in common use. Case studies of drug-related adverse events are valuable in teaching*

practical therapeutics, both as an aid to understanding risk management and to avoid the excessively didactic approach which has in the past burdened the undergraduate curriculum.

Such comments are fully supportive of the concerns previously expressed, with one important exception. *Is it 'reasonable (and proper) that details of doses should be looked up rather than committed to memory' when the lack of knowledge of drug dose is the single most common cause of medication error?* It was surely not the wish of the report to perpetuate this major cause of error, which may yet again highlight the crucial importance of recording and publishing errors to enable a global understanding of the causes of errors in medication. Similarly, a discrete discussion with a Dean of a Medical School is unlikely to affect anything other than a local change. Surely all medical schools should be made aware of the problem. Indeed, in the Summary to the report (point 5) it is stated that:

Drug prescribing and administration errors occur with unacceptable frequency, particularly among recently qualified doctors. It is recommended that steps are taken with Medical Schools to ensure that therapeutics and risk management are thoroughly covered in core curricula.

And in the Conclusions, Recommendation 5, it is stated that:

Medical schools should ensure that their core curricula provide a thorough knowledge of safe drug prescribing and administration. Proper assessment in these areas is essential to minimise the occurrence of therapeutic errors, particularly during general professional training.

The inevitable conclusion is that a prescriber of a drug must be professionally and morally aware of all of the salient factors to ensure the safe use of that drug in practice. With the exception of medicines that are used only rarely, or which require complex calculations and specialised preparation (*see* page 134), knowledge of doses of common drugs is as essential for safe practice as is an understanding of their pharmacological and therapeutic properties and 'contra-indications, drug interactions and toxicities' (*see* above). Most often the prescriber will be a physician, but it is not immediately clear why a physician is assumed to be able to retain complex information about drug interactions yet have difficulty with drug doses.

However, the above report is surely to be congratulated on raising the concept of a 'learning curve', previously discussed briefly on pages 64–5 and illustrated in Figure 6.10.

Perhaps the most interesting account of a 'learning curve' is to be found in the authoritative evidence given to the Bristol Royal Infirmary Inquiry into paediatric surgery.[50] The evidence was of course directed towards learning surgical techniques and 'managing the learning curve'. It was provided from the following and instructive testimonies:

89 *Dr. Underwood:*
I believe it may be possible to shorten a learning curve by good theoretical knowledge of the new procedure, observing others with experience, training alongside others and then working with decreasing supervision by the experienced operator, in the same way that a trainee learns new skills.

90 *Mr. Wishart:*
Suggested the following steps could be taken:

- *private preparation which includes reading, attending meetings, courses etc.*
- *visiting centres of 'excellence' and observing there*
- *visiting centres of 'excellence' and having an opportunity to assist the experienced surgeon at an operation*
- *attending workshops dedicated to promoting technical proficiency in specific procedures*
- *inviting experts to operate or assist the surgeon in his own centre.*

92 *Professor Angelini explained how he approached a new procedure:*
Any time I have embarked on a new surgical procedure, and this has happened on several occasions since 1992, I usually have gone to visit centres where those procedures were carried out, and subsequently have invited the experts to Bristol to help me with the surgery. This has often been with regard to both surgical and anaesthetic expertise.

93 *Professor Sir Kenneth Calman:*
I was involved surgically, for about eight years, mainly on transplantation and vascular surgery. During that process, the senior consultant I worked with took a year out to go and work in the United States on liver transplantation. He would not have done a liver transplant on his own in this country without a year's experience with one of the most outstanding liver transplant surgeons in the world. That would be the way he would deal with an entirely new procedure; he would normally go somewhere where they are doing it and learn how it is done, come back with the skills and expertise and build up a team.

94 *Sir Barry Jackson discussed the extent to which there were formal requirements to be followed, in the following exchange:*
Q . . . what would be the expectation as to the practical steps that had had to be taken before a person could be confident that actually they would not be harming their patient if they embarked on something relatively new?
A . . . There was nothing laid down about this. It was not formalised. It was up to an individual surgeon to take what steps they

considered necessary to enable them to carry out that operation with a clear conscience.

Q . . . So perhaps there might be a range of steps available to them. The obvious one would be to review the literature to make sure they were familiar at least in theory with the steps that needed to be taken in performing this new technique. That presumably is something that everybody would have been aiming to do during the period with which we are concerned?

A . . . Yes, well, without either reading the literature, reading the technique in an article . . .or seeing a video, and videos were widely used at this time, or having seen the operation in somebody else's operating theatre when visiting another surgeon, I do not think any surgeon would embark on a new operation without one or other of those steps being taken before they put, as we say in the trade, knife to skin.

95 *Mr Dussek recommended in his paper* 'Avoiding the Learning Curve':
Surgeons should not be performing operations until they are competent to do so at an accepted general level of risk. Every surgeon should feel confident that he has the necessary education and experience to perform a new operation skilfully and that this skill should extend where necessary to the peri-operative management. Funding should be available for surgeons to attend the necessary training courses . . . . Consultants must relinquish a historical reluctance to ask other consultants to help. With the emergence of the new 'Calman trainees' with possibly less surgical experience than their predecessors, this is going to be of increasing importance.

In a footnote to the above accounts, Mr Barry Jackson, President of the Royal College of Surgeons of England, told the inquiry that the Royal Colleges have since sought to respond to the issue of the 'learning curve' through a system called SERNIP (the Safety and Efficacy Register, New Interventional Procedures), introduced in 1996. Mr Jackson explained how SERNIP functioned as follows. New techniques should be referred to this new body for a careful assessment as to whether or not this was a technique that could be recommended to trusts and purchasers for widespread implementation, or whether it needed further refinement or proper controlled trial assessment, or whether it was found wanting.

It is clear that at least for new surgical procedures, and even for highly qualified professionals, a proven competence will be required before the patient is exposed to unnecessary risk. *Should not similar procedures be required of the healthcare professional in the prescribing, administration or dispensing of new drugs?* And for the trainee or junior doctor, the use of all drugs is a new or relatively new experience. *Surely they require the greatest assistance and advice of all.* To expose patients to the unnecessary risk of an unsupervised learning curve becomes increasingly difficult to distinguish from reckless behaviour and negligence. The conclusions of the above report, chaired by Professor Wood, are surely correct. And the recommendations become even more urgent if Mr Dussek's comments that some consultants have been reluctant to seek advice from their colleagues have substance (providing a regrettable role model for junior staff), and that truncated periods of training (i.e. 'Calman trainees') may produce junior staff who require even more help.

Secondly, the lack of guidance by the GMC on the core component of the course *may* have resulted in the construction of different curricula by the various medical schools. Therefore graduates from different universities may have a different knowledge and competency base. This creates uncertainty and becomes problematic for a future employer who may increasingly require evidence of a specific core knowledge base, competences and a fitness for purpose. This relates directly to the accountability of medical education, which is of pressing importance and provides a major challenge.[51] A crucial feature in such deliberations is the positioning of the patient 'centre stage' in the new NHS.[52]

Thirdly, the dissolution of specialities within a broader and unproven educational imperative precludes an external assessment or understanding of an individual student's knowledge of pharmacology, biochemistry or other disciplines. Rothman[53] has elegantly expressed the problem as follows:

> 'How much science is enough? In a problem-based environment that consists primarily of clinical problems selected to reflect the spectrum of common medicine, and ordered to respect one of a variety of views concerning the optimum path from novice to expert, can it be assumed that:
> a. the basic knowledge required to effectively address these problems can be learned in the process of addressing these same problems.
> b coherent, useful and reasonably enduring structures of basic science knowledge will emerge as a result of this process.
> c a body of basic science knowledge sufficient for the needs of soon to be encountered clinical training and clinical practice will also emerge.
> d motivation and skills that will allow the continued renewal of this basic knowledge resource will be developed.

Fourthly, there is no evidence that problem-based learning results in greater effectiveness of knowledge acquisition or clinical skills.[53,54] Even its supporters admit that the benefits appear to evolve around an enhanced work environment for students and faculty,[55,56] and that it is time to rethink the promise of problem-based learning for the acquisition of basic knowledge and clinical skills, and to move on.[53,57] Furthermore, Schmidt[46] has recently questioned many of the assumptions underlying self-directed learning. Thus:

> the direction that learning takes in these curricula is only to a limited extent in the hands of the student, the skills acquired do

not visibly transfer to professional practice, and the importance of the skills for professional practice is possibly somewhat overrated by those who preach educational innovation.

However, Schmidt would probably consider that the primary pedagogic attraction of problem-based learning is that it supports the development of teamworking and valuing the role of others. This helps to meet the NHS Plan objective of 'identifying shared learning opportunities', but is not the best method of teaching facts and figures. It is emphasised that although student-directed learning may have uncertain long-term consequences, in its own right it has immediate and sizeable cognitive and motivational effects and is used as an important but not overly dominant feature of many degree courses. Time and experience will show whether problem-based learning has created a satisfactory beginning for the development of a competent physician.

However, time is not available to hospitals, which have an immediate duty of care to the patient, and where the moral, professional and legal problems transcend the luxury of educational theory. Consider the conclusions reached by Leape and colleagues,[58] Dean and colleagues,[59] Wilson and colleagues,[60] the Cambridgeshire Health Authority inquiry into methotrexate toxicity,[61] and the report on the prevention of intrathecal medication errors,[49] where a basic cause of medication error was a lack of knowledge (of some of the most elementary principles of pharmacology and therapeutics), and where some prescribers reported 'no training in drug dosing or in the practicalities of prescribing'.

Clearly, and particularly within the perspective of increasing litigation and in a culture where all healthcare staff and patients will be expected to report errors, hospitals cannot expose patients to clinical staff of unknown competence.

The second dilemma

This relates to the proposals in the NHS Plan, published in July 2000, to reduce the length of the medical degree from five to four years for undergraduate entry programmes and from four- to three-year accelerated courses for graduate entry, in order to produce more doctors in a shorter time period.[62] The BMA strongly believes that graduate courses can be effectively implemented if the appropriate level of funding is provided. However, with regard to a truncation of the undergraduate course, the BMA believes that it is imperative that all of the courses lead to a defined standard of achievement, and that evidence is needed to establish whether 'fitness for practice' can be successfully achieved for some doctors at an earlier age, how accelerated undergraduate programmes will affect the stress levels of medical students, and whether the PRHO year may have to be increased to two years in order to fulfil the EU requirements of 5500 hours of theoretical and practical instruction for the basic medical training.[63] Experience in hospital and general practice is vitally important for the inculcation and refinement of clinical skills. The proposal of a potential reduction in the training programme has been met with consternation at the threat of a potential decline in clinical competence.

The third dilemma

This relates to issues of multiprofessional education. One reason for these 'top-down' initiatives[64] is to facilitate integrated care through professional integration. The delivery of an effective clinical agenda in acute and primary care requires that the diverse and expert professional knowledge and skills of staff are brought together in cohesive teams.[65] The theme of interprofessional learning has been emphasised for the care of particular client groups, with the focus on post-qualifying education for professionals.[66,67] This is quite different to the recommendations of the Schofield Report,[68] where a new 'generic carer' was suggested to replace nurses, and a common foundation programme provided for all future healthcare professionals. It is also different to the recommendation in the Bristol Royal Infirmary Inquiry, which suggested that under the heading 'competent healthcare professionals':

> 72 *Medical schools, schools of nursing and management schools should be encouraged to develop joint courses. Future healthcare professionals must work in multidisciplinary teams; shared learning should therefore begin as soon as possible. A common curriculum for the first year of undergraduate education of all healthcare professionals should be developed through a pilot project.*[69]

Although it is very important that healthcare professionals work together (*see* pages 247 and 258), the merits of teaching undergraduate medical students, biomedical science students, physiotherapists, diagnostic radiographers, therapeutic radiographers, nurses and others in a single group are unproven.[70–72] Teaching basic sciences to students with disparate backgrounds (with regard to prior learning), interests and learning styles within a single group is certainly a major challenge to the teacher in terms of engaging the students and maintaining their individual attention. Not infrequently it results in informal remedial teaching of the disadvantaged groups by concerned staff, or over-teaching of others.[73] This is quite distinct from important attempts to ensure that healthcare staff will work together to meet patient needs by joint training for all health professionals in communication skills, valuing each others' roles, ethics and NHS principles.[74] However, a pilot project on shared learning between nursing and medical undergraduate students while on placement confirmed the complexities of organising and delivering a shared learning programme across differing curricula.[75]

But Leinster, Dean of the new medical school at the University of East Anglia, is reported to provide a different perspective.[76] He suggests a radically new curriculum to reflect the time that will come when the terms 'doctor' and 'nurse' will be obsolete, and where health professionals will be judged not by their labels but by their competencies. He has argued that as the boundaries between the professions merge, so must their education, and criticised the GMC 1993 curriculum as 'irrelevant and encouraged superficial learning'. What the modern medical graduate needs is the ability to 'access, evaluate and use new information'. It is anticipated that the curriculum will be problem based and well positioned to develop multiprofessional learning. Also of interest is the requirement for academic staff to spend half their time teaching and half researching, which is intended to counter the impression that many universities regard teaching as the poor relation compared to research. A comparison of the competencies attained by students attending the University of East Anglia with those of students attending other universities is awaited with considerable interest.

Preserving and enhancing the level of the unique knowledge and skills base of nursing, medicine, pharmacy and all the other healthcare professions, while acknowledging their interdependence for the delivery of safe and co-ordinated care,[68,70,77] still represents the primary and challenging goal. A more balanced steering, although problematic, may come from the NHS Plan and the move towards Core Benchmarking Statements by the Quality Assurance Agency (*see* page 162).

The fourth dilemma

This is that many teachers in medical schools may be unaware of the extent of prescriber-related drug-induced adverse events and medication errors in the developed world of medical practice. Moreover, on the evidence that is available, it has not been acknowledged previously that *the single most frequently reported factor leading to medication errors is lack of knowledge.* Such information may be crucial for future course revision.

For example, in an attempt to gain a greater understanding of the reasons for non-optimal prescribing, Boreham and colleagues[78] applied error analysis techniques to errors made by final-year medical students in a classroom experiment based on a real-life case that involved adjusting a patient's phenytoin dosage in order to achieve better control of seizures. *Within this teaching paradigm, the root cause of errors was the lack of a knowledge base which integrated scientific knowledge with clinical know-how.* The authors indicated that the study raises important questions about the design of the medical curriculum:

> *First, the techniques of process-tracing, knowledge elicitation and error analysis offer significant insights into students' failure to acquire cognitive skill. They provide a way of relating what knowledge students have acquired to the clinical reasoning strategies they follow, and thence to the effectiveness or otherwise of their medical decisions. Thus they can serve as powerful tools for developing medical education. Second, the results draw attention to the need*

for a thorough understanding of basic medical science. Some con-
temporary medical educators query the emphasis traditionally
placed on learning the basic medical sciences as subjects in their
own right. However, most of the hazardous dose recommendations
were apparently associated with a poor understanding of the phar-
macokinetics of phenytoin. This suggests that, although clinical
reasoning on the basis of scientific knowledge alone can generate
error because scientific generalisations might not indicate the action
needed in individual cases, when science is used in appropriate
combination with clinical know-how, the greater the students'
scientific understanding, the less the chance of hazardous prescrib-
ing. The use of knowledge of the basic and clinical sciences clearly
relies on the retrieval of relevant information and an understanding
of its use.

It would be of considerable interest to develop the model in other therapeutic areas in order to investigate further the importance of basic science to safe medical practice.

Within the above perspectives the reader may wish to consider the proposal of the Royal Australian College of General Practitioners for the weightings to define professional competence, subject to a major review every five years:[79]

1   cognitive skills (66%: divided into recall of knowledge, 14%; interpretive skills, 18%; problem solving, 34%)
2   affective (interpersonal) skills (26%)
3   psychomotor (manual and perceptual) skills (8%).

Review of *Tomorrow's Doctors* and bench marking for medicine

It is not known whether the present changes in medical education have contributed to medication errors in the last decade. The worst-case scenario would be that medication and other errors continue at present levels or increase. In July 2001, the GMC's Education Committee commenced a consultation exercise with Deans of Medicine, Royal Medical Colleges, patient organisations and others on a review of *Tomorrow's Doctors*, with new recommendations on undergraduate medical education. The recommendations do not appear to represent a major change of direction from the 1993 document, which 'continues to avoid all reference to traditional subjects and disciplines'.[80,81] The Quality Assurance Agency has also instigated a consultation for medicine benchmarking statements.[82] Both consultation documents provide a valuable opportunity for further debate on medical education.

This could include a reflection on the basic ethos of course design and the logistics of its teaching. For example, the consultation document includes a significant new section on the inclusion of complementary and alternative medicines within future courses. Certainly society has a major interest in and use for such procedures and products (*see* page 236). However, it is not clear that all schools of medicine, pharmacy, nursing and other disciplines even have the necessary expertise to teach the courses (*see* page 236). Natural products have long been the focus of pharmacognosy and phytochemistry. However, this particular discipline has rarely featured as a major research area, and inevitably the relentless pressures of the research agenda on all UK universities have generally driven academic appointment committees to prioritise and support existing research strengths rather than potential teaching needs. Indeed, there has been a quite deliberate intention to focus the entire research strengths of some departments on a very restricted locus of interests. The consequences of this for the expertise required (or neglected) for teaching require urgent debate.

It would be extremely unfortunate if fundamental inadequacies in under-graduate course design were perceived to contribute to patient injury, disability and death. In addition, the QAA has recently indicated that universities also will have to take full responsibility for the quality of their students' work placement or study-abroad programmes. It is designed to ensure that all student placements have explicit learning outcomes.[83] This is a major initiative and it will be subject to much discussion.

Pharmacology teaching to pharmacy students

The new academic four-year pharmacy degree course

In 1997, the UK schools of pharmacy welcomed the first intake of students to the new four academic year pharmacy degree courses. In some schools of pharmacy the course integrates the academic studies with two six-month periods of professional training within a 5-year degree programme. The three academic year course had been in existence for over 35 years, and there was concern that the increases in knowledge in the physical, chemical, biological, medical and social sciences, together with those of information technology, were not being fully addressed in the pharmacy curriculum.

Although this is a common difficulty in the teaching of most vocational degree subjects, pharmacy was fortunate that the Accreditation Body for the UK undergraduate degree programmes, the Royal Pharmaceutical Society of Great Britain, was insistent upon, and championed the extension of the course to four academic years. The Indicative Syllabus prepared by the Education Division of the Society provides the bedrock of the knowledge base on which to build future competencies. The vast majority of the full curriculum and not less than 50% of the final year is core content. Thus it ensures the same basic teaching and learning experience in the different schools of pharmacy, and graduates with a predictable level of knowledge and skills. At least 35% of the curriculum deals with the actions and uses of drugs in medicine, irrespective of specialisation in the final year. Students are encouraged to take responsibility for their own learning both within the degree course and as a basis for later continuing education and professional development.

There was much discussion within pharmacy schools and the profession about the nature of the new course. There was also acknowledgement of the rapidly changing role of the pharmacist in both primary and secondary healthcare. A crucial feature was to introduce new material for these projected roles while maintaining a sensible balance between the scientific and professional components of the course. The outcome for pharmacy students is an education which provides one of the most detailed learning experiences of the isolation, characterisation, analysis, formulation and design of medicines, their manufacture and use to be found in any undergraduate course.

Within the QAA's Subject Benchmark Statement for pharmacy,[84] the programme outcomes match those set out in the degree descriptor for a qualification at Masters (M) level – that is:

> *a critical awareness of current problems and/or new insights, much of which is at, or informed by, the forefront of their academic discipline or area of professional practice; a comprehensive under-standing of techniques applicable to their own research; an ability to evaluate critically current research and advanced scholarship.*

The defining feature of the pharmacist has always been the knowledge and skills required for the preparation and supply of effective medicines, and advice on their safe use. The development of relevant undergraduate and, increasingly, postgraduate courses and experiences will enable the relevant knowledge and skills base to deliver the elements of pharmaceutical care and medicines management for the patient.

More immediately, the course was designed to provide students with a knowledge and understanding of aspects of drug action and therapeutics to ensure their fitness for preregistration practice. With regard to the comments of the Cambridge Inquiry, some courses have modules which focus exclusively on infectious and neoplastic disease, to reflect the frequently problematic nature of the drugs used in the treatment of the latter.

Most schools of pharmacy use lectures, tutorials, small-group workshops and practical classes to optimise the teaching and individual learning experience. For example, the modules for understanding the pharmacology of drug action may employ practical classes in which the students themselves take different medicines to reinforce the theory. For example, diuretic drugs are archetypal medicines that are believed to be 'safe', yet have been consistently responsible for a significant number of emergency hospital admissions for over 35 years. The students take different types of diuretic drugs and measure their urine output, sodium and potassium levels to demonstrate their very powerful but different effects. The measurement of basal levels of sodium and potassium demonstrates how little potassium is available for inappropriate excretion and so how easily, even with normal doses of diuretic drugs, the patient can become hypokalaemic, with all the attendant and serious adverse consequences of this condition.

Equally importantly, the experience facilitates the retention of basic and important pharmacological knowledge and principles and provides the basis for student analyses of case studies and problem-based activities in small-group and tutorial sessions. The integrative teaching and student-centred learning are designed to enhance safe, effective and authoritative understanding of drug treatment and advice.

However, it remains curious that, having produced a graduate in a school of pharmacy, medicine or some other health discipline, the academic world remains in ignorance of the relevance of the academic attainment or degree classification/grade to the future professional competence of the student. In summary, having produced a graduate, the academic world has had no objective measure of his or her professional success (or possible failure), and therefore the success or otherwise of their educational programmes. However, this situation may now change, and it is related directly to attempts to improve academic provision, accountability and patient safety.

Holding the undergraduate courses in healthcare accountable for their provision

There are four established or emergent factors that will assist higher education in enhancing the quality of its provision, and in measuring the success of its undergraduate courses:

1   the professional/accreditation bodies
2   the employer
3   the student
4   the law (*see* Chapter 15).

The professional/accreditation bodies

The General Medical Council (GMC), the Royal Pharmaceutical Society and other professional bodies have well-established roles to protect patients and guide clinical professionals by:

• identifying and assuring the educational standards required for entry to the register
• keeping an up-to-date register of qualified professional staff
• issuing guidance to the public and the profession on the standards expected of registered professionals
• dealing with clinical staff whose fitness to practice is in doubt.

Although the UK Council of Health Regulators may play an important role in the regulation of professional bodies, self-regulation can reflect the important differences between professions. Using statutory instruments and persuasion, the accreditation bodies govern the content and influence the resourcing of the undergraduate courses. This is a well-established role and, for example, the Royal Pharmaceutical Society has a proven record of refusing to accredit courses that do not achieve the required standards.[85] The Society also has a Preregistration Examination which all pharmacy graduates are required to pass for registration. This provides an effective mechanism for ensuring that the periods of academic *plus* clinical training have been adequate for registration.

All professional bodies are carefully reviewing their codes of ethics to ensure contemporary and respectable standards to fulfil the Government's requirements for health self-regulatory bodies. An extract from the Pharmaceutical Society's Code of Ethics relevant to key responsibilities of the pharmacist, professional competence and supervision of trainees can be found in Appendix 7. The revision seeks to identify through standards of professional performance the personal responsibilities associated with the roles that pharmacists wish to undertake. The membership has welcomed these initiatives and the introduction of an increased lay involvement within the perspective of consistency of regulation between the healthcare professions. The Society's Disciplinary Committee also ajudicates on allegations of pharmacy malpractice within the perspective of the revised Code of Ethics.[86]

In addition, the GMC has revised its guidance to the profession. The GMC Professional Conduct Committee considers offences of 'serious professional misconduct' (the legal phrase which has framed all allegations of misconduct against doctors) to include cases of negligence and 'the public has higher expectations of doctors and members of other self-governing professions. Their governing bodies are under a corresponding duty to protect the public against the genially incompetent as well as the deliberate wrongdoers' (*David Noel McCandless v The General Medical Council*, 1995).[87]

Until recently, the hearings at the GMC were related to conduct rather than to delivery of clinical care to patients. The case of Dr Oliver Archer in 1983 was perhaps a turning point and a catalyst for change. Despite being very concerned about the lack of treatment of a seriously ill boy, and acknowledging that the standard was unacceptable, serious professional misconduct remained unfound.[88]

In 1985, in the *Blue Book* (the Council's guidance to the profession), two paragraphs related to standards of care (the first since the establishment of the GMC by the Medical Act of 1858), and the subsequent introduction of new legal procedures and a new allegation of 'seriously deficient performance' culminated in the publication *Good Medical Practice* in 1995, which set out for the first time the duties and attributes of a good doctor (*see* Appendix 7). The new performance procedures came into force in 1997, and provide a solid expectation of a high level of clinical care. Details of the GMC's fitness-to-practise procedures can be found in Townsend,[88] and personal learning plans are being developed across the whole spectrum of medical education, as well as continuing professional development for experienced clinicians.[89]

However, it remains an uncomfortable time for the GMC. Issues of its governance[90,91] or its plans for revalidation[92] create a sensitive balance between the interests of the public, the profession (who pay for the GMC) and government. The medical profession has always believed in self-regulation. The question raised is whether or not this will continue.[93] In addition, the Consumers' Association has called for an even further increase in lay representation on disciplinary committees. It has also called for the GMC to significantly improve its handling of complaints and to have powers to strike doctors off for life. Williams, Principal Health Researcher for the Consumers' Association and *Health Which?* stated:

> *The GMC has got a long way to go before public confidence will be fully restored in its ability to put patients before doctors. These two measures are small steps down the long path towards a regulatory body that can deliver for patients.*[94]

Rising expectations by patients and consumer organisations, proposals for all professionals of regular revalidation, and personal and peer audit will all facilitate progression to show a fitness for practice. Most importantly, all such activities that are designed to improve the quality of care should act to reduce errors and complaints. *It is logical to introduce these philosophies at the beginning of undergraduate education.*[89] Barach and Moss emphasise that safety is a patient's right and the obligation of all healthcare professionals, and they ask the question 'How long, though, should we wait before all medical schools and training programmes include safety of patients as a central objective?'.[95] Even so, it will remain a major challenge to predict poor performance before the occurrence of unsafe acts and unprofessional behaviour.

There has been no known interaction between the accreditation bodies and higher education either to identify or to prevent error-inducing behaviour before the event, or indeed after the occurrence of serious errors in practice. Yet it would be of interest if an audit of academic and professional profiling found a positive correlation between poor professional standards or incompetence, and a particular level of prior academic performance/conduct at graduation. If this was demonstrated, it might aid the development of a constructive response to the low-level performer. This might then involve a strengthening of academic support and more focused attempts to assist with and improve the performance of the student who may develop into the professional with difficulties or at risk.

The employer

It is anticipated that, ideally, employers of graduate healthcare staff should have well established training and assessment programmes for the clinical tuition of junior staff. This would ensure that the knowledge and skills base of such programmes could become ever more precisely defined to ensure a smooth transition from undergraduate tuition through graduation and clinical training to professional competence. It would also provide a level of protection for the trainee as well as the employer in terms of potential litigation. Moreover, assessment at the commencement of training provides a direct measure of graduate competence and prior tuition that can be related to individual academic institutions. This may become even more urgent if the 'Russell Group' of universities (the universities of Birmingham, Bristol, Cambridge, Edinburgh, Glasgow, Leeds, Liverpool, Manchester, Newcastle upon Tyne, Nottingham, Oxford, Sheffield, Southampton and Warwick, Imperial College of Science, Technology and Medicine, King's College London, the London School of Economics and Political Science, and University College London) are successful in demanding the abolition of all teaching-quality assessment, in defiance of ministers and students. It is reported that this group is stating that quality inspectors should rely only 'on the outputs of internal audit processes'.[96] In response, the president of the National Union of Students is reported as stating that:

> The NUS is appalled at the suggestions from the Russell Group to abolish all forms of teaching-quality assurance in higher education. Students who are now contributing more than £1.6 billion to the sector need to feel confident that their expectations of a course will be fully met and that there are effective quality assurance procedures in place.[96]

The Minister for Higher Education recently told vice-chancellors that they 'need to think about how the needs of students and employers are being met', and added that she would be looking at the consultation to ensure a balance between accountability and inspection.[96]

In a preliminary study, McPherson and colleagues[97] measured pharmacy preregistration trainee baseline clinical competence in the South Thames NHS Trusts at the start of the preregistration year using a questionnaire and the Objective Structured Clinical Examination (OSCE). The objective was to link the level of clinical competence to key characteristics of the graduate and their past experience. The Royal Pharmaceutical Society precisely defines a number of competences that all preregistration trainees must achieve in order to be eligible for registration as pharmacists.[98]

There was a significant positive correlation between the classification of undergraduate degree and OSCE performance. Due to the small sample sizes it was not possible to identify relationships between OSCE performance and specific schools of pharmacy or past experiences. However, this situation will change with the assessment of more students and an increase in the size of the database. Therefore comment on the relative performance of an individual school of pharmacy should finally prove possible.

The OSCE performance can provide a useful formative assessment technique to guide preregistration training. For example, the overall level of clinical competence was low and the candidates experienced difficulty in mathematical manipulations relevant to pharmacokinetic equations. A common error was one of magnitude (e.g. a recommended loading dose of gentamicin ranged from 3 mg, an ineffective dose causing serious patient harm, to 3 g, a high toxic dose again causing patient harm). This highlighted a concern that many graduates do not question or consider their answers within a practical context. They appeared to *lack knowledge of the consequences of the doses that they calculate* (that is, the patient could die from either untreated infection or drug-induced toxicity).

A deficiency in the numerical skills of students has also been noted by the Royal Pharmaceutical Society in its preregistration examination and it is further developing numerically based questions in order to determine more thoroughly each candidate's numerical competency.[99] Physicians make similar numerical errors.[100] However, for pharmacists the errors are more serious since, first, their advice on drug doses is frequently sought by ward staff, and second, there is no check on their errors other than by the patient or nurse. A more formal dissemination of knowledge between academia, the accreditation bodies and the employers with respect to such problems may lead to a concerted effort by all three groups to improve professional competence.

McPherson and colleagues conclude that *their observations provide clear implications for syllabus and curriculum development teams at schools of pharmacy, and that future studies will compare baseline with end-of-year performance.*

Battles and Shea,[101] in analysing the errors of medical student trainees in the UK and the USA, reached the same conclusion:

> *in each case, the analysis revealed in striking clarity deficiencies of educational content and problems of program structure . . . doing a root-cause analysis in conjunction with a near-miss event-reporting system can be a valuable source of documented information to guide needed educational and system changes to graduate medical educa-tion programs.*

The student

All university courses have some form of Staff Student Liaison Committee which regularly seeks feedback and acts on student concerns. This formal feedback may not happen from the preregistration year, particularly if the students have physically left the university campus. Yet this is a crucial feature of training, and comments from students provide an authoritative perspective. The past president of the British Pharmaceutical Students' Association commented on the preregistration year for pharmacy students:

> *In recent years much effort has been put into updating the com-petencies within the preregistration experience. We need to ask whether the pre-reg year is the best way to identify, give, monitor and provide feed back on professional training. The people who are least happy with the preregistration year are the very people it is*

designed to help – pharmacy graduates. So why are they unhappy, what can be done to change this and who's responsible for the change? There are Society guidelines for the recruitment of students, but there seems to be little enforcement of these rules. The Society tries hard to control what is learnt during the pre-reg year, but it seems unwilling to extend this control to include dealing with problems. It is not just the students who have difficulties: many tutors are faced with intricate situations with little in the way of a formalised system to back them up. Do students know what they should expect from a placement and how to take action if it's not delivering? With students investing so much money on training to become a pharmacist, it is hardly surprising that they are starting to expect a lot more from today's preregistration year. The tutor is probably one of the most influential people in a young pharmacist's development, yet the support and training they get is minimal. It takes time, experience and academic training to become a lecturer at university, yet it is the pre-reg tutors who are relied on to produce the finished product. This begs the question: 'Are tutors the best way to deliver preregistration training?' I think that they have an important role but what I would like to see is the on-the-job experience gained during a shorter placement brought back into the universities, where it can be examined and put into context by the trainee. A split pre-reg year such as the one offered by Bradford (where sandwich students also have an academic tutor), goes some way towards addressing this problem. I also question the ability of the pre-reg year to produce pharmacists that are fit for the purpose. If we are to take on the roles in Pharmacy in the Future, *then surely these should be covered in undergraduate education and pre-reg training? It is time for a common sense revolution in pre-registration training.*[102]

The problems faced by medical students in the integration of education with service needs, clinical practice and tuition have also proved particularly challenging, and these are reviewed separately in Chapter 14.

Chapter 14

The problematic nature of the preregistration period of general clinical training

Summary: Medical students and the preregistration house officer (PRHO) year

- Prior to 1953 in the UK, medical students entered medical practice straight from medical school.
- Subsequently, a one-year period of compulsory and supervised general clinical training in hospital was introduced. At present this must include 4 months in medicine and 4 months in surgery, and may include 4 months in general practice.
- Theoretically, the clinical duties of medical students were supposed to include *an important educational component and supervision by senior medical staff.*
- The reality of preregistration was described as 'dominated by service work (frequently of an inappropriate nature) to the exclusion of education' with the result that 'the large amount of practical training gained in the preregistration year with little teaching or direct supervision may result in confidence without competence' and lack of appropriate skills.
- Indeed, there was clear evidence that many PRHOs were effectively encouraged to teach themselves, with hours of duty ranging in one study from 83 to 101 hours per week. This is widely considered to be unsafe and a most regrettable if not unpleasant start to a clinical career.
- The GMC have introduced clear recommendations to improve the quality of general clinical training in *The New Doctor.*
- The essential requirements for improvements in the preregistration period have been described as:
  1 protected time for teaching by senior staff
  2 the continuous availability of senior staff for supervision and support
  3 a well-designed rotational scheme for training

> 4 effective formative assessment
> 5 enhancement of the teaching skills of consultants and senior-grade staff
> 6 regular appraisal of posts by the postgraduate dean and the doctors in training.

Introduction

In the early 1950s in the UK, it had become apparent that the increasing complexity of medical practice was causing concern that medical graduates could still enter independent practice straight from medical school. In 1953, a one-year period of compulsory and supervised general clinical training in hospital was introduced. This has continued in the UK with a medical education ending with a year as a preregistration house officer (PRHO) that provides the general clinical experience (at present this must include four months in medicine and four months in surgery, and may include four months in general practice), which is required before full registration with the GMC.

The educational component of the PRHO year is acknowledged in the statutory responsibility that the universities have for this year. However, the PRHO year has had an increasingly troubled existence for the junior doctors. These problems have related to the excessive workloads of the service provision, the frequently inappropriate nature of the work, the frequent absence of educational provision and the fact that there is little if any direct clinical supervision.

PRHO workloads, inappropriate duties, lack of educational component and inappropriate supervision

In 1990, Leslie and colleagues[1] determined the hours, volume and type of work of PRHOs in the Royal Infirmary, Edinburgh's largest teaching hospital. Information was collected in February 1989 by independent observers and not by self-recorded and exaggerated allegations.

The following findings emerged.

- The hours of duty ranged from 83 to 101 hours each week.
- The longest period of duty was 58 hours.
- Between 50% and 71% of house officers' time was spent on patient-oriented

duties during the day. This decreased to between 21% and 53% during the night.
- It was concluded that more house officers were needed and, as a result, three extra PRHOs were appointed. This reduced the period of duty to an average of 72 hours a week.

One year later, in a juniors' hours-of-work survey it was reported that one in four junior doctors were working over 83 hours a week.[2] In the same year (1991), a PRHO and a senior house officer were convicted of manslaughter following a therapeutic tragedy. The legal correspondent of the *British Medical Journal* wrote:

> *Bringing the full weight of the criminal law to bear on two fledgling doctors will do little to remedy a system which lets juniors loose on patients with too little training, too little support, and too little sleep.*[3]

In 1992, Richards, on behalf of the Council of Deans of United Kingdom Medical Schools and Faculties,[4] prepared a paper entitled 'Educational improvement of the preregistration period of general clinical training'. It was designed to encourage debate and noted that house officer posts were no longer acceptable for a variety of reasons, including the following:

- *long hours of far more demanding work than before*
- *inadequate support resulting in much time spent on inappropriate duties and on tasks such as audit*
- *a far greater and faster throughput of patients*
- *higher expectations by patients of their doctors and by doctors and their families of their personal lives*
- *educationally the preregistration is also unsatisfactory and has recently been described as 'dominated by service work to the virtual exclusion of education' with the result that 'the large amount of practical training gained in the preregistration year with little teaching or direct supervision may result in confidence without competence'.*[5]

It was also noted that:

> *education is likely to be even less adequate if, as expected, the balance of basic medical education shifts from training to education, becoming less comprehensive and factual and more intellectually stimulating. Much is and can only be learned by experience. But experience needs to be supplemented by an appropriately designed programme of education and assessment, commonplace at this stage of education in the United States, but rare in the United Kingdom, and for which house officers would have little time and less energy.*

To ease the problems, the Council of Deans made the following proposals.

- The preregistration period of general clinical training should be extended to two years, with the main aim of improving practical supervision and education.
- On qualification the new doctor will be appointed as one of a pair of first- and second-year house officers to a post in which each will have appropriate individual professional responsibility for a share of the patients.
- The second-year house officer will provide immediate supervision of the first-year house officer.
- The registrar and consultant would continue to be in support, subject to commitments in outpatient clinics, theatres and outside the hospital.

The paper achieved its objective of encouraging a vigorous debate (*see BMJ* article).[6] For example, Andrews, Chairman of the Medical Students Group, stated that:

> *The educational aims are laudable. It surprises people to learn that the preregistration year is supposed to have an educational content; my recently qualified colleagues do not recognise this aspect . . . . Being supervised by somebody with, at best, no more experience than at present (half the experience twice the time yields the same final experience) does not improve the quality of care.*

Bahrami, of the Department of Postgraduate Medical Education, University of Leeds, was equally direct:

> *Although there are some superficial attractions in Peter Richards's proposed changes for the preregistration period of general clinical training, the root cause of the problem has not been addressed. The reasons for dissatisfaction with the preregistration year are mainly lack of supervision and training and excessive hours of work. The proposal as it stands, having acknowledged these problems, leaves the responsibility for supervision and training in the hands of another junior doctor, who would have a mere six months' more experience in the post. Clearly, the effectiveness of such training and the wisdom of such an arrangement are open to debate . . . . The more crucial requirement that any supervision must be provided by the consultant and senior-grade staff has been made conditional on their availability and other service commitments, including work outside the hospital.*
>
> *In effect, there will be hardly any change from the present situation, except the remote possibility of a small reduction in the number of hours worked each week . . . . I believe that the proposal is superficial and irrelevant.*
>
> *The essential requirements for any improvement in the preregistration period must include at least the following:*
>
> - *protected time for teaching by senior staff*
> - *the continuous availability of senior staff for supervision and support at all times*

- *a well-designed rotational scheme of training during the preregistration period*
- *effective formative assessment*
- *enhancement of the teaching skills of consultants and senior-grade staff*
- *regular appraisal of posts by the postgraduate dean or the dean's representatives, or both, and the doctors in training.*

The proposals from the Council of Deans reflected the culture of an earlier decade. The reader may be surprised that those with a legal responsibility for the preregistration year could, in effect, advocate that the students were to teach themselves. However, shadowing junior or senior colleagues may act to reduce anxiety, increase confidence and enhance social and communication skills. Moreover, there are genuine concerns that European directives may actually restrict the hours worked to a degree that may adversely limit the learned knowledge and skills base. However, that being the case, it is even more important that the students derive maximum benefit within the limited time available. In this respect, experienced teachers and tutors may provide an optimal learning experience.

For example, would the reader be prepared to drive their car if it had recently had the brakes, steering and suspension serviced or repaired by a junior and unqualified mechanic with little or unknown skills and experience who had received instruction from a similarly unqualified junior? Should patients not receive a standard of care at least as high as that afforded to their cars?

It is hardly surprising that the recommendations of the GMC in 1992 stated that:

> *The goodwill of consultants and of principals in general practice to be appointed as educational supervisors is essential if house officers' expectations are to be fulfilled. This will be forthcoming only if there is full discussion between the universities and all concerned with the preregistration year, and a realisation by all of the importance of the year to the young doctor . . . . The educational supervisor should help with both professional and personal development and be aware of the PRHO's individual needs . . . provide feedback on their clinical progress . . . and should personally undertake, and not delegate, their tutorial functions.*[7]

This was followed by the publication of *The New Doctor* by the GMC in 1996, which includes detailed 'Recommendations on General Clinical Training made under Section 5 of the Medical Act 1983'.[8] There were eight key themes.

1 *General clinical training is the final year of basic medical education. Due regard must be paid to the educational needs of PRHOs, who are learning to become doctors by providing a service.*
2 *These recommendations apply to the training of all PRHOs, regardless of the university from which they graduated.*

3 *All PRHOs need high-quality education and training, which includes proper clinical and educational supervision and appropriate provision for their welfare.*

4 *Those responsible for facilitating PRHO learning and assessing PRHO progress require training for and support in these roles.*

5 *Lines of accountability must be established by the universities with responsibility for overseeing the preregistration year, in conjunction with the providers of PRHO training. This will involve the postgraduate deans and clinical tutors, as well as the PRHOs' educational supervisors.*

6 *PRHOs for their part must demonstrate that by the end of the preregistration year they have made the clinical and educational progress required of a doctor who is to be fully registered with the GMC.*

7 *The GMC's guidance on good medical practice should underpin the work of PRHOs and the doctors from whom they learn.*

8 *These recommendations should be fully implemented by April 2000. The GMC will be monitoring progress towards that end, and will be looking to the universities, in consultation with health authorities and NHS trusts, to put in place the necessary arrangements.*

The 47-page document is essential reading for all PRHOs and those involved in their academic and clinical education. It provides a definitive understanding of what must be achieved, as well as a fundamental basis for the development of good medical practice without which improvements in patient safety and treatments will be difficult to achieve.

However, the reality of educating and training preregistration house officers was clearly a complex problem requiring sophisticated negotiating skills to secure a solution. Wilson[7] ascertained the opinions, attitudes and requirements of consultants responsible for preregistration house officers under the headings of professional details, present training arrangements, effectiveness of current training, and perceived help required for implementing the recommendations. The setting consisted of two teaching hospitals and nine district hospitals in Yorkshire involving 33 consultants (19 physicians and 14 surgeons). All of the hospitals held induction courses, but few of the consultants were personally involved. It was established that the traditional ward round with clinical meetings provided the main educational provision for house officers as a team activity. Only eight consultants held one-to-one teaching sessions or tutorials, and most consultants estimated that their total teaching time was less than 30 minutes a week. In total, 24 respondents stated that they delegated some of the responsibilities for house-officer teaching to other junior medical staff and to ward sisters. The apprenticeship experience was regarded by almost all of the consultants as the most powerful contribution to house-officer training. In response to the question 'How do you currently assess the effectiveness of your teaching?', 25 respondents replied that they did not, and only five actively sought feedback from their house officers. Although there was support for educational supervisors and the introduction of a structured educational programme, pressure on consultants to work faster and to participate in audit and management, coupled with a reduction in junior doctors' hours, were considered to mitigate against the educational developments.

There was wide agreement that house-officer training is unsatisfactory. Furthermore, consultants receive no training in educational methods. Most would welcome such training, but it was felt that there must be conceptual, contractual and financial changes to secure an educational role before the preregistration year could have a proper educational value.

In a review of the preregistration year, Lowry[9] noted that the GMC recommendations may all be worthy aims, but that:

> they are so far removed from the reality of most house officers' experiences as to be laughable. How is a consultant physician or surgeon in a busy hospital supposed to find time for the formal educational supervision suggested, much less the pastoral aspects? Who is going to train consultants in the necessary counselling and facilitating skills? Who will provide the cover for house officers attending their education sessions? Is it realistic to expect junior house officers to admit to their consultants that they are over-burdened when their career progression depends on getting a good reference? Unless some of these problems can be overcome, the GMC's recommendations will be impossible to implement.

The training of junior doctors and senior house officers was subsequently highlighted in a number of papers and reports in 1997–98 by Kelly and Murray,[10] the Royal Colleges[11] and the General Medical Council,[12] with progress in developing training programmes to improve junior doctor education.[13] However, within a high-workload environment there is:

> great reliance on individual doctors recognising their learning needs and making the most of educational opportunities . . . when the clinical situation and available time coincide. Co-operative learning occurs when small groups of trainees work together to maximise their own and each others' learning.[14,15] However, in a study of paediatric senior house officers, 19% did not have the opportunity to meet others; the reasons were quoted as being too busy, working in a shift system or no team meetings taking place.[14] Some of the junior doctors also mentioned having to work on their own with little consultant contact. The paediatric SHOs felt that the co-operative learning shown to occur was their main source of education, as one-to-one teaching did not often occur and, when it did, the educational content was minimal. Some of the SHOs also found there was little co-operation between junior and senior medical staff. Nevertheless, there was clear support and enthusiasm for co-operative learning

situations, since these provide quality education when compared with any service-based training experienced in their present posts.

The PRHO year and the inconstant acquisition of clinical skills

In a critical incidence study conducted in 1991, Calman and Donaldson[16] had also expressed concern about the lack of basic clinical skills of new medical graduates. It is instructive to review the progress that has been made since the mid-1990s.

Bax and Godfrey[17] identified a group of core clinical skills and found that 50% were learned before graduation and the remainder during the preregistration year. However, Jones and colleagues[18] have reported that even in a medical school with defined core skills and a new curriculum, difficulties remain apparent in the preparation of undergraduates for the preregistration house year. Subsequently, Goodfellow and Claydon[19] have described undergraduate medical training in the UK as follows:

> *Undergraduate medical training varies between medical schools but generally follows the recommendations set out in the General Medical Council document* Tomorrow's Doctors, *which portrays undergraduate training as the first step in a continuum of education. The document regards the endpoint of undergraduate training as the start of the preregistration year, and declares that newly qualified doctors must be well prepared for the responsibilities of house officers. The undergraduate course contains many components, but an essential part of the recommendations is the concept of a core content of knowledge and practical skills to be attained by all students. Regarding essential practical skills, the GMC recommendations specify only basic and advanced life support, venepuncture and insertion of an intravenous cannula. However, the document states that this is a restricted list and that medical schools should construct a list of those procedures in each of which they will require all students to have demonstrated competence by the time that they qualify.*

In an interesting development in 1999, a group of medical students at Sheffield University were reported to have expressed concern about their lack of clinical skills in the approach to their final examinations.[19] They were asked to nominate up to ten clinical skills which they felt would be used regularly during the house year and in which they should be competent. They identified eight tasks which had previously been selected by other authors as 'core skills'.[17] This information was used by Goodfellow and Claydon[19] to design a questionnaire to assess the adequacy of training that the medical students had

Table 14.1: The number and percentage of skills (in parentheses) performed by final-year medical students during their undergraduate years[19]

Skill	Range					Median
	0	1–4	5–20	21–40	>40	
Intravenous cannulation	0 (0)	11 (13)	44 (54)	31 (38)	14 (17)	5–20
Venepuncture	0 (0)	4 (5)	19 (23)	29 (35)	48 (59)	21–40
	Range					
	0	1–4	5–10	11–20	>20	
Rectal examination	5 (0)	70 (86)	19 (23)	4 (5)	2 (2)	1–4
	Range					
	0	1–2	3–10	11–20	>20	
Nasogastric tube	77 (94)	21 (26)	1 (1)	1 (1)	0 (0)	0
Suturing	34 (41)	28 (34)	29 (35)	6 (7)	4 (5)	1–2
Arterial blood gas	13 (16)	38 (46)	33 (40)	13 (16)	3 (4)	1–2
Catheter	321 (38)	40 (49)	25 (31)	3 (4)	0 (0)	1–2

Note: The questionnaire asked the students to quantify the numbers of each skill performed during the entire undergraduate course into ranges. The questionnaire was filled in by 122 students, representing 75% of the students sitting finals.

received. In addition, because of the increasing number of medico-legal issues surrounding needlestick injury, and the risk of disease transmission by this route, student recall of training with regard to the avoidance of such injury was also assessed.

The results showed that a substantial number of final-year students had little if any experience of some of the clinical skills listed in Table 14.1. For example, many had negligible experience of performing ECGs, and around 30% had never passed a urinary catheter. The investigation also showed that the skills assessed are in routine use by most house officers. In addition, the authors looked at the amount of training that house officers received after qualification. The data in Table 14.2 indicate that most house officers did not recall receiving any further training in the selected core skills. *It appeared that many practical skills are employed during the house-officer year despite inadequate training, and with no supervision to ensure correct technique. Of the eight skills studied, most had been performed very few times by the students at qualification. Less than half of the current preregistration house officers could recall training being given in any of the skills studied. There were no significant differences in house-officer training between teaching and district general hospitals. With*

Table 14.2: Percentage of house officers who recalled receiving training in a skill after qualification (numbers are shown in parentheses)[19]

Skill	Training recalled	Training given	Not answered
Intravenous cannulation	60 (50)	38 (32)	2 (2)
Venepuncture	79 (66)	19 (16)	2 (2)
Rectal examination	90 (76)	7 (6)	2 (2)
Nasogastric tube	84 (71)	14 (12)	1 (1)
Suturing	68 (51)	31 (26)	1 (1)
Arterial blood gas	85 (71)	14 (12)	1 (1)
Catheter	56 (47)	43 (36)	1 (1)
Electrocardiogram	80 (67)	19 (16)	1 (1)

Note: The questionnaire was filled in by 84 preregistration house officers who were within 2 weeks of finishing their house year. There were 68 house officers from teaching hospitals and 16 house officers from District General Hospitals; 37 house officers were from surgical specialities and 47 were from medical specialities.

regard to needlestick injuries, nearly two-thirds of preregistration house officers were unable to recall any training at either undergraduate or post-graduate level.

The original concerns expressed by the medical students towards the end of their undergraduate training seem to be borne out by the findings of this study. *The students had received clinical skills teaching in the traditional ward 'firm' setting, in which there was no clear time allocation for learning of specific skills and no documentation required. The students described the acquisition of skills as haphazard and random.* Although the 'core skills' had been previously identified at this institution,[17] the students had not received written information about these skills.

In their discussion, the authors noted that:

> *Each of the hospitals where the preregistration house officers worked had an induction programme, from two days to one week in duration. At the two teaching hospitals the induction courses included a clinical skills teaching session that included urinary catheterisation, intravenous cannulation, arterial blood sampling and electrocardiography. The District General Hospitals did not teach, on their induction courses, any of the core skills we studied. No hospital included documented formal needlestick training in its induction programme.*
>
> *We are not suggesting that Sheffield is worse than other schools in these respects; this kind of clinical 'firm' teaching has been the traditional way to impart both clinical knowledge and clinical skills in most medical schools throughout the UK. With the advent of new medical curricula and the development of skills-training centres,*

better methods of teaching may emerge . . . . The findings on rectal examination are of particular concern. Lack of experience in this part of complete examination of the patient may be explained partly by the current medico-legal climate, in which the public is increasingly resistant to medical student involvement. In addition, clinical experience as an undergraduate is known to depend on which clinical firm the students are attached to.[20] House officers who have not learned essential clinical skills may find the initial part of their preregistration house year especially taxing.[16] Although a large number of clinical skills are attained during the preregistration house year,[17] our survey indicates that few are taught formally . . . . What can be done to make the training of undergraduates and preregistration house officers closer to a continuum? Logbooks and skills laboratories for undergraduates (now used at Sheffield), and induction courses for house officers, could help. A logbook indicates that procedures have been completed, but it does not certify competence, and important details of patient interactions tend to be omitted. What of skills laboratories? These are well established in the UK and provide an environment for structured learning and feedback.[21] They do not offer 'real patient experience', but undergraduates find them helpful,[21] for example, with regard to objective structured clinical examinations.[22,23] We aim to assess the impact of a skills laboratory and logbooks in Sheffield by repeating the survey in two years' time. In our study no formal preregistration house-officer training in needlestick injury could be traced, and less than half of the preregistration house officers could recall any training being given. This is an important issue in view of the risks to healthcare workers from bloodborne pathogens in the workplace, especially since acquisition of a transmissible pathogen may preclude further work in the health service. One study indicates that about 50% of ward-based doctors sustain a needlestick injury in two years, and that the risk is similar for clinical medical students.[24] According to Hettiaratchy and colleagues,[25] most junior doctors in the UK do not routinely wear gloves for venepuncture, and only 17.5% of needlestick injuries are reported. This matter requires urgent attention at both undergraduate and house-officer levels.

However, the concerns extend beyond the UK.

In Australia, a survey by Spike and Veitch[26] in 1988 of sixth-year medical students in Queensland revealed that only two out of 47 procedural skills considered to be essential for general practice had been performed alone by 80% or more students, and six of the essential skills had not been performed by more than 80% of students. In a later study by Roche and colleagues[27] of the perceptions by trainees of the quality and extent of training received for interactional and technical skills in all teaching hospitals in New South Wales, this was reported to be generally poor in terms of time and educational strategies used. Fewer than one in three trainees considered themselves to be competent in interactional skills, and one in three trainees doubted their competence in technical skills.

In America, 60 medical schools participated in a survey on how they taught clinical procedures to medical students prior to their clinical rotations.[28] More than 75% of the schools offered nothing other than an introduction to phlebotomy. Koenig and Chu[29] reported a study of fourth-year medical students' knowledge of the protective equipment required to safely complete ten common clinical procedures, in which the mean percentage of correct answers given by the responding students was 67%. In a survey of third-year medical students about their experience of 18 skills that are generally recognised as required learning for the third-year surgical clerkship, experience with 10 out of the 18 clinical skills was significantly below the overall competency level required.[30]

In an assessment of the adequacy of training and supervision of interns in Norway, substantial variation was found in skills among respondents from different hospitals and various emergency medical skills. Half of the 'medical' house officers and 65% of the 'surgical' house officers reported that they had received no introductory information or supervision before attending for hospital duties.[31] Two-thirds did not participate in an educational programme, 80% did not receive feedback on their work, and most house officers received no evaluation of their work at all.[32]

The above investigations provide a valuable learning experience for medical education and clinical tuition, and they reveal a serious problem. A significant number of medical students have been receiving an unacceptable level of educational or clinical tuition. This immediately opens to question the competence and safety of the practitioner, with the risk to his or her professional reputation, the reputation of the academic and clinical institutions and, most important of all, the safety of the patient. It is not surprising that there has been much debate about improving the PRHO year and, in particular, about how best to prepare students for their clinical role.

First, it is likely that most medical schools are attempting or have already been able to establish the essential clinical, professional and personal skills that are required on graduation, and secondly there is a need to assess whether and when these skills have been acquired. The skills necessary are those which are required by the majority of clinical firms and which have been established by survey. The experience of the Sheffield Medical School provides a useful insight into the process, with full consultation between the consultants in clinical firms taking undergraduates and postgraduates from Sheffield, house officers starting their preregistration year, house officers ending their preregistration year, and undergraduates starting their final year.[17] Of 35 skills listed on the questionnaire, 26 skills were identified as core practical skills. In total, 15 of the core skills had been acquired by the majority of students by the time they graduated, of which 13 skills were acquired prior to the final undergraduate year. Core skills that were not required as an undergraduate were acquired as a PRHO. The survey acted as a quality-control mechanism for teaching at both the undergraduate and postgraduate levels. With regard to the importance of needlestick injuries, the annual *Student Handbook* of the University of Leeds School of Medicine, session 2001/2002, describes in detail the duties and responsibilities with respect to the handling, use, disposal and duty of care of sharps, and the combating of occupational hazards.[33] There is undoubtedly a continuum of improvement of safe practice in the educational and clinical environments.

The concept of supervision

In her exploration of the concept of supervision, its functions and the qualities required for it to be effective, good practice was defined by Freeth[34] as follows:

- clearly contracted
- shared discussion about expectations, aims and functions
- discussion about responsibilities and accountability, especially concerning the welfare of patients
- development of a good working alliance in a non-threatening atmosphere
- attitude of openness to learning
- ability to choose one's supervisor, which enhances engagement in the process (often impractical)
- preferably not with one's consultant (often impractical)
- addressing the needs of the supervisee, not the supervisor
- ability to review the process and quality of supervision itself.

However, Freeth indicates that the reality is different:

> *Unfortunately, the hierarchical, competitive and defensive climate in which the medical profession operates is not conducive to providing the functions of effective peer supervision, especially if there is not an impartial and skilled facilitator. Presently, most of the functions of supervision, particularly education and support, usually occur informally between doctors in the mess or along hospital corridors. These opportunities are extremely valuable. They will also work well if a team is supportive and has a learning culture. However, the medical profession needs to seriously question how much this form of support, on an ad hoc basis, can and should be relied on. Issues such as confidentiality and accountability need to be considered, in addition to whether informal arrangements alone can guarantee effectiveness in fulfilling the various aims and functions of supervision.*[34]

The reader may be deeply troubled to learn that junior medical staff at the commencement of their clinical training and career have such inconstant, irregular and unconvincing assistance in their educational provision. If the findings of the studies are generally recognised, there would appear to be cultural and resourcing problems of major magnitude which will inevitably compromise the provision of patient care and the education of the trainee. Both of these are unacceptable. To suggest that 'progress in education is required to strengthen the level of existing hospital training'[14] would appear to be an understatement. It is not apparent that the employer has an understanding of the knowledge and skills base of the junior doctor on appointment, or that the employer has shown due diligence in the subsequent supervision of junior staff. This is acknowledged in *Supporting Doctors, Protecting Patients: Current Approach to Poor Clinical Performance in the NHS.*

The appropriate delegation and supervision of clinical work is described as follows:

> *5.10   An important issue for doctors in training is the way in which clinical work is delegated to them by more senior staff and, more generally, how their work is supervised.*
>
> *5.11   Delegation of clinical responsibilities to a junior doctor based on a broad assumption of their competencies rather than a proper understanding of them can pose a potential danger to patients. Moreover, superficial or haphazard supervision of a doctor in training may not only give them an inadequate training, but may also fail to recognise or correct a problem in their knowledge or skills. Poor supervision and inappropriate delegation are bad for patients and bad for doctors in training. We are aware that some Royal Colleges and professional bodies have developed guidance for their Fellows and Members. We propose that comprehensive guidance is produced on this subject with appropriate involvement of the NHS.*[35]
>
> *2.25   Recent changes to the management of training for junior doctors have helped to improve the situation by creating a proper structured training and annual review for doctors in the specialist registrar grade. Mechanisms for dealing with the problems of the poorly performing trainee are, however, still not entirely satisfactory.*

The Bristol Royal Infirmary Report also indicates, under the rubric 'competent healthcare professionals', that:

> *78   Where surgeons or other clinicians undertake an invasive procedure for the first time, they should be properly trained and directly supervised, if the procedure is already established. In the case of a new, untried invasive clinical procedure, they must seek permission from the local research ethics committee. Patients are entitled to know what experience the surgeon or clinician has before giving consent.*[36]

It is also re-emphasised from the report on intrathecal medication errors (*see* page 283) that:

15 In the short term, reductions in working hours will relieve fatigue but at the expense of:

- *increased work intensity for staff when on duty*
- *increased cross-cover between specialities*
- *reduced formal supervision of inexperienced by more experienced staff*
- *less opportunity for more formal training (induction courses, speciality tutorials and audit meetings).*

This provides a most disturbing insight into the training of medical staff. In summary, it would appear that there may be an increase rather than a decrease in opportunities for errors.

Nevertheless, in the event of litigation involving a trainee, it remains implicit that a basal level of student performance obtained at the commencement of graduate tuition and following clinical supervision may inevitably be called into question. Again, from the report *Supporting Doctors, Protecting Patients*:

2.29 The system has recently been introduced and is evolving. A trainee who is performing poorly may blame the trainer for inadequate supervision or unfair assessment. Some consultant trainers are inexperienced in providing reports which are sufficiently well documented to stand up on appeal. Trainees threatened with delayed progress or removal from training are naturally eager to defend themselves and may take their case through to an Employment Tribunal [35]

Collaboration between the professions may help to address some of the problems. For example, at the Countess of Chester Trust, the pharmacists produce discharge prescriptions as part of a programme to reduce junior doctors' hours. The benefits included fewer errors and queries and less financial waste.[37] At Manchester Medical School, medical students are being taught safe prescribing by the School of Pharmacy (Collett, personal communication). However, neither of these well-intentioned initiatives can eradicate the deficits in clinical training caused by lack of resources. It is the quality of clinical supervision which is a key factor and which has been defined as 'a designated interaction between two or more practitioners within a safe and supportive environment, which enables a continuum of reflective, critical analysis of care, to ensure quality patient services'.[38]

The level of supervision of clinical activity will vary between professions and at different levels. Thus the Royal College of Anaesthetists defines three levels of supervision where first, the consultant is present and available to provide immediate help and advice to the trainee who examines and manages the patient, secondly as above but the consultant is present elsewhere in the hospital although he or she can be contacted for immediate advice, and thirdly, the consultant is not present in the hospital but can be contacted for immediate advice and can return to the hospital.[39] This can be usefully contrasted with community nursing, where a degree of reflective and critical practice is frequently achieved by solitary practitioners in the patient's home. The essential aim for all professions is to ensure that the skills are equal to the task in hand. *Competence rather than qualifications has been described as the key to safe supervision and delegation.*[40]

Chapter 15

Litigation and negligence

Summary: Litigation, negligence and the criminal law

- Litigation may be increasingly important in holding the academic and clinical professions accountable for their provision. Even a pre-registration pharmacy trainee (and his supervisor) in the UK was subject to a police prosecution and criminal charge. This reflects major and increasing concern about the standards of medical care and legal redress.
- Legal negligence requires evidence of a duty of care, a breach of that duty, and loss caused or materially contributed to that breach.
- In some countries the criminal law is routinely used to assess medical negligence. In the UK there has been an eightfold increase during the 1990s in the number of manslaughter charges brought against doctors; no less than 50% of the doctors so charged were junior doctors. With the threat of imprisonment, this is a serious development.
- Reckless behaviour or gross negligence is at the heart of a manslaughter charge, and its seeds may be sown in complacency and arrogance. Both can begin to be addressed at the undergraduate level and in clinical training, and before incompetence is revealed on the very public stage of a criminal court, to tarnish the entire profession.
- Frustration may have driven the new initiatives of prosecution through the criminal justice system to ensure that patients seek a just and fair remedy. However, whether this will be achieved using criminal proceedings remains to be seen.

Introduction

The third and increasingly important factor that will hold academic teaching (and the professions) accountable for the quality of its provision is litigation. Errors committed in healthcare, particularly those committed by trainee healthcare students, may increasingly call into question the adequacy of undergraduate course provision and/or clinical supervision.

This is within the perspective of enormous reforms in the process of civil law in the UK, in the prosecution of medical malpractice (*see* page 111) and, increasingly, the use of criminal proceedings for serious incidents.

The litigation process and the changing face of negligence

In a judgement of 1954, in *Roe vs Minister of Health*,[1] two men were recorded to have suffered severe injuries after receiving spinal anaesthetics. Unbeknown to anyone, and therefore held not to be capable of reasonable discovery, the glass of the ampoules was flawed, and phenol had penetrated it, causing the injuries. Lord Denning, in considering the essential distinction between negligence and misadventure, stated:

> *It is so easy to be wise after the event and to condemn as negligence that which is only misadventure. We ought always to be on our guard against it, especially in cases against hospitals and doctors. Medical science has conferred great benefits on mankind, but those benefits are attended by considerable risks . . . we cannot take the benefits without taking the risks . . . we must insist on due care for the patient at every point, but we must not condemn as negligence that which is only a misadventure.*

For both the patient and the doctor the distinction is fundamental. An injury arising from negligence will carry an attribution of blame to the doctor and the possibility of the patient having a right to compensation; neither necessarily follow from a misadventure. In determining the possibility of negligence following an act or omission by a doctor, one applies the following triad:

- a duty of care
- breach of that duty
- loss caused or materially contributed to that breach.

There must be a synthesis of all three factors to generate the legal definition of negligence. This provides for intriguing interrelationships, as illustrated in the cases described by Griffiths.[2] It is quite possible for a doctor to be negligent in the usual sense of the word, but due to good luck the patient escapes harm, does not suffer loss, and therefore the act is not one of legal negligence. Therefore the crucial task is for the court to distinguish between negligence and misadventure which hinges on a breach of a duty of care.

In the landmark judgement concerning the case of a Mr Bolam,[3] who was given electroconvulsive therapy during which he sustained a fracture of the vertebra, Mr Justice McNair, in his direction to the jury, stated the following:

> *I must tell you what in law we mean by 'negligence'. In the ordinary case which does not involve any special skill, negligence in law*

*means a failure to do some act which a reasonable man in the
circumstances would, or the doing of an act which the reasonable
man in the circumstances would not do; and if the failure or the
doing of that act results in injury, then there is a cause of action.
How do you test whether this act or failure is negligent? In the
ordinary case it has been said you judge it by the action of the man
in the street. He is the ordinary man. In one case it has been said
that you judge it by the conduct of the man on the top of the
Clapham omnibus. But where you get a situation which involves
the use of some special skill or competence, then the test as to
whether there has been negligence or not is not the test of the man
on top of a Clapham omnibus, because he has not got this special
skill. The test is the standard of the ordinary skilled man exercising
and professing to have that special skill. A man need not possess the
highest expert skill: it is well established by law that it is sufficient if
he exercises the ordinary skill of an ordinary competent man
exercising that particular art . . . . At the same time that does not
mean that a medical man can obstinately and pig-headedly carry on
with some old technique if it has been proved to be contrary to what
is really substantially the whole of informed medical opinion.*

In summary, the law opted for a subjective assessment of competence rather
than an objective test. The court has attempted to test both the patient's rights
and the doctor's responsibilities, but also the latter's rights as well. The jury
found the doctor not guilty of negligence because he acted, as Mr Justice McNair
said, 'in accordance with a practice accepted as proper by a reasonable body of
medical men skilled in that area'.

This followed *Hunter v Hanley*[4] when, on appeal, Lord President Clyde set
out the definition for medical negligence as follows:

*the true test for establishing negligence and diagnosis or treatment
on the part of the doctor is whether he has been proved to be guilty
of such failure as no doctor of ordinary skill would be guilty of if
acting with ordinary care . . . it must be established that the course
the doctor has adopted is one which no professional man of
ordinary skill would have taken if he had been acting with
ordinary care.*

These judgements have been interpreted and expanded by further rulings.
However, the principle is *that the standard is set by ordinary doctors* and
does not have to be the most expert or even the best, but has been entrenched in
law as 'the accepted medical practice'. In court, the issue of whether or not there
has been a breach of a duty of care is a decision for the judge to make after
hearing evidence from independent experts.

However, and more recently, in *Bolitho and others v City and Hackney
Health Authority*,[5] Lord Browne-Wilkinson sounded a clear warning to experts
who may seek to defend what is illogical or indefensible:

In my view the court is not bound to hold that a defendant doctor escapes liability for negligent treatment or diagnosis just because he leads evidence from a number of medical experts who are genuinely of the opinion that the defendant's treatment or diagnosis accorded with sound medical practice . . . the court has to be satisfied that the exponents of the body of opinion relied on can demonstrate that such opinion had a logical basis. In particular cases involving, as they often do, the weighing of risks against benefits, the judge before accepting a body of opinion as being responsible, reasonable or respectable will need to be satisfied that, in forming their views, the experts have directed their minds to the question of comparative risks and benefits and have reached a defensible conclusion on the matter.

Bolitho very firmly reminds the trial judge of the power he has in deciding what value he places on an expert opinion, and this is demonstrated in *Marriot v West Midlands Health Authority and others*.[6]

Although the *Hunter v Hanley/Bolam* criteria, for assessing whether or not a doctor's clinical act or omission is negligent, is the law, every clinical case is now subject to close scrutiny for the following reasons.[2]

1 *The case may not be clearly delineated as clinical; it may reflect a systems breakdown or a failure of management.*
2 *Is it the defendant's practice which is respectable or is it really an indefensible practice that is supported by respectable doctors? It was implicit in the Bolam judgement that 'the ordinary skill of an ordinary competent man exercising that particular art' was in fact respectable (can it be concluded that medical management which results in a general level of injury, disability or death to approximately 1 in 10 patients is respectable?).*
3 *There is authority for the view that even in professional negligence cases, compliance with approved practice is not conclusive in favour of the defendant.*
4 *Is the practice outdated? Is it irrelevant? Is it logical?*
5 *Does the practice conform to any relevant protocol?*
6 *Where evidence shows that a lacuna in professional practice exists by which risks of grave danger are knowingly taken, then however small the risk, the court must anxiously examine that lacuna – particularly if the risk can be easily and inexpensively avoided (Hucks v Cole).*[7]

Bearing the above in mind, the reader may have assumed that patients are entitled 'to care and treatment of an appropriate standard informed by current knowledge'. However, the assumption is sorely challenged in the devastating report on the NHS following the Bristol Royal Infirmary Inquiry. With respect to 'care of an appropriate standard', the report concludes as follows:

90 Until well into the 1990s, the notion that there should be explicit standards of care which all healthcare professionals should seek to meet and which would apply to patients across the NHS simply did not exist . . .

91 . . . In particular, there is no mechanism for surveillance to ensure that patterns of poor performance are recognised and addressed.[8]

Patients, healthcare managers and the courts do not appear to regard the payment of money by an indemnifier as punishment for fault or protection of the public. The new accountability for poor medical performance may increasingly be found in the professional regulatory bodies and the criminal law. The removal of the ability to practise or imprisonment are ultimate sanctions.[8]

Negligence and the criminal law

For many years, malpractice in the UK by healthcare professionals (i.e. individuals claiming to be experts possessing specialist knowledge and skills) resulted in action being taken against the professional in a civil court. The action invariably followed the insurance, resulting in a claim for financial compensation followed by a disciplinary hearing of the professional body. However, there is evidence that this situation may be changing to involve a police investigation and charges brought by the Crown Prosecution Service of manslaughter and criminal proceedings.

A criminal prosecution with the real threat of a police investigation and imprisonment is a very serious development. Although extremely concerning for the professions, it has four advantages for the patient and society. First, it will focus attention on an issue and be treated by all parties with a gravity that simply cannot be attained in any other way. Secondly, the investigation will be immediate and professional, thirdly, it will be independent, and finally it may provide a fairer mechanism of redress for the patient (and for society).

Healthcare professionals can be convicted of manslaughter by a jury if the evidence is persuasive that someone has died as a result of their gross negligence (defined as a wholly irresponsible disregard of a serious risk to others, of which the defendant is aware or 'to which he has made himself wilfully blind').[8] In summary, the jury taking into account the risk of death involved must decide whether the defendant's conduct was so bad that it was of a criminal nature.

The shift to include prosecution under criminal proceedings may first reflect the deterioration in the confidence of the public and judges in the medical and other healthcare professions. This is clear from the lecture presented by Lord Woolf, Lord Chief Justice at the Wolfson Institute, on 17 January 2001.[9]

Lord Woolf called for:

> a less deferential approach by the courts to the medical profession and an end to the assumption that 'doctor knows best'. Public confidence had been dented by a series of well-publicised scandals . . . in the past courts had been excessively deferential to the medical profession but this 'automatic assumption of beneficence' had been dented. It is unwise to place any profession or any other body providing services to the public on a pedestal where their actions cannot be subject to close scrutiny.

He also called for:

> courts to take a more robust view of negligence by the medical profession and not be deterred by the accepted test for negligence that what had been done 'was in accord with a respectable body of medical opinion'. I cannot help believing that the behaviour of those involved in the recent scandals betrays a lack of appreciation of the limits of their responsibility. They were not motivated by personal gain, but they had lost sight of their power and authority. They acted as though they were able to take any action they thought desirable, irrespective of the views of others. The over-deferential approach is captured in the phrase 'doctor knows best'. The contemporary approach is a more critical one. It could be said that doctor knows best if he acts reasonably and logically and gets his facts right.

Lord Woolf noted in his most serious comment that the following factors had also made judges less deferential:

- the difficulties people experienced in bringing successful claims
- an increasing awareness of patients' rights
- the closer scrutiny of doctors by courts in countries such as Canada and Australia
- the scale of medical negligence litigation, which was a 'disaster area'.

This indicated that the health service was not giving sufficient priority to avoiding medical mishaps and treating patients justly when mishaps occurred. Lord Woolf further noted the increasing number of complaints to the General Medical Council, and the fact that the Medical Protection Society reported that it was taking as many calls from whistleblowers in a month as it used to take in a year.[10] Most of the callers were young GPs who were unhappy about the practice of their seniors. For the first time, GMC guidelines have placed a legal responsibility on doctors to report incompetent colleagues.

Perhaps the serious error of the British Medical Association in emailing doctors a circular relevant to Dr Shipman's criminal history during his actual trial, and after the jury had retired, was simply the final affront to the due process of law. Mr Justice Forbes accepted that there was no intention to prejudice the trial:

> However, I am satisfied that those documents were capable of
> prejudicing the fairness of this trial. It would have been almost
> impossible to resist an application to discharge the jury. If the jury in
> this case had been discharged, it would have been almost impos-
> sible to retry Dr Shipman either on the charges with which he is
> convicted or on any other offences. Had the jury been discharged,
> there would have been no possibility of a retrial. The outrage and
> horror that the public would necessarily have felt cannot possibly be
> exaggerated.

The BMA offered the judge the association's sincerest apologies. However, the judge indicated that 'this is such a serious matter it would not be appropriate for me to accept the apology to bring the matter to an end'.

He decided that there was a *prima facie* case to answer, and referred the case to the Attorney-General for contempt of court.[11]

However, the mounting concerns have not been expressed solely by the legal profession. Sir Donald Irvine, President of the GMC, at the Annual Lloyd Roberts Lecture at the Royal Society of Medicine in January 2001[10] criticised the medical profession, management and governments for the crisis in the NHS, including complacency about poor practice. In a scathing indictment he stated that:

> systems directed at the employer and producer rather than the
> patient had contributed substantially to the formation of protective
> attitudes, too much sloppy management and the toleration of too
> much poor or unacceptable practice. There are deep-seated flaws in
> the culture and regulation of the medical profession, and serious
> deficiencies in the management and capacity of the NHS. The
> cultural flaws in the medical profession show up as excessive
> paternalism, lack of respect for the patients and their right to
> make decisions about their care, and secrecy and complacency
> about poor practice.

The numerous recommendations of the Bristol Royal Infirmary Inquiry, the most detailed investigation ever undertaken into the practices of the NHS, simply and fully confirm the devastating conclusions drawn by Sir Donald Irvine.[12]

Concerns have also been expressed by the media which raise public aware-ness to a high level. For example, in the UK in 2000, in response to the reporting of medical errors, Channel 4 television ran an unprecedented and detailed series of documentaries entitled *Doctors on Trial*, reporting on high-profile medical errors and the health of the medical profession. On 1 October 2000, Channel 4 also screened a film called *Innocents*, a dramatic reconstruction of the events leading up to the tragedy at the Bristol Royal Infirmary. The series culminated in a televised debate entitled *Doctors on Trial* before a representative studio jury of 250 people selected by the National Opinion Polls. The presenter, in emphasising that the overwhelming number of doctors are dedicated to their vocation, work extremely hard and save countless lives, questioned 'whether doctors collectively as a profession have created a culture where misconduct is able to flourish'.

Leading members of the medical and healthcare professions were cross-examined by counsel, and the audience finally voted on the subject of the debate: 'Doctors are accused of too often placing their own interests above their patients, fostering a closed working culture, and resisting necessary change within the health service'. The verdict was 44% guilty, 56% not guilty. The presenter concluded 'that doctors are clearly doing a good job in difficult circumstances, and the time for using them as whipping posts for the ills of the health service must come to an end'. It is unlikely that the medical and other healthcare professions derived much solace from the verdict; nearly half of their patients – a quite astonishing proportion – believed that there was substance in the accusation.

And yet the medical profession continues to receive the highest of accolades from the public in terms of trustworthiness. In the most recent survey by MORI, on behalf of the BMA, in response to the straight question 'Who do you trust?', nine out of 10 people placed doctors at the top of the list (see Box 15.1). The results refer to data obtained in 2001 and results have been recorded consistently over recent years.[13] Establishing the relationship between the perceived 'creation of a culture where misconduct is allowed to flourish' and 'Who do you trust?', would make for a fascinating study.

Box 15.1: The response of the UK public to the question 'Who do you trust to tell the truth?' The survey was undertaken by MORI for the BMA in March 2001 and reviewed by Corrado in August 2001[13]

Doctors	89%
Teachers	86%
Professors	78%
Judges	78%
Clergymen/priests	78%
Television newsreaders	75%
Scientists	65%
The police	63%
The ordinary man and woman in the street	52%
Pollsters	46%
Civil servants	43%
Trade union officials	39%
Business leaders	27%
Government ministers	20%
Journalists	18%
Politicians generally	17%

Reckless behaviour or gross negligence is at the heart of a manslaughter charge, and its seeds may be sown in complacency and arrogance. There is evidence that the inept not only reach erroneous conclusions but also over-estimate their abilities.[14] However, in the case of physicians, complacency and arrogance may conspire with an absence of knowledge and understanding or lack of skills, with a tragic outcome. The investigation into the workings of the NHS in the Bristol heart surgery scandal and its extensive reporting described the culture as one of 'institutional arrogance', 'arrogance born of indifference', a 'macho medical culture', 'tribalism', and a 'club culture' among some doctors and NHS staff that contributed to many children receiving inadequate care, where more than 30% more children died than might be expected, as a result of substandard care.[15–17] Of greatest concern, the culture of secrecy was believed to extend far beyond the hospital itself.

However, there is reason for cautious optimism. The BMA has pledged support for the implementation of Professor Kennedy's recommendations from the Bristol Royal Infirmary Inquiry. Dr Ian Bogle, Chairman of the BMA Council, stated:

> I would like to express my apologies and sympathy to the parents of the Bristol babies who died or suffered damage. We let them down. We are absolutely determined to see that some good comes out of the tragedy by working with Government and with colleagues throughout the NHS to detect problems at an early stage, to provide better information for parents and to improve safety and quality.
>
> The whole of the medical profession has learned from the Bristol tragedy. It started a process of soul searching which has changed medicine for the better. I welcome the Health Secretary's commitment to encouraging a new climate of trust and openness and his acknowledgement of the skill and commitment of NHS staff. Doctors and the whole of the NHS have been developing new systems and a new culture both before and during the time that the inquiry was running, but we now need to study Professor Kennedy's report in depth to see what further lessons can be learned and what needs to be done.[18]

The divide between science and the practice of medicine was summarised by Sir David Weatherall as follows:

> the principal problem for those who educate our doctors of the future is how, on the one hand, to encourage a lifelong attitude of critical, scientific thinking to the management of illness and, on the other, to recognise that moment when the scientific approach, because of ignorance, has reached its limits and must be replaced by sympathetic empiricism. Because of the dichotomy between the self-confidence required at the bedside and self-critical uncertainty essential in the research laboratory, it may be difficult to achieve

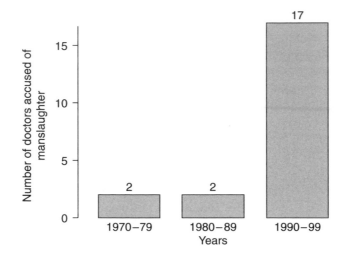

Figure 15.1: The number of doctors accused of manslaughter in the UK over the last 30 years. The analysis was of the deaths of patients due to medication errors. A total of 17 doctors (1990–99) were involved in 13 cases. Prepared from the data of Ferner.[21]

> *this balance. Can one person ever combine the two qualities? Possibly not, but this is the goal to which medicine must aspire . . . . If the medical students of the future, together with biomedical scientists, fully appreciate and accept these complexities for what they are . . . both should achieve a level of humility that will tend to reduce the stresses and strains between the investigators and practitioners.*[19]

A quiet and reassuring confidence at the bedside is an essential practitioner skill and quite distinct from arrogance. Arrogance or a presumptuous disdain for the views of others, is unpleasant but, more importantly, it is also unsafe. Arrogance purports to self-importance or perhaps an indiscernible blending into cultural misfeasance and incompetence that becomes increasingly difficult to distinguish from reckless behaviour. Rule violations (i.e. staff acting wilfully beyond their competence) by healthcare staff were the third commonest cause of error.[20] The confident administration of vincristine via a route which induces catastrophic consequences may be perceived to belie knowledge of its use. And behaviour that appears to be negligent, reckless or wholly irresponsible has serious legal implications.

In a review of the literature relating to manslaughter charges brought against doctors, Ferner[21] recorded an eightfold increase in the 1990s compared with the previous two decades (*see* Figure 15.1). Within the period 1998–2000 alone, the following cases involving fatalities caused by healthcare staff were each prosecuted as one of manslaughter:

- the administration of a lethal dose of 100 mg diamorphine; the doctor was sentenced to 12 months' imprisonment, and suspended for two years[22]
- the administration of a lethal dose of methadone by a police surgeon, who was too ill to stand trial, but the judge ordered that the charge lie on the file[23]
- the administration by an anaesthetist of nitrous oxide instead of oxygen to a boy with Goldenhar's syndrome; sentenced to six months' imprisonment[24]
- the administration of vincristine intrathecally by a specialist registrar in paediatric anaesthesia to a 12-year-old boy; before the trial more evidence of significant systems failures was identified as a factor in the boy's death and the crown offered no evidence and the doctors were acquitted[25]
- the administration of 300 mg of morphine by a nurse to the wrong patient, who sought help from a doctor and other nurses. The patient recovered, then subsequently died. They were acquitted in a complex ruling[26]
- the preparation of a medicine containing an excessive amount of chloroform and its dispensing by a preregistration pharmacy student under the guidance of a tutor pharmacist, resulting in the death of a 3-week-old child. The defendants pleaded guilty to a charge of not supplying 'a medicine of the nature or quality demanded' (a Medicines Act 1968, Section 4 offence). The Crown Prosecution Services asked the judge to rule that there had been no criminal intent, and to direct not-guilty verdicts.[27]

The latter case was unusual in that a charge was brought by the Crown Prosecution Service (CPS) against a preregistration pharmacy graduate who was neither a healthcare professional nor on a professional register. Statutory regulations and standards relevant to inexperienced staff are discussed below.

Litigation, negligence and inexperienced staff

In the case of the dispensing error of the pharmacy preregistration student and tutor pharmacist, and the CPS' request inviting the not-guilty verdict, comments were raised about the limited experience of medicine preparation afforded by the university training and the clinical preregistration training arrangements that the student had received.[27–29] Mr Justice Forbes said it was clear that the defendants were not criminally responsible for the death of Matthew Young, but that 'each of you failed to show due diligence in the dispensing of the solution'.[27]

As a consequence of this case, the Royal Pharmaceutical Society's director of professional standards commented as follows:

> *All community pharmacists who take on preregistration trainees need to have an understanding of the basic knowledge and skill levels they are likely to get from a raw graduate. What needs to be picked up in the training year will depend on the basal level of competence of graduates.*[27]

Subsequently, the Statutory Committee of the Royal Pharmaceutical Society decided to take no action against the preregistration trainee. The committee's chairman, Lord Fraser, said that behind the Medicines Act offence lay a very real, very public tragedy. The committee reiterated that there was a real importance in having structured supervision for preregistration students, and that the significance of this could not be sufficiently stressed. The student had started afresh his preregistration training and the committee was impressed by the full reports on his training and the significant degree of support being offered to him. The committee hoped that confidence in his abilities would return, and that thereafter he would follow a successful career in pharmacy.[30]

The case raised extremely important issues that need to be explored further for an understanding of the level of knowledge and skills that are required of all trainee and healthcare practitioners. And how would a supervisor assess the basal level of competence of a graduate?

Similar comments may also apply to the death of Mr Jowett, an 18-year-old patient, following the intrathecal injection of vincristine on 4 January 2001 at the Queens Medical Centre in Nottingham. The death was the subject of a police investigation where two doctors were suspended.[31]

Mr Jowett's death occurred just one day after the inquest on Ms Horn, a 23-year-old patient who died in 1998 after a doctor made a similar mistake at Leicester Royal Infirmary in 1990. Ms Horn died after eight years of living as a paraplegic and requiring 24-hour care. The error was admitted and described as 'a genuine mistake made from a lapse of concentration'. The coroner recorded a verdict of accidental death.[32]

More recently, the Nottinghamshire coroner found mistakes at every level of medical management in the death of Mr Jowett. He rejected relatives' calls for a verdict of unlawful killing, and decided that Mr Jowett died an accidental death. However, the coroner added that Mr Jowett had been let down by many people:

> *Clearly there is the medical and nursing staff but there is also the pharmacy people who arranged for the bringing of drugs on to the ward. There is a question of hospitals letting down medical teams in not training their staff. There are also questions for the drug industry* and the Department of Health.*[33]

---

* The manufacturer clearly warned, no less than five times, of the dangers in the use of vincristine – *see* Box 12.3, page 153.

The Department of Health's inquiry listed 48 separate factors;[34] a synopsis and the recommendations can be found in Appendix 8. The inquiry and the media reporting of the tragedy make uncomfortable reading. Professor Liam Donaldson was acerbic in comment, saying that there had been a 'chilling series of blunders and oversights'. And Mr Jowetts' father made the following comment:

> They told us he would probably die [after the injection]. Sometimes there were six nurses around the bed, holding him down because he was in that much pain. He seemed to level out, then deteriorate. It was not until about two or three days before he died that we gave up hope.[33]

It was reported that neither doctor was trained to inject the drug, both of them failed to read the label on the syringe, and each thought that the other had sufficient knowledge to be aware of what was being done.[33,35]

Lord Denning began to address the difficult questions about the consequences of negligence of junior staff nearly 50 years ago. In a case where a simple error by junior doctors in their use of an anaesthetic killed a patient, the Court of Appeal decided that the hospital authorities had to share the blame.

> It would be in the highest degree unjust that hospital authorities, by getting inexperienced doctors to perform their duties for them, without adequate supervision, should be able to throw all responsibility on to those doctors as if they were fully experienced practitioners . . . [hospitals] should not leave patients in inexperienced hands without proper supervision.
>
> Jones v Manchester Corporation[36]

The sharing of blame to the apportioning of blame was further explored in a complaint against a provider made in *Wilsher v Essex Area Health Authority*,[37] in which a baby born prematurely had received improper treatment (the patient received excessive oxygen which was implicated as one of the causes for him becoming blind), due in part to the failure to supervise an inexperienced doctor. It was his defence that he should be judged to a standard reasonably expected of a junior doctor, and therefore he should not be considered negligent for his failure. In the Court of Appeal, all members exonerated the junior doctor from blame in this case because he did take the reasonable step of asking for the assistance of a senior colleague.

However, the comments of the Appeal Court, with respect to a doctor's expertise or lack of it, were instructive. Lord Mustill accepted that all doctors learn their expertise on the job, that this is inevitable and desirable, that hospitals make their contribution to medical practice by training young doctors and derive benefit since they are able to employ many more doctors than would be possible if all were expected to be fully qualified, and that patients are well served by these arrangements. On the other hand, if the standards of care expected from doctors related to the individual's degree of training and experience, then the rights of the patient would:

> *vary according to the chance of recruitment and rostering. The patient's right to complain of faulty treatment will be more limited if he has been entrusted to the care of a doctor who is a complete novice in the particular field (unless he can point to some fault of supervision in a person up the hierarchy) than if he has been in the hands of a doctor who has already spent months on the same ward.*

This he found unacceptable:

> *It would be a false step to subordinate the legitimate expectation of the patient that he will receive from each person concerned with his care a degree of skill appropriate to the task which he undertakes, to an understandable wish to minimise the psychological and financial pressures on hard-pressed young doctors.*

He concluded that negligence ought to be assessed according to the post which the doctor occupies, rather than the skill which could be expected of him individually. Glidewell took a similar view saying:

> *the law requires the trainee or learner to be judged by the same standard as his more experienced colleagues. If it did not, inexperience would frequently be urged as a defence to an action for professional negligence.*

However, in a dissenting judgement, Sir Nicolas Brown-Wilkinson preferred the contrary view where the standard of care should be assessed according to the expertise and skill of the individual doctor. He noted that some junior doctors might lack even the degree of understanding to assess their own competence:

> *the position of the houseman in his first year after qualifying . . . who has just started in a specialist field in order to gain the necessary skill in that field is not capable of such an analysis. The houseman takes up his post in order to gain full professional qualification . . . . In my judgement such doctors cannot in fairness be said to be at fault if, at the start of their time, they lack the very skills which they are seeking to acquire.*

Instead, the vice-chancellor blamed the registrar responsible for the supervision, who had checked the patient and failed to note the error. However, rather than deprive the plaintiff of any form of remedy, the vice-chancellor advised that an action be considered against the health authority for its failure to provide hospital staff with sufficient skill to undertake the duties assigned to them. He said:

> In my judgement, a hospital authority which so conducts its
> hospital that it fails to provide doctors of sufficient skill and
> experience to give the treatment offered at the hospital, may be
> directly liable in negligence to the patient.

The negligence revolved around the failure to ensure that experienced staff were
available to provide the appropriate supervision of junior staff. But if a junior
doctor makes an error of judgement occasioned by fatigue or excessive workload, or other systems errors beyond his or her control, to which other junior
doctors would also succumb, ought they to be held personally liable? Possibly
not – see *Johnstone v Bloomsbury Health Authority*.[38]

Issues of resourcing as contributory factors to negligence or poor standards are
inevitably assessed on their merits. For example, and again focusing on a case
that involved a failure to ensure that experienced staff were available to
supervise junior staff, in *Bull v Devon Health Authority*,[39] the defendant's
system for summoning a consultant urgently to an obstetrics unit broke down.
As a consequence the plaintiff suffered brain damage. The defendants explained
that the system for summoning consultants from one site to another was 'par
for the course', and that to require anything else was unrealistic. Lord Mustill
rejected this defence:

> I see nothing ideal about a system which would have given the
> mother and child the protection against emergencies when it was
> needed . . . . The system should have been set up so as to produce a
> registrar or consultant on the spot within 20 minutes, subject to
> some unforeseeable contingency. In the present case there was an
> interval of about an hour during which the mother and child were at
> risk, with nobody present who could do anything if an emergency
> were to develop. The trend of the evidence seems to me manifestly
> that this interval was too long.

The Bristol Royal Infirmary Inquiry was also specific in emphasising the
distinction between the inadequacy of resources and other issues relating to
tragic outcomes:

> Conclusions on the adequacy of the service: 39 *It is crucial,
> however, to make clear the following. The inadequacy in resources
> for PCS at Bristol was typical of the NHS as a whole. From this, it
> follows that whatever went wrong at Bristol was not caused by lack
> of resources. Other centres laboured under the same or similar
> difficulties. For example, the shortage in qualified nurses and in
> cardiologists was a national phenomenon, affecting all centres. We
> therefore emphasise the point again that, while underfunding
> blighted the NHS as a whole, it does not alone provide the
> explanation for what went wrong at Bristol.*[40]

Finally, and similarly to the study by McPherson and colleagues,[41] there is a
question of whether it will be a requirement to establish basal performance of

all healthcare graduates at the commencement of professional training to establish 'due diligence' in the allocation of duties and training. It may be questioned whether this is a formidable task or perhaps a straightforward procedure that could be addressed using generic tests or examinations developed with the assistance of the accreditation bodies and employers.

Clearly there are major and increasing concerns about the standards of medical care and legal redress. Patients may be dismayed to read from the comments of Lord Woolf that the deferential behaviour of the legal system towards the medical profession may have influenced judgement. Frustration may have driven the new initiatives of prosecution through the criminal justice system to ensure that patients may seek a just and fair remedy. However, whether this will be achieved using criminal proceedings remains to be seen, although this is the normal practice in some European countries.[42]

Nevertheless, important principles emerge from some of the above prosecutions that are relevant to education and healthcare. The prosecution of the pharmacy preregistration student and his clinical tutor for the dispensing of a lethal medication gave rise to numerous articles and correspondence within the pharmaceutical press which questioned the teaching of pharmacy undergraduates, where 'academics must shoulder some of the blame'.[29]

Can it be right that a pharmacy student can graduate without the necessary knowledge and skills to prepare appropriate dilutions?[27] Can it be correct that a medical student can enter clinical training without being taught the principles of how to administer drugs?[43] Junior doctors appear to be at particular risk. In the review of recent manslaughter charges directed against 17 physicians, no less than nine were junior doctors.[21] Their number is disproportionate to the number of registered physicians. Does this reflect personal failings, inadequate undergraduate tuition, poor clinical supervision, excessive workloads, or a combination of these factors? In any event, *it appears almost inevitable that the academic and clinical training that has been afforded to trainee graduates who find themselves as future defendants will be brought into question.*

Increasingly, the public perception of the stature of the professions is being driven by the media in reporting catastrophic events and the most regrettable behaviour of the professions' least able or most notorious members. Attempts to recognise, prevent or neutralise professional incompetence and malfeasance at an early stage are a crucial goal with regard to patient safety. A strong case could be made that this should commence at the beginning of education and professional instruction and addressed as a concordance with the support of the appropriate accreditation/professional bodies, future employers and patient and carer groups.

Implications for professional and continuing education and professional aspirations in healthcare

Summary: Professional aspirations in healthcare

- The development of patient-centred medicine is designed to ensure that during patients' passage through the healthcare system they are entitled to respect and honesty and be involved, wherever possible, in decisions about their care. It will also enhance the personal responsibilities of both patients and healthcare professionals.
- The competence of the healthcare professional will be a central issue with regard to changing roles in medication review and prescribing. Such interventions should begin to address the problems that patients experience in securing and using safe treatments. The room for improvement is enormous and is reflected in the increased knowledge and skills that will be required to practise safe therapeutics.
- This is a serious issue. It is emphasised that this is a very real challenge, and it is imperative that the practitioners are properly trained to perform the very challenging role of *the prescriber*.
- This will also occur at a time when some patients have unprecedented access to information via computers and the Internet, and when they are being actively encouraged to report all errors and near misses in their own or other patients' treatments.
- Given the developing breadth of expertise that is required to provide a safe and effective healthcare system, it is inevitable that this can only be realistically achieved using the diverse and specialist knowledge and skills distributed within and between the healthcare professions, *working in partnership with the patient to a new concordance.*
- *This has important implications for the education and training of present and future healthcare staff.*

Professional and continuing education

Whatever the successes and limitations of the undergraduate teaching, bearing in mind that there are processes in place to rectify problems, continuing professional education and training will be the single most important goal to secure the continued competence and registration of any practitioner in any profession.

It is just 30 years ago that Dr Edward Rosenew, Vice-President of the American College of Physicians, estimated the half-life of medical knowledge to be only five years.[1] Moreover, it is over 25 years since Dubin[2] and Lindsay and colleagues[3] developed the idea of 'knowledge half-life', which was defined as the time span between the completion of formal undergraduate education and the time when the person will be half as competent to meet the needs of his or her profession. This value was reported to be five years in engineering and medicine. Somewhat tongue-in-cheek, and assuming that the rate of progress stays the same, by the time the professional is about to retire (say 40 years of eight half-lives of practice) they would possess less than 1% of the knowledge required to practise their profession. It is salutary to consider that in some American states, evidence of continuing medical education has been required by statute for over 25 years for periodic re-registration of the licence to practise.[3] In summary, the acquisition of new knowledge is essential for continued competence,[4] and the fight against professional obsolescence should begin in the undergraduate curriculum.[5]

In healthcare this will be at different levels to match individual interests and abilities and service needs. It will involve both the maintenance and updating of knowledge and competences at a variety of levels, including certification, diplomas, Masters degrees and more recently doctoral programmes, to encompass the enormous range of abilities and interests within the professions. Many of these activities are already deeply entrenched and will provide a perpetual springboard for intellectual satisfaction, personal achievement and, above all, maintained or continued improvements in personal competence to secure patient safety.

It is to be hoped that a new body, namely the Medical Education and Standards Board,[6] which is designed to provide a coherent, robust and accountable approach to postgraduate medical education, will secure the very high standards that are required. It remains a challenging task.

In a study undertaken by the Professional Associations Research Network in Bristol, a survey of over 400 professional associations assessed attitudes to continuing professional development (CPD).[7] The main barriers to CPD were found to be lack of time; lack of money; lack of access to relevant activities; a workplace culture hostile or indifferent to CPD; lack of incentives to doing CPD; overly constraining CPD; and lack of professional support. In addition, professionals were against just having a checklist to tick, as this could lead to falsification. Peer observation was considered to be a more reliable methodology. In an article questioning whether or not CPD is the panacea that can restore trust in doctors, accountants and other professionals, Phillips stated the obvious:

> *for doctors, fitness to practise is literally a matter of life and death!*[8]

Professional aspirations in healthcare

Knowledge and understanding based on sound scientific and clinical principles are crucial for future success. There are real challenges facing medicine, nursing, pharmacy and other healthcare professions and genuine opportunities for making a vital contribution to healthcare.

The development of patient-centred medicine

> *Patients in their journey through the healthcare system are entitled to be treated with respect and honesty and to be involved, wherever possible, in decisions about their care.*
>
> *62   Partnership between patient and healthcare professional is the way forward. The exchange and provision of information is at the core of an open and honest relationship between healthcare professionals and patients. There are four fundamental principles which should in future underpin any policy aimed at meeting patients' needs for information. First, trust can only be sustained by openness. Secondly, openness means that information be given freely, honestly and regularly. Thirdly, it is of fundamental importance to be honest about the twin concerns of risk and uncertainty. Lastly, informing patients, and in the case of young children their parents, must be regarded as a process and not a one-off event.*
>
> *63   Hospitals must have an integrated system of support and counselling for patients and carers, staffed by well-trained professionals with links to outside. Such a system is central to care, not an add-on.*
>
> *64   There should be a clear system in the form of a 'one-stop shop' in every trust for addressing the concerns of patients about the care provided or the conduct of a healthcare professional.*[9]

The above recommendations were taken from the Bristol Royal Infirmary Inquiry, and although there are a number of issues specific to the provision of acute healthcare services for children, the majority of the concerns and recommendations apply throughout primary and secondary care in the NHS.

An early exponent of patient-centred medicine was the psychotherapist Balint,[10] who believed in putting the patient at the centre of the consultation.

To achieve a satisfactory outcome in the consultation, Pendleton and colleagues[11] also emphasised the importance of the doctor in eliciting the patient's ideas, expectations and concerns. Subsequently, the agenda has been progressed to enable a more accurate characterisation of the patient's problem and a shared solution.[12] The extremes are the traditional doctor-led directives and paternalism to consumer choice, but with the treatment choice being delegated to the patient. Shared decision making may allow variation in the balance of information and power according to the particular circumstances. The process is one of negotiation where the clinician must respect the legitimacy of the patient's views and the patient must accept a shared responsibility for the clinical decision. The desire for participation varies with age, cultural background, educational status and disease type.[13–15] For example, some South-East Asian cultures consider that surgery may cause the person concerned to be physically incomplete in the next life.[16] However, Navajo families believe that direct information about the risks of procedures or a diagnosis is harmful, and that talking about death can actually hasten its arrival.[17,18] Factors such as these definitely complicate the processes of shared decision making.[19] Moreover, not all patients wish to make decisions. For example, in a sample consisting of over 1000 women with breast cancer, 34% wanted to delegate the decision to the doctor, 44% wanted to collaborate and 22% wanted to select their own treatment.[20]

However, there remains much evidence to indicate that outcomes of compliance, health status and patient satisfaction improve when patients are better informed,[15,21] although it would be ingenuous not to believe that shared decision making may have an uneasy demeanour. The recent medical advice in the UK for the use of the triple vaccine for the prevention of measles, mumps and rubella was not accepted by some parents for their children. However, the 'greater good for society' of following the guidelines effectively negated individual choice.[22] Similarly, it has been noted that an increased choice for patients might mean more strokes and heart attacks for patients, because the latter are not as enthusiastic as their doctors about receiving treatment for mild to moderate hypertension.[23] However, the healthcare practitioner should exercise care to ensure that increased morbidity or mortality is not attributed to the professional care.

With regard to medication, it has been assumed for many years that the prescribing and dispensing of the drug to the patient with instructions was sufficient to ensure its sensible use. There were few attempts to monitor its use and value. The problems that were revealed by the inquiry of the Royal Pharmaceutical Society of Great Britain in partnership with Merck Sharp and Dohme, which concerned the difficulties patients experience in taking their medicines, were noted on page 30.[24] In some cases prescriptions were collected but they were never used.[25] An interesting perspective is gained on problems of compliance from a US study which may be relevant to compliance difficulties in the UK.[26] Physicians treating hypertension were unanimous that one of the most important factors for patient compliance was drug cost, which was as important as unpleasant adverse effects and other factors (*see* Table 16.1).

Table 16.1: Percentage of physicians responding to the question, 'What do you think are some of the important factors that affect patient compliance with antihypertensive drug therapy?'[26]

Factors affecting compliance	Cardiologists (%)	Internists (%)	General/family practitioners (%)
Drug costs	97.0	96.7	98.0
Unpleasant adverse effects	95.0	95.1	94.5
Dosing schedule	91.6	90.2	92.8
Inadequate patient education	79.7	78.7	82.6
Lack of patient involvement in treatment plan	61.8	64.8	69.5
Disease severity	36.9	42.6	41.3

Note: A questionnaire was sent to a random sample of 10 000 physicians (taken from the American Association's Physician Masterfile in 1996) practising in those specialties most likely to treat hypertension, including cardiology, general and geriatric internal medicine, and general and family practice. The study explored how well physicians who treat hypertension know the indications and contraindications for particular antihypertensive therapies, and how closely their opinions and practice of hypertension treatment agree with national guidelines. A total of 1023 (10.2%) physicians responded to the survey (see also Figure 16.2).

In a study of user healthcare strategies in the treatment of asthma among South Asian and white cultural groups in the UK, 55% of the respondents reported that they took their medication as prescribed. However, on closer analysis around 59% of interviewees reported that they sometimes stopped taking their prescribed medications, and this was comparable across ethnic groups.[27] The top three reasons for these patients stopping their prescribed medicines were as follows:

- feeling well (48%)
- side-effects (28%)
- fear of dependency (14%).

The reluctance to admit to non-standard medication usage indicated an awareness that drug taking might be perceived negatively by practitioners. In addition, usage of alternative therapies was widespread. No less than 84% of patients who had stopped their medication were also using a complementary or holistic approach to asthma self-management (e.g. food avoidance (47%), exercise (36%), food inclusion (31%), home remedies (31%), aromatherapy (10%), Chinese medicine (7%) and homoeopathy (7%)).

In a review of antihypertensive therapy, Collins and colleagues[28] suggested that 'actual compliance with the antihypertensive therapy might reduce stroke risks by about one half and chronic heart disease by about one-fifth within a few years'.

A similar situation may exist in the treatment of many other illnesses. Non-compliance may be a matter of choice or part of the illness or treatment. For example, in anorexia a lack of self-care is built into the condition, or secondary to symptoms in depression or schizophrenia, or it may be the result of a side-effect of medication such as sedation or weight gain.[29] Alternatively, it may result from poor levels of understanding, the tedium of facing a chronic condition or hostility towards healthcare professionals.

The scale of the problem is illustrated by the oral hypoglycaemic treatment of type II diabetes. Only 31% of the sulphonylurea-only group and 34% of those taking metformin adhered to therapy, and these figures dropped to 13% in patients taking both drugs. Furthermore, there was a decrease in adherence of 22% for each increase in frequency of daily dose.[30]

However, whatever the cause, Lacey[29] has emphasised that a multidisciplinary team has an advantage in providing greater continuity of care and allowing access to several healthcare professionals rather than one (to whom the patient might not respond).

Neglect of the needs of the patient is demonstrated by the fact that it is only now that the EU Readability Guideline for patient information leaflets is establishing their suitability for patients by user testing. It is surely absurd that one in five people in the UK is reported to be unable to read the print on medicine labels because it is too small.[31] Yet it remains clear that the mandatory comprehensive medicine information leaflets supplied as package inserts do not guarantee that all patients will be aware of the leaflet, and only a minority will read some of it.[32–34]

The concept of using patient information leaflets as prophylaxis against patients presenting with symptoms of minor illness was investigated by Heaney and colleagues[33] and Little and colleagues.[35] In these substantial studies which used nearly 10000 and about 4000 patients, respectively, there was no or only a limited impact on consultation rates. The results are probably not too surprising, as general practitioner training emphasises the need for a continuing presence to modify health-seeking behaviour. This is probably best achieved within a consultation and within context, and as part of a multifaceted approach. Indeed, the limitations of the instructional approach are now well recognised and are being replaced by a more detailed interaction with the patient that is known as concordance or partnership.[36] It was designed to help the patient to benefit much more from their medication and to include a reduction in the quite extraordinary rates of medication non-compliance.

The consequences of the patient's failure to take their medication correctly in terms of the development of adverse drug events or medication errors have been incalculable, as has the financial cost of medicines wastage and the consequences of ADEs. However, concordance also extends into other areas.

Understanding the patient's experience following the administration of a drug is becoming a key focus of the pharmaceutical and medical sciences for three further reasons.

1 Patient 'experience measures' are primary measures and indeed the only reliable measures that we have for phenomena such as pain and other subjective observations. The patient is uniquely positioned to report symptoms and their reductions for such disorders.
2 Furthermore, patient outcome measures such as quality of life (QoL) and activities of daily living (ADL) have become important for differentiating drug activities within a therapeutic class. Such experiences have been crucial to establishing the success of certain drugs.
3 Early warning systems such as the UK's Yellow Card scheme and prescription event monitoring for adverse drug events associated with new and other medicines partly rely on the patient spontaneously reporting adverse symptoms to the healthcare professional. A more formal and direct patient-instigated form of surveillance may be appropriate. For example, leaflets issued by community pharmacists encouraging patients to report adverse symptoms to their doctor increased the number of symptoms reported,[37] post-marketing surveillance of medicines by patients in the USA recorded that common ADRs were reliably reported,[38–40] in an Australian study patients were shown to identify established ADRs from symptom lists distributed by community pharmacists,[41] and in The Netherlands the reporting by patients of known and unknown adverse drug reactions may contribute to their earlier detection than is recorded by healthcare professionals (*see* Figure 16.1).[42] It was concluded that patient reporting may play an additional role in pharmacovigilance.

In the UK, the Consumers' Association, *Health Which?*, has called for the creation of a system for patients to report drug side-effects directly to the Medicines Control Agency. The Managing Editor of *Health Which?* stated that:

> *Patients should have a role in reporting side-effects of drugs – their experiences are absolutely valid and should be taken into account alongside monitoring of side-effects by healthcare professionals. The Medicines Control Agency should at least consider the pros and cons of this. Doctors continue to under-report suspected adverse reactions to drugs. And in the UK, patients have been largely excluded from the side-effects-reporting system. We strongly believe that the system needs to be overhauled to give everyone a better picture of potential side-effects. The Medicines Control Agency should consider extending the black triangle scheme to patient information. This could help boost the number of side-effects reports for new drugs about which there is little information.*[43]

Patients may also describe the nature of drug-induced side-effects more accurately than is recorded by their doctor. In breast cancer patients receiving tamoxifen or goserelin, symptoms that were recorded often varied from those described by patients, with side-effects being overlooked. In total, 99% of patients experienced adverse symptoms, but only 89% had side-effects recorded. Few doctors noted the severity of the symptoms, and they tended to stress the

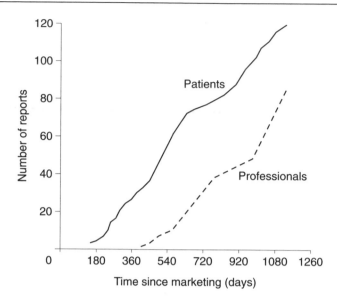

Figure 16.1: A comparison of the time to reporting of suspected adverse drug reactions (cumulative number) associated with the use of paroxetine received from patients and healthcare professionals since marketing $(t = 0)$ in The Netherlands. Prepared from the data of Egberts *et al.*[42]

least common side-effects. In total, 91% of patients believed that their treatment caused hot flushes, but this was listed on only 47% of records; 80% reported that they had gained weight, but only 21% had this symptom marked on their notes. Professor Fallowfield, who led the study, believed that 'overstretched cancer doctors simply don't have the time to spend listening to their patients'.[44]

However, it is not only patients but perhaps also their carers who can report such information. The carer's contribution in primary care was described by Banks[45] as follows:

> *The importance of care provided by family, parents and friends has been increasingly recognised over the last decade. For every 1000 patients in a practice population, there will be 120 carers supporting relatives or friends because of illness, disability or frailty. It is likely that just over 40% of the carers will be men. A large proportion of the carers will be aged between 45 and 64, but there will also be children supporting family members. The personal and emotional care that unpaid carers provide in treatment and 24-hour supervision is valued at nearly £34 billion per annum, and could never be replaced by health and social care services.*[46]

It is clear that carers play an indispensable and unique role in healthcare. They can make a vital contribution to the planning and development of services, and carer issues are being increasingly addressed within Primary Care Investment Plans.

In the UK, the patient together with primary care will be assuming centre-stage in the future healthcare system. Attempts to engage with the patient in order to improve their medication paradigm and response to treatment require a meaningful partnership with the patient. This necessitates the provision of information with understanding and continued support and assistance with the measurement of outcomes. For example, inappropriate prescribing of unnecessary drugs or those with an absolute contraindication is associated in the elderly with higher admission rates due to ADRs.[47]

The recent *National Service Framework for Older People*, published in March 2000,[48] and in particular *Medicines and Older People: implementing medicines-related aspects of the NSF for older people*,[49] published at the same time, define the standards for health and social services to ensure a high quality of care. The latter framework was produced because the majority of older people are taking prescribed medicines in conjunction with the other medicines that they buy themselves, and ensures that:

> *older people have ready access to the right medicine, at the right dose and in the right form. Achieving greater partnership in medicine taking between patients and health professionals, improving choice and addressing the information needs of older people and their carers can help meet these standards.*

Effective interventions include the following:

- *prescribing advice support*: to primary care groups and trusts and to individual prescribers to improve the quality of prescribing
- *active monitoring of treatment*: to ensure that the medicines are effective and remain so, and to detect any potential medicine-related problems at an early stage
- *review of repeat-prescribing systems*: to improve the control of prescribing
- *medication review with individual patients and their carers*: to explain why periodic review, not only of prescribed medicines, but also of those purchased over the counter, herbal and homoeopathic remedies, and medicines shared between friends, is important
- *education and training*: to monitor continuously the evidence base for the interventions in order to ensure their suitability and safety.

Such interventions would begin to address the problems that patients experience in securing and using safe treatments. For example, the key problems associated with repeat medication include unnecessary therapy, ineffective therapy, no or inadequate routine monitoring, inappropriate choice of therapy/dosing schedule and admitted non-compliance. Although the effective management of repeat prescribing remains a substantial task,[49] there is evidence from controlled trials of pharmacist-conducted medication reviews that these difficulties can be identified and resolved with the physician.[50–52] The vigilance of the community pharmacist in dispensing repeat prescriptions could help greatly to reduce preventable problems.[53] Patel reports the case of one elderly patient who had taken, exceptionally, 63 medicines in a two-year period without any review of her medication.[54] Bradford Health Authority established a scheme whereby community pharmacists carried out domiciliary visits to older people and made recommendations to the patients' GPs about the changes needed. Common problems raised by patients included unrelieved symptoms (36%), difficulty in remembering the dose of medicine (35%) and side-effects (27%).[55]

A call for specialist pharmacists to review medication in residential homes has been made in a joint report by the Royal College of Physicians, the Royal College of Nursing and the British Geriatrics Society. Improvements in safety and cost savings would be considerable, and medication review and patient education can significantly improve knowledge and compliance.[56–58] The problems revealed in such investigations are both ominous and profound. In a major study of pharmacist-conducted medication review, modifications were required for half of all the medicines prescribed, with recommendations to stop medication in 47% of the cases, and in two-thirds of these there was no stated reason for the medicine being taken.[59,60] A follow-up study showed that the reduction in the number of prescribed medicines had no adverse effect on morbidity or mortality.[61]

Concordance reflects the fact that the decades of compartmentalised patient care provided by the various professions and organised to protect a sectional interest have had some success but also frequent and lamentable failures in the totality of patient care. This chapter documents some of the serious consequences to patients of failures within the healthcare system. Frequently this has occurred because the healthcare practitioner has exceeded his or her knowledge base and competence. The powerful synergistic potential of the knowledge base and skills of a full partnership of the healthcare staff, together with that of the patient and carer, may prevent many of these failures. The Forum on Team-working in Primary Healthcare was established in 1999 as a joint initiative between the Royal Pharmaceutical Society and the British Medical Association following discussions between numerous healthcare professional groups.[62] Speaking at the report's launch, the forum's chairman indicated that 'The government's plan for the NHS calls for continued professional co-operation and development, and it is clear that the future of primary healthcare lies in the team approach'.[62]

Medical information systems are beginning to provide clinical guidelines for populations on a global scale, and managed care systems will increasingly control how care will be provided. Primary healthcare providers are taking a central role and patient stays in hospital are becoming abbreviated. Increasingly, wellness and prevention programmes are designed to keep people and patients out of the healthcare systems.

'Medicines: the future horizon'

In his address to the British Pharmaceutical Conference in September 2000,[63] Lord Hunt, Parliamentary Under-Secretary for Health, outlined three particular challenges facing pharmacy:

1 to meet patients' changing needs to ensure that people could obtain medicines and pharmaceutical advice easily
2 to provide more support in the use of medicines, with extra help for those who needed it to get the maximum benefit from their medicines; too many medicines were wasted and far too many patients suffered avoidable side-effects
3 to give patients confidence that the advice they receive is good advice.

This meant 'making sure that professional education and training met the needs of tomorrow's world, and making sure that pharmacists were keeping their skills up to date'.

Lord Hunt also said that new legislation would extend prescribing rights as a way of matching the right skills to the tasks to be done.

Medicines management was a key issue, and the Royal Pharmaceutical Society had already done a huge amount of work to define and promote the concept of concordance. The appointment of a new chief pharmaceutical officer with the specific remit of bringing together all of the key people to implement a national strategy for integrating partnerships in medicines at all levels of the NHS is a major undertaking.[64]

Clinical governance had been introduced throughout the NHS to deliver quality standards, and pharmacists were already making significant contributions through monitoring prescribing. The date set by government for the introduction of medicines management is 2004. There were 116 applications from primary care organisations to take part in the first year of the programme, with 26 successful bids.[65] The nature of these investigations has been briefly reported elsewhere,[66] the National Prescribing Centre is developing a section for its website (www.npc.co.uk) and the Modernisation Board has also set up a website (www.pharmacyinthefuture.org.uk) involving eight pharmacy organisations to enhance progress.[67] They will address the following pivotal issues:

• delivering a measurable gain in healthcare to the patient
• constructing a new approach to patient care by developing the partnership between the patient, pharmacist, physician and other members of the healthcare team
• facilitating collaboration between the healthcare professions in primary care
• maximising the use of the skills and training of the healthcare professionals
• delivering measurable improvements in value for money in medicines prescribing, and reducing wastage.

The President of the Royal Pharmaceutical Society has emphasised that *Medicines: the Future Horizon* provides a watershed for the pharmacy profession, and that the Society's council was considering ways in which it could support the process and prepare the profession for its future responsibilities.[68]

Adapting prescribing in the new NHS: changes in the prescribing role

The education now available to pharmacy students provides one of the most detailed learning experiences with regard to drugs and their use of any undergraduate course. How can this be best used at the professional level? When the Health and Social Care Bill[69] becomes law, it will amend existing legislation to allow prescribing by pharmacists, ophthalmic opticians, osteopaths, dental auxiliaries, chiropodists and practitioners registered under the Professions Supplementary Medicine Act 1960 or the Health Act 1999. There are also provisions to establish local pharmaceutical services.

Pharmacists and primary care prescribing

The Nuffield Inquiry in 1986 and the Joint Working Party Report (Pharmaceutical Care) in 1993 identified the potential role for community pharmacists in advising GPs on prescribing. Keele University's IMPACT programme in 1994 used specially trained pharmacists to deliver prescribing advice to GPs, and funding by the Department of Health in 1995 ensured that by 1996 schemes were running in nine family health service authorities involving over 60 community pharmacists. The programme has developed rapidly, and pharmaceutical advisers are increasingly involved in medication review for patients on long-term treatment, repeat-prescribing-system reviews, some disease-management clinics, drug alerts, prescription fraud and other duties. Significant new posts continue to be created in primary care groups, which will convert to primary care trusts, and in general practice. Indeed, there are now over 500 adviser posts in primary care in the UK, and these will be supported by core competency frameworks and continuing professional development. Such programmes provide convincing evidence of the real benefits to professional collaboration in improved patient care.

Nurse prescribing

District nurses and health visitors successfully lobbied for prescribing rights for a limited range of items, and a *Nurse Prescribers' Formulary* was developed as an addendum to the *BNF*. The formulary was constructed mainly to cater for these professionals' needs when working at some distance from their NHS trust or GP surgery. Some practice nurses have also since been trained in nurse prescribing. Nurses undergo special training before they are allowed to prescribe, and an evaluation of the scheme indicates its success. The schemes appear to have met with approval by both the medical and nursing professions. It is the proposed extension of the *Nurse Prescribers' Formulary* that has occasioned a consultative document. The Royal Pharmaceutical Society has welcomed proposals for extended nurse prescribing, provided that public safety remains the paramount consideration.[70] The contribution of pharmacists to the previous training of nurse prescribers had been highly valued by the nurses who had been trained.[70]

In the Department of Health document, *Consultation on Proposals to Extend Nurse Prescribing*,[71] five options are identified in the extension involving the inclusion of General Sales List and Pharmacy medicines and licensed Prescription Only Medicines (POMs).

The consultation document requested views on the extension of nurse prescribing with regard to the principles, potential medical conditions, options for extending the *Nurse Prescribers' Formulary*, nurses who may train to prescribe, and plans for their preparation and training. The principles described were patient safety, better and more convenient care for patients, an extension of nurse prescribing which will reflect what is needed to manage patients' medical conditions, and convenient access to treatment. This will help to define the range of suitable interventions, which medicines might be added to the *Nurse Prescribers' Formulary*, what kind of training and support nurses will need, and which nurses will need prescribing training. Decisions will be driven by patient and local service needs, nurses will take full clinical responsibility for their decisions, and pharmacists and the Prescription Pricing Authority need to be able to identify easily those nurses who are entitled to prescribe, and what they can prescribe.

The Medical Conditions were described as follows:

> The current Nurse Prescribers' Formulary *is fairly limited in the conditions which it covers, concentrating on dressings and appliances, though it does also include a limited number of medicines, including some prescription-only medicines. Informal discussions with the health professions have indicated that the formulary needs to be extended to cover other and broader medical conditions, so that patients are able to gain access to the medicines they need more easily, and so that the skills of nurses are better used. Examples of these additional groups of medical conditions include:*
>
> * *treatment for minor injuries and ailments*
> * *health maintenance*
> * *chronic disease management*
> * *palliative care.*

McGavock[72] has expressed grave concern about the extension of nurse prescribing (although the sentiment could be expressed against any potential prescriber) in that the public has a right to expect that every nurse prescriber should be formally trained by university-level experts with at least six months' full-time teaching followed by one year of supervised prescribing, with legal responsibility for extended nurse prescribing resting with the nurse. Certainly the knowledge base required for nurse prescribing as described by Courtenay and Butler[73] is currently only found in pharmacy, medical and pharmacology degrees. This would presumably require the taking of major sections of these degrees. The degree of information or knowledge that is required would theoretically be dependent on the breadth of the prescribing authority envisaged.[74] However, the breadth and other issues require clarification. This is clearly evident from a report on a recent seminar on prescribing issues.[75]

The meeting was opened by Dr June Crown, Chairman of the Review of Prescribing Supply and Administration of Medicines, who emphasised that the review had been necessary because of the changes in professional education and training, patient expectations, professional relationships and the range and complexity of medicines, and had demonstrated the confidence that the Government had in the staff working for the NHS. Prescribing rights for those professionals named 'professions supplementary to medicine' would be enabled 'when the case is made'. However, the Chairman of the Crown Report commented that:

> the current extension of nurse prescribing was not the route she would have recommended to take prescribing forward safely. She felt that specialist nurses in whom we had confidence to prescribe should have been the focus. Caution was needed to ensure that walk-in centres and direct-access centres did not create problems; they were a potentially difficult area to manage.

At the same seminar, Professor While, Professor of Community Nursing, spoke about the difficulty of translating into practice the lessons learned from the nurse-prescribing pilot projects, which could not necessarily be used to inform the future. All specialist community nurses had now been trained to become prescribers, but they were a heterogeneous group – they did not all have the same education, background or experience:

> There seemed to be two groups forming: prescribers and reluctant prescribers. Three months after training, some had not prescribed at all; increasing anxiety and the lack of confidence had meant that they could not put pen to paper. There had been a lack of research into aspects of nurse prescribing. The enablers and inhibitors to prescribing had not been identified. The way forward was to recognise that the nurses' role needed to be adjusted in order to accommodate prescribing. Robust nurse prescriber education was required together with a recognition of the ongoing education needs of nurse prescribers. There were difficulties educating people halfway through their professional lives, and compensation was needed for varied educational experience. Professor While believed that nurses had had an idea, which was just a contextual idea, foisted upon them. There was confusion and extra bureaucracy as a result, which was not beneficial from a patient viewpoint. It was a difficult path to

tread. She did not want to imply that nurses were not up to the challenge, but that there was a need to recognise that challenge.[75]

In an overview of prescribing for all professions, a primary care trust executive committee chairman emphasised that the corporate nature of PCTs provided the best opportunity that the NHS had ever had, and that safe, economical and effective prescribing was a team responsibility – the key was teamwork.

There can be no doubt that patient safety now rules supreme in the NHS, that medication errors are one of the most frequent causes of medical error, that prescription medicines are probably the fourth to sixth commonest cause of death and a leading public health problem, that the traditional prescriber has made most errors, and that the detection and reporting of errors by the patients and healthcare staff will proceed at an unprecedented level. *The future prescriber of whatever denomination has a most daunting task to improve the standards of prescribing and this will be assessed under intense patient and public scrutiny.* The reluctance of some trained prescribers to assume a prescriber's role must be respected – it is difficult to imagine a more hazardous beginning for a very difficult task. It is taken that the Department of Health will not progress anything that is suspect, unsafe or unsound, *to either the healthcare professional or the patient.*

To prescribe drugs safely is a major undertaking. To prescribe for minor ailments and self-limiting conditions is a relatively low-risk activity. However, there is a fundamental contradiction in attempting to extend the formulary to cover other and 'broader medical conditions', and yet attempt to define for these specific medical treatments a limited prescribing formulary that could be described as safe practice. It is implicit in this approach that one is considering the defined and discrete use of a number of formulary-based medicines for a clearly defined service need. The treatment of minor ailments and conditions may be relatively simplistic. However, this can be vastly different to the treatment of chronic and other illnesses which may require or involve multiple drug treatments and a much greater knowledge base. Precisely the same comments also apply to medication review.

For example, in chronic disease management one identifies a disease and the drug treatment(s) relevant to that disorder. However, the problem in the real world is that patients frequently exit hospital with a discharge prescription for many medicines (*see* Figure 6.7), perhaps from different specialists, or are receiving treatments for co-existing conditions in primary care. Alternatively, but just as likely, the patient may already be taking an ill-defined number of medicines purchased from a pharmacy or shared with friends (*see* page 224). Prescribing potent medicines comes at a very real cost, *both to the prescriber and to the patient* (also *see* Chapter 8).

Hypertension is one of the most prevalent chronic diseases seen in medical practice, affecting some 50 million people in the USA alone. The treatment of hypertension illustrates the profound depth of knowledge and understanding required for its safe treatment. It:

involves a knowledge of and choice among a bewildering array of medications with varied pharmacologic mechanisms, such as alpha- and beta-adrenergic blockade, calcium channel blockade, angiotensin-converting enzyme inhibition, diuresis, and vasodilation, and the indications and contraindications for each. Within each of these major classes there are important subclasses, such as thiazide versus potassium sparing diuretics and dihydropyridine versus other calcium-channel blockers, adding further complexity to the decision making.[26]

Cardiovascular specialists may be best trained to treat hypertension, but most hypertensive patients are seen and treated in primary care. The quality of care for this condition depends on the effective dissemination of information from clinical research to clinical practice. In the presence of ongoing educational efforts, a recent survey explored how well US physicians who treat hypertension know the indications and contraindications for particular antihypertensive therapies, and how closely their opinions and practice of hypertension treatment agree with national guidelines. The physicians (cardiologists, internists and general/family practitioners) had to answer four questions and amongst all respondents 37.3% answered all four knowledge questions correctly and 78.8% correctly answered at least three. The proportion of physicians that correctly identified the preferred drug class is shown in Figure 16.2, increasing from 25.7% for general/family practitioners to 49.5% for cardiologists. However, the respondents were less compliant with the recommended preference for evidence-based prescribing of diuretics and beta-blockers. It was concluded that the national efforts to educate physicians about the increasingly complex armamentarium for hypertension, and to persuade them to base their prescribing on the results of randomised, controlled trials of primary prevention, must be continued.[26]

Thus, the survey addressed questions relating to routine treatments of hypertension by physicians. The increasingly complex nature of prescribing is described by O'Rourke and Richardson for the management of hypertension when blood pressure is difficult to control.[76] It involves:

inaccurate blood pressure measurements, white-coat hypertension, disease progression, suboptimal treatment, non-compliance with prescribed treatments, coexisting conditions, secondary hypertension and substances in the diet or as medication that may oppose antihypertensive treatment (caffeine, alcohol, cocaine, medications containing sodium (e.g. antacids or parenteral antibiotics), amphetamines, appetite suppressants or nasal decongestants, non-steroidal anti-inflammatory agents, steroids, monoamine oxidase inhibitors and many other drugs) and even withdrawal from antihypertensive agents such as clonidine or beta-blockers. Furthermore, several disorders may coexist in patients with hypertension to either increase blood pressure or interfere with its treatment, and these include anxiety disorders, obesity, smoking, alcohol abuse, acute or chronic pain, pregnancy and sleep apnoea.

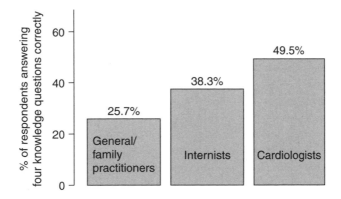

Figure 16.2: A questionnaire was sent to a random sample of 10 000 physicians (taken from the American Association's Physician Masterfile in 1996) practising in those specialties most likely to treat hypertension, including cardiology, general and geriatric internal medicine, and general and family practice. The study explored how well physicians who treat hypertension know the indications and contraindications for particular antihypertensive therapies, and how closely their opinions and practice of hypertension treatment agree with national guidelines. A total of 1023 (10.2%) physicians responded to the survey. Five groups of drugs were identified and the physicians were asked (a) Which classes of drugs are primarily used for high-renin hypertensive patients and also used to treat congestive heart failure, (b) Which classes of drugs are most appropriate in treating hypertensive patients with angina or post-myocardial infarction? (c) Which classes of drugs are contraindicated in the presence of renal decompensation and can cause dehydration? (d) Response to question 'In your opinion, at which systolic and diastolic blood pressure would you consider a patient to have mild, moderate and severe blood pressure?', assessed in relation to the Fifth Joint National Committee on the Detection, Evaluation and Treatment of High Blood Pressure.[26]

The authors conclude that there is little evidence beyond expert opinion to guide clinicians in the treatment of this condition.

Thus for a prescriber to treat hypertension safely, a thorough understanding of the pharmacology and therapeutics of drug action that extends far beyond the confines of antihypertensive therapy is necessary. *Precisely the same comments can be made for many other chronic disorders.* If the prescriber is aware of such problems, and has been intensively trained, then they may not exceed their authority and seek help when required. However, the third commonest cause of medication error is the prescriber acting (perhaps unknowingly) beyond their competence. Moreover, such comments do not apply just to prescription medicines. Many patients now take herbal medications, and not withstanding the fact that healthcare professionals may be concerned about the frequent absence of evidence to secure their use, they may interact significantly with other drugs and procedures.

For example, can the reader identify which of the following herbal products should be discontinued, or continued at the same dose, or have the dose increased before the patient undergoes surgery? Consider *Echinacea*, *Ephedra*, garlic, *Ginkgo*, ginseng, kava, St John's wort and valerian in the context of this question. The pharmacological effects of these products and their deleterious effects on perioperative care have recently been summarised by Ang-Lee and colleagues, and the answer is that all of these compounds should be discontinued in order to prevent adverse effects on the vascular and other systems and herb–drug interactions.[77]

Do patients understand the importance of pharmacodynamic and pharmacokinetic drug effects and interactions? Have healthcare professionals been properly taught about the interactions of herbal preparations with prescription medicines and operative procedures?[78] Indeed, have healthcare professionals been trained in the pharmacology and clinical value of natural products and other complementary and alternative medicines in their own right? This issue is addressed for the new medical curriculum in the *New Doctor* consultative document. But do schools of medicine, nursing and other healthcare disciplines have staff with the necessary knowledge and skills base in pharmacognosy/ phytochemistry/pharmacology to have credibility, competence and expertise in teaching about natural products? What components of the present courses will have to be jettisoned to allow the inclusion of new material? Furthermore, although pharmacognosy has traditionally been a pharmacy-based discipline, it may even be questioned whether or not all schools of pharmacy have maintained expertise in this area. The subject itself may have been jettisoned to provide room for teaching on the latest advances in molecular biology, genetics and other disciplines. In addition, the division between competing pressures of research and teaching in UK universities has generally prioritised the appointment of new staff to support and enhance existing research strengths. It is not surprising that, in the USA, a survey of pharmacy schools in 1998 revealed that 13 out of 50 schools reported that herbal medicines were not discussed at all, and in those that responded, the number of contact hours for both herbal and complementary and alternative medicine (CAM) ranged from 1.5 to 67 hours among 36 of the 50 schools.[79]

This is not a trivial issue. The rapidly developing interest in CAM by society is now obvious. Examples include herbal medicines, Chinese or Ayurvedic medicines, orthomolecular therapies, acupuncture, aromatherapy, reflexology, massage, relaxation therapies, naturopathy and homoeopathy.[80] The information that is available for the lay reader on these subjects both in magazines and on the Internet is enormous and incessant and some Internet sites on herbal medicines offer sound advice. For example, *The Herbal Encyclopedia* emphasises:

> *that herbs are medicines which should be treated with the very same respect as prescription drugs; that more is not better; dosage needs to be carefully controlled; one dose does not fit all; doses need to be based on the illness treated, your past and present medical history, your age, your weight and other factors. A*

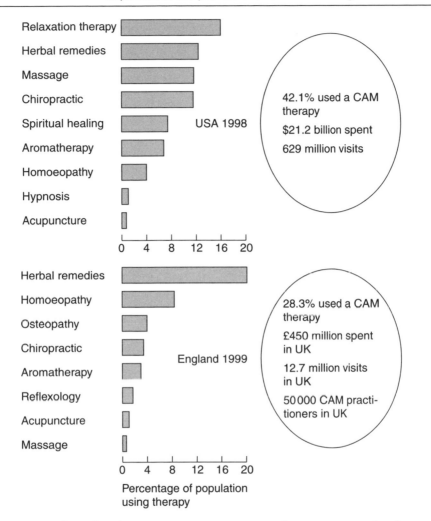

Figure 16.3: The developing interest in complementary and alternative medicine (CAM) in the USA and the UK, and the percentage of the population that uses different types of therapy.[80]

> *healthcare professional can help you choose the proper combinations and dosages ... tell your doctor what you are taking ... some herbs have serious adverse reactions when improperly used with prescription drugs ...*[81]

Given the account above, Waltz's belief that the healthcare professional can help in the choice of proper combinations and dosages appears optimistic at best.

The extent of the interest in CAM in the USA and the UK is clear from the data shown in Figure 16.3.[80] However, lack of convincing evidence for a treatment or procedure that can be distinguished from a placebo response has, for some healthcare staff, occasioned concern about or even disbelief in CAM.[82,83] And some of these therapies – for example, homoeopathy – directly challenge our basic scientific understanding. In addition, there may be genuine concerns about the safety of some products or therapies. For example, from July 2001 a permanent ban was imposed on *Aristolochia* species because they pose a serious risk to public health – aristolochic acids are mutagenic, carcinogenic and cause kidney damage. A ban on other species is inevitable, since a number of plants have similar common or Pin Yin names, and Chinese herbal tradition allows the interchange of plants with similar medicinal properties.[84]

A recent edition of *Current Problems in Pharmacovigilance* indicates that the use of *Psoralea corylifolia* fruit in unlicensed herbal preparations is causing concern because the fruit is known to contain furanocoumarin psoralen, which is known to cause phototoxicity. The level of psoralen in the fruit may vary considerably, and thus preparations made by herbalists could contain variable amounts of the compound. A safe dose of psoralen has not yet been established. It was concluded that patients who are treated with non-standardised, uncontrolled herbal preparations derived from *Psoralea corylifolia* fruit are at risk of serious skin reactions, and that traditional Chinese medicines which contain *Psoralea corylifolia* should not be used.[85]

However, irrespective of the frequent controversy about the efficacy or otherwise of such treatments, the crucial and undeniable observation is that CAM *is* used by a significant and probably increasing number of patients, and some alternative therapies may or may not interact with other medicines. The future healthcare professional has little option other than to understand about their use. Yet how, for future students, a major and significant body of new knowledge is to be introduced into an already fully demanding curriculum is unclear. Ignoring the problem is no longer an option, as there are clear hazards associated with the unthinking use of some of these treatments, whether or not their use is combined with that of conventional medicines. What is not acceptable in terms of patient safety is the development of double standards in the assessment procedures for chemicals described as 'conventional medicines' and chemicals described as 'alternative natural products'. It is particularly concerning that in one report from the USA, 38.5% of patients using CAM did not disclose this fact to their doctor.[86] This reflects a clear and immediate danger.

Many of the above issues were addressed at the Sixty-First Congress of the International Pharmaceutical Federation in Singapore in 2001.[87] A Centre for Integrative Therapies in Pharmaceutical Care, which deals with substance-based alternative therapies, was set up in 1999 with a website to help healthcare professionals to obtain appropriate information (www.mcp.edu/altmed). However, further referenced material is clearly required.

To return to the role of the prescriber, it is clear that the prescriber's responsibilities can be found, possibly unexpectedly, within a disconcertingly broadening perspective. Section 16 of the consultative document on nurse prescribing states:

> *The Department of Health favours one* Formulary for Nurse Pre-scribing, *with individual nurses using their professional judgement to decide the items within it that they are competent to prescribe. There is a parallel here with doctors and dentists, who although authorised under the Medicines Act to prescribe any medicine, would not necessarily choose to do so. Clearly, the type and extent of a training programme for nurses is a key issue.*

It is not clear why the Department of Health wishes to perpetuate an inherently unsafe system. Surely it is unsafe for *any prescriber* to be able to prescribe *any* formulary drug based on a subjective assessment of personal competence. In the event of misadventure, the new Civil Procedure Rules will require evidence of good practice, and this in turn will require objective evidence of appropriate knowledge and skills. However, it is clear that it is the type of programme and training for all prescribers (including nurses) which is the pivotal issue and which will finally identify their remit and responsibilities.

The announcement in November 2001 of compulsory guidelines aimed at preventing intrathecal chemotherapy disasters is a watershed in regulating the prescribing, preparation, supply and administration of such drugs. NHS trusts were given just three weeks to check that they complied with the new compulsory guidelines for safe intrathecal chemotherapy.[88] The essential core of the new guidelines is a register of those who have been *trained and certified as competent* to prescribe, prepare, dispense, supply, check or administer intrathecal chemotherapy. *Formal assessment will be required.* Thus, drug preparation is only permitted by pharmacy staff who are so registered; prescribing is restricted to consultants and registrars, as is administration (full guidance can be found at www.doh.gov.uk/intrathecalchemotherapy/index.html).

The stringency of the regulations is intended to relegate intrathecal errors (which are extremely rare) to history. But the new regulations are a turning point in recognising the seriousness with which damage to patients caused by either a lapse in judgement or the incompetent use of any therapeutic agent is viewed. For example, does it make sense that there is no formal recognition of staff competence for the administration of chemotherapy by oral and parenteral routes other than intrathecal, which continues to involve a serious and predictable adverse event profile and places countless more patients at risk? Does it make sense that there are other numerous groups of drugs which require great skill in their use but are used by staff of essentially unproven competence? But more positively, we finally begin to recognise, take hold of and address a major problem – the poor or incompetent use of medicines.

In the NHS Plan that was presented to Parliament by the Secretary of State for Health in July 2000,[6] it is envisaged that by:

> *the year 2001, around 23 000 nurses will have the right to prescribe a limited range of medicines. We will then extend both the range of medicines which can be prescribed and the numbers of nurses who can do so. The introduction this year of 'Patient Group Directions', which enable nurses and other professionals to supply medicines to*

patients according to protocols authorised by a doctor or pharmacist, will mean that by 2004 a majority of nurses should be able to prescribe.

The close collaboration by all members of the healthcare team and patients in the careful prescribing, monitoring and taking of medication is a goal worthy of their united and unremitting efforts.

Caution: a prescribing role *per se*?

The final report on the review of prescribing, supply and administration of medicines by Dr Crown was published in March 1999, and sought to provide a robust framework for prescribing which would improve patient care.[89] It advocates two new types of prescribers, as independent or dependent, as reviewed by Livingstone.[90] In particular, there has been much discussion of pharmacists and nurses contributing to a prescribing role. Both groups may wish to consider that *it requires a knowledge and understanding considerably beyond the skills and knowledge base that is required for the dispensing or administration of drugs.*

The number of errors committed in dispensing is low, and a credit to the care taken by pharmacy in both primary and secondary care. This figure is much lower than those recorded in either the prescribing or the administration stages of a drug being given to the patient. Dispensing normally involves double checking, which has contributed to the low error rates. However, and more importantly, *for many years the mandatory recording of errors and their careful analysis in major community pharmacy concerns* (e.g. Boots and Lloyds pharmacies), at all levels of the organisation, has a proven record of achievement which demonstrates that systems which do not hide and punish error effectively learn, correct and improve to maintain a high level of safe performance.

However, caution is needed – comparisons of degrees of error between the prescribing, administration and dispensing roles should be approached with care.

It must be understood that *prescribing carries far more risks than dispensing*, and that healthcare staff are required and patients are now being invited and encouraged to report all future medication errors and 'near misses'.

However, the doctor, pharmacist, nurse or other healthcare worker who wishes to offer a greater contribution to the advising/prescribing role now has the great advantage of being able to begin to understand some of the causes of error in the prescribing process.

> A major and fundamental problem has been *lack of knowledge of the drug or patient.*

Future prescribers must be absolutely clear that, before approaching the prescriber's role and the patient, they have the knowledge and skills necessary to perform one of the most demanding tasks in therapeutics.

The importance of collaboration and concordance

Collaboration, concordance or partnership at all levels to ensure that the patient receives an effective and safe treatment will be a most important and perhaps the major and continuing goal[91] (*also see* www.concordance.org/). It has been described as 'the fortunate collision between the prescriber's biomedical representation of illness and the patient's real-world view'.[92]

The Forum on Teamworking in Primary Care is supported by the British Dental Association, the Patients' Association and many others to facilitate understanding and progress.[93]

Certainly, electronic prescribing and recording of patient data can reduce errors of communication and support clinical decision making by doctors, nurses and pharmacists (*see* page 127).[94,95] The Government initiative, 'Information for Health', may also finally include social and community care records.[96] However, computer-held records are only as reliable as the software and the data entered.[97] *And there is no software available that can meaningfully predict the consequences of the interaction of a patient's prescribed medication armamentarium, involving perhaps a dozen drugs, with variables such as age, coexisting conditions, disease progression, non-compliance, self-medication, and the taking of recreational drugs such as alcohol and smoking.*

The patient's best chance of surviving their illness and medication still depends on an experienced clinical practitioner.

Electronic databases are not a panacea. Their introduction cannot eliminate all errors associated with prescribing (*see* page 129), and invariably they require attention at the user–system interface to prevent the introduction of new problems. In addition, a number of pharmacy computer systems have been shown to have limited reliability when used to detect prescription errors,[94,98,99] and pharmacists should not rely exclusively on these systems, nor should they routinely override alerts. Medication errors resulting in litigation will not be excused because of a reliance on computer-related prescribing.

However, the provision of information from a computer, the Internet and elsewhere is quite distinct from a knowledge base that comes from years of experience and an authoritative understanding of drug action and therapeutic potential that can be related to an individual patient.

Moving from an information-based to a knowledge-based healthcare system

Knowledge and understanding cannot be accessed from a laptop computer at the patient's bedside. The laptop simply provides information, as do patient chart records. This is a crucial point which is illustrated by the following account.

Lesar and colleagues,[100] in an analysis of medication-prescribing errors in a teaching hospital, found that no less than 30% of potentially severe or serious errors (61 cases) concerned allergic drug reactions where patients with confirmed histories of allergic drug reactions were prescribed either the medication to which the patient was allergic, an agent of the same pharmacological class, or a drug of a chemical class with a high frequency of cross-reactivity. Similarly, Leape and colleagues[101] found instances where an allergy to a drug was clearly indicated on the patient's hospital chart record, yet an order for the same drug was written immediately below it! Even more alarmingly, Preston and colleagues,[102] in an analysis of patients with an established allergy to penicillin, found that the agents substituted for penicillin were actually potentially *more* toxic in 70% of cases. In a primary care study, no less than 13% of patients with an adverse drug event which required hospitalisation had a fully documented previous reaction to the causative drug,[103] and all such drug/allergy interactions are potentially fatal!

A recent and poignant case was that of care worker Teresa Innes who, prior to her admittance to a UK hospital for the treatment of a leg infection, was apprehensive for her safety. This same hospital had previously determined that she was severely allergic to penicillin and had warned her of the serious dangers of any such future treatments. Therefore before entering hospital she had taken a number of precautions:

- her GP was requested to phone the hospital beforehand to warn them of her sensitivity
- she wore a bracelet stating that she should not be administered penicillin
- she took a letter with her from her GP detailing her condition
- she warned a surgeon of her sensitivity after her admission, which was noted
- she checked that her medical notes clearly stated that she should not be given penicillin.

After entering hospital and whilst waiting for the operation to proceed, doctors decided to administer the antibiotic Magnapen by drip to fight the infection. Ms Innes immediately had an anaphylactic response, resulting in brain damage and coma. It is reported that the surgeon who suggested the drug and the junior doctor who wrote the prescription were unaware of her allergy, and that the nurse who administered the drug was unaware that Magnapen is penicillin-related.[104] Not withstanding the valiant attempts of Ms Innes and her GP to ensure her survival at the hands of the healthcare system, they failed.

In 1998, the FDA warned physicians against the inappropriate use of cisapride, employing prominent publication of case reports, label changes and 'Dear Health Care Professional' letters. In the year before the warning the proportions of patients taking cisapride (where its use was contraindicated) in three sites were 26%, 30% and 60%, respectively. In the year after the warnings, the corresponding figures were 24%, 28% and 58%, respectively.[105]

Patient information leaflets on the use of isophane insulin in pen injectors indicate the importance of tipping for resuspension to ensure adequate mixing and injection, but only 9% of patients were found to have adequately accomplished the task.[106,107]

The lessons of history are clear:

> Providing information does *not* necessarily guarantee its sensible use, even when it may prevent serious injury to or death of the patient.

The above examples call into question the competence of healthcare staff and patients in interpreting the information that is already in their possession. Their knowledge base and understanding were apparently inadequate for the task in hand. It is not immediately clear why the presentation of the same cautionary data on a computer screen would encourage a more thoughtful response.

Similarly, it is clear that those patients who now arrive at the doctors' surgery armed with printouts from the Internet and other literature sources about the latest available treatments (Poste has reported that 40% of patients in America now send emails to their doctor and 22% arrive to see their physician with printouts[108]) have far more information. However, it is equally clear that the patient cannot interpret the data without expert help. It is significant that 89% of adult patients in the UK have never used the Internet when they or their family members were ill, because they were concerned that they would wrongly diagnose themselves or take the wrong medicine.[109]

Even experts in the healthcare sciences accessing research papers outside their immediate area of expertise in genetics or molecular biology, for example, may not understand the vocabulary of the science, let alone the meaning of the research. Physicians have expressed concern that, without genetics training, they are ill equipped to interpret genetic tests and provide counselling. In an attempt to develop a genetic testing guideline for the mutation of BRCA1 and BRCA2, which predicts a predisposition to breast and ovarian cancer, with all the associated risk factors, the guideline grew into a seven-page spreadsheet which only trained genetic personnel could interpret, and there are around 4000 genetic disorders each with its own unique risk factors and environmental and behavioural interactions.[110]

The problems inherent in translating information into knowledge are highlighted by the latest major research initiatives undertaken within the Engineering and Physical Sciences Research Council (EPSRC) and the Medical Research Council (MRC). The EPSRC has established no less than four new interdisciplinary research collaborations (IRCs) and one collaboration with the MRC to help to identify and solve the major problems of information technology and information overload. These six-year programmes involve 20 universities and around 45 companies, and will investigate how digital technology can be developed to move data at speeds of up to a hundred million million bits of information a second, and how this raw information can be organised, filtered and managed. Professor Brady, who leads the new IRC 'from medical images and signals to clinical information', has emphasised that:

> clinicians face huge floods of data; they are now almost overwhelmed by the rate at which images and signals come at them. We plan to use image and signal processing in a way that condenses the amount of information and presents it in a way that aids rather than hinders decision-making.[111]

However, information is normally of little value without knowledge and understanding. Data and information represent only the very beginnings of a difficult journey on the path towards knowledge. The journey from 'File-server' to 'Knowledge-server' remains an intriguing goal!

A model of a knowledge-based information system indicating the hierarchy of data, information, knowledge and finally wisdom is shown in Figure 16.4. Data are transformed by processing (by humans or machines) into information which has little intrinsic value. The crucial step is the transformation of information into knowledge, which requires existing heuristics and rules, which are essential to reach conclusions and make inferences, and for decision making and problem solving.[112] When tempered by judgement and a system of values, and enhanced by accumulating experiences and learning, prudence, insight, instincts, intuition and discernment, wisdom may develop, this being a lifelong endeavour which enhances the highest level of understanding.

The pressures of undergraduate student life or personal inclination ensure that most students focus on the second stage of information in order to pass their exams. For most healthcare students it is likely that true understanding and knowledge begin to develop during the period of clinical training. However, there remain concerns that the distributive importance of knowledge and information may change, effectively flattening the pyramidal structure, with an increasing number of practitioners being found within the 'information box'.

In summary, the experiences and understanding of the 'knowledgeable few' may be translated downwards in clinical guidelines that amount to a series of instructions to those who have a reduced level of expertise or competence. If this is the actuality, then the guidelines may indeed ensure a better level of clinical care. Together with the respectability of many of the guidelines, they may also afford some defence in the event of adverse reactions. The concern is that fewer practitioners would attempt to achieve the higher levels of

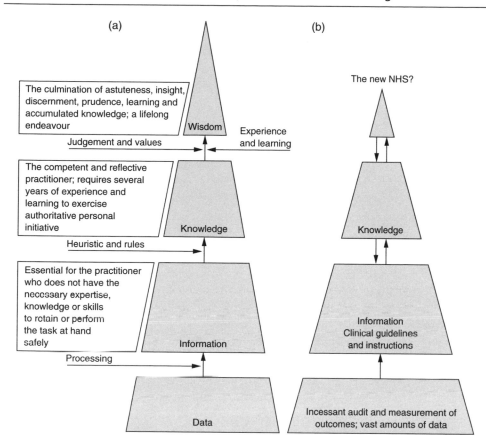

Figure 16.4: (a) A model hierarchy of data-processing into information which, when combined with heuristics and rules, will yield knowledge. When knowledge is tempered by judgement and a value system together with experience and learning, then knowledge becomes wisdom. Prepared from Partridge and Hussain.[112] (b) Potential changes in the distribution of the hierarchy in the NHS caused by increasing emphasis on the information stage and the introduction of clinical guidelines, and the relevance of the stages to the changing face of clinical competence.

professional development, resulting in an increasing number of less knowledgeable practitioners. Indeed, would professionals be required at all for many of the tasks if the response simply required adherence to a series of instructions?

When guidelines are not sensibly defended to guide the actions of the attendant physician, then one cannot blame the physician for departing from the guidelines. However, the reality is that the physician would have to fully defend any such departure from the guidelines (an onerous task), which effectively merge into instructions.

Chapter 17

Future directions for professional expertise in healthcare: a conundrum

Summary: The increasing need for professional expertise: a conundrum

- The incessant progression of knowledge leads inexorably to the focusing and refinement but also the narrowing of highly specific skills.
- However, in what has been described as one of the great issues for medicine in the twenty-first century, fewer and fewer patients will present with a disease involving only one system.
- In future we may have to revive the role of the generalist to 'try to put the human organism back together again and see how it works as a whole'.

In summary, the ever-increasing workloads, an ever-increasing database, the relentless march of knowledge and the erosion of learned material inevitably conspire to limit and define professional competence.

This affects all professions. A visit to many law firms will reveal experts in criminal, company, planning, probate, family, patenting and other law specialisms. A visit to an accountancy practice will reveal specialists in national insurance, insolvency, capital gains tax, inheritance tax, income, VAT and others, all within the same firm. And yes, some of these initiatives have been driven by the concern that staff may provide inadequate professional advice with potential litigation. However, the individual limitations *were* acknowledged, to ensure that both the staff and their clients were suitably protected.

It is clear that the advances in the pharmaceutical and medical sciences are no less profound. It appears inevitable that the manifestations of effective and safe healthcare require the working together of those with diverse and specialised knowledge and skills that are necessarily distributed both within and between the healthcare professions. This has clearly occurred within secondary care, with varying degrees of success, and is beginning to occur within primary care.

The growth of specialisms in postgraduate education in the medical sciences began about 70 years ago. However, it is only within the last 20 years that the growth has been exceptional, as exemplified by the American experience (see Figure 17.1). Since 1980, the number of specialities/subspecialities of certificated and accredited programmes has increased dramatically. As of January 2000, the Accreditation Council for Graduate Medical Education (ACGME) accredited nearly 7700 residency programmes in 103 specialities.[1] There have been attempts to limit this growth, but the desire for special recognition of narrower and narrower areas of knowledge and/or techniques is substantial. Will Europe follow the US in the provision of specialist skills? It would appear inevitable, but the growth of specialisms comes at a cost.

In 1966, the Citizens Commission on Graduate Medical Education[2] concluded that 'The rise in specialization has been accompanied by an alarming decline in the number of physicians who devote themselves to continuing and comprehensive care of the whole individual'.

More recently, in the USA there have been substantial pressures to increase the number of primary care physicians and to reduce the number of specialists and subspecialists, but this was in response to economic initiatives.

However, in a discussion of the major issues for medicine in the twenty-first century, Sir David Weatherall neatly summarised the problem as follows:[3]

> with the increasing aged populations, fewer and fewer patients are being encountered who have disease involving only one system. Our teaching hospitals of the future will have to revive the central role of the generalist just as, when the Humane Genome Project is complete, the next generation of biologists will have to take a more holistic view and, using biomathematical approaches that have not yet even been dreamed of, try to put the human organism back together and see how it works as a whole.

Such concerns are deceptively simplistic as we approach one of the greatest problems already challenging safe and effective treatments. It is implicit within Sir David's comments that the 'generalist' would be required to have the knowledge and skills to safely address dysfunction of the whole patient. In brief, if acting individually, he or she would surely require to a considerable degree the knowledge and skills of different specialists to address different system dysfunctions; this does not appear possible. Alternatively, the generalist may play the crucial role in attempting to bring together the deliberations of the individual 'specialists' to ensure an effective and safe coherence between the various individual specialist prescribed treatments. This reveals both the advantages and the shortcomings of 'specialisms' and the 'specialist'.

A perspective on the depth of the problem of 'specialisms' has been apparent for generations and has been recorded by John Ralston Saul in his elegant discourse *Life in a box: specialization and the individual.*[4]

> *The rise of the professional was intimately linked throughout the industrial revolution with individual responsibility, to the degree*

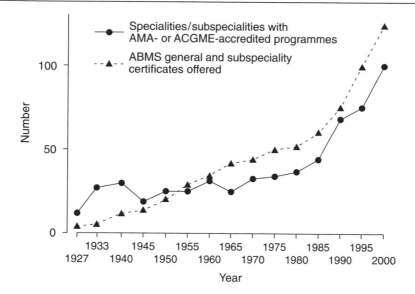

Figure 17.1: Growth of specialisations in graduate medical education for accreditation and certification between 1927 and 2000 in the USA. AMA, American Medical Association; ACGME, Accreditation Council for Graduate Medical Education; ABMS, American Board of Medical Specialists. Prepared from the data of Donini-Lenho and Hedrick.[1]

that he was competent. Thus the value of individualism was pegged to the soaring value of specialization. This was both the measure of his worth and the sum of his contribution to society as a whole. The assumption seemed to be that this new professionalism would lead to bodies of expertise joining together in a sort of populist meritocracy . . . . The professional did indeed find that he could build his personal empire; but curiously enough, the more expert he became, the more his empire shrank. On the one hand, because he was a virtually all-powerful retainer of information, expertise and responsibility over a tiny area, his co-operation was essential to others who, although within his general discipline, were themselves experts in other tiny areas. Obviously, the co-operation of the whole group, with each other and with society as a whole, was also essential to the general population. On the other hand, as these tiny areas of absolute responsibility proliferated, each individual was more securely locked in his confining cell of expertise. Inevitably, he became increasingly powerless in society as a whole. While our mythology suggests that society is like a tree with the ripening fruits of professional individualism growing thick upon it, a more accurate image would show a maze of corridors, blocked by endless locked doors, each one leading in or out of a small cell . . . .

Judge Learned Hand, then a graduating Harvard student, spoke of this modern malaise to his classmates on their convocation day in 1893:

> *'Civilization implies specialization, specialization is forgetfulness of total values and the establishment of false ones, that is philistinism. A savage can never fall into this condition, his values are all real, he supplies his own wants and finds them proceeding from himself, not an estimate of those of others. We must in practice be specialists; the division of labour ordains us to know of one subject and little of others; it forces Philistinism down our throats whether we like it or not'.*

Hand spent his life on the bench attempting to bring his assumption of morality and common sense to bear on his judgements. He wanted to link his own specialization to the outer world. For that he was respected as the greatest magistrate in America. He was not, however, named to the Supreme Court. It could be argued that, despite the best will in the world from those who are in what we call positions of responsibility, the system invariably manages not to reward those who succeed in communicating between boxes without respecting established structure . . . . During working hours a man's obligations to his employment function force him to restrain his views on this, his area of expertise. He is also silent on other people's areas of expertise. After all, the aim of structure is smooth functioning, not public criticism. And the expert's desire not to be criticized by those outside his box restrains him in turn from criticizing them. When he leaves his office/function at the end of the day, he is theoretically free. In reality, were he to engage in independent public comment on his area of expertise, while on his own time, he would find himself in serious trouble with the system that employs him. Such comment would be considered a form of treason . . . . Substantive nonconformity is treated as irresponsible and unprofessional. To do so would be to endanger a safe position inside a box. But the middle class male and female are products of an educational and social system which tells them that a successful life requires the penetration of an expert's box and the occupation of as much space as possible within and for as long a period of time as possible. Sensibly enough, few would risk losing that. This fear of acting in an irresponsible manner has struck a death blow to public debate among educated citizens.

One of the expert's most successful discoveries was that he could defend his territory by the simple development of a specialized language incomprehensible to others . . . . Subject after subject and profession after profession have now had the general understanding of their functions ripped out of the public's hands by the experts . . . . The new specialized terminology amounts to a serious attack on language as a tool of common understanding. Their standard procedure when faced by outside questioning is to avoid answering and instead to discourage, even to frighten off the questioner, by implying that he is uninformed, inaccurate, superficial and, invariably, overexcited. If the questioner has some hierarchical power, the expert may feel obliged to answer with greater care . . . . The primary instigators of obstruction are the very people who should have been devoted to the increasing of communication – the professors. They have turned their universities into temples of expertise, pandering to modern society's weakness for exclusivity . . . . They, the custodians of the Western, intellectual tradition, now devote themselves to the prevention of integrated thought. Because professors both train society's youth and catalogue current events, they have become the official guardians of the boxes in which the educated live.

Specialist skills in healthcare are essential yet evolve into ever narrower domains, to the extent that a specialist's competence and authority is tightly proscribed. Increasingly, our aged population is presenting with co-morbidity requiring attention from different specialists with different treatments, possibly little known to each other, and where the effects of such combined treatments, not unexpectedly, are possibly beyond the competence of any individual specialist to predict. In the UK, the patient's general practitioner has assumed the responsibility for managing the totality of his or her treatment (*see* Figure 17.2). But has society afforded the general practitioner the necessary resources of time and continued professional development to achieve such competence necessary for the safe delivery of healthcare?

The problem is a paradox – we require general practitioners to be highly skilled, yet we charge them with a duty of comprehensive healthcare for the whole individual. This issue has not been resolved, although primary care groups illuminate at least one constructive engagement. And others are being developed. Assistance from other healthcare professionals appears inevitable.

In August 2001, the Department of Health launched a new report, *The Expert Patient*, which described how the NHS will enable patients with chronic or long term medical conditions to become decision makers in their treatments and care.[5] It is recommended that over a six-year period user-led self-management training programmes for patients with chronic illness should be introduced, with pilot programmes being set up initially within primary care trusts. This will be accompanied by a national training and co-ordinating centre designed to provide healthcare, social services and professionals within the voluntary sector with up to date information on the provision of self-management.

The proposals set out in the report are based on the belief that many patients with chronic illnesses have a wealth of knowledge and experience about the management of their own condition and, with support and training, should be able to take the lead in their treatment. It is about the creation of a cadre of

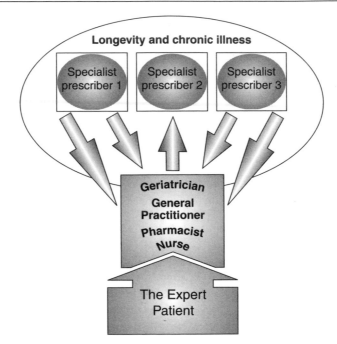

Figure 17.2: A diagrammatic presentation of the pivotal conundrum of modern medicine; how to bring together in a skillful and coherent manner specialisms, longevity and chronic illness to ensure that the totality of the combined treatments for more than one system dysfunction is effective and safe? The model depicts the demanding responsibility placed on the patient's geriatrician and healthcare team, with assistance from the patient who will be required to develop expert knowledge of their own illness.[5]

expert patients – people who have the confidence, skills, information and knowledge to play a central role in the management of life with chronic diseases, and to minimise the impact of disease on their lives. It cannot be doubted that in the UK and most other developed countries the predominant disease pattern is one of chronic rather than acute illness. The data presented in Figure 17.3 shows the extent of the problem. In the UK, at any one time, as many as 17.5 million adults may be living with a chronic disease, with some 75% of older people falling into this category. Thus, within the UK:

- arthritis affects about 8.5 million, which includes some 14 500 children
- asthma is estimated to affect over 3.4 million people, including 1.5 million children
- diabetes mellitis prevalence is thought to be in the region of 1.5 million diagnosed cases
- heart failure has been estimated to affect about half a million people
- multiple sclerosis is estimated to affect 80 000–90 000 people
- epilepsy affects more than 420 000 people.

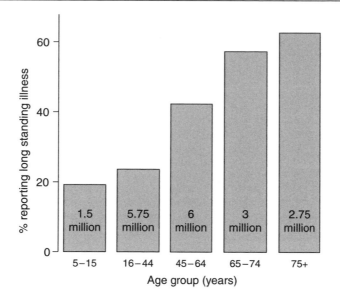

Figure 17.3: The numbers of people in the UK reporting (in millions and expressed as a percentage in age groups) that they suffer from a long standing illness.[5]

And there are inequalities between social groups, as significantly more unskilled men and women report a longstanding illness than their professional counterparts.[5]

Although people have specific needs to their individual disease, they also have common requirements:

- know how to recognise and act upon symptoms
- deal with acute attacks or exacerbations of the disease
- make the most effective use of medicines and treatments
- comprehend the implications of professional advice
- establish a stable pattern of sleep and rest and dealing with fatigue
- access social and other services
- manage work and the resources of employment services
- access chosen leisure activities
- develop strategies to deal with the psychological consequences of the illness
- learn to cope with other people's response to their chronic illness.

These are admirable goals. The challenge for the NHS, working in partnership with patient organisations and others, is to fundamentally shift the way we manage long-term illness, a shift which will empower and liberate patients to play a central role in decisions about their illness.

Yet this does not abrogate the responsibility of the healthcare professional. Within primary care there is concern about the isolation of any lone practitioner in any of the healthcare professions. If it is assumed that medical specialists within secondary care expertly prescribe some 20 or so different drugs, and feel reasonably confident yet cautious about their use; the data reported by Taylor and Bond[6] (*see* Figure 3.2) indicate that some medical practitioners in primary care routinely prescribe over 200 drugs, while some prescribe less than 50 drugs.

Has society behaved in a reasonable manner in asking a practitioner who has many additional and varied duties to attempt to achieve sole competence in safely prescribing so many drugs? The converse is also true. How can some doctors provide so relatively few treatments? It is surely of urgent importance that we develop further supportive roles to encourage safe practice. Practitioners in primary care play a crucial role in preventing ill health and dealing with a host of illnesses before they develop into serious disease. They and their patients deserve society's best efforts to help them to achieve these important goals.

However, in all such concerns it is implicit that doctors will continue to serve their patients and that their numbers will be sufficient to fulfil the projected needs of the NHS. But how certain can we be that this assumption is correct? A major National Survey of General Practitioner Opinion commissioned by the General Practitioners' Committee (GPC) of the British Medical Association was recently conducted in order to assess a wide range of issues relevant to the future of UK healthcare provision.[7] The report was published in October 2001, and just a few of the answers to numerous and very detailed questions are shown in Figure 17.4.

If the results are representative of most UK general practitioners, the analysis leaves no room for complacency. The low morale is evidenced by the fact that 96% of doctors agree or agree strongly that too much is being asked of general practice, nearly 30% of doctors are considering a career change involving a move outside general practice, nearly 50% of doctors are reluctant to recommend general practice to junior doctors, excessive and unmanageable stress is experienced by around 20% of doctors (with a further 60% finding it excessive but manageable), and a quarter of doctors want to leave general practice. Although the survey was conducted to help the GPC to set the negotiating priorities for the current round of contract talks,[8] concern is obvious. And although over 60% of general practitioners are committed to the concept of clinical governance, it must be extremely regrettable that under 'point 53' of the document, no less than 77.2%, 83.3% and 86.9% agreed or agreed strongly that 'the introduction of clinical governance, appraisal and revalidation', respectively, will make some doctors retire early from general practice.

It is not possible to conclude whether or not the dissatisfaction of many general practitioners with the circumstances of their work is substantially different to that which could be found among nurses, pharmacists, teachers, academics, policemen and others. However, even if others do feel disadvantaged, this would not devalue the results found for the general practitioners, but rather it reflects an even greater and more widespread problem with major and diverse consequences. In brief, having focused on audit and governance to enhance standards – a logical and inevitable endeavour, but with the equally inevitable bureaucracy and endless piles of paper and emails – it would

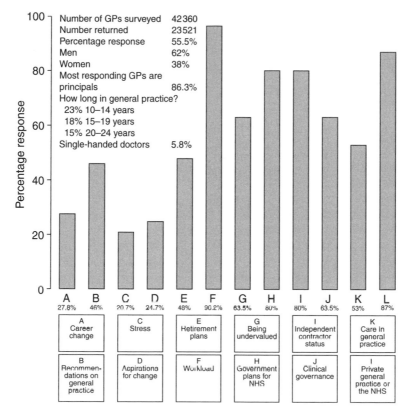

Number of GPs surveyed 42360
Number returned 23521
Percentage response 55.5%
Men 62%
Women 38%
Most responding GPs are
principals 86.3%
How long in general practice?
23% 10–14 years
18% 15–19 years
15% 20–24 years
Single-handed doctors 5.8%

A	B	C	D	E	F	G	H	I	J	K	L
27.8%	46%	20.7%	24.7%	48%	90.2%	63.5%	80%	80%	63.5%	53%	87%

A Career change	C Stress	E Retirement plans	G Being undervalued	I Independent contractor status	K Care in general practice
B Recommen- dations on general practice	D Aspirations for change	F Workload	H Government plans for NHS	J Clinical governance	L Private general practice or the NHS

Figure 17.4: A selection of opinions from the National Survey of General Practitioner Opinion, October 2001. A, 27.8% are considering a career change outside general practice; B, 46% would not recommend general practice to an undergraduate or junior doctor; C, 20.7% find that their work-related stress is both excessive and unmanageable; D, 24.7% of GPs want to leave general practice; E, When they became GPs, 18% of respondents planned to retire before reaching the age of 60 years, whereas now 48% plan to do so; F, 96.2% agree or strongly agree that too much is being asked of general practice; G, 63.5% strongly agree that general practice is undervalued; H, more than 80% of GPs feel that the Government's plans for the NHS are not achievable within the proposed time scale; I, 80% of GPs wish to retain the option of independent contractor status; J, 63.5% of GPs are committed to the concept of clinical governance; K, 53% of GPs believe that the care which patients receive in general practice is better than it was 5 years ago; L, 87% want most GP services to be provided by the NHS, and 87% would prefer to work in the NHS, provided that workload and pay were comparable. Data were taken from the National Survey of General Practitioner Opinion overall results top-line report prepared for the General Practitioners' Committee, British Medical Association.[5]

be of more than academic interest to determine the precise point at which a job becomes so unpleasant or almost impossible to undertake successfully that it effectively self-destructs – and people simply walk away. Is this already occurring in general practice?

This question needs to be debated on another occasion, but does it really make sense to dramatically increase student intakes (*see* Figure 13.1) in an attempt to fill present vacancies and subsequent service needs, when some existing students in medicine, nursing and other disciplines on graduating already either never seek a career in healthcare or quickly leave the service (notwithstanding the appreciable costs to both the students and society)? Perhaps proportionally more students may, from the increased numbers enrolled, find their way at least temporarily into the NHS. However, is this a triumph of illusion and misjudgement based on short-term fears, short-term views, short-term relationships, short-term compromise and short-term correction of an inherently flawed system? Would it be more effective in both financial and human terms to cautiously increase student numbers *and* attempt to provide jobs which are pleasant, satisfying and naturally attractive to our young people who would be pleased to remain in post? There is little point in having meticulously designed systems of audit and regulated procedures for a demoralised or absent workforce. Most of these issues relate to inadequate resourcing. It is possible that the NHS may already be addressing the problem.

It appears that pharmacy is the first single professional group to be targeted by the DoH under its *Improving Working Lives* initiative. It is intended to result in sufficient numbers of motivated staff being employed in the NHS, to deliver the standards of care envisaged in the NHS Plan.[9] Focus is on flexible working, the working environment, professional development, cross-sector working and other activities.

Will the future beckon to a fascinating new reality?

Chapter 18

Conclusions

A concern to report and then reduce drug-induced adverse events and medication errors has opened Pandora's box. The patient has emerged and requested that healthcare should have the resource, knowledge and skills necessary to provide a high-quality service and be accountable for its actions. Both patients and governments urgently seek safe healthcare systems and a reduction in the number of errors caused by medical management, which are a major cause of injury, disability and death in the developed world. The unacceptable human cost is mirrored by the unacceptable financial cost.

One of the greatest barriers to improving patient safety has been a lack of awareness of the extent to which errors occur. They have been unrecognised, under-reported or unacknowledged by many clinical staff and by the academic staff who teach undergraduate students in healthcare. While reporting of errors needs to be improved, it is also essential to begin the process of error reduction, which is a powerful tool for the setting and enforcing of standards of safety.

Some errors are a result of human slips, lapses or mistakes, but they frequently occur as a consequence of a systems failure. A reporting and understanding of the causes of errors is required in order to learn from errors to prevent their recurrence. The number of errors reported may initially appear to increase to reflect previous under-reporting or, within the UK, increased healthcare activity. The reduction of system (latent) errors, so making it easier for staff to do the right thing and more difficult for them to do the wrong thing, is considered to be the most effective way of reducing future errors. Rather than blaming the individual, the error becomes a learning experience.

Two important mechanisms which have already been identified for reducing the rate of latent errors are improved computer technology to make available electronically essential patient and prescribing information, and also the inclusion of a pharmacist within the medication team (this alone is reported to reduce prescribing errors by around 65%).

It is frequently suggested that to focus on human (active) errors is only to address a single retrospective incident. This view is inaccurate. With regard to the active errors in medication that are made by individuals, the most frequent cause of error was identified as a lack of knowledge. The prescriber or administrator of the drug was in ignorance of simple pharmacological knowledge (e.g. doses or concepts) *that effectively precluded safe therapy*. This is a most important observation, and not merely because it was the most frequent cause of prescriber error. This simply should not happen. It is a serious problem since the prevention of system failures will be compromised if the clinical practitioners are not working within their required competence.

This has important implications for the education of healthcare staff and is reviewed within the perspective of two undergraduate teaching programmes for medical and pharmacy students. In particular, the challenge of attempting the design of curricula in the presence of an ever-increasing information database, and the concerns raised by the lack of a core curriculum, a reduction in the coverage of the basic sciences, the cleansing of identifiable disciplines such as pharmacology and other traditional subjects, the decrease in the factual content and the reduction in the assessments of content (factual knowledge) in the new medical courses is deeply concerning. Similarly, the quality of the preregistration house officer year with regard to the inculcation of clinical knowledge and skills has been described by students as haphazard and random.

Consideration is given to the implications of the types and causes of medication errors for the projected changes in prescriber status in the new NHS. Emphasis is given to the crucial importance of training to ensure that new prescribers are properly prepared for their new roles, as well as to just how difficult the prescriber's role may be in terms of the multitudinous and perhaps unexpected factors that can influence medication. The widespread and uncontrolled use of herbal preparations that may adversely interact with dispensed medicines provides just one worrying example of this.

The patient's contribution to adverse drug events or medication errors reflects a major failure to take the drugs as instructed. It is simply not known how much illness continues or is not treated because of either intentional or non-intentional non-adherence. The opportunity for improving healthcare, reducing adverse events and medication errors and eradicating financial waste is enormous. However, it will require much greater involvement and education of the patient and carer with their therapy and the healthcare staff.

Future directions for the use of professional expertise in healthcare focused on increasing safety for the patient will inevitably develop further, with the bringing together of the knowledge and skills necessarily distributed within and between different professions. Indeed, it is difficult to see how the extensive and ever-developing knowledge and skills base which is now essential for the safe and effective use of medicines could be found anywhere except within specialisms and different professions working with the patient to a new concordance.

This has important implications for the education and training of present and future healthcare staff, and for the changes envisaged in professional responsibilities within the NHS. However, even if we accept the vital moral and professional imperative of reducing harm to patients, and actually improving their treatments (which essentially has been beyond the scope of the present book), an equally important if not greater challenge remains. This relates to the incessant demands on the academic and clinical environments to teach, and on our students to learn, an ever broader base of subjects within the perspective of incessant audit, governance and the attendant bureaucracy and extraordinary piles of paper and associated ephemera. Already some students who qualify in medicine, nursing or the other healthcare professions never enter those professions, or quickly leave after a brief exposure to them. Similarly, some healthcare professionals are leaving or retiring early and even refusing 'golden handcuffs' to remain within the system. In brief, the jobs on offer are perceived to be relatively unattractive or unpleasant. An attempt to provide jobs which are not overly bureaucratic and which are interesting, satisfying and attractive to our young people may perhaps be a more rational approach to meeting future service needs than simply feeding an ever greater number of students through the educational system.

In their article entitled 'Safe healthcare: are we up to it?', Leape and Berwick[1] reached the following conclusions:

> *If we can mobilise our resources and make safety our priority, healthcare can make tremendous strides in the next few years. But today's culture of blame and guilt too often shackles us. Harder still, we must now accomplish this cultural change under the spotlight of a newly aroused public that, given our track record, is understandably doubtful that healthcare can, on its own, do what needs to be done. Indeed, the public's doubt in our commitment may be all too well founded. Healthcare's track record of failure to act on over three decades of accumulating evidence of medical errors offers plenty of ammunition to those who claim that we may need to be forced to do what is, at bottom, right.*
>
> *The need is obvious, and the mandate is clear. Will we respond adequately and fast enough? Will hospitals and healthcare organisations get serious enough, soon enough, about patient safety? Can we accept the legitimacy of the public's right to know when serious accidents occur, and can we honour the publics legitimate expectation that we will admit our mistakes, investigate them, and make the changes necessary to prevent them in future?*
>
> *Are we ready to change? Or will we procrastinate and dissemble – to lament later when the inevitable regulatory backlash occurs? It may seem to some that the race for patient safety has just begun, but the patience of the public we serve is already wearing thin. They are asking us to promise something reasonable, but more than we ever promised before: that they will not be harmed by the care that is supposed to help them. We owe them nothing less, and that debt is now due.*

Appendix 1

Adverse drug reactions

Adverse drug reactions have been classified by Edwards and Aronson[1] into the following six types, with a useful mnemonic.

1 *Dose related (or Augmented)*: the response is predicted to occur in most or all patients, is related to the established pharmacological actions of the drug, and has a low mortality. Examples include neuroleptic-induced neurological toxicity, digoxin toxicity, anticholinergic effects of tricyclic antidepressants.

Management: reduce dose or withhold, consider effects of concomitant therapy.

2 *Non-dose related (or Bizzare)*: uncommon and unpredictable, not related to the known pharmacology or dose, with a high mortality. Examples include immunological reactions to penicillin or other drugs.

Management: withhold, and avoid in future.

3 *Dose and time related (Chronic)*: uncommon and related to the cumulative dose. Examples include hypothalamic–pituitary–adrenal suppression by corticosteroids.

Management: reduce dose or withhold; withdrawal may have to be prolonged.

4 *Time related (or Delayed)*: uncommon, usually dose related and occurs or becomes apparent some time after the use of the drug. Examples include neuroleptic-induced tardive dyskinesias (after many years) or diethylstilbes-trol-induced vaginal adenocarcinoma (in the next generation).

Management: often intractable; no effective treatment.

5 *Withdrawal (or End of use)*: uncommon, and usually occurs soon after drug withdrawal. Examples include myocardial ischaemia following beta-blocker withdrawal, opiate withdrawal syndrome.

Management: reintroduce and withdraw slowly.

6 *Unexpected failure of therapy (Failure)*: common and dose related. Examples include inadequate dosage of oral contraceptive, inadequate course of antibiotics.

Management: increase dosage or extend treatment; consider effects of concomitant therapy.

Edwards and Aronson detail the diagnosis and attribution of causality, and the management and surveillance systems for the detection, prediction and prevention of adverse drug events, as far as is possible. *The above classification of adverse drug events can be extended, to include a category of predictable failures from intentional therapeutic paradigms.*

7 *Predictable failures from a designed therapeutic protocol (Clinical Guidelines)*: inevitable re-emergence of original symptoms and pathology in some patients after the intentional reduction of drug dose or failure of treatment. Examples include inadequate dosage of proton-pump inhibitors for gastro-oesophageal reflux disorder, inadequate drug regimen of anti-emetics in cancer patients.

Management: administration of the effective dose regimen.

Reference

1 Edwards IR and Aronson JK (2000) Adverse drug reactions: definitions, diagnosis and management. *Lancet.* **356**: 1255–9.

Definitions of causation and preventability scales as used in the Quality in Australian Health Care Study[1]

Causation

Causation was present if the adverse event (AE) was caused by medical management rather than the disease process. It included acts of omission (failure to diagnose or treat) and acts of commission (incorrect treatment or management).

A scale of 1 to 6 was used to determine whether an AE was caused by healthcare management or the disease processes:

1 = virtually no evidence of management causation
2 = slight to modest evidence of management causation
3 = management causation not likely, less than 50–50 but close call
4 = management causation more likely than not, not more than 50–50 but close call
5 = moderate to strong evidence of management causation
6 = virtually certain evidence of management causation.

Preventability

Preventability of an AE was defined as 'an error in management due to failure to follow the accepted practice at an individual or system level'. Accepted practice was taken to be 'the current level of expected performance for the average practitioner or system that manages the condition in question'.

The degree of preventability was scored on a scale of 1 to 6, grouped into three categories as follows.

No preventability:
1 = virtually no evidence of preventability.

Low preventability
2 = slight to modest evidence of preventability
3 = preventability not likely, less than 50–50 but close call.

High preventability:
4 = preventability more likely than not, more than 50–50 but close call
5 = strong evidence of preventability
6 = virtually certain evidence of preventability.

Examples of adverse event classification

Complication, no causation (no adverse event)
An elderly man was admitted to hospital after a fall leading to a fractured neck of femur, which was managed by early fixation without complication. Three days later the patient had a major upper gastrointestinal bleed and died of the consequences of hypotension and anaemia. There was no history of gastro-intestinal bleeding or its investigation, nor any reason for having a high index of suspicion. The situation appeared to have been promptly recognised and assessed.

This patient had a complication which caused death, but this was judged not to be caused by healthcare management.

Adverse event, no preventability
A 50-year-old woman underwent coronary angiography for unstable angina. During the angiogram she sustained an anaphylactic reaction to the contrast, with cardiac arrest. She was able to be resuscitated promptly, without permanent sequelae, and hospitalisation was prolonged by 10 days. Evidence for prior contrast reactions was sought and not found.

This patient had a complication, disability and causation, and thus experienced an adverse event. It was judged not to have been preventable.

Adverse event, high preventability
An 87-year-old woman with osteoporosis underwent open reduction and internal fixation with an Austin–Moore prosthesis and received antibiotic therapy for a urinary tract infection. Five days after the operation it was noted that the patient had developed bilateral decubitus ulcers on her heels. No pressure-area care had been documented. The ulcers, which required daily dressings by a community nurse, were still required at discharge. The patient's hospital stay was extended to 37 days.

This patient had an adverse event resulting in disability and prolonged hospital stay, with a high degree of preventability.

Reference

1 Wilson RM *et al.* (1995) The Quality in Australian Health Care Study. *Med J Aust.* **163**: 458–71.

Potential severity classification for order errors[1]

A Potentially fatal or severe

1 The dose ordered for a medication with a low therapeutic index was greater than 10 times the normal dose.
2 A dose was ordered for a medication with a very low therapeutic index that would potentially result in pharmacological effects or serum concentrations associated with severe or fatal toxic reactions.
3 A drug was ordered that had the potential to produce a severe or life-threatening reaction in the patient (i.e. anaphylaxis).
4 The dose of a life-saving drug or a drug being used for a severe illness was too low for the patient being treated.

B Potentially serious

1 The dose ordered for a medication with a low therapeutic index was greater than 4 to 10 times the normal dose.
2 A dose was ordered for a medication with a very low therapeutic index that would potentially result in serious toxic reactions.
3 The dose ordered for a drug used for a serious illness was too low for the patient.
4 The wrong medication was ordered, with potential serious toxic reactions or inadequate therapy for a serious illness.
5 A route was ordered for a medication that could potentially produce serious toxic reactions or inadequate therapy for a serious illness.
6 A medication order was written illegibly or in such a manner as to result in an error that could produce serious toxic reactions or inadequate therapy for a serious illness.
7 Duplicate therapy with potential for serious toxic reactions was prescribed.

C Potentially significant

1   The dose ordered for a medication with a low therapeutic index was 1.5 to 4 times the normal dose, with potential toxic reactions because of the high dose.
2   The dose ordered for any medication was at least five times greater than normal, with potential for adverse effects because of the high dose.
3   The dose ordered was inadequate to produce therapeutic effects.
4   The wrong route of administration was ordered, with potential for increased adverse effects or inadequate therapy.
5   The wrong medication was ordered for a non-serious illness and/or there was potential for side-effects from the drug.
6   A medication order was written illegibly or in such a manner as to result in an error producing adverse effects or inadequate therapy.
7   Duplicate therapy was prescribed with a potential for additive toxic reactions.

D Problem orders

1   Duplicate therapy was prescribed without potential for increased adverse effects.
2   The order lacked specific drug, dose, dosage strength, formulation, route or frequency information.
3   The wrong route was ordered without potential for toxic reactions or therapeutic failure.
4   The dose of medication was five times greater than normal, but without toxic potential.
5   An errant order was written that was unlikely to be carried out given the nature of the drug, dosage forms, route ordered, missing information, etc.

• Errors were assigned to a specific error class if the error detected fulfilled any of the listed criteria for each class.
• Adapted from Foli HL *et al.* (1987) Medication error prevention by clinical pharmacists in two children's hospitals. *Pediatrics.* **79**: 718–22.

Examples of significant prescribing errors detected and averted

Errant orders with potential for 'severe' or 'serious' adverse consequences

- Prescribing medication to which the patient had a documented allergy (61 cases).
- Ordering antibiotics for serious infections for the wrong patient.
- Five- to tenfold overdoses of glyburide.
- Oral hypoglycaemic agents for the wrong patient.
- Glyburide and glypizide in full doses concurrently.
- Four- to tenfold overdoses of heparin bolus or infusion.
- Tenfold overdose of protamine sulphate.
- Warfarin three times a day instead of once a day.
- Propranolol hydrochloride, 10 mg intravenous push.
- Azathioprine ordered instead of zidovudine.
- Ccfazolin to treat enterococcal infections.
- Oral vancomycin to treat systemic infection.
- Ceftizoxime sodium instead of ceftazidime to treat pseudomonal infection.
- Intravenous colchicine, 1 mg every 4 hours, as a standing order.
- 30 U regular insulin instead of isophane insulin suspension.
- Phenytoin once a day instead of three times a day.
- Vasopressin, 0.4 U per hour instead of 0.4 U per minute for bleeding varices.

Orders with potential for some adverse consequences (significant errors)

- Threefold overdose of buprenorphine.
- Standard-release isosorbide dinitrate ordered once a day.
- Verapamil, 240 mg once a day, ordered as non-sustained-release tablet.
- Triazolam ordered every 4 hours.
- Scopolamine transdermal patch ordered once a day instead of every three days.
- Tenfold overdose of trifluoperazine.
- Ketoconazole, 200 mg four times a day instead of once a day.
- Allopurinol, 600 mg four times a day instead of once a day.
- Ibuprofen, 800 mg every four hours.
- Gentamycin, 80 mg every 8 hours in patients with elevated serum creatinine levels.

Reference

1 Lesar TS *et al.* (1990) Medication prescribing errors in a teaching hospital. *JAMA.* **263**: 2329–34.

Appendix 4

Medication error report form[1]

Report by (circle)   Dr   Nurse   Pharmacist
Location (circle)   PCW   PCICU

Please tick the category of medication error you wish to report.

SUPPLY ERROR
- ☐ Stock: inadequate/expired
- ☐ Drug information problem
- ☐ Labelling error
- ☐ Dispensing error
- ☐ Other (please specify)

ADMINISTRATION ERROR
- ☐ Dose omission/delay
- ☐ Incorrect dose given
- ☐ Incorrect administration technique/rate
- ☐ Other (please specify)

PRESCRIPTION ERROR
- ☐ Chart incomplete (e.g. name or weight missing/unsigned)
- ☐ Incorrect dose
- ☐ Incorrect frequency
- ☐ Illegible
- ☐ Drugs accidentally omitted
- ☐ Drug interaction
- ☐ Transcription error
- ☐ Other (please specify)

> Was the error detected before the drug was given?   Yes/No

Details of the event (including any clinical consequences):

_____

_____

_____

Date: Signature: Print name:

This report can be submitted anonymously.

Classification of errors by Wilson *et al.*[1]

A Three broad categories: prescription, administration and supply.
B Also classified as serious (capable of producing permanent organ damage or death) or not serious, and outcome was graded according to the outcome described by Hartig *et al.*[2]

Level 0: error prevented by staff surveillance.

Level 1: error occurred but there was no patient harm.

Level 2: error occurred; increased monitoring was required, but no change in clinical status.

Level 3: error occurred; change in clinical status, or need for increased laboratory monitoring, but no ultimate harm.

Level 4: error occurred; extra treatment requirement, or increased length of stay resulted.

Level 5: error occurred; permanent patient harm resulted.

Level 6: error occurred resulting in the death of the patient.

References

1 Wilson DG *et al.* (1998) Medication errors in paediatric practice: insights from a continuous quality improvement approach. *Eur J Paediatrics.* **157**: 769–74.

2 Hartig SC, Denger SD and Schneider PJ (1991) A severity-indexed incident-report-based medication error reporting program. *Am J Hosp Pharm.* **48**: 2611–16.

An identification of 16 major systems failures underlying the errors and proximal causes of adverse drug events and potential adverse drug events[1]

1 *Drug knowledge dissemination (98 errors)*
   Physicians made prescribing errors that appeared to be due to deficiencies of knowledge about the drug and how it should be used. This included incorrect doses, forms, frequencies and routes of administration, as well as errors in the choice of drug. Examples include failure to order a test dose of amphotericin B and an order for amitriptyline for an elderly patient (amitriptyline is strongly anticholinergic, and gerontologists recommend using other antidepressants in the elderly). Nurses also made errors related to lack of understanding of the drug, but these were less frequent and less likely to lead to an ADE.

2 *Dose and identity checking (40 errors)*
   The systems for verifying that the proper drug is delivered in the proper dose sometimes failed in both the pharmacy dispensing and nursing administration stages. A significant cause of identity errors was look-alike packaging and sound-alike names, as drug quality control of these functions still relies completely on inspection.

3 *Patient information availability (37 errors)*
   Information about the patient's condition, results of laboratory tests, current medications and recent doses (particularly of narcotics) was sometimes not easily accessible when it was needed, leading to prescribing errors as well as inappropriate administration of ordered drugs. Pharmacists sometimes lacked information about clinical characteristics of patients and results of laboratory tests that would have enabled them to interpret an improper order. Although most of the required patient information was available somewhere, it was not always readily accessible. For example,

from a remote location a covering physician often could not easily determine all of the medications that the patient had recently received.

4 *Order transcription (29 errors)*

The need to transcribe physicians' orders manually on to medication sheets led to errors because unit secretaries lack medical training and physicians' handwriting is often illegible. Error detection depends on subsequent inspection by a nurse.

5 *Allergy defence (24 errors)*

Patients sometimes received medication to which they had known allergies, even when the physician had noted the allergy in the admission work-up, and even when a notation was present on the medication administration record. The system depends on manual checks which are unreliable, and the system did not ensure that physicians, nurses and pharmacists had drug allergy information when they needed it.

6 *Medication order tracking (18 errors)*

The system for processing a medication order, from ordering through to administration of the drug to the patient is complex, involving multiple individuals, groups and departments. There is no mechanism for easily identifying at any instant where the order or medication is in the process. Consequently, a great deal of time is wasted by nurses and others in finding out where an order or medication is. It is sometimes difficult to tell from the data recorded if or when the medication has been given, missed, discontinued or changed. Because doses are sometimes recorded in more than one location, it may be difficult to determine the extent of cumulative doses of some drugs (especially narcotics).

7 *Interservice communication (17 errors)*

Communication between personnel from different services was rather poor. For example, it was sometimes difficult for a nurse or pharmacist to determine which physician had written an order for a drug or dose that seemed inappropriate and to contact that physician. Nurses also sometimes had difficulty in contacting pharmacists.

8 *Device use (12 errors)*

The variety of types of infusion pumps (eight in one hospital) makes it difficult for nurses to obtain and maintain the expertise necessary to use them properly.

9 *Standardisation of doses and frequencies (12 errors)*

There are no hospital-wide standards for dosing schedules, and even generally accepted doses and dosing schedules were often not followed by physicians. In addition, the hours when medications are given vary among patient care units. Lack of standardisation of orders greatly increase the time and thought that must be given to medication by the nurses, and also increases the likelihood of errors. In one hospital, physicians used six different variants of the 'K-scale' (a graduated scale for giving potassium replacement).

10 *Standardisation of drug distribution within unit (11 errors)*

Medications are delivered by pharmacy technicians to a central repository bin on each floor, but what happens next varies from unit to unit, as well as by time of day. There is no standardised system for ensuring that the medications get to the correct medication drawer at the right time for use by the patient.

11 *Standardisation of procedures (10 errors)*
The locations and use of medication drawers, order sheets, medication administration records and IV supplies vary substantially from unit to unit. Because physicians, pharmacists and nurses care for patients on many different units, these variations lead to reduced efficiency and increased risk of error.

12 *Preparation of IV medications by nurses (6 errors)*
Approximately 40% of IV medications are prepared by nurses in the units. In addition, for some medications the doses are calculated and drawn up by the nurse from bulk supplies on the floor. Each of these operations provides opportunities for multiple errors – in calculating the amounts, drawing up, mixing and labelling.

13 *Transfer/transition problems (4 errors)*
Errors in administration of drugs sometimes occurred when a patient was in physical transition from one place to another, such as during transfer from one unit to another, or when off the unit (e.g. for an X-ray or test). This appeared to result in part from ambiguity about who was responsible for the patient and in part from suspension of the usual unit procedures that help to ensure the safe administration of drugs to patients.

14 *Conflict resolution (4 errors)*
Although there are some procedures for dealing with conflicts (e.g. when a nurse or pharmacist questions a physician and is rebuffed), many nurses and pharmacists were unaware of the procedures or did not feel that they were workable or effective.

15 *Staffing and work assignments*
Three deficiencies were noted.
1 Excessive workloads due to inability to match staffing assignments to the clinical load when there were fluctuations in patient census and severity of illness. **2** Variations in the availability of experienced nurses, so that novice nurses were sometimes inadequately supervised and assisted. **3** The structure of the patient care environment, so that most nurses work autonomously most of the time. The latter deficiency sometimes led nurses to fail to seek assistance when it was needed. Staffing and work assignment deficiencies were thought to be major causes of a large number and range of errors.

16 *Feedback about adverse drug events*
Physicians and nurses received little follow-up information about drug-related errors, even when they were discovered.

Reference

1 Leape LL *et al.* (1995) Systems analysis of adverse drug events. ADE Prevention Study Group. *JAMA.* **274**: 35–43.

Policy on the rights of patients in medical education[1]

For educational activities that are not part of clinical care

- Patients must understand that medical students are not qualified doctors (and not 'young doctors', 'my colleagues' or 'assistants').
- Clinical teachers and students must obtain explicit verbal consent from patients before students take case histories or physically examine them, making sure that they understand the primarily educational purpose of their participation.
- Clinical teachers and students should never perform physical examinations or present cases that are potentially embarrassing for primarily educational purposes without the patient's verbal consent, including consent for the number of students present. When individual students are conducting such examinations, a chaperone should usually be present.
- Students should never perform any physical examination on patients under general anaesthetic for primarily educational purposes without the patient's prior written consent, which should be placed in the notes. Patients who are otherwise unconscious or incompetent must be involved in primarily educational activity only with the explicit agreement of their responsible children and after consent from parents (children) or consultation with relatives (adults).
- Clinical teachers should obtain the patient's explicit verbal consent for students to participate in treatment (suturing, taking blood, delivering babies, etc.). Procedures that do not require immediate supervision should be undertaken only if there is recorded evidence of competence.
- Students must respect the confidentiality of all information communicated by patients in the course of their treatment or participation in educational activity. Patients should understand that students may be obliged to inform a responsible clinician about information that is relevant to their clinical care.
- Clinical teachers are responsible for ensuring that these guidelines are followed. If students are asked by anyone to do anything to the contrary, they must politely refuse, referring to these guidelines. Encouraging students to ignore these guidelines is unacceptable.

Reference

1 Doyal L (2001) Closing the gap between professional teaching and practice. *BMJ.* **322**: 685–6.

Example statements of professional ethics and duties[1,2]

Key responsibilities of a pharmacist

Pharmacists understand the nature and effect of medicines and medicinal ingredients, and how they may be used to prevent and treat illness, relieve symptoms or assist in the diagnosis of disease. Pharmacists in professional practice use their knowledge for the well-being and safety of patients and the public.

- *At all times pharmacists must act in the interests of patients and other members of the public, and seek to provide the best possible healthcare for the community in partnership with other health professions. Pharmacists must treat all those who seek their professional services with courtesy, respect and confidentiality. Pharmacists must respect patients' rights to participate in decisions about their care and must provide information in a way in which it can be understood.*
- *Pharmacists must ensure that their knowledge, skills and performance are of a high quality, up to date, evidence based and relevant to their field of practice.*
- *Pharmacists must ensure that they behave with integrity and probity, adhere to accepted standards of personal and professional conduct and do not engage in any behaviour or activity likely to bring the profession into disrepute or undermine public confidence in the profession.*

Professional competence

The public, the profession and the NHS expect pharmacists to develop their professional performance to provide a high level of care to patients.

a *Pharmacists must continually review the skills and knowledge required for their field of practice, identifying those skills or knowledge most in need of development or improvement and audit.*
b *Pharmacists must, each year, undertake a minimum of 30 hours' continuing professional development structured to meet their personal needs, and be able to provide evidence of such.*
c *Pharmacists must be ready and able to provide information and advice about any medicine supplied by them or under their authority.*
d *Pharmacists giving advice to prescribers, patients and others must be able to demonstrate competence and knowledge of medicines within the relevant therapeutic class.*

KA3 Preregistration tutors and pharmacists supervising preregistration trainees

Preregistration tutors and pharmacists supervising preregistration trainees must ensure that:

a *they reflect on work processes and outcomes, evaluate their own performance and take action to develop their expertise and knowledge*
b *preregistration trainees receive wide-ranging experience of professional practice within the pharmacy location*
c *they review the progress of preregistration trainees regularly and provide constructive and honest feedback, encouraging trainees to self-appraise their performance*
d *preregistration trainees understand and learn how to comply with the key responsibilities of a pharmacist, and that the training meets the trainees' needs*
e *preregistration trainees are properly supervised, in particular in relation to their responsibilities for services to the public*
f *assessments of a student's performance provided to the Society are honest and objective. The public may be put at risk if a tutor or supervising pharmacist confirms the competence of a trainee who has not attained a satisfactory standard.*

The Duties of a Doctor *place the patient's needs at the very centre of such duties.*

Patients must be able to trust doctors with their lives and well-being. To justify that trust, we as a profession have a duty to maintain a good standard of practice and care and to show respect for human life. In particular, as a doctor you must:

- *make the care of your patient your first concern*
- *treat every patient politely and considerately*
- *respect patients' dignity and privacy*
- *listen to patients and respect their views*
- *give patients information in a form that they can understand*
- *respect the rights of patients to be fully involved in decisions about their care*
- *keep your professional knowledge up to date*
- *recognise the limits of your professional competence*
- *be honest and trustworthy*
- *respect and protect confidential information*
- *make sure that your personal needs do not prejudice your patient's care*
- *act quickly to protect patients from risk if you have good reason to believe that you or a colleague may not be fit to practice*
- *avoid abusing your position as a doctor*
- *work with colleagues in the ways that best serve patients' interests.*

References

1 Ed. (2001) Code of ethics revision. *Pharm J.* **266**: 325–32.
2 Townsend A (2000) The role of the General Medical Council. In: M Drury (ed.) *Clinical Negligence in General Practice.* Radcliffe Medical Press, Oxford, 27–42.

Appendix 8

The prevention of intrathecal medication errors: a report to the Chief Medical Officer[1]

A synopsis

One of the recommendations in *An Organisation With a Memory* was 'by 2001, to reduce to zero the number of patients dying or being paralysed by malad-ministered spinal injections'. The scope of the report was to identify the factors contributing to the hazard, to consult widely across disciplines to identify interventions which may reduce intrathecal errors and their effectiveness and practicability, to set out the steps required to achieve the goal of zero incidents, and to consider (where relevant) strategies to reduce the overall burden of adverse events in the NHS.

Only about five cases are known to have occurred in the NHS in the last decade, which when combined with an estimated denominator of 15 000 intrathecal cytotoxic treatments a year, would suggest a rate of around 3 per 100 000 such treatments.

- All hospitals have taken steps to prevent it happening.
- It is a rare event.
- The consequences are invariably devastating and usually fatal.
- Recovery measures taken after the event are of little or no benefit.

The target of zero incidence is therefore extremely demanding but entirely appropriate. To the personal tragedy of the affected patients and their families must be added the unquantifiable human costs to the health professionals involved and the damage to public confidence in the NHS.

> *In view of public concern over this repeated mishap, there should be a single national document setting out safe practices for the admin-istration of intrathecal chemotherapy.*

The attitude of the report to the taxonomy of hazards was interesting, since (the classification):

both influences and reflects our understanding of them. In medicine, the usual aim is to base classifications on causes. Such an approach is problematic for adverse health care events, since the causes are usually multiple, interacting and often individually trivial . . . . A useful taxonomy (of hazards) should direct attention to the most promising preventative strategy by focusing on the key characteristic which might be modified.

At its simplest, the problem considered here could be seen as a drug administration error specific to the administration of vinca alkaloids. Preventative measures would then be directed towards ensuring that drugs of this class are only injected intravenously, as intended.

Two broad preventative strategies are distinguished here.

The first, which encompasses all of the precautions currently implemented within the NHS to prevent intrathecal injection errors, can be termed the human factor approach. It includes the following:

- training and education
- ward procedures and protocols
- pharmacy procedures and protocols.

The second strategy is to seek a design solution of 'engineering safety' (e.g. connectors used in medical devices).

Proposals for immediate action

Recommendation 1

The NHS should issue national guidance on safety procedures to be followed during the administration of intrathecal chemotherapy. This guidance should incorporate best medical, ward and pharmacy practice from the many local protocols which have been written.

Recommendation 2

Within each clinical service in which cytotoxic chemotherapy is given, there should be an agreed and regularly updated list of individuals permitted to administer intrathecal chemotherapy. The named individuals must have received training on the protocol to be followed and have been provided with current copies of that protocol. Trust chief executives should be responsible for ensuring that this safeguard is implemented forthwith as part of clinical governance.

Recommendation 3

National NHS guidance should include measures to ensure that administration of intravenous and intrathecal cytotoxic agents is carried out by different trained staff, at different times and in different clinical locations. Drugs should be checked by two staff with chemotherapy training. Trusts should specify local implementation arrangements as attachments to the national guidance.

The above measures would have prevented past incidents of intrathecal alkaloid injection. Together, they provide multiple robust levels of security and can be implemented with minimum delay.

Recommendation 4

The dispensing of vinca alkaloids either **1** in a non-Luer syringe or **2** only in 50-mL or 100-mL bags for intravenous infusion should be urgently explored.

The latter needs to be piloted to ensure that pharmaceutical and nursing concerns about extravasation can be resolved.

Strategic initiatives to be taken forward concurrently

Recommendation 5

Medical schools should ensure that their core curricula provide a thorough knowledge of safe drug prescribing and administration. Proper assessment in these areas is essential to minimise the occurrence of therapeutic errors, particularly during general professional training.

Recommendation 6

Policy decisions are required on a possible programme of redesign of connecting devices. The costs, benefits, risks and feasibility of such a programme will need to be examined in the light of quantitative data on adverse events arising from misconnections and disconnections in the NHS. Research is likely to be required for risk assessment and health economic analysis.

Reference

1 Department of Health (2001) *The Prevention of Intrathecal Medication Errors. A report to the Chief Medical Officer*. Department of Health, London; www.doh.gov.uk/imeprevent

References

Chapter 1

1 Barach P and Moss F (2001) Delivering safe health care. Safety is a patient's right and the obligation of all health professionals. *BMJ.* **323**: 585–6.
2 Metropolitan Insurance Company (1992) Anti-arthritic medication usage: 1991. *Stat Bull.* **73**: 25–34.
3 Laine L (2001) Approaches to nonsteroidal anti-inflammatory drug use in the high-risk patient. *Gastroenterology.* **120**: 594–606.
4 Wolfe MM, Lichtenstein DR and Singh G (1999) Gastrointestinal toxicity of nonsteroidal anti-inflammatory drugs. *NEJM.* **340**: 1888–99.
5 Tramer MR *et al.* (2000) Quantitative estimation of rare adverse events which follow a biological progression; a new model applied to chronic NSAID use. *Pain.* **85**: 169–82.
6 Singh G and Triadafilopoulos G (1999) Epidemiology of NSAID-induced gastrointestinal complications. *J Rheumatol.* **26 (Supplement 56)**: 18–24.
7 Dalby K (2001) How to avoid common prescribing errors. *Prescriber.* **5 June**: 83–6.
8 Cunningham G *et al.* (1997) Drug-related problems in elderly patients admitted to Tayside hospitals: methods for prevention and subsequent reassessment. *Age Ageing.* **26**: 375–82.
9 Gabriel SE, Jaakkimainen L and Bombardier C (1991) Risk for serious gastrointestinal complications related to use of nonsteroidal anti-inflammatory drugs: a meta-analysis. *Ann Intern Med.* **115**: 787–96.
10 Griffin MR *et al.* (1991) Nonsteroidal anti-inflammatory drug use and increased risk for peptic ulcer disease in elderly persons. *Ann Intern Med.* **114**: 257–63.
11 Bloom BS (1988) Cost of treating arthritis and NSAID-related gastrointestinal side-effects. *Aliment Pharmacol Ther.* **2 (Supplement 1)**: 131–8.
12 Erstad BL (2001) Proton-pump inhibitors for acute peptic ulcer bleeding. *Ann Pharmacother.* **35**: 730–40.
13 Silverstein FE *et al.* (1995) Misoprotol reduces serious gastrointestinal complications in patients with rheumatoid arthritis receiving nonsteroidal anti-inflammatory drugs. A randomised, double-blind, placebo-controlled trial. *Ann Intern Med.* **123**: 241–9.
14 Tramer MR (2000) Aspirin, like all other drugs, is a poison. *BMJ.* **321**: 1170–71.
15 Ingram M (2001) Painkiller risks. *The Times.* **22 May**.

16 Moores KG (2001) COX-2-selective NSAIDs: mission not yet accomplished. *World Drug Inform.* **12**: 1–7; http://www.uiowa.edu/~idis.

17 Moskowitz RW (2000) *Statement made at the Fifteenth European United League Against Rheumatism Congress, 10 July, Nice, France*; http://www.docguide.com.

18 Wolfe SM (2001) *Statement made at the open public hearing of the US Food and Drug Administration Arthritis Advisory Committee Meeting, 8 February*; http://www.fda.gov/ohrms/dockets/ac/01/transcripts/3677t2.rtf.

19 Mukherjee D, Nissen SE and Topol EJ (2001) Risk of cardiovascular events associated with selective COX-2 inhibitors. *JAMA.* **286**: 954–9.

20 National Institute for Clinical Excellence (2001). *Guidance on the Use of Cyclo-Oxygenase Inhibitors, Celecoxib, Rofecoxib, Meloxicam, and Etodolac for Osteoarthritis and Rheumatoid Arthritis.* Technology Appraisal Guidance No. 27. National Institute for Clinical Excellence, London; www.nice.org.uk/pdf/coxiifullguidance.pdf.

21 Adcock H (2001) NICE guidance on COX-2 inhibitors welcomed, but some questions remain. *Pharm J.* **267**: 146.

22 Ed. (2001) NPA disagrees with CSM safety judgements on POM-to-P switches. *Pharm J.* **267**: 142.

23 Moore TJ, Psaty BM and Furberg CD (1998) Time to act on drug safety. *JAMA.* **279**: 1571–3.

24 Ray WA, Griffin MR and Avorn J (1993) Evaluating drugs after their approval for clinical use. *JAMA.* **329**: 2029–32.

25 Wong ICK (1990) Pharmacovigilance resources in the United Kingdom. *Pharm J.* **263**: 285–8.

26 Ed. (1999) 'Yellow card' reporting now allowed for all community pharmacists. *Pharm J.* **263**: 776.

27 Ed. (1999) Full steam ahead on ADR reporting. *Pharm J.* **263**: 769.

28 Ed. (2002) Black triangle scheme flawed, says the Consumers' Association. *Pharm J.* **266**: 526.

29 Barbone F *et al.* (1998) Association of road traffic accidents with benzodiazepine use. *Lancet.* **352**: 1331–6.

30 Wang PS *et al.* (2001) Hazardous benzodiazepine regimens in the elderly: effects of half-life, dosage and duration on risk of hip fracture. *Am J Psychiatry* **158**: 892–8.

31 Hardman JG *et al.* (eds) (1996) *Goodman and Gilman's The Pharmacological Basis of Therapeutics* (9e). McGraw-Hill, New York, 57–8.

32 Young LY and Koda-Kimble MA (1995) *Applied Therapeutics: the clinical use of drugs.* Applied Therapeutics Inc., Vancouver.

33 Ed. (2000) Editor's choice: facing up to medical error. *BMJ.* **320**.

34 Leape LL *et al.* (1991) The nature of adverse events in hospitalised patients. Results of the Harvard Medical Practice Study II. *NEJM.* **324**: 377–84.

35 McDonald CJ, Weiner M and Hui SL (2000) Deaths due to medical errors are exaggerated in Institute of Medicine report. *JAMA.* **284**: 93–5.

36 Kohn LT, Corrigan JM and Donaldson MS (1999) *To Err is Human: building a safer health care system.* Institute of Medicine National Academy Press, Washington, DC.

37 Davis RM and Pless B (2001) BMJ bans 'accidents': accidents are not unpredictable. *BMJ.* **322**: 1320–1.

38 Doege TC (1978) An injury is no accident. *NEJM.* **298**: 509–10.

39 http://www.claims-line-direct.co.uk/.

40 Furedi F (2001) The blame game. *New Scientist.* **25 August**.

41 Department of Health (2000) *An Organisation With a Memory.* The Stationery Office, London; http://www.doh.gov.uk/orgmemreport/orgmemexecsum.htm.

42 Department of Health (2001) *Building a Safer NHS for Patients.* The Stationery Office, London; www.doh.gov.uk/buildsafenhs.

43 Eisenberg J (2000) *Report of the Quality Interagency Coordination Task Force (QuIC) to the President. Doing what counts for patient safety: federal actions to reduce medical errors and their impact.* Rockville, MD; www.Quic.org.

44 Ed. (2001) Editor's choice: promoting safety and quality. *BMJ.* **323**.

Chapter 2

1 Edwards IR and Aronson JK (2000) Adverse drug reactions: definitions, diagnosis and management. *Lancet.* **356**: 1255–9.

2 Barker KN and McConnel WE (1962) The problem of detecting medication errors in hospital. *Am J Hosp Pharm.* **19**: 361–70.

3 Davis N (2000) Initiatives for reducing medication errors: the time is now. *Am J Health Syst Pharm.* **57**: 1487–92.

4 Schimmel EM (1964) The hazards of hospitalization. *Ann Intern Med.* **60**: 100–1.

5 Borda IT, Slone D and Jick H (1968) Assessment of adverse reactions within a drug surveillance program. *JAMA.* **205**: 645–7.

6 Karch FE and Lasagna L (1975) Adverse drug reactions. A critical review. *JAMA.* **234**: 1236–41.

7 Jick H (1984) Adverse drug reactions: the magnitude of the problem. *J Allergy Clin Immunol.* **74**: 555–7.

8 Lazarou J, Pomeranz BH and Corey PN (1998) Incidence of adverse drug reactions in hospitalised patients: a meta-analysis of prospective studies. *JAMA.* **279**: 1200–5.

9 Brennan TA *et al.* (1991) Incidence of adverse events and negligence in hospitalised patients. Results of the Harvard Medical Practice Study I. *NEJM.* **324**: 370–76.

10 Hiatt HH *et al.* (1989) A study of medical injury and medical malpractice. *NEJM.* **321**: 480–84.

11 Leape LL (2000) Institute of Medicine medical error figures are not exaggerated. *JAMA*. **284**: 95–7.

12 Leape LL *et al.* (1991) The nature of adverse events in hospitalized patients. Results of the Harvard Medical Practice Study II. *NEJM*. **324**: 377–84.

13 Leape LL *et al.* (1993) Preventing medical injury. *Qual Rev Bull*. **19**: 144–9.

14 Thomas EJ *et al.* (2000) Incidence and types of adverse events and negligent care in Utah and Colorado. *Med Care*. **38**: 261–71.

15 Phillips DP Christenfeld N and Glynn LM (1998) Increase in US medication-error deaths between 1983 and 1993. *Lancet*. **351**: 643–4.

16 Ferner RE and Anton C (1998) Increase in US medication-error deaths. *Lancet*. **351**: 1655–6.

17 Manasse HR (1998) Increase in US medication-error deaths. *Lancet*. **351**: 1655.

18 Rooney C (1998) Increase in US medication-error deaths. *Lancet*. **351**: 1656–7.

19 Phillips DP, Christenfeld N and Glynn LM (1998) Increase in US medication-error deaths. *Lancet*. **351**: 1657.

20 Wilson RM *et al.* (1995) The Quality in Australian Health Care Study. *Med J Aust*. **163**: 458–71.

21 Vincent C, Neale G and Woloshynowych M (2001) Adverse events in British hospitals: preliminary retrospective record review. *BMJ*. **322**: 517–19.

22 Department of Health (2000) *An Organisation with a Memory*. The Stationery Office, London; http://www.doh.gov.uk/orgmemreport/orgmemexecsum.htm.

23 Cullen DJ *et al.* (1995) The incident reporting system does not detect adverse drug events: a problem for quality improvement. *J Comm Qual Improv*. **21**: 541–8.

24 Reinstein PF and Robinson JI (1994) *Annual Adverse Drug Experience Report*. Division of Epidemiology and Surveillance, Food and Drug Administration, US Department of Health and Human Services, Rockville, MD.

25 Moore TJ, Psaty BM and Furberg CD (1998) Time to act on drug safety. *JAMA*. **279**: 1571–3.

26 Kessler DA (1993) Introducing MedWatch: a new approach to reporting medication and device adverse effects and product problems. *JAMA*. **269**: 2765–8.

27 Ed. (2000) NIH under fire over gene therapy trials. *Nature*. **405**: 237.

28 Ed. (2000) Gene therapy institute denies that errors led to trial death. *Nature*. **403**: 820.

29 Ed. (2000) US government shuts down Pennsylvania gene therapy trials. *Nature*. **403**: 354.

30 Ed. (2000) Gene therapy's trials. *Nature*. **405**: 599.

31 Wadman M (2001) Johns Hopkins researchers fume over government crackdown. *Nature*. **412**: 363.

32 Begley S, Foote D and Rogers A (2001) Dying for science. *Newsweek.* **30 July**: 34.

33 Ferner RE and Cook M (1993) Adverse drug reactions: who is to know? *BMJ.* **307**: 480–81.

34 Akwagyriam I *et al.* (1996) Drug history taking and the identification of drug-related problems in an accident and emergency department. *J Accident Emerg Med.* **13**: 166–8.

35 Hughes DK (1999) *Anonymous reporting of medication errors.* MSc Thesis. John Moores University, Liverpool.

36 Department of Health (2000) *An Organisation With a Memory.* The Stationery Office, London, 62; http://www.doh.gov.uk/orgmemreport.htm.

Chapter 3

1 Beard K (1992) Adverse reactions as a cause of hospital admission in the aged. *Drugs Aging.* **2**: 356–67.

2 Roughead EE *et al.* (1998) Drug-related hospital admissions: a review of Australian studies published 1988–1996. *Med J Aust.* **168**: 405–8.

3 Schneitman-McIntire O *et al.* (1996) Medication misadventures resulting in emergency department visits at an HMO medical center. *Am J Health Syst Pharm.* **53**: 1416–22.

4 Willcox SM, Himmelstein DU and Woolhandler S (1994) Inappropriate drug prescribing for the community-dwelling elderly. *JAMA.* **272**: 292–6.

5 Lazarou J, Pomeranz BH and Corey PN (1998) Incidence of adverse drug reactions in hospitalized patients: a meta-analysis of prospective studies. *JAMA.* **279**: 1200–5.

6 Jick H (1984) Adverse drug reactions: the magnitude of the problem. *J Allergy Clin Immunol.* **74**: 555–7.

7 Gandhi TK *et al.* (2000) Drug complications in outpatients. *J Gen Intern Med.* **15**: 149–54.

8 Darchy B *et al.* (1999) Iatrogenic diseases as a reason for admission to the intensive-care unit: incidence, causes and consequences. *Arch Intern Med.* **159**: 71–8.

9 Trunet P *et al.* (1980) The role of iatrogenic disease in admissions to intensive care. *JAMA.* **244**: 2617–20.

10 Lakshmanan MC, Hershey CO and Breslau D (1986) Hospital admissions caused by iatrogenic disease. *Arch Intern Med* **146**: 1931–4.

11 Bhasale AL *et al.* (1998) Analysing potential harm in Australian general practice: an incident-monitoring study. *Med J Aust.* **169**: 73–6.

12 Merlo J *et al.* (2001) Prescriptions with potential drug interactions dispensed at Swedish pharmacies in January 1999: cross-sectional study. *BMJ.* **323**: 427–8.

13 Wilson T, Pringle M and Sheikh A (2001) Promoting patient safety in primary care: research, action and leadership are required. *BMJ.* **323**: 583–4.

14 Taylor R (1998) National and international patterns of drug use. In: FD Hobbs and CP Bradley (eds) *Prescribing in Primary Care.* Oxford University Press, Oxford, 9–35.

15 Primatesta P and Poulter NR (2000) Lipid concentrations and the use of lipid-lowering drugs: evidence from a national cross-sectional survey. *BMJ.* **321**: 1322–5.

16 Department of Health (1995) *Variations in Health.* The Stationery Office, London; http://www.doh.gov.uk.

17 Patel MG *et al.* (1999) Anomalous prescribing patterns of lipid-lowering drugs. *Pharm J.* **263 (Supplement)**: R15.

18 Department of Health (1999) *Saving Lives: our healthier nation (White Paper)* and *Reducing Health Inequalities (an Action Report).* Department of Health, London; http://tap.ccta.gov.uk/doh/coin4.nsf.

19 Taylor RJ and Bond CM (1991) Change in the established prescribing habits of general practitioners: an analysis of initial prescriptions in general practice. *Br J Gen Pract.* **41**: 244–8.

20 Ed. (1994) GPs' prescribing is irrational, says Audit Commission. *BMJ.* **308**: 675.

21 McGrath AM and Jackson GA (1996) Survey of neuroleptic prescribing in residents of nursing homes in Glasgow. *BMJ.* **312**: 611–12.

22 Treloar A, Beats B and Philpot M (2000) A pill in the sandwich: covert medication in food and drink. *J R Soc Med.* **93**: 408–11.

23 Bootman JL, Harrison DL and Cox E (1997) The healthcare cost of drug-related morbidity and mortality in nursing facilities. *Arch Intern Med.* **157**: 2089–96.

24 Sullivan SD, Kreling DH and Hazlet TK (1990) Noncompliance with medication regimens and subsequent hospitalizations: a literature analysis and cost of hospitalization. *J Res Pharm Econ.* **2**: 19–33.

25 Einarson TR (1993) Drug-related hospital admissions. *Ann Pharmacother.* **27**: 832–40.

26 Marinker M (1996) *Partnership in Medicine Taking: a consultative document.* The Royal Pharmaceutical Society of Great Britain and Merck Sharp and Dohme, London.

27 Hummer M and Fleischhacker WW (1999) Compliance and outcome in patients treated with antipsychotics: the impact of extrapyramidal symptoms. In: G Mallarkey (ed.) *Managing Schizophrenia.* Adis International, Auckland, 49–57.

28 Rovelli M *et al.* (1989) Noncompliance in organ transplant recipients. *Transplant Proc.* **21**: 833–4.

29 Cox A and Marriott J (2000) Dealing with dispensing errors. *Pharm J.* **264**: 724.

30 Kayne S (1996) Negligence and the pharmacist: dispensing and prescribing errors. *Pharm J.* **257**: 32–5.

31 Department of Health (2001) *Building a Safer NHS for Patients.* The Stationery Office, London; www.doh.gov.uk/buildsafenhs.

32 Murdoch A (2001) Pharmacy Director, Lloyds Pharmacy, personal communication.

33 Ed. (2001) Boots to launch non-threatening risk assessment programme for dispensing. *Pharm J.* **266**: 802.

34 Spencer MG and Smith AP (1993) A multicentre study of dispensing errors in British hospitals. *Int J Pharm Pract.* **2**: 142–6.

Chapter 4

1 Bates DW, Leape LL and Petrycki S (1993) Incidence and preventability of adverse drug events in hospitalised adults. *J Gen Intern Med.* **8**: 289–94.

2 Bates DW *et al.* (1995) Incidence of adverse drug events and potential adverse drug events. Implications for prevention. ADE Prevention Study Group. *JAMA.* **274**: 29–34.

3 Phillips DP, Christenfeld N and Glynn LM (1998) Increase in US medication-error deaths between 1983 and 1993. *Lancet.* **351**: 643–4.

4 Department of Health (2001) *Building a Safer NHS for Patients.* The Stationery Office, London; http://www.doh.gov.uk/buildsafenhs.

5 Lesar TS *et al.* (1990) Medication prescribing errors in a teaching hospital. *JAMA.* **263**: 2329–34.

6 Wilson DG *et al.* (1998) Medication errors in paediatric practice: insights from a continuous quality improvement approach. *Eur J Pediatrics.* **157**: 769–74.

7 Hartig SC, Denger SD and Schneider PJ (1991) A severity-indexed incident-report-based medication error reporting program. *Am J Hosp Pharm.* **48**: 2611–16.

8 Andrews LB *et al.* (1997) An alternative strategy for studying adverse events in medical care. *Lancet.* **349**: 309–13.

9 Donchin Y *et al.* (1995) A look into the nature and causes of human errors in the intensive care unit. *Crit Care Med.* **23**: 294–300.

10 Dearden CH and Rutherford WH (1985) The resuscitation of the severely injured in the accident and emergency department – a medical audit. *Injury.* **16**: 249–52.

Chapter 5

1 Leape LL *et al.* (1991) The nature of adverse events in hospitalized patients. Results of the Harvard Medical Practice Study II. *NEJM.* **324**: 377–84.

2 Lesar TS *et al.* (1990) Medication prescribing errors in a teaching hospital. *JAMA.* **263**: 2329–34.

3 Lesar TS, Briceland L and Stein DS (1997) Factors related to errors in medication prescribing. *JAMA.* **277**: 312–17.

4 Leape LL *et al.* (1995) Systems analysis of adverse drug events. ADE Prevention Study Group. *JAMA.* **274**: 35–43.

5 Dean B *et al.* (2000) Prescribing errors in hospital inpatients: why do they occur? *Pharm J.* **265**: R17.

Chapter 6

1 Brennan TA *et al.* (1991) Incidence of adverse events and negligence in hospitalized patients. Results of the Harvard Medical Practice Study I. *NEJM.* **324**: 370–76.

2 Wilson RM *et al.* (1995) The Quality in Australian Health Care Study. *Med J Aust.* **163**: 458–71.

3 Bates DW *et al.* (1999) Patient risk factors for adverse drug events in hospitalised patients. ADE Prevention Study Group. *Arch Intern Med.* **159**: 2553–60.

4 Department of Health (2001) *National Service Framework for Older People.* Department of Health, London.

5 Department of Health (2000) *Prescriptions Dispensed in the Community Statistics for 1989–1999: England.* Department of Health, London.

6 Bajekal M *et al.* (1999) Cardiovascular disease '98. In: B Erens and P Primatesta (eds) *Health Survey for England. Volume 1: Findings.* The Stationery Office, London.

7 Denham MJ and Barnett NL (1998) Drug therapy and the older person. Role of the pharmacist. *Drug Safety* **19**: 243–50.

8 Cunningham G *et al.* (1997) Drug-related problems in elderly patients admitted to Tayside hospitals: methods for prevention and subsequent reassessment. *Age Ageing.* **26**: 375–82.

9 Mannesse CK *et al.* (2000) Contribution of adverse drug reactions to hospital admission of older patients. *Age Ageing.* **29**: 35–9.

10 Mannesse CK *et al.* (1997) Adverse drug reactions in elderly patients as contributory factor for hospital admission. *BMJ.* **315**: 1057–8.

11 Merlo J *et al.* (2000) *All prescriptions with potential drug interactions dispensed at all Swedish pharmacies in January 1999.* Paper presented in part at the International Society of Pharmacoepidemiology Annual Meeting in Barcelona, Spain, 19–23 August 2000.

12 Merlo J *et al.* (2001) Prescriptions with potential drug interactions dispensed at Swedish pharmacies in January 1999: cross-sectional study. *BMJ.* **323**: 427–8.

13 Nathan A *et al* (1999) 'Brown bag' medication reviews as a means of optimizing patient's use of medication and of identifying potential clinical problems. *Fam Pract.* **16**: 278–82.

14 Royal Pharmaceutical Society of Great Britain (1997) *From Compliance to Concordance – Achieving Partnership in Medicine-Taking*. Royal Pharmaceutical Society of Great Britain, London.

15 Royal College of Physicians (2001) *The National Sentinel Clinical Audit of Evidence-Based Prescribing for Older People by the Royal College of Physicians*. Royal College of Physicians, London.

16 Andrews LB *et al.* (1997) An alternative strategy for studying adverse events in medical care. *Lancet.* **349**: 309–13.

17 Wilson DG *et al.* (1998) Medication errors in paediatric practice: insights from a continuous quality improvement approach. *Eur J Paediatrics.* **157**: 769–74.

18 Cullen DJ *et al.* (1997) Preventable adverse drug events in hospitalised patients: a comparative study of intensive care and general care units. *Crit Care Med.* **25**: 1289–97.

19 Tarnow-Mordi WO *et al.* (2000) Hospital mortality in relation to staff workload: a 4-year study in an adult intensive-care unit. *Lancet.* **356**: 185–9.

20 Ed. (2000) Hospital doctors under pressure: new roles for the healthcare workforce. *Pharm J.* **264**: 682.

21 Sexton JB, Thomas EJ and Helmreich RL (2000) Error, stress and teamwork in medicine and aviation: cross-sectional surveys. *BMJ.* **320**: 745–9.

22 Fallowfield LJ, Lipkin M and Hall A (1998) Teaching senior oncologists communication skills: results from Phase 1 of a comprehensive longitudinal programme in the UK. *J Clin Oncol.* **16**: 1961–8.

23 Fallowfield LJ *et al.* (2001) Psychiatric morbidity and its recognition by doctors in patients with cancer. *Br J Cancer.* **84**: 1011–15.

24 Fallowfield LJ *et al.* (20001) Teaching senior nurses how to teach communication skills in oncology. *Cancer Nurs.* **24**: 185–91.

25 Jenkins V, Fallowfield LJ and Saul J (2001) Information needs of patients with cancer: results from a large study in UK cancer centres. *Br J Cancer.* **84**: 48–51.

26 Charter D (2001) Doctors are too stressed to relate to frightened patients. *The Times.* **26 June**.

27 Department of Health (2001) *The Prevention of Intrathecal Medication Errors. A report to the Chief Medical Officer.* Department of Health, London; www.doh.gov.uk/imeprevent.

28 Department of Health (2000) *The NHS Plan. A plan for investment, a plan for reform.* The Stationery Office, London; www.hmso.govt.uk.

29 Ed. (2001) New junior doctors face long hours at work. BMA online. Wednesday 1 August 2001; http://www.bma.org.uk/pressrel.nsf.

30 Lesar TS *et al.* (1990) Medication prescribing errors in a teaching hospital. *JAMA.* **263**: 2329–34.

31 Wu AW *et al.* (1991) Do house officers learn from their mistakes? *JAMA.* **265**: 2089–94.

32 Thomas EJ *et al.* (2000) Incidence and types of adverse events and negligent care in Utah and Colorado. *Med Care.* **38**: 261–71.

33 Brennan TA *et al.* (1991) Hospital characteristics associated with adverse events and substandard care. *JAMA.* **265**: 3265–9.

34 Thomas EJ, Orav EJ and Brennan TA (2000) Hospital ownership and preventable adverse events. *J Gen Intern Med.* **15**: 211–19.

35 Allison JJ *et al.* (2000) Relationship of hospital teaching status with quality of care and mortality for Medicare patients with acute MI. *JAMA.* **284**: 1256–62.

36 Medicines Resource Centre (1997) The 'atypical' antipsychotics: clozapine, risperidone, sertindole and olanzepine. *MeReC Bull.* **8**: 25–8.

37 Hummer M and Fleischhacker WW (1999) Compliance and outcome in patients treated with antipsychotics: the impact of extrapyramidal symptoms. In: G Mallarkey (ed.) *Managing Schizophrenia.* Adis International, Auckland, 49–57.

38 Buchanan RW and Carpenter WT (1999) Targeted maintenance treatment in schizophrenia: issues and recommendations. In: G Mallarkey (ed.) *Managing Schizophrenia.* Adis International, Auckland, 35–40.

39 Jann MW and Cohen LJ (1999) Economic considerations and formulary management of oral antipsychotics. In: G Mallarkey (ed.) *Managing Schizophrenia.* Adis International, Auckland, 77–91.

40 Casey DE (1995) Motor and mental aspects of extrapyramidal syndromes. *Int Clin Psychopharmacol.* **10 (Supplement 3)**: 105–14.

41 Kane J *et al.* (1988) Clozapine for the treatment-resistant schizophrenic. A double-blind comparison with chlorpromazine. *Arch Gen Psychiatry.* **45**: 789–96.

42 Taylor D (1999) Switching from typical to atypical antipsychotics: practical guidelines. In: G Mallarkey (ed.) *Managing Schizophrenia.* Adis International, Auckland, 41–8.

43 Geddes J *et al.* (2000) Atypical antipsychotics in the treatment of schizophrenia: systematic overview and meta-regression analysis. *BMJ.* **321**: 1371–6.

44 Kapur S and Remington G (2000) Atypical antipsychotics. *BMJ.* **321**: 1360–61.

45 National Institute for Clinical Excellence (2000) NICE issues guidance on proton pump inhibitors (PPI) for dyspepsia; http://www.nice.uk.org/nice-web/article.asp?a=3589.

46 Cottrill M (2000) Counting the cost of the NICE guidelines on PPIs. *Guidelines Pract.* **3**: 22.

47 Colin-Jones D (2000) Competitor queries 'on demand' PPI use. *Pharm J.* **265**: 437.

48 Epstein O (2000) Competitor queries 'on demand' PPI use. *Pharm J.* **265**: 437.

49 Leape LL *et al.* (1991) The nature of adverse events in hospitalized patients. Results of the Harvard Medical Practice Study II. *NEJM.* **324**: 377–84.

50 Antiemetic Subcommittee of the Multinational Association of Supportive Care in Cancer (1998) Prevention of chemotherapy- and

radiotherapy-induced emesis: results of the Perugia Consensus Conference. *Ann Oncol.* **9**: 811–19.

51 Olver N (1998) Methodology of trials for treating nausea and vomiting. In: MA Dicato (ed.) *Medical Management of Cancer-Treatment-Induced Emesis*. Martin Dunitz, London, 9–24.

52 Morrow GR and Roscoe JA (1998) Anticipatory nausea and vomiting: models, mechanisms and management. In: MA Dicato (ed.) *Medical Management of Cancer-Treatment-Induced Emesis.* Martin Dunitz, London, 149–66.

53 Popescu RA and Cunningham D (1998) Prevention of nausea and vomiting in repeat courses. In: MA Dicato (ed.) *Medical Management of Cancer-Treatment-Induced Emesis*. Martin Dunitz, London, 132–48.

54 Swinbourne AL and Tattersall MHN (1998) Patients' point of view. In: MA Dicato (ed.) *Medical Management of Cancer-Treatment-Induced Emesis*. Martin Dunitz, London, 195–203.

55 Ed. (2000) AstraZeneca Industrial Achievement Award Lecture. The pharmaceutical industry and the evolution of molecular medicine. *Pharm J.* **265**: 766.

56 Ed. (2001) The human genome. *Nature.* **409**: 745–964.

57 Richards T (2001) Three views of genetics: the enthusiast, the visionary and the sceptic. *BMJ.* **322**: 1016.

58 Ed. (2001) Editor's choice: bringing ordinary doctors into the genetics party. *BMJ.* **322**.

59 Akhtar S (2002) Pharmacogenomics: are pharmacists ready for genotyped prescribing? *Pharm J.* **268**: 296–9.

Chapter 7

1 Bates DW *et al.* (1997) The costs of adverse drug events in hospitalised patients. Adverse Drug Events Prevention Study Group. *JAMA.* **277**: 307–11.

2 Classen DC *et al.* (1997) Adverse drug events in hospitalised patients. Excess length of stay, extra costs, and attributable mortality. *JAMA.* **277**: 301–6.

3 Thomas EJ *et al.* (1999) Costs of medical injuries in Utah and Colorado. *Inquiry.* **36**: 255–64.

4 Bloom BS (1988) Cost of treating arthritis and NSAID-related gastro-intestinal side-effects. *Ailment Pharmacol Ther.* **2 (Supplement 1)**: 131–8.

5 Bootman JL, Harrison DL and Cox E (1997) The health care cost of drug-related morbidity and mortality in nursing facilities. *Arch Intern Med.* **157**: 2089–96.

6 Johnson JA and Bootman JL (1997) Drug-related morbidity and mortality and the economic impact of pharmaceutical care. *Am J Health Syst Pharm.* **54**: 554–8.

7 Weiden PJ and Olfson M (1995) Cost of relapse in schizophrenia. *Schizophr Bull.* **21**: 419–29.

8 Wilson RM *et al.* (1995) The Quality in Australian Health Care Study. *Med J Aust.* **163**: 458–71.

9 Moore N *et al.* (1998) Frequency and cost of serious adverse drug reactions in a department of general medicine. *Br J Clin Pharmacol.* **45**: 301–8.

10 Department of Health (2000) *An Organisation With a Memory.* The Stationery Office, London; http://www.doh.gov.uk.

11 Vincent C, Neale G and Woloshynowych M (2001) Adverse events in British hospitals: preliminary retrospective record review. *BMJ.* **322**: 517–19.

12 Drury M (2000) Cause and effect. In: M Drury (ed.) *Clinical Negligence.* Radcliffe Medical Press, Oxford, 1–12.

13 Localio AR *et al.* (1991) Relation between malpractice claims and adverse events due to negligence. Results of the Harvard Medical Practice Study III. *NEJM.* **325**: 245–51.

14 Andrews LB *et al.* (1997) An alternative strategy for studying adverse events in medical care. *Lancet.* **349**: 309–13.

Chapter 8

1 Brennan TA *et al.* (1991) Incidence of adverse events and negligence in hospitalized patients. Results of the Harvard Medical Practice Study I. *NEJM.* **324**: 370–76.

2 Wilson RM *et al.* (1995) The Quality in Australian Health Care Study. *Med J Aust.* **163**: 458–71.

3 Lazarou J, Pomeranz BH and Corey PN (1998) Incidence of adverse drug reactions in hospitalized patients: a meta-analysis of prospective studies. *JAMA.* **279**: 1200–5.

4 Department of Health)2001) Health Laboratory Service; http://www.doh.gov.uk.

5 Kirkland KB *et al.* (1999) The impact of surgical-site infections in the 1990s: attributable mortality, excess length of hospitalization, and extra costs. *Infect Control Hosp Epidemiol.* **20**: 725–30.

6 Centers for Disease Control and Prevention (1996) *National Nosocomical Infection Surveillance System. Semi-annual report.* Centers for Disease Control and Prevention, Atlanta, GA.

7 Steel K *et al.* (1981) Iatrogenic illness in a general medical service at a university hospital. *NEJM.* **304**: 638–42.

8 Davis N and Cohen MR (1981) *Medication Errors: causes and prevention.* George F. Stickley Co., Philadelphia, PA.

9 Dubois RW and Brook RH (1988) Preventable deaths: who, how often and why? *Ann Intern Med.* **109**: 582–9.

10 Bates DW *et al.* (1995) Incidence of adverse drug events and potential adverse drug events. Implications for prevention. ADE Prevention Study Group. *JAMA.* **274**: 29–34.

11 Classen DC *et al.* (1991) Computerized surveillance of adverse drug events in hospital patients. *JAMA.* **266**: 2847–51.

12 Andrews LB *et al.* (1997) An alternative strategy for studying adverse events in medical care. *Lancet.* **349**: 309–13.

13 Hall MJ and Lawrence L (1996) *Ambulatory Surgery in the United States.* National Center for Health Statistics, Hyattsville, MD.

14 Primatesta P and Poulter NR (2000) Lipid concentrations and the use of lipid-lowering drugs: evidence from a national cross-sectional survey. *BMJ.* **321**: 1322–5.

15 Patel MG *et al.* (1999) Anomalous prescribing patterns of lipid-lowering drugs. *Pharm J.* **263 (Supplement)**: R15.

16 Department of Health (2000) *An Organisation With a Memory.* The Stationery Office, London; http://www.doh.gov.uk.

17 Marinker M (1996) *Partnership in Medicine Taking: a consultative document.* The Royal Pharmaceutical Society of Great Britain and Merck Sharp and Dohme, London.

18 Bates DW, Leape LL and Petrycki (1993) Incidence and preventability of adverse drug events in hospitalized adults. *J Gen Intern Med.* **8**: 289–94.

19 Wilson DG *et al.* (1998) Medication errors in paediatric practice: insights from a continuous quality improvement approach. *Eur J Paediatrics.* **157**: 769–74.

20 Leape LL *et al.* (1991) The nature of adverse events in hospitalized patients. Results of the Harvard Medical Practice Study II. *NEJM.* **324**: 377–84.

21 Leape LL *et al.* (1995) Systems analysis of adverse drug events. ADE Prevention Study Group. *JAMA.* **274**: 35–43.

22 Bates DW *et al.* (1999) Patient risk factors for adverse drug events in hospitalized patients. ADE Prevention Study Group. *Arch Intern Med.* **159**: 2553–60.

23 Tarnow-Mordi WO *et al.* (2000) Hospital mortality in relation to staff workload: a 4-year study in an adult intensive-care unit. *Lancet.* **356**: 185–9.

24 Sexton JB, Thomas EJ and Helmreich RL (2000) Error, stress and teamwork in medicine and aviation: cross-sectional surveys. *BMJ.* **320**: 745–9.

25 Lesar TS *et al.* (1990) Medication prescribing errors in a teaching hospital. *JAMA.* **263**: 2329–34.

26 Thomas EJ, Orav EJ and Brennan TA (2000) Hospital ownership and preventable adverse events. *J Gen Intern Med.* **15**: 211–19.

27 Localio AR *et al.* (1991) Relation between malpractice claims and adverse events due to negligence. Results of the Harvard Medical Practice Study III. *NEJM.* **325**: 245–51.

Chapter 9

1 Department of Health (2000) *An Organisation With a Memory.* The Stationery Office, London; http://www.doh.gov.ukorgmemreport/orgmemexecsum.htm.

2 Kohn LT, Corrigan JM and Donaldson MS (1999) *To Err is Human: building a safer health system.* Institute of Medicine National Academy Press, Washington, DC, 3–4.

3 Leape LL *et al.* (1991) The nature of adverse events in hospitalized patients. Results of the Harvard Medical Practice Study II. *NEJM.* **324**: 377–84.

4 Wilson RM *et al.* (1995) The Quality in Australian Health Care Study. *Med J Aust.* **163**: 458–71.

5 Edwards IR and Aronson JK (2000) Adverse drug reactions: definitions, diagnosis and management. *Lancet.* **356**: 1255–9.

6 National Patient Safety Foundation (1997) *Agenda for Research and Development in Patient Safety;* http://www.ama-assn.org/med-sci/npsf/pr1997.htm.

7 Perrow C (1984) *Normal Accidents.* Basic Books, New York.

8 Cooper JB *et al.* (1978) Preventable anesthesia mishaps: a study of human factors. *Anesthesiology.* **49**: 399–406.

9 Reason J (1990) *Human Error.* Cambridge University Press, Cambridge.

10 News (1994) Doctor charged over death. *The Guardian.* **3 July**.

11 Lesar TS *et al.* (1990) Medication prescribing errors in a teaching hospital. *JAMA.* **263**: 2329–34.

12 Leape LL (1994) Error in medicine. *JAMA.* **272**: 1851–7.

13 Gilovich T (1993) *How We Know What Isn't: the fallibility of human reason in everyday life.* The Free Press, New York.

14 Piatelli-Palmarini M (1994) *Inevitable Illusions: how mistakes of reason rule our minds.* John Wiley & Sons, New York.

15 Rasmussen J and Jensen A (1974) Mental procedures in real-life tasks: a case study of electronic trouble shooting. *Ergonomics.* **17**: 293–307.

16 Tversky A and Kahneman D (1981) The framing of decisions and the psychology of choice. *Science.* **211**: 453–8.

17 Vaughan D (1996) *The Challenger Launch Decision.* The University of Chicago Press, Chicago.

18 Kohn LT, Corrigan JM and Donaldson MS (eds) (1999) *To Err is Human: building a safer health system.* Institute of Medicine National Academy of Science, Washington, DC, xi–x.

19 Veatch RM (1989) *Cross-Cultural Perspectives in Medical Ethics.* Jones and Bartlett Publishers, Boston, MA.

20 Kohn LT, Corrigan JM and Donaldson MS (eds) (1999) *To Err is Human: building a safer health system. Executive Summary.* Institute of Medicine National Academy of Sciences, Washington, DC.

21 Brennan TA *et al.* (1991) Incidence of adverse events and negligence in

hospitalized patients. Results of the Harvard Medical Practice Study I. *NEJM*. **324**: 370–76.

22 Brodie I (2000) Clinton acts to cut hospital errors. *The Times*. **23 February**.

23 McDonald CJ, Weiner M and Hui SL (2000) Deaths due to medical errors are exaggerated in Institute of Medicine report. *JAMA*. **284**: 93–5.

24 Leape LL (2000) Institute of Medicine medical error figures are not exaggerated. *JAMA*. **284**: 95–7.

25 Brennan TA (2000) The Institute of Medicine report on medical errors – could it do harm? *NEJM*. **342**: 1123–5.

26 Department of Health (1997) *The New NHS: modern, dependable*. Department of Health, London.

27 Department of Health (1998) *A First-Class Service: quality in the new NHS*. Department of Health, London.

28 Alexander A (2001) Why the Shipman inquiry is a question of confidence. *The Times (Law section)* **26 June**: 5.

29 Wilson-Smith CQ (2001) The current climate. In: *Clinical Negligence: an update on current law and issues*. Clinical Negligence Group, London.

30 Dinnen MW *et al.* (1999) *Incident Reporting in the NHS. Department of Health Health Care Risk Report*. Department of Health, London.

31 Department of Health (2000) *The Government's Expenditure Plans 2000–2001*. The Stationery Office, London.

32 Department of Health (2001) *Building a Safer NHS for Patients*. The Stationery Office, London; www.doh.gov.uk/buildsafenhs.

33 Department of Health (1999) *The Report of the National Confidential Enquiry into Perioperative Deaths 1997/1998*. DoH, London.

34 Department of Health (2000) *An Organisation With a Memory*. The Stationery Office, London, 49.

35 Department of Health (1999) *Supporting Doctors, Protecting Patients*. A consultation paper on preventing, recognising and dealing with poor clinical performance of doctors in the NHS in England. DoH, London.

36 Smith D and Elliot D (1999) *Moving Beyond Denial: exploring the barriers to learning from crisis*. University of Sheffield, Sheffield.

37 Firth-Cozens J (2000) Teams, culture and managing risks. In: C Vincent (ed.) *Clinical Risk Management*. BMJ Books, London.

38 Wason P (1960) On the failure to eliminate hypotheses in a conceptual task. *Quart J Exp Psychol*. **xii, Part 3**.

39 Department of Health (2000) *An Organisation With a Memory*. The Stationery Office, London.

40 Boseley S (2001) Heart specialists raise new child tragedy fears. *The Guardian*. **13 February**: 6.

41 *Learning from Bristol. The Report of the Public Inquiry into Children's Heart Surgery at the Bristol Royal Infirmary 1984–1995. The Bristol Royal Infirmary Inquiry, July 2001*; http://www.bristol-inquiry.org.uk.

42 Department of Health (2000) *An Organisation With a Memory*. The Stationery Office, London, 61.

43 Spink A (2001) Professional negligence: an update on current law and

issues. *Professional Solutions and Services*. **1 February**; http://www.prosols.uk.com.

44 The Institute for Safe Medication Practices (ISMP) (2001); www.ismp.org.

45 The Institute for Healthcare Improvement (IHI) (2001); www.ihi.org.

46 The Agency for Healthcare Research and Quality (AHRQ) in the USA (2001); www.ahcpr.gov/qual/errorsix.htm.

47 The Joint Commission on the Accreditation of Health Care Organizations (JCAHO) (2001); www.jcaho.org.

48 The Australian Patient Safety Foundation (APSF) (2001); www.apsf.net.au.

49 European Foundation for the Advancement of Healthcare Practitioners (2001); www.efahp.org.

50 Patient Safety Center, American Society of Health-System Pharmacists (2001); www.ashporg/patientsafety/index.

51 Reason J (2000) Human error: models and management. *BMJ*. **320**: 768–70.

52 Reinertsen JL (2000) Let's talk about error. *BMJ*. **320**: 730.

53 Hiefetz T (1984) *Leadership Without Easy Answers*. Bellknap Press, Cambridge, MA.

54 Department of Health (2001) *Building a Safer NHS for Patients*. The Stationery Office, London, 38.

Chapter 10

1 Ineson N (2000) Risk management in general practice. In: M Drury (ed.) *Clinical Negligence in General Practice*. Radcliffe Medical Press, Oxford, 127–54.

2 Conolly WB (1991) General priciples. In: JPW Varian (ed.) *Handbook of Medicological Practice*. Butterworth-Heinemann, Oxford, 47–82.

3 Vincent C, Young M and Phillips A (1994) Why do people sue doctors? A study of patients and relatives taking legal action. *Lancet*. **343**: 1609–13.

4 Drury M (2000) Complaints and the National Health Service. In: M Drury (ed.) *Clinical Negligence in General Practice*. Radcliffe Medical Press, Oxford, 13–24.

5 Powell PV (1995) An audit of the handling of medical negligence complaints by a health board. *Health Bull (Edinb)*. **53**: 196–205.

6 Department of Health and Social Security (1983) *National Health Service Management Inquiry (Griffiths Report)*. HMSO, London.

7 Department of Health (1989) *Working for Patients*. DoH, London.

8 Drury M (2000) Cause and effect. In: M Drury (ed.) *Clinical Negligence in General Practice*. Radcliffe Medical Press, Oxford, 1–12.

9 Pickering J (2000) The process of the law. In: M Drury (ed.) *Clinical Negligence in General Practice*. Radcliffe Medical Press, Oxford, 73–110.

10 *Blackburn v Newcastle Health Authority*.

11 Walker S (2000) NHS litigation. *Medicolegal J*. **68**: 3–15.

12 Gibb F (2001) How litigation is losing out to mediation. *The Times (Law section).* **26 June**.

13 Ince & Co. (2001) *The Dispute Revolution: a brief guide to mediation and ADR.* Ince & Co., London.

14 Gibb F (2001) No compensation for those who find litigation too expensive. *The Times (Law section).* **3 July**: 3.

15 Department of Health (2001) *National Statistics. Handling complaints: monitoring the NHS complaints procedures. England, financial year 1999–00.* Department of Health, London; www.doh.gov.uk/nhscomplaints.

16 Evans E (2001) Patients' concerns are still not being heeded. *BMJ.* **323**: 1065.

17 Dinnick S (2000) Defending allegations of negligence – the role of the medical defence organisations. In: M Drury (ed.) *Clinical Negligence in General Practice.* Radcliffe Medical Press, Oxford, 155–68.

Chapter 11

1 Bridge LJ, in *R v Secretary of State ex parte Hinks* (1992) 1 BMLR 93, 96 (the case was decided in 1980).

2 British Orthopaedic Association (1993) *The Management of Skeletal Trauma in the United Kingdom.* BOA, London.

3 Department of Health (2000) *The NHS Plan. A plan for investment, a plan for reform.* The Stationery Office, London.

4 Charter D (2001) Doctors in crisis complaints soar. *The Times.* **15 February**.

5 *Learning from Bristol. The Report of the Public Inquiry into Children's Heart Surgery at the Bristol Royal Infirmary 1984–1995. The Bristol Royal Infirmary Inquiry. July 2001. Synopsis. Point 14*; http://www.bristol-inquiry.org.uk.

6 *Learning from Bristol. The Report of the Public Inquiry into Children's Heart Surgery at the Bristol Royal Infirmary 1984–1995. The Bristol Royal Infirmary Inquiry. July 2001. The safety of care. Points 86 and 87*; http://www.bristol-inquiry.org.uk.

7 Walker S (2000) NHS litigation. *Medicolegal J.* **68**: 3–15.

8 Department of Health (2001) *The Prevention of Intrathecal Medication Errors. A report to the Chief Medical Officer.* The Stationery Office, London.

9 Department of Health (1998) *A First-Class Service: quality in the new NHS.* The Stationery Office, London.

10 Phillips DP, Christenfeld N and Glynn LM (1998) Increase in US medication-error deaths between 1983 and 1993. *Lancet.* **351**: 643–4.

11 Hall MJ and Lawrence L (1996) *Ambulatory Surgery in the United States.* National Center for Health Statistics, Hyattsville, MD.

12 Brennan TA *et al.* (1991) Incidence of adverse events and negligence in hospitalized patients. Results of the Harvard Medical Practice Study I. *NEJM.* **324**: 370–76.

13 Thomas EJ, Orav EJ and Brennan TA (2000) Hospital ownership and preventable adverse events. *J Gen Intern Med.* **15**: 211–19.

14 Allison JJ *et al.* (2000) Relationship of hospital teaching status with quality of care and mortality for Medicare patients with acute MI. *JAMA.* **284**: 1256–62.

15 Wilson RM *et al.* (1995) The Quality in Australian Health Care Study. *Med J Aust.* **163**: 458–71.

16 Daly K, Beale R and Chang RW (2001) Reduction in mortality after inappropriate early discharge from intensive-care unit: logistic regression triage model. *BMJ.* **322**: 1261–2.

17 Sherman J and Landale J (2001) Ministers' plea to foreign doctors. *The Times.* **20 August**.

18 Charter D (2001) Doctor recruits put off by NHS image. *The Times.* **20 August**.

19 Morris N (2001) Recruiting drive fails to fill NHS vacancies. *The Independent.* **11 April**.

20 Gartside R (2001) Only radical change can tackle community pharmacist workload and shortages. *Pharm J.* **267**: 226.

21 Carr-Brown J and Rufford N (2001) Patients win fight for surgery abroad. *The Sunday Times.* **26 August**.

22 Ed. (2000) Emergencies may slip through NHS Direct net, says Health Which. *Pharm J.* **265**: 220.

23 Lattimer V *et al.* (1998) Safety and effectiveness of nurse telephone consultation in out-of-hours primary care: randomised controlled trial. The South Wiltshire Out-of-Hours Project (SWOOP) Group. *BMJ.* **317**: 1054–9.

24 Department of Health (2001) *Building a Safer NHS for Patients.* The Stationery Office, London; http://www.doh.gov.uk/buildsafenhs.

25 Reason J (2000) Human error: models and management. *BMJ.* **320**: 768–70.

26 National Patient Safety Foundation at the American Medical Association (1999) *Agenda for Research and Development in Patient Safety*; http://www.ama-assn.org/medsci/npsf/research/research.htm.

27 Kohn LT, Corrigan JM and Donaldson MS (eds) (1999) *To Err is Human: building a safer health system.* Institute of Medicine National Academy Press, Washington, DC, 58.

28 Kohn LT, Corrigan JM and Donaldson MS (eds) (1999) *To Err is Human: building a safer health system.* Institute of Medicine National Academy Press, Washington, DC, 49–68.

29 Department of Health (2000) *Pharmacy in the Future – Implementing the NHS Plan. A programme for pharmacy in the National Health Service.* Department of Health, London.

30 Kelly G (2000) Electronics, clinicians and the NHS. *BMJ.* **321**: 846–7.

31 Bates DW (2000) Using information technology to reduce rates of medication errors in hospitals. *BMJ.* **320**: 788–91.

32 Ed. (2000) Robotic dispensing device installed at St Thomas's hospital. *Pharm J.* **265**: 653–5.

33 Cook R and Woods D (1994) Operating at the sharp end: the complexity of human error. In: MS Bogner (ed.) *Human Error in Medicine.* Erbaum, Hillsdale, NJ.

34 Norman D (1993) *Things That Make Us Smart: defending human attributes in the age of medicine.* Lawrence Erbaum Associates, Menlo Park, CA.

35 Bates DWT *et al.* (1999) The impact of computerised physician order entry on medication error prevention. *J Am Med Inform Assoc.* **6**: 313–32.

36 Carter *et al.* (1996) *The Computer-Based Patient Record. The Jacobi Medical Center Experience, Second Annual Nicholas E Davis CPR Recognition Proceedings (Computer-Based Patient Record Institute).*

37 Evans RS *et al.* (1998) A computer-assisted management program for antibiotics and other anti-infective agents. *NEJM.* **338**: 232–8.

38 Nightingale PG *et al.* (2000) Implementation of rules-based computerised bedside prescribing and administration: intervention study. *BMJ.* **320**: 750–3.

39 NHS Executive and University of Newcastle (2001) *PRODIGY: practical support for clinical governance.* Sowerby Centre for Health Informatics at Newcastle. Winter/Spring Edition; http://www.prodigy.nhs.uk.

40 Langdorf MI *et al.* (2000) Physician versus computer knowledge of potential drug interactions in the emergency department. *Acad Emerg Med.* **7**: 1321–9.

41 Reason J (1990) *Human Error.* Cambridge University Press, Cambridge.

42 Ed. (2001) Welcome for proposed extension of nurse prescribing. *Pharm J.* **266**: 108–9.

43 Weinger MB *et al.* (1998) Incorporating human factors into the design of medical devices. *JAMA.* **280**: 1484.

44 American Society of Health-System Pharmacists (1996) Consensus statement. Top priority actions for preventing adverse drug events in hospitals. *Am J Health Syst Pharm.* **53**: 747–51.

45 Kohn LT, Corrigan MS and Donaldson MS (eds) (1999) *To Err is Human: building a safer health system.* Institute of Medicine National Academy Press, Washington, DC, 183–97.

46 Bates DW *et al.* (1998) Effect of computerized physician order entry and a team intervention on prevention of serious medication errors. *JAMA.* **280**: 1311–16.

47 Bates DW *et al.* (1994) Potential identifiability and preventability of adverse events using information systems. *J Am Med Inform Assoc.* **1**: 404–11.

48 Gebhart F (1999) Facility slashes drug errors via bar-coding. *Drug Topics.* **1**: 44.

49 Bates DW *et al.* (1995) Incidence of adverse drug events and potential

adverse drug events. Implications for prevention. ADE Prevention Study Group. *JAMA.* **274**: 29–34.

50 Kohn LT, Corrigan JM and Donaldson MS (eds) (1999) *To Err is Human: building a safer health system.* Institute of Medicine National Academy Press, Washington, DC.

51 Cohen M (1997) Important error prevention advisory. *Hosp Pharm.* **32**: 489–91.

52 Lesar TS (1998) Errors in the use of medication dosage equations. *Arch Pediatr Adolesc Med.* **152**: 340–44.

53 Paterson DL, Robson JM and Wagener MM (1998) Risk factors for toxicity in elderly patients given aminoglycosides once daily. *J Gen Intern Med.* **13**: 735–9.

54 Slaughter RL and Cappelletty DM (1998) Economic impact of aminoglyco-side toxicity and its prevention through therapeutic drug monitoring. *Pharmacoeconomics.* **14**: 385–94.

55 Clinical Initiatives Centre (2000) *Reducing Adverse Events: best practices in reporting and prescribing.* Clinical Initiatives Center, Advisory Board Company, Washington, DC.

56 National Patient Safety Partnership (1999) *Healthcare Leaders Urge Adoption of Methods to Reduce Adverse Drug Events. News release;* http://www.nursingworld.org/pressrel/1999/st0512.htm.

57 Hatoum HT *et al.* (1986) An eleven-year review of the pharmacy literature: documentation of the value and acceptance of clinical pharmacy. *Drug Intell Clin Pharm.* **20**: 33–48.

58 Schumock GT *et al.* (1996) Economic evaluation of clinical pharmacy services: 1988–1995. *Pharmacotherapy.* **19**: 1188–208.

59 Bond CA, Raehl CL and Franke T (1999) Clinical pharmacy services and hospital mortality rates. *Pharmacotherapy.* **19**: 556–64.

60 Bond CA, Raehl CL and Pitterle ME (1994) National clinical pharmacy services study. *Pharmacotherapy.* **14**: 282–304.

61 Bond CA, Raehl CL and Franke T (2000) Clinical pharmacy services, pharmacy staffing, and the total cost of care in United States hospitals. *Pharmacotherapy.* **20**: 609–21.

62 Leape LL *et al.* (1999) Pharmacist participation in physician rounds and adverse drug events in the intensive care unit. *JAMA.* **282**: 267–70.

63 Gattis WA *et al.* (1999) Reduction in heart failure events by the addition of a clinical pharmacist to the heart failure management team: results of the Pharmacist in Heart Failure Assessment Recommendation and Monitoring (PHARM) Study. *Arch Intern Med.* **159**: 1939–45.

64 Boorman S and Cairns C (2000) Another way forward for pharmaceutical care: a team-based clinical pharmacy service. *Pharm J.* **264**: 343–6.

65 Hall SN (1970) *Report on the Working Party of the Hospital Pharmaceutical Service.* HMSO, London.

66 Committee on Hospital Scientific and Technical Services (1968) *Report.* HMSO, London.

67 Bradley TJ, Round AP and Ramsden M (2000) The success of an evidence-

based rational prescribing intervention: a retrospective study. *Pharm J.* **265**: 26–9.

68 Krska J *et al.* (2000) Providing pharmaceutical care using a systematic approach. *Pharm J.* **265**: 657–60.

69 Watson MC and Sharp DJ (2001) General practitioners' opinions of educational outreach visits from community pharmacists as a method of providing prescribing information. *Pharm J.* **266**: 20–22.

70 Pringle M (2000) The future of community pharmacy: the Royal College's challenge for pharmacy. *Pharm J.* **265**: 441.

71 Department of Health (2001) *National Clinical Assessment Authority*; http://www.ncaa.nhs.uk.

Chapter 12

1 Kohn LT, Corrigan JM and Donaldson MS (eds) (1999) *To Err is Human: building a safer health system.* Institute of Medicine National Academy Press, Washington, DC, 146.

2 Barach P and Small SD (2000) Reporting and preventing medical mishaps: lessons from non-medical near-miss reporting systems. *BMJ.* **320**: 759–63.

3 Brennan TA *et al.* (1991) Incidence of adverse events and negligence in hospitalized patients. Results of the Harvard Medical Practice Study I. *NEJM.* **324**: 370–6.

4 Hicks LK *et al.* (2001) Understanding the clinical dilemmas that shape medical students' ethical development: questionnaire survey and focus group study. *BMJ.* **322**: 709–10.

5 Doyal L (2001) Closing the gap between professional teaching and practice. *BMJ.* **322**: 685–6.

6 Wilson DG *et al.* (1998) Medication errors in paediatric practice: insights from a continuous quality improvement approach. *Eur J Paediatrics.* **157**: 769–74.

7 Foli HL *et al.* (1987) Medication error prevention by clinical pharmacists in two childrens's hospitals. *Pediatrics.* **79**: 718–22.

8 Ferner RE (2000) Medication errors that have led to manslaughter charges. *BMJ.* **321**: 1212–16.

9 Lesar TS *et al.* (1990) Medication prescribing errors in a teaching hospital. *JAMA.* **263:** 2329–34.

10 Health and Public Policy Committee of the American College of Physicians (1988) Improving medical education in therapeutics. *Ann Intern Med.* **108**: 145–7.

11 Reason J (1990) *Human Error.* Cambridge University Press, Cambridge.

12 Cook RI, Render RI and Woods DD (2000) Gaps in the continuity of care and progress on patient safety. *BMJ.* **320**: 791–4.

13 Espinosa JA and Nolan TW (2000) Reducing errors made by emergency physicians in interpreting radiographs: longitudinal study. *BMJ.* **320**: 737–40.

14 Department of Health (2000) *An Organisation With a Memory.* The Stationery Office, London; http://www.doh.gov.uk/orgmemreport/ orgmemexecsum.htm.

15 Wilson T, Pringle M and Sheikh A (2001) Promoting patient safety in primary care: research, action and leadership are required. *BMJ.* **323**: 583–4.

16 Leape LL *et al.* (1995) Systems analysis of adverse drug events. ADE Prevention Study Group. *JAMA.* **274**: 35–43.

17 Lesar TS, Briceland L and Stein DS (1997) Factors related to errors in medication prescribing. *JAMA.* **277**: 312–17.

18 Dean B *et al.* (2000) Prescribing errors in hospital inpatients: why do they occur? *Pharm J.* **265**: R17.

19 Battles JB and Shea CE (2001) A system for analysing medical errors to improve GME curricula and programs. *Acad Med.* **76**: 125–33.

20 Leape LL *et al.* (1991) The nature of adverse events in hospitalized patients. Results of the Harvard Medical Practice Study II. *NEJM.* **324**: 377–84.

21 Cambridge Health Authority (2000) *Methotrexate Toxicity: an inquiry into the death of a Cambridgeshire patient in April 2000.* Cambridge Health Authority, Cambridge; http://www.cambs-ha.nhs.uk/ publications.

22 Edwards IR and Aronson JK (2000) Adverse drug reactions: definitions, diagnosis and management. *Lancet.* **356**: 1255–9.

23 British Medical Association and Royal Pharmaceutical Society of Great Britain (March, 1999) *British National Formulary 37.* British Medical Association and Royal Pharmaceutical Society of Great Britain.

24 Data Pharm Publications (1999) *ABPI Compendium of Data Sheets and Summaries of Product Characteristics 1999–2000.* Data Pharm Publications, London.

25 Gebhart F (1999) Facility slashes drug errors via bar-coding. *Drug Topics.* **1**: 44.

26 Huxley TH (1881) General address on the connection of the biological sciences with medicine. *Lancet.* **2**: 272–6.

27 Reid R (1974) *Microbes and Men.* British Broadcasting Corporation, London.

28 Martindale W and Westcott WW (eds) (1885) *The Extra Pharmacopoeia with the Additions Introduced into the British Pharmacopoeia* (14e). Wyman and Sons, London.

29 Parfitt K (ed.) (1999) *Martindale: the complete drug reference* (32e). Pharmaceutical Press, London.

30 Heydorn WE (1997) New drugs approved by the FDA in Part 2. *Pharm News.* **5**: 28–33.

31 Van den Haak M (2001) Fewer new launches in 2000. *CMR Int News.* **19**: 10–14.

32 Department of Health (1999) *Supporting Doctors, Protecting Patients. A consultation paper on preventing, recognising and dealing with poor clinical performance of doctors in the NHS in England.* DoH, London; http://www.doh.gov.uk/cmoconsult1.htm.
33 Department of Health (2001) *Assuring the Quality of Medical Practice. Implementing Supporting Doctors, Protecting Patients.* DoH, London.

Chapter 13

1 Department of Health (2000) *The NHS Plan. A plan for investment, a plan for reform.* The Stationery Office, London.
2 Sanders C (2001) Moves to get the NHS fighting fit. *The Times Higher Educ Suppl.* **8 June**: 6–7.
3 Ed. (2001) Medical applications in freefall. *The Times Higher Educ Suppl.* **27 July**: 2.
4 Ed. (2001) Crisis looming for pharmacy courses? *Pharm J.* **267**: 251.
5 Goddard A (2001) A-level horde prompts calls for more cash. *The Times Higher Educ Suppl.* **17 August**: 1.
6 Royal Pharmaceutical Society of Great Britain (2001) *Pharmacy Student Analysis 1999–2000.* Compiled within the RPSGB Education Division with the co-operation of the Heads of Schools of Pharmacy. Royal Pharmaceutical Society of Great Britain, London.
7 Thomson A (2001) Growth is blamed for fall in standards. *The Times Higher Educ Suppl.* **11 May**: 8.
8 Charatan F (2000) Applications to US medical schools fall by a fifth. *BMJ.* **321**: 1177.
9 Ed. (2001) US faces pharmacist shortage. *Pharm J.* **266**: 376; www.bhpr.hrsa.gov:80/healthworkforce/pharmacist.html.
10 Hackett G (2001) Architect of AS-level doubts own exam. *The Sunday Times.* **10 June**: 5.
11 Thomson A (2001) Growth is blamed for fall in standards. *The Times Higher Educ Suppl.* **11 May**: 8.
12 Baldwin DC Jr *et al.* (1996) Cheating in medical school: a survey of second-year students at 31 schools. *Acad Med.* **71**: 267–73.
13 Rennie SC and Crosby JR (2001) Are 'tomorrow's doctors' honest? Questionnaire study exploring medical students' attitudes and reported behaviour on academic misconduct. *BMJ.* **322**: 274–5.
14 Sierles F, Hendricks I and Circle S (1980) Cheating in medical school. *J Med Educ.* **55**: 124–5.
15 Smith R (2000) Cheating at medical school. *BMJ.* **321**: 398.
16 Van Luijk SJ *et al.* (2000) Assessing professional behaviour and the role of academic advice at the Maastricht Medical School. *Med Teacher.* **22**: 168–72.

17 Wagner RF Jr (1993) Medical student academic misconduct: implications of recent case law and possible institutional responses. *Acad Med.* **68**: 887–9.

18 Walker J (1998) Students' plagiarism in universities: what are we doing about it? *Higher Educ Res Dev.* **17**: 887–9.

19 Albanese M (2000) The decline and fall of humanism in medical education. *Med Educ.* **34**: 596–7.

20 Institute of Health and Community Studies (1999) *Managing Medical Performance. The report of a seminar for chairs of health authorities and NHS trusts, 17 March, London.* Institute of Health and Community Studies, Bournemouth.

21 General Medical Council (1993) *Tomorrow's Doctors: recommendations on undergraduate medical education. Report of the Education Committee.* General Medical Council, London.

22 Boud D and Feletti G (1991) *The Challenge of Problem-Based Learning.* Kogan Page, London.

23 Ed. (1974) The McMaster philosophy. An approach to medical education – McMaster education. *J Med Educ.* **49**: 1040–50.

24 Fowell SL *et al.* (2000) Student assessment in undergraduate medical education in the United Kingdom, 1998. *Med Educ.* **34 (Supplement 1)**: 1–49.

25 The Quality Assurance Agency for Higher Education (1998) *Subject Overview Report Medicine;* http://www.qaa.ac.uk.

26 The Quality Assurance Agency for Higher Education (1999) *Subject Review Report, November 1998;* http://www.qaa.ac.uk.

27 The Quality Assurance Agency for Higher Education (1998) *Subject Review Report, 1998;* http://www.qaa.ac.uk.

28 The Quality Assurance Agency for Higher Education (1999) *Follow-Up Report on Action Taken in Response to Subject Review, 1999;* http://www.qaa.ac.uk.

29 Bateman DN, McInnes GT and Webb DJ (1999) Clinical pharmacology and therapeutics in a changing world. *Br J Clin Pharmacol.* **48**: 1–3.

30 Anderson J (1993) The continuum of medical education. The role of basic medical sciences. *J R Coll Phys Lond.* **27**: 405–7.

31 Beaty HN (1990) Changes in medical education should not ignore the basic sciences. *Acad Med.* **65**: 675–6.

32 Walley T and Webb DJ (1997) Developing a core curriculum in clinical pharmacology and therapeutics: a Delphi study. *Br J Clin Pharmacol.* **44**: 167–70.

33 Walley T and Webb DJ (1997) Core content of a course in clinical pharmacology. *Br J Clin Pharmacol.* **44**: 171–4.

34 Thomas SHL (2000) *Student Formulary for Students Qualifying in 2003.* University of Newcastle, Newcastle-upon-Tyne.

35 McCrorie P (2000) The place of the basic sciences in medical curricula. *Med Educ.* **34**: 594–5.

36 Lloyd-Jones G, Walley T and Bligh J (1997) Integrating clinical pharmacology in a new problem-based medical undergraduate curriculum. *Br J Clin Pharmacol.* **43**: 15–19.

37 Doig K and Werner E (2000) The marriage of a traditional lecture-based curriculum and problem-based learning: are the offspring vigorous? *Med Teacher.* **22**: 173–8.

38 Barrows HS and Tamblyn RM (1980) *Problem-Based Learning: an approach to medical education.* Pringer, New York.

39 Albanese MA and Mitchell S (1993) Problem-based learning: a review of literature on its outcomes and implementation issue. *Acad Med.* **68**: 52–81.

40 Slotnick HB (2000) How doctors know when to stop learning. *Med Teacher.* **22**: 189–96.

41 David T *et al.* (1999) *Problem-Based Learning in Medicine.* Royal Society of Medicine Press Ltd, London.

42 Norman GR and Schmidt HG (1992) The psychological basis of problem-based learning: a review of the evidence. *Acad Med.* **67**: 557–65.

43 Dickson D (1993) Backlash threatens biomedicine. *Nature.* **365**: 5.

44 Wiesberg SP (2001) Genetics and preventive medicine. *JAMA.* **286**: 1634.

45 Phillips AJ (2001) The challenge of gene therapy and DNA delivery. *J Pharm Pharmc.* **53**: 1169–74.

46 Schmidt HG (2000) Assumptions underlying self-directed learning may be false. *Med Educ.* **34**: 243–5.

47 Hofstra ML *et al.* (1988) Invloed van ervaring op diagnostische prestaties van huisartsen (The influence of experience on diagnostic accuracy of family physicians). *Huisarts En Wetenschap.* **31**: 282–4.

48 Snell L *et al.* (2000) A review of the evaluation of clinical teaching: new perspectives and challenges. *Med Educ.* **34**: 862–70.

49 Department of Health (2001) *The Prevention of Intrathecal Medication Errors. A report to the Chief Medical Officer.* Department of Health, London.

50 *Learning from Bristol. The Report of the Public Inquiry into Children's Heart Surgery at the Bristol Royal Infirmary 1984–1995. The Bristol Royal Infirmary Inquiry. July 2001. Care in the operating theatre and the 'learning curve'; the 'learning curve'; managing the 'learning curve';* http://www.bristol-inquiry.org.uk.

51 Murray E *et al.* (2000) The accountability of clinical education: its definition and assessment. *Med Educ.* **34**: 871–9.

52 Department of Health (2001) *Building a Safer NHS for Patients.* The Stationery Office, London.

53 Rothman AI (2000) Problem-based learning – time to move forward? *Med Educ.* **34**: 509–10.

54 Colliver JA (2000) Effectiveness of problem-based learning curricula: research and theory. *Acad Med.* **75**: 259–66.

55 Albanese M (2000) Problem-based learning: why curricula are likely to show little effect on knowledge and clinical skills. *Med Educ.* **34**: 729–38.

56 Bligh J (2000) Problem-based learning: the story continues to unfold. *Med Educ.* **34**: 688–9.

57 Norman GR and Schmidt HG (2000) Effectiveness of problem-based learning curricula: theory, practice and paper darts. *Med Educ.* **34**: 721–8.

58 Leape LL *et al.* (1995) Systems analysis of adverse drug events. ADE Prevention Study Group. *JAMA.* **274**: 35–43.

59 Dean B *et al.* (2000) Prescribing errors in hospital inpatients: why do they occur? *Pharm J.* **265**: R17.

60 Wilson DG *et al.* (1998) Medication errors in paediatric practice: insights from a continuous quality improvement approach. *Eur J Paediatrics.* **157**: 769–74.

61 Cambridge Health Authority (2000) *Methotrexate Toxicity: an inquiry into the death of a Cambridgeshire patient in April 2000.* Cambridge Health Authority, Cambridge; http://www.cambs-ha.nhs.uk/publications.

62 Department of Health (2000) *The NHS Plan. A plan for investment, a plan for reform. Shorter courses.* Department of Health, London.

63 BMA (2001) *Shorter undergraduate medical courses and graduate entry into medicine.* BMA online. http://www.bma.org.uk/public/webdocs.nsf/webprevw/shortercourses.

64 Department of Health (1996) *Primary Care: choice and opportunity.* HMSO, London.

65 Parsell G and Bligh J (1998) Interprofessional learning. *Postgrad Med J.* **74**: 89–95.

66 Sainsbury Centre for Mental Health (1997) *Pulling Together. The future roles and training of mental health staff.* Sainsbury Centre for Mental Health, London.

67 Standing Committee on Postgraduate Medical and Dental Education (SCOPME) (1997) *Multiprofessional Working and Learning: sharing the educational challenge.* SCOPME, London.

68 Schofield M (1996) *The Future Healthcare Workforce: the Steering Group Report.* Lilly Laboratories, Manchester.

69 *Learning from Bristol. The Report of the Public Inquiry into Children's Heart Surgery at the Bristol Royal Infirmary 1984–1995. The Bristol Royal Infirmary Inquiry. July 2001. Competent healthcare professionals;* http://www.bristol-inquiry.org.uk.

70 Fraser D *et al.* (2000) A university department merger of midwifery and obstetrics: a step on the journey to enhancing interprofessional learning. *Med Teacher.* **22**: 179–83.

71 Pirrie M *et al.* (1998) Multiple-professional education. Part 2. Promoting cohesive practice in healthcare. *Med Teacher.* **20**: 409–16.

72 Ross F and Southgate L (2000) Learning together in medical and nursing training: aspirations and activity. *Med Educ.* **34**: 739–43.

73 Wilson T and Mires GJ (2000) A comparison of performance by medical and midwifery students in multiprofessional teaching. *Med Educ.* **34**: 744–6.

74 Department of Health (2000) *The NHS Plan. A plan for investment, a plan*

for reform. Changes for nurses, midwives, therapists and other NHS staff. Department of Health, London.

75 Roberts C *et al.* (2000) Not so easy as it sounds: a qualitative study of a shared learning project between medical and nursing undergraduate students. *Med Teacher.* **22**: 386–91.

76 Sanders C (2001) An unconventional treatment. *The Times Higher Educ Suppl.* **26 October**: 21.

77 Freeth D and Chaput De Saintonge DM (2000) Helping medical students become good house officers: interprofessional learning in a skills centre. *Med Teacher.* **22**: 392–8.

78 Boreham NC, Mawer GE and Foster RW (2000) Medical students' errors in pharmacotherapeutics. *Med Educ.* **34**: 188–93.

79 Heywood J (1999) *Assessment in Higher Education: student learning, teaching, programmes and institutions.* Jessica Kingsley Publishers, London.

80 Cato G (2001) *Review of Tomorrow's Doctors: consultation on new recommendations on undergraduate medical education;* www.gmc-uk.org.

81 General Medical Council (2001) *Draft Recommendations on Undergraduate Medical Education. Consultation copy.* General Medical Council, London.

82 The Quality Assurance Agency for Higher Education (2001) *QAA consultation: benchmarking academic standards. Medicine;* http://www.qaa.ac.uk/crntwork/benchmark/phase2/medicine.pdf.

83 Baty P (2001) QAA issues rules for placements. *The Times Higher Educ Suppl.* **17 August**: 4.

84 The Quality Assurance Agency for Higher Education (2001) *QAA consultation: benchmarking academic standards. Pharmacy;* http://www.qaa.ac.uk/crntwork/benchmark/phase2/pharmacy.pdf.

85 Ed. (2000) Society withholds accreditation from Liverpool MPharm degree. *Pharm J.* **265**: 218.

86 Ed. (2001) Code of Ethics revision. *Pharm J.* **266**: 325–32.

87 *David Noe McCandless v The General Medical Council*, 1995.

88 Townsend A (2000) The role of the General Medical Council. In: M Drury (ed.) *Clinical Negligence in General Practice.* Radcliffe Medical Press, Oxford, 27–42.

89 Challis M (2000) AMEE Medical Education Guide No. 19. Personal learning plans. *Med Teacher.* **22**: 225–36.

90 Dewar S and Finlayson B (2001) Reforming the GMC. *BMJ.* **322**: 689–90.

91 General Medical Council (2001) *Protecting Patients: a summary consultative document.* General Medical Council, London; www.gmc-uk.org/consultation/default.htm.

92 Beecham L (2000) GMC to consult on next stage of revalidation. *BMJ.* **320**: 1425.

93 Smith R (2001) Approaching the abyss. *BMJ.* **322**: 1196.

94 Consumers' Association (2000) *GMC Reform Must Move Up a Gear, says CA;* http://www.which.net/whatsnew/pr/feb00/general/gmcreform.html.

95 Barach P and Moss F (2001) Delivering safe health care. Safety is a patient's right and the obligation of all health professionals. *BMJ*. **323**: 585–6.

96 Baty P (2001) Russel elite go for jugular of ailing QAA. *The Times Higher Educ Suppl.* **21 September**: 1.

97 McPherson GS, Davies JG and McRobbie D (1999) Preregistration trainee clinical competence: a baseline assessment. *Pharm J.* **263**: 168–70.

98 Royal Pharmaceutical Society (1998) *Preregistration Training Manual.* Royal Pharmaceutical Society, London.

99 Royal Pharmaceutical Society (1997) *Preregistration Bulletin.* Royal Pharmaceutical Society, London.

100 Lesar TS (1998) Errors in the use of medication dosage equations. *Arch Pediatr Adolesc Med.* **152**: 340–44.

101 Battles JB and Shea CE (2001) A system for analysing medical errors to improve GME curricula and programs. *Acad Med.* **76**: 125–33.

102 Wicks N (2001) Is the pre-reg year missing the point? *Chem Druggist.* **17 November**: 14.

Chapter 14

1 Leslie PJ *et al.* (1990) Hours, volume and type of work of preregistration house officers. *BMJ*. **300**: 1038–41.

2 Ford J and Simpson P (1991) Juniors' hours-of-work survey: additional findings. *BMJ*. **302**: 118.

3 Dyer C (1991) Manslaughter convictions for making mistakes. *BMJ*. **303**: 1218.

4 Ed. (1992) Educational improvement of the preregistration period of general clinical training. *BMJ*. **304**: 625–7.

5 Dowling S and Barrett S (1991) *Doctors in the Making: the experience of the preregistration year.* School for Advanced Urban Studies, University of Bristol, Bristol.

6 Ed. (1992) Improving preregistration training. *BMJ*. **304**: 980–81.

7 Wilson DH (1993) Education and training of preregistration house officers: the consultants. *BMJ*. **306**: 194–6.

8 General Medical Council (1996) *The New Doctor. Protecting patients, guiding doctors. Recommendations on General Medical Training made under Section 5 of the Medical Act 1983.* General Medical Council, London.

9 Lowry S (1993) The preregistration year. *BMJ*. **306**: 196–8.

10 Kelly D and Murray TS (1997) An assessment of hospital training for general practice in the West of Scotland. *Educ Gen Pract.* **8**: 220–26.

11 Royal College of Physicians and Surgeons (1997) *Review of Working Patterns, Training and Experience of Medical SHOs.* RCPS, London.

12 General Medical Council (1998) *The Early Years: Recommendations on Senior House Officer Training*. General Medical Council, London.

13 Hargreaves D and Southworth G (1997) *On-the-Job Training for Physicians: A practical guide*. Royal Society of Medicine, London.

14 Gibson DR and Campbell RM (2000) The role of co-operative learning in the training of junior hospital doctors: a study of paediatric senior house officers. *Med Teacher*. **22**: 297–300.

15 Gibson DR and Campbell RM (2000) Promoting effective teaching and learning: hospital consultants identify their needs. *Med Educ*. **34**: 126–30.

16 Calman KC and Donaldson M (1991) The pre-registration house officer year: a critical incident study. *Med Educ*. **25**: 51–9.

17 Bax NDS and Godfrey J (1997) Identifying core skills for the medical curriculum. *Med Educ*. **31**: 347–51.

18 Jones A, McArdle PJ and O'Neill PA (2001) How well prepared are graduates for the role of pre-registration house officer? A comparison of the perceptions of new graduates and educational supervisors. *Med Educ*. **35**: 578–84.

19 Goodfellow PB and Claydon P (2001) Students sitting medical finals – ready to be house officers? *J R Soc Med*. **94**: 516–20.

20 Seabrook MA *et al*. (2000) Consistency of teaching in parallel surgical firms: an audit of student experience at one medical school. *Med Educ*. **34**: 292–8.

21 du Boulay C and Medway C (1999) The clinical skills resource: a review of current practice. *Med Educ*. **33**: 185–91.

22 Das M, Townsend A and Hasan MY (1998) The views of senior students and young doctors of their training in a skills laboratory. *Med Educ*. **32**: 143–9.

23 Bradley P and Bligh J (1999) One year's experience with a clinical skills resource centre. *Med Educ*. **33**: 114–20.

24 de Vries B and Cossart YE (1994) Needlestick injury in medical students. *Med J Aust*. **160**: 398–400.

25 Hettiaratchy S *et al*. (1998) Glove usage and reporting of needlestick injuries by junior hospital medical staff. *Ann R C Surg Engl*. **80**: 439–41.

26 Spike NA and Veitch PC (1991) Competency of medical students in general practice procedural skills. *Aust Fam Phys*. **20**: 586–7.

27 Roche AM, Sanson-Fisher RW and Cockburn J (1997) Training experiences immediately after medical school. *Med Educ*. **31**: 9–16.

28 Nelson MS and Traub S (1993) Clinical skills training of US medical students. *Acad Med*. **68**: 926–8.

29 Koenig S and Chu J (1993) Senior medical students' knowledge of universal precautions. *Acad Med*. **68**: 372–4.

30 Wade TP, Edwards JC and Kamininski DL (1993) Clinical skills acquired during third-year surgical clerkships. *Am J Surg*. **166**: 292–9.

31 Falck G, Brattebo G and Aarseth O (1995) Is the training of interns in practical clinical skills adequate? *Tidsskr Nor Laegeforen*. **115**: 2091–5.

32 Aarseth O, Falck G and Brattebo G (1995) Do the interns receive the

supervision they are supposed to get? *Tiddsskr Nor Laegeforen.* **115**: 2087–90.

33 Levine M and Iredale A (2001) *University of Leeds School of Medicine Student Handbook. Session 2001/2002.* University of Leeds, Leeds.

34 Freeth R (2001) Supervision. *BMJ Classified.* **15 September**: 2–3.

35 Department of Health (1999) *Supporting Doctors, Protecting Patients. A consultation paper on preventing, recognising and dealing with poor clinical performance of doctors in the NHS in England.* Department of Health, London; http://www.doh.gov.cmcoconsult1.htm.

36 *Learning from Bristol. The Report of the Public Inquiry into Children's Heart Surgery at the Bristol Royal Infirmary 1984–1995. The Bristol Royal Infirmary Inquiry. July 2001. Competent healthcare professionals;* http://www.bristol-inquiry.org.uk.

37 Young H (1999) *An Evaluation of Discharge Prescription Writing by Clinical Pharmacists.* Countess of Chester NHS Trust.

38 General Dental Council (1997) *Curriculum for Dental Therapists.* General Dental Council, London.

39 Royal College of Anaesthetists (2000) *The Intercollegiate Committee for Training in Paediatric Intensive-Care Medicine.* Royal College of Anaesthetists, London.

40 Harrison A (2001) Competence is the key to safe supervision and delegation. *Pharm J.* **267**: 89–91.

Chapter 15

1 *Roe v Minister of Health* (1954) 2 All ER: 131.

2 Griffiths JR (2000) The law of negligence. In: M Drury (ed.) *Clinical Negligence in General Practice.* Radcliffe Medical Press, Oxford, 43–72.

3 *Bolam v Friern Hospital Management Committee* (1957) 2 All ER: 118.

4 *Hunter v Hanley* (1955) Session Cases: 200.

5 *Bolitho and others v City and Hackney Health Authority* (1998) Lloyds LR Med: 26.

6 *Marriot v West Midlands Health Authority and others* (1999) Lloyds LR Med (Part 1, February 1999): 23.

7 *Hucks v Cole* (1968, reported in 1993) 4 Med LR: 393.

8 *Learning from Bristol. The Report of the Public Inquiry into Children's Heart Surgery at the Bristol Royal Infirmary 1984–1995. The Bristol Royal Infirmary Inquiry. July 2001. Care of an appropriate standard;* http://www.bristol-inquiry.org.uk.

9 Gibb F (2001) Doctor doesn't know best, says Wolf. *The Times.* **18 January**.

10 Hall C (2001) Presentation by Sir Donald Irvine, President of the GMC, at the Annual Lloyds Roberts Lecture at the Royal Society of Medicine, 16 January 2001. *The Daily Telegraph.* **17 January**.

11 Duce R and Jenkins R (2000) BMA criticised over contempt. *The Times*. **2 February**.

12 *Learning from Bristol. The Report of the Public Inquiry into Children's Heart Surgery at the Bristol Royal Infirmary 1984–1995. The Bristol Royal Infirmary Inquiry. July 2001. Final Report, Section Two, Recommendations*; http://www.bristol-inquiry.org.uk.

13 Corrado M (2001) No-one likes us, or do they? *Sci Public Affairs*. **August**: 14–15.

14 Kruger J and Dunning D (1999) Unskilled and unaware of it: how difficulties in recognizing one's own incompetence lead to inflated self-assessments. *J Pers Soc Psychol*. **77**: 1121–34.

15 Rogers L (2001) NHS damned for 'culture of arrogance': report condemns Bristol scandal. *The Sunday Times*. **11 February**.

16 *Learning from Bristol. The Report of the Public Inquiry into Children's Heart Surgery at the Bristol Royal Infirmary 1984–1995. The Bristol Royal Infirmary Inquiry. July 2001*; http://www.bristol-inquiry.org.uk.

17 Hawkes N (2001) Hospital club culture led to over 30 deaths. *The Times*. **19 July**.

18 *BMA pledges support for follow-up action on Bristol Inquiry Report*. BMA Online, Wednesday 18 July 2001; http://www.bma.org.uk/pressrel.nsf.

19 Weatherall D (1999) The conflict between the science and the art of clinical practice in the next millennium. In: DC Grossman and H Valtin (eds) *Great Issues for Medicine in the Twenty First Century. Ethical and social issues arising out of advances in the biomedical sciences*. The New York Academy of Sciences, New York, 240–6.

20 Leape LL *et al.* (1995) Systems analysis of adverse drug events. ADE Prevention Study Group. *JAMA*. **274**: 35–43.

21 Ferner RE (2000) Medication errors that have led to manslaughter charges. *BMJ*. **321**: 1212–16.

22 Stokes P (1998) Suspended jail term for doctor in lethal injection case. *Daily Telegraph*. **28 November**.

23 Stokes P (1999) Surgeon too ill to stand trial. *Daily Telegraph*. **17 March**.

24 News (1999) Anaethetist jailed over death. *Daily Telegraph*. **30 July**.

25 Clough S (1999) Doctors cleared of killing boy, 12, in cancer jab mix-up. *Daily Telegraph*. **6 January**.

26 Stokes P (1999) Patient died after nurse's morphine tablet blunder. *Daily Telegraph*. **5 September**.

27 Ed. (2000) Boots pharmacist and trainee cleared of baby's manslaughter, but fined for dispensing a defective medicine. *Pharm J*. **264**: 390.

28 Rome CM (2000) Serious questions. *Pharm J*. **264**: 468.

29 Shallal A (2000) Defect in training format. *Pharm J*. **264**: 468–9.

30 Ed. (2001) No action taken against preregistration student involved in 'peppermint water' tragedy. *Pharm J*. **267**: 212.

31 Laville S, Hall C and NMcIlroy AJ (2001) Cancer boy dies after doctor's drugs blunder. *Daily Telegraph*. **3 February**.

32 Weaver M (2001) Girl died after eight years as a paraplegic. *Daily Telegraph*. **3 February**.

33 Charter D (2001) Every part of the NHS to blame for boy's death. *The Times*. **20 April**.

34 Department of Health (2001) *The Prevention of Intrathecal Medication Errors. A report to the Chief Medical Officer*. Department of Health, London.

35 Charter D (2001) Series of blunders lead to fatal errors. *The Times*. **20 April**.

36 Cited in Boardman H *et al*. (2001) A pharmacy workforce survey in the West Midlands: (4) morale and motivation. *Pharm J*. **267**: 685–90.

37 Murphy J (2001) Roll call of resignations exposes GP crisis. *Sunday Telegraph*. **11 November**.

38 *Johnstone v Bloomsbury Health Authority* (1991) 2 All ER: 293.

39 *Bull v Devon Health Authority* (1993) 4 Med LR 117 (decided in 1989).

40 *Learning from Bristol. The Report of the Public Inquiry into Children's Heart Surgery at the Bristol Royal Infirmary 1984–1995. The Bristol Royal Infirmary Inquiry. July 2001. Conclusions on the adequacy of the service;* http://www.bristol-inquiry.org.uk.

41 McPherson GS, Davies JG and McRobbie D (1999) Preregistration trainee clinical competence: a baseline assessment. *Pharm J*. **263**: 168–70.

42 Jourdan S, Rossi ML and Goulding J (2000) Italy: medical negligence as a crime. *Lancet*. **356**: 1267–8.

43 Teahon K and Bateman DN (1993) A survey of intravenous drug administration by preregistration house officers. *BMJ*. **307**: 605–6.

Chapter 16

1 Rosenew EC (1971) *Medical knowledge self-assessment programs*. Paper presented at 173rd Annual Meeting of the Medical and Chisurgical Faculty of State of Maryland, Baltimore, 1971.

2 Dubin SS (1972) Obsolescence or life-long learning: a choice for the professional. *Am Psychol*. **27**: 486–98.

3 Lindsay CA, Morrison JL and Kelley EJ (1974) Professional obsolescence: implications for continuing professional development. *Adult Educ*. **25**: 3–22.

4 Walker VL and Lowenthal W (1981) Perceptions by undergraduate students toward continuing education. *Am J Pharm Educ*. **45**: 268–72.

5 Kell C and Van Deursen R (2000) The fight against professional obsolescence should begin in the undergraduate curriculum. *Med Teacher*. **22**: 160–63.

6 Department of Health (2000) *The NHS Plan. A plan for investment, a plan for reform*. The Stationery Office, London.

7 Freeman A, Davies K and Phillips M (2001) *Continuing Professional*

Development in the UK: attitudes and experiences of practitioners. Parn Publications; www.parn.org.uk.

8 Sanders C (2001) Answer to a question of trust? *The Times Higher Educ Suppl.* **17 August**: 21.

9 *Learning from Bristol. The Report of the Public Inquiry into Children's Heart Surgery at the Bristol Royal Infirmary 1984–1995. The Bristol Royal Infirmary Inquiry. Respect and honesty. July 2001.* http://www.bristol-inquiry.org.uk.

10 Balint M (1957) *The Doctor, His Patient and the Illness*. Pitman, London.

11 Pendleton D *et al.* (1984) *The Consultation: an approach to learning and teaching*. Oxford University Press, Oxford.

12 Elwyn G, Edwards A and Kinnersley P (1999) Shared decision-making in primary care: the neglected second half of the consultation. *Br J Gen Pract.* **49**: 477–82.

13 Aneel A, Rosen P and Hjortsberg C (1997) Choice and participation in the health services: a survey of preferences among Swedish residents. *Health Policy.* **40**: 157–68.

14 Casileth BR *et al.* (1980) Information and participation preferences of hospitalised adult cancer patients. *Health Policy.* **92**: 832–4.

15 Greenfield S *et al.* (1988) Patients' participation in medical care: effects on blood sugar control and quality of life in diabetes. *J Gen Intern Med.* **3**: 448–57.

16 Fadiman A (1997) *The Spirit Catches You and You Fall Down*. Farrar, Straus and Giroux, New York.

17 Kravitz RL and Melnikow J (2001) Engaging patients in medical decision making. The end is worthwhile, but the means need to be more practical. *BMJ.* **323**: 584–5.

18 Carrese JA and Rhodes LA (1995) Western bioethics on the Navajo reservation: benefit or harm. *JAMA.* **274**: 826–9.

19 Braddock CHI *et al.* (1999) Informed decision making in practice: time to get back to basics. *JAMA.* **282**: 2313–20.

20 Degner LF *et al.* (1997) Information needs and decisional preferences in women with breast cancer. *JAMA.* **277**: 1485–92.

21 Hope T (1996) *Evidence-Based Patient Choice*. King's Fund, London.

22 Ed. (2001) GMC to rule on the ethics of treatment choice over MMR vaccination. *Pharm J.* **267**: 183.

23 Editorial (2001) Editor's choice: promoting safety and quality. *BMJ.* **323**.

24 Marinker M (1996) *Partnership in Medicine Taking: a consultative document*. The Royal Pharmaceutical Society of Great Britain and Merck Sharp and Dohme, London.

25 Ed. (2000) Huge waste of medicines claimed. *Pharm J.* **264**: 238.

26 Huse DM *et al.* (2001) Physicians knowledge, attitudes, and practice of pharmacological treatment of hypertension. *Ann Pharmaco.* **35**: 1173–9.

27 Lowmax H, Brooks FR and Mitchell M (2001) Understanding user healthcare strategies: experiences of asthma therapy among South Asians and white cultural groups. In: S Gillam and F Brooks (eds) *New Beginnings:*

towards patient and public involvement in primary healthcare. King's Fund, University of London, London.

28 Collins R *et al.* (1990) Blood pressure, stroke and coronary heart disease. Part 2. Short-term reductions in blood pressure: overview of randomised drug trials in their epidemiological context. *Lancet.* **335**: 827–38.

29 Lacey H (1999) A part of the illness. *Pharm J.* **263**: 922.

30 Ed. (2000) Aherence to oral hypoglycaemic treatment low, study shows. *Pharm J.* **264**: 429.

31 Small-print dangers. The Royal National Institute for the Blind; www.rnib.org.uk.

32 NHS Centre for Reviews and Dissemination (1999) Getting evidence into practice. *Effect Health Care Bull.* **5**: 1.

33 Heaney D *et al.* (2001) Assessment of impact of information booklets on use of healthcare services: randomised control study. *BMJ.* **322**: 1218–21.

34 Oxman AD *et al.* (1995) No magic bullets: a systematic review of 102 trials interventions to improve professional practice. *Can Am Med Assoc J.* **153**: 1423–31.

35 Little P *et al.* (2001) Randomised control trial of self-management leaflets for minor illness provided by post. *BMJ.* **322**: 1214–17.

36 Gillam S and Brooks F (2001) *New Beginnings: towards patient and public involvement in primary healthcare.* King's Fund, University of London, London.

37 Campbell A and Howie J (1988) Involving the patient in reporting adverse drug reactions. *J R C Gen Pract.* **38**: 370–71.

38 Fisher S *et al.* (1994) Patient drug attributions and postmarketing surveillance. *Pharmacotherapy.* **14**: 202–9.

39 Fisher S *et al.* (1987) Patient-initiated postmarketing surveillance: a validation study. *J Clin Pharmacol.* **27**: 843–54.

40 Fisher S, Kent TA and Bryant SG (1995) Postmarket surveillance by patient self-monitoring – preliminary data for sertraline versus fluoxetine. *J Clin Psychiatry.* **56**: 288–96.

41 Mitchell *et al.* (1994) Adverse drug reactions: can consumers provide early warning? *Pharmacoepidemiol Drug Safety.* **3**: 257–64.

42 Egberts TCG *et al.* (1996) Can adverse drug reactions be detected earlier? A comparison of reports by patients and professionals. *BMJ.* **313**: 350–51.

43 Let consumers report drug side-effects, says *Health Which?* 10 April 2001; http://www.net/whats new/pr/apr01/health/sideeffects.html.

44 Poole O and Booth J (2001) Breast cancer drug problems 'ignored'. *Sunday Telegraph.* **12 August**.

45 Banks P (2001) Carer's contribution in primary care. In: S Gillam and F Brooks (eds) *New Beginnings: towards patient and public involvement in primary healthcare.* King's Fund, University of London, London.

46 Nuttal SR *et al.* (1994) Financing long-term care in Great Britain. *J Inst Actuaries.* **121**: 1–68.

47 Lindley CM *et al.* (1992) Inappropriate medication is a major cause of adverse drug reactions in elderly patients. *Age Ageing.* **21**: 294–300.

48 Department of Health (2001) *National Service Framework for Older People.* Department of Health, London.

49 Department of Health (2001) *Medicines and Older People: implementing medicines-related aspects of the NSF for older people.* Department of Health, London.

50 Mackie CM *et al.* (2000) A randomised controlled trial of medication review in patients receiving polypharmacy in a general practice setting. *Pharm J.* **265**: R7. **Suppl.**: Pharmacy Practice Research, British Pharmaceutical Conference, Birmingham, 10–13 September 2000.

51 Petty DR *et al.* (2000) Pharmacist-conducted clinical medication review clinic: consultation generator or saver. *Pharm J.* **265**: R29. **Suppl.**: Pharmacy Practice Research, British Pharmaceutical Conference, Birmingham, 10–13 September 2000.

52 Tully M and Cantrill J (1999) Role of the pharmacist in evidence-based prescribing in primary care. In: M Gabbay (ed.) *The Evidence-Based Primary Care Handbook.* Royal Society of Medicine Press, London.

53 Bond C *et al.* (2000) Repeat prescribing: a role for community pharmacists in controlling and monitoring repeat prescriptions. *Br J Gen Pract.* **50**: 271–5.

54 Patel H (2001) Medicines management is not about rocket science. *Pharm J.* **266**: 730.

55 Naylor DM and Oxley DV (1997) Assessing the need for a domiciliary pharmaceutical service for older patients using a coding system to record and quantify data. *Pharm J.* **258**: 479–84.

56 Bero LA *et al.* (2000) Expanding the roles of outpatient pharmacists: effects on health services utilisation, costs and patient outcomes. *Cochrane Database Syst Rev.* **Issue 2**.

57 Lowe CJ *et al.* (2000) Effects of a medicine review and education programme for older people in general practice. *Br J Clin Pharmacol.* **50**: 172–5.

58 Williams SE, Bond CM and Menzies C (2000) A pharmaceutical needs assessment in a primary care setting. *Br J Gen Pract.* **50**: 95–9.

59 Furniss L, Craig SK and Burns A (1978) Medication use in nursing homes for elderly people. *Int J Geriatr Psychiatry.* **13**: 433–9.

60 Furniss L *et al.* (1998) Medication reviews in nursing homes: documenting and classifying the activities of a pharmacist. *Pharm J.* **261**: 320–23.

61 Furniss L *et al.* (2000) Effects of a pharmacist's medication review in nursing homes: randomised controlled trial. *Br J Psychiatry.* **176**: 563–67.

62 Ed. (2000) Report suggests that teamworking benefits primary healthcare. *Pharm J.* **265**: 672.

63 Ed. (2000) Keynote speech: plan sets out how pharmacy can build a future for itself, says minister. *Pharm J.* **265**: 397–400.

64 Lowe C (2001) What medicines management means. *Pharm J.* **267**: 206–7.

65 Ed. (2001) First national medicines management pilot sites announced by government. *Pharm J.* **267**: 75.

66 Thompson F (2001) What will the successful medicines management pilot sites be offering? *Pharm J.* **267**: 83.

67 Thompson F (2001) Where to go for help when you want to put Government policy into practice. *Pharm J.* **267**: 80.

68 Ed. (2000) A watershed for the profession, says the President. *Pharm J.* **265**: 400–2.

69 Department of Health (2001) *Health and Social Care.* DoH, London; www.doh.gov.uk/caretrusts/emergframe.htm.

70 Ed. (2001) Welcome for proposed extension of nurse prescribing. *Pharm J.* **266**: 108–9.

71 Department of Health (2001) *Consultation on Proposals to Extend Nurse Prescribing.* Department of Health, London; http://www.doh.gov.uk/nurseprescribing.

72 McGavock H (2000) My grave concern over nurse prescribing. *Prescriber.* **19 December**: 45.

73 Courtenay M and Butler M (1998) Nurse prescribing – the knowledge base. *Nursing Times.* **94**: 40–42.

74 Ed. (2000) Major expansion for nurse prescribing? *Pharm J.* **265**: 673.

75 Alexander A (2001) Prescribing: an agenda for all professions. South East Pharmaceutical Industry Group with support from the Wessex and the London Thames Valley Pharmaceutical Groups, Guildford, 22 May 2001. *Pharm J.* **267**: 28–9.

76 O'Rourke JE and Richardson WS (2001) Evidenced-based management of hypertension. What to do when blood pressure is difficult to control. *BMJ.* **322**: 1299–32.

77 Ang-Lee MK, Moss J and Yuan CS (2001) Herbal medicines and perioperative care. *JAMA.* **286**: 208–16.

78 Ed. (2001) Use of herbal medicines could pose risk to patients undergoing surgery. *Pharm J.* **267**: 79.

79 Ed. (2001) Complementary medicine – popular, but full potential remains untapped. *Pharm J.* **267**: 328–9.

80 Ed. (2001) Hype, hope and healing. Complementary therapies: are they a passing fashion or a wake-up call for conventional medicine? New Scientist finds out what really works. *New Scientist.* **26 May**: 28–53.

81 Waltz L (2001) *The Herbal Encyclopedia: safety with herbs.* www.wic.net/waltzark/Safety.htm.

82 Everitt BS (1999) Alternative therapies: panaceas or placebos? In: *Chance Rules. An informal guide to probability, risk and statistics.* Springer-Verlag, New York, 157–72.

83 Shapiro AK and Shapiro E (1997) *The Powerful Placebo.* The Johns Hopkins University Press, Baltimore, MD, 1–280.

84 Ed. (2001) Aristolochia ban to be permanent. *Pharm J.* **266**: 138.

85 Ed. (2001) *Psoralea corylifolia* fruit in traditional Chinese medicines

causing severe skin reactions. *Curr Prob Pharmacovigilance.* **27**: 12; http://www.mca.gov.uk.

86 Eisenberg DM *et al.* (1998) Trends in alternative medicine use in the United States, 1990–97. Results of a follow-up national survey. *JAMA.* **280**: 1569–75.

87 Ed. (2001) Pharmacists' interactions with complementary and alternative medicines. Sixty-First Congress of the International Pharmaceutical Federation, Singapore, 2–6 September 2001. *Pharm J.* **267**: 359–60.

88 Thompson M (2001) Compulsory guidelines aim to stop intrathecal chemotherapy disasters. *Pharm J.* **267**: 707.

89 Crown J (1999) *Review of Prescribing, Supply and Administration of Medicines. Final report.* Department of Health, London; www.doh. gov.uk/prescribe.

90 Livingstone C (1999) Prescribing medicines – a new job for some health professionals. *Pharm J.* **262**: 702–4.

91 Hughes DS *et al.* (1999) Collaborative medicines management. *Pharm J.* **263**: 170–72.

92 Webb D *et al.* (1999) Concordance: last link in the chain? *Pharm J.* **263**: 782.

93 Ed. (2000) Report suggests that teamworking benefits primary healthcare. *Pharm J.* **265**: 672.

94 Teich JM *et al.* (1999) The Brigham integrated computing system (BICS): advanced clinical systems in an academic hospital environment. *Int J Med Inform.* **54**: 197–208.

95 Nightingale PG *et al.* (2000) Implementation of rules-based computerised bedside prescribing and administration: intervention study. *BMJ.* **320**: 750–53.

96 Wickramaratna V (1999) Implementing the 'Information for Health' initiative in the NHS. *Pharm J.* **263**: 135.

97 Institute for Safe Medication Practice (1999) Over-reliance on pharmacy computer systems may place patients at great risk; http://www.ismp.org.

98 Bates DW *et al.* (1999) The impact of computerised physician order entry on medication error prevention. *J Am Med Inform Assoc.* **6**: 313–32.

99 Bates DW *et al.* (1998) Effect of computerized physician order entry and a team intervention on prevention of serious medication errors. *JAMA.* **280**: 1311–16.

100 Lesar TS *et al.* (1990) Medication prescribing errors in a teaching hospital. *JAMA.* **263**: 2329–34.

101 Leape LL *et al.* (1995) Systems analysis of adverse drug events. ADE Prevention Study Group. *JAMA.* **274**: 35–43.

102 Preston SL, Briceland LL and Lesar TS (1994) Accuracy of penicillin allergy reporting. *Am J Hosp Pharm.* **51**: 79–84.

103 Gandhi TK *et al.* (2000) Drug complications in outpatients. *J Gen Intern Med.* **15**: 149–54.

104 Brooke C (2001) Horrific blunders leave mother in coma. *Daily Mail.* **9 November**: 1.

105 Smalley W *et al.* (2000) Contraindicated use of cisapride: impact of food and drug administration regulatory action. *JAMA.* **284**: 3036–9.
106 Jehle PM *et al.* (1999) Inadequate suspension of neutral protamine Hagendorn (NPH) insulin in pens. *Lancet.* **354**: 1604–7.
107 Ed. (1999) Study finds patients do not mix cartridge insulin properly before use. *Pharm J.* **263**: 1778.
108 AstraZeneca Industrial Achievement Award Lecture (2000) The pharmaceutical industry and the evolution of molecular medicine. *Pharm. J.* **265**: 766.
109 Ed. (2000) National Opinion Polls for Druids. Most patients have never used the Internet. *Pharm J.* **265**: 615.
110 Weiland AJ (2000) The challenges of genetic advances. *Healthplan.* **41**: 24–30.
111 Ed. (2000) Looking to the digital future. *EPSRC Newsline.* **16**: 6–11.
112 Partridge D and Hussain KM (1995) Introduction to knowledged-based systems. In: *Knowledge-Based Information Systems.* McGraw-Hill Book Company, London, 1–19.

Chapter 17

1 Donini-Lenhoff FG and Hedrick HL (2000) Growth of specialization in graduate medical education. *JAMA.* **284**: 1284–9.
2 Citizens Commission on Graduate Medical Education (1996) *The Graduate Education of Physicians.* American Medical Association, Chicago, IL.
3 Weatherall D (1999) The conflict between the science and the art of clinical practice in the next millennium. In: DC Grossman and H Valtin (eds) *Great Issues for Medicine in the Twenty-First Century. Ethical and social issues arising out of advances in the biomedical sciences.* New York Academy of Sciences, New York, 240–46.
4 Saul JR (1993) *Voltaire's Bastards: the dictatorship of reason in the West.* Vintage Books, New York, 466–98.
5 Department of Health (2001) *The Expert Patient: a new approach to chronic disease management for the 21st century.* DoH, London.
6 Taylor RJ and Bond CM (1991) Change in the established prescribing habits of general practitioners: an analysis of initial prescriptions in general practice. *Br J Gen Pract.* **41**: 244–8.
7 *National Survey of GP Opinion: overall results top-line report, October 2001, prepared for General Practitioners' Committee, British Medical Association, London;* http:/www.bma.org.uk.
8 British Medical Association (2001) *Radical Action Required to Keep Family Doctors in the New NHS. Major GP opinion survey shows half of*

all family doctors plan to retire early. British Medical Association, London; http://www.bma.org.uk.

9 Ed. (2001) NHS targets pharmacists and staff to improve the quality of working lives. *Pharm J.* **267**: 373.

Chapter 18

1 Leape LL and Berwick DM (2000) Safe healthcare: are we up to it? *BMJ.* **320**: 725–6.

The author and publisher gratefully acknowledge the following sources of information and materials used in this book:

Adis International Ltd; American Medical Association; Blackwell Scientific Ltd; BMJ Publishing Group; The Clinical Disputes Forum; The Clinical Negligence Group; CMP Information Ltd; Datapharm Publications; Department of Healthcare Education, University of Liverpool; Eli Lilly and Company Ltd; Engineering and Physical Sciences Research Council; Harvey Whitney Books Company; The Herbal Encyclopedia; Institute of Health and Community Studies, Bournemouth University; The Lancet; National Academy Press; Nature; New England Journal of Medicine; News International; Oxford University Press; The Pharmaceutical Journal; Royal Pharmaceutical Society of Great Britain; Quality Assurance Agency for Higher Education; Royal Society of Medicine Press Ltd; Springer-Verlag; The Stationery Office; The Times Higher Education Supplement; Which? Online.

Index